MAKING OUR SCHOOLS
MORE EFFECTIVE

ABOUT THE AUTHOR

Martin Patchen, Ph.D., is professor emeritus of sociology at Purdue University. He has taught and done research on a variety of educational issues. He is the author of six previous books, including *Black-White Contact in Schools: Its Social and Academic Effects.*

MAKING OUR SCHOOLS MORE EFFECTIVE

What Matters and What Works

By

MARTIN PATCHEN

CHARLES C THOMAS · PUBLISHER, LTD.
Springfield · Illinois · U.S.A.

Published and Distributed Throughout the World by

CHARLES C THOMAS • PUBLISHER, LTD.
2600 South First Street
Springfield, Illinois 62704

© 2004 by CHARLES C THOMAS • PUBLISHER, LTD

ISBN 0-398-07490-9 (hard)
ISBN 0-398-07491-7 (paper)

Library of Congress Catalog Card Number: 2003068702

Printed in the United States of America
JW-R-3

Library of Congress Cataloging-in-Publication Data

Patchen, Martin.
    Making our schools more effective : what matters and what works / by Martin
Patchen.
        p. cm.
    Includes bibliographical references and index.
    ISBN 0-398-07490-9 (hard) — ISBN 0-398-07491-7 (pbk.)
    1. School improvement programs—United States.   I. Title.

LB2822.82.P36 2004
371.2'00973—dc22

                                                                    2003068702

BK
$ 49.95

To my wife, Nancy,
with appreciation for her help and support
to me in writing this book
and in all other ways.

PREFACE

Another book on school reform? Given the outpouring of books on this subject, a potential reader might ask what this book can add to our understanding of how to make schools more effective.

Books on school reform have focused on many specific aspects of the subject. Some books are descriptive case studies of individual schools or particular school systems. Some books have focused on, and sometimes advocated, reform efforts of a particular type. Such reform efforts include (among others) changes in teaching methods; in curriculum; in grouping of students by ethnicity, ability, gender, or interests; in greater accountability for teachers and for schools; in the decision-making processes of schools; and in the freedom of parents to choose a school for their children. Some books concerned with educational reform focus on particular groups of students (African-Americans, Latino-Americans, and so on). A few books have been more comprehensive, but these generally have discussed a succession of particular topics in relative isolation from each other.

The outpouring of research and ideas about improving the schools has provided us with much useful information and many valuable ideas. However, the current state of our knowledge is rather disorganized. Professional educators and laypersons alike are confronted with an often bewildering variety of different findings and different prescriptions for reform. It is difficult to digest all of this literature—to judge how good the evidence is for particular suggested reforms, which influences on educational outcomes are crucial and which are less important, and how various sets of evidence and various suggested changes may or may not fit together. Thus, there is a need for the broad range of research and ideas on improving our schools to be summarized, evaluated, and brought together within a coherent framework.

This book is intended to provide such a synthesis. It summarizes and evaluates work bearing directly on the classroom situation, work focusing on the characteristics and organization of the individual school, and work dealing with the ways in which schools relate to parents and the community. It summarizes and evaluates evidence concerning what works and what does not work, what is important and what is less important in affecting student learning. It attempts to provide a holistic picture of problems and possible solutions by showing how processes at different "levels" are connected; that is, how what goes on in the classroom between teachers and students is related to the organization of the individual school and how it is run, which, in turn, is related to the organization of the school system and its relationship to the community.

By summarizing evidence concerning which programs are most effective in the schools, this book is intended to contribute to successful school policy. It is not written to advocate my own ideas about school policy but, rather, to present as objectively as possible relevant evidence for and against particular policies and approaches.

The book does not present a blueprint or formula by which schools can provide effective education to all students. Neither does it propose improved educational programs in detail. However, the information presented on what factors are most strongly related to student learning, and on what has worked to improve education, does suggest the general directions and emphases that are likely to be most successful. Conclusions about the policy implications of research evidence are presented at the end of each chapter. Discussion about desirable school policy also is presented in the final chapter.

Several emphases and limitations of the book should be noted. I give the greatest attention to the outcome of schooling that both the public and the schools see as most important—student learning. Since available data on learning usually are the result of standard achievement tests, much of the evidence I review is based on such evidence. While this type of data provides only a partial assessment of student learning, results based on such data, combined with other information, do show a coherent picture of what kinds of schools are most effective.

I give less attention to outcomes of schooling other than student learning. At times I do discuss evidence that helps explain why students drop out of school. Several other outcomes, including student attendance and parent and student satisfaction, also receive some attention. However, several potential outcomes of schooling that often are seen as desirable, especially shaping students who have good character and who are good citizens, are given little attention. My relative neglect of these nonacademic outcomes is not because I think they are unimportant, but primarily because it is difficult to cover all outcomes in one book. How schools affect the character and civic participation of young people are important topics and deserve attention and study by others.

In reviewing the evidence on various aspects of schooling, I try to draw generalizations about what kinds of programs and practices generally are most effective, especially for raising academic achievement. In some places I discuss the ways in which certain school characteristics may have stronger effects on particular groups of students, such as African-Americans.

However, I give only a little attention to how effective practices may differ somewhat for different subjects and different grade levels. Such a more fine-grained analysis is beyond the scope of this book Other books that focus on particular aspects of schooling, such as instructional methods or assessment of learning, are able to consider more fully how the best approaches need to be modified according to the particular setting.

This book focuses primarily on research on schools in the United States. Some evidence from schools in other countries is presented, but there is not an extensive comparison among schools in different countries. Although beyond the scope of this book, systematic comparisons of the educational systems in various countries are very useful. Other books provide more of this type of information, and we can learn much from seeing what is being done elsewhere in the world.

Even with the limitations of its coverage, this book covers a broad range of topics that are relevant to school effectiveness. For each topic, there undoubtedly is some research that I have not cited. However, by looking at the long list of references in the notes to each chapter, the reader can see that my coverage of relevant literature is extensive.

In sum, this book provides a broad and integrative review of research on what makes for effective schools, focusing on factors that affect academic achievement, especially in American schools. Such a comprehensive overview of this material has been rare. The book should give the reader a broad perspective on the research concerning school improvement, pointing to what kinds of policies and programs seem most effective and how the various reform efforts relate to each other. It is intended to be of interest to a wide audience, including educators, faculty and students in education and sociology, parents of students, and members of the broader public interested in educational issues.

A few words about my own background. I am a sociologist and have taught and done research at universities for almost all of my adult life. In recent years, I taught a course on the Sociology of Education. Some of my research has been done in high schools, and I have spent some time visiting schools at various levels (elementary, middle school, and high school), observing classes and talking with principals, teachers, and students.

But this book is not based on my limited personal experiences in K–12 schools. It is based primarily on an exhaustive review of research by educators, sociologists, psychologists, economists, and others who have studied the schools. What I have brought primarily to this work is my general knowledge about research methods, my knowledge of a broad range of research in this area, and what I hope is some ability to bring together this material in a coherent and understandable way. The reader may judge the result.

Martin Patchen

ACKNOWLEDGMENTS

I would like to thank the many people who helped me in writing this book.

William McInerny of the School of Education at Purdue University gave me valuable insights about research in education. A number of principals and many teachers and students in the schools of Lafayette and of Tippecanoe County in Indiana took time to tell me about the problems and successes of life in their schools. Edward Eiler, superintendent of the Lafayette schools, shared with me some of his perspectives about the challenges that educators face today. I am grateful to all of them for their time and their assistance.

I also benefited from the comments of many people on one or more chapters of the book. They include Nancy Patchen, Elizabeth Grauerholz, Jan McLean, Elizabeth Heilman, James Lehman, Maureen Hallinan, James Hougland, Jr., George Horwich, James Russell, Mary Jo Sparrow, Ernest McDaniel, Donald Ferris, and William Asher. I appreciate each of them taking the time to give me their perspectives and comments.

The figures for the book were prepared by Dawn Fisher. I thank her for her good work and her willingness to help.

The manuscript for the book was typed by Candy Lawson, who is extremely able and efficient, is a pleasure to work with, and possesses a rare talent for deciphering my scrawls. I was fortunate to have her work with me.

CONTENTS

MAKING OUR SCHOOLS
MORE EFFECTIVE

Chapter One

ISSUES IN PUBLIC EDUCATION

Every year we pump more money into our public school system, and every year the system gets worse. . . . Meanwhile, nearly 90% of American children are stuck in a failing system.

> Campaign for America's Children,
> coheaded by former U.S. Secretary
> of Education William J. Bennett.[1]

When one actually examines the evidence, one discovers that it simply will not support the fiction that America has a generally failing system of education. This claim is nonsense.

> David Berliner and Bruce Biddle, *The Manufactured Crisis.*[2]

As the above quotations illustrate, there are great differences in opinion about the general quality of American public schools. But however differently people assess the overall state of the schools, almost all agree that they can and should be improved.

Public schools in America have accomplished a great deal, including providing a high school education to a large majority of American youth. There are many fine public schools—both elementary schools and high schools—that provide an excellent education to their students. But it also is clear that many students, especially many poor and minority youth, are leaving school with weak skills (in writing, mathematics, and other areas) that leave them poorly prepared for skilled jobs or for higher education.[3]

Concern with real or alleged deficiencies in public education have led many people—business leaders, government officials, educators, and others—to press for "reforms" in the schools. A variety of changes have been made in many schools, including requiring more academic courses, testing students more often, having smaller classes, and creating new charter schools, in an effort to improve student learning. However, there has been and continues to be vigorous debate about what kinds of school changes are desirable and about the best ways to educate our children.

Among the issues on which there are different viewpoints are the following:

1. What subjects and skills should be taught in the schools?
2. What methods should teachers use to teach and manage their classes?
3. How often and in what ways should students' learning be tested or otherwise assessed?
4. How should schools be organized and run, with respect to both their academic programs and to the working relationships among their staff members?
5. How should the student body of a school be composed, especially in terms of its total size and its racial/ethnic makeup, in order to promote successful learning?
6. What are the effects on schools and students of giving parents a choice among schools, both within the public school system (for example, creating charter schools) and in private schools (as with voucher plans)?
7. What are the reasons for the disparities in school achievement between minority youth and non-Hispanic white youth, and how can this achievement gap be eliminated?

This chapter first briefly discusses each of these questions. I look at some of the specific aspects of each issue and at some of the historical and social context of these issues. I also consider different viewpoints relevant to each of these issues and the types of information needed to provide better answers to these important questions.

WHAT SHOULD SCHOOLS
TEACH THEIR STUDENTS?

What youth are taught in American schools has been a continuing source of controversy over the course of our history. School has been seen variously as the place where young people should be prepared for the world of work and careers; to be good citizens; to have good values and good character; and to learn to live satisfying and healthy personal lives. Different groups—business organizations, religious groups, government officials, educators, and others—have advocated particular objectives and curricula suited to their objectives.[4]

A major and recurring disagreement has concerned the extent to which education, especially at the secondary level, should focus on academic subjects or on the "practical."[5] As public high schools expanded in the late 1800s and early 1900s, their initial emphasis on academic subjects (math, science, English, etc.) declined. Manual training high schools were opened in many cities to teach mechanical skills to secondary school students. Within regular high schools, enrollments in core academic subjects decreased while enrollments in "personal development" courses (such as those in hygiene, driver's education, and family life) increased.

What many people saw as a "dilution" of school curricula has led to periodic efforts to strengthen the academic content of students' education. Such efforts were strong in the 1950s, when many Americans worried about a scientific competition with the Soviet Union, and also have been prominent in recent decades, as business leaders and others have questioned whether American students are learning enough basic academic skills. Recently many states have mandated an increase in the number of core academic courses, such as those in math and science, that all students are required to take.

Debate continues over the extent to which schools should focus on developing their students' personal, practical, or artistic knowledge and skills, as opposed to exclusive or near-exclusive focus on their knowledge of basic academic subjects. Should students be offered, or required to take, courses in sex education? drugs? driver's education? financial management? family life? physical education? music? arts? How much of their course work should be electives? (Some writers have said that permitting a large number of electives leads to a "shopping mall high school.")[6] While most people will find a variety of courses to be useful, clearly there are limits on the amount of time and resources a school has available, and choices must be made.

A related issue is whether all of our youth should receive a similar academic training or whether various groups of students should be given different types of education. Before the twentieth century, high schools generally offered traditional academic programs. But in the late nineteenth and early twentieth centuries, as the proportion of the nation's youth attending high school grew rapidly, many high schools began to offer different types of education for students of differing abilities and interests.

Many educators in the early twentieth century saw a varied curriculum as satisfying the needs of less affluent youth and thus making the schools more democratic. By providing a variety of new courses and curriculum tracks, educators also were trying to engage adolescents' interest enough for them to stay in school. Employers welcomed the creation of vocational programs that would train prospective workers in the skills needed in business and industry.[7]

Providing different programs of education for different groups of students has aroused considerable opposition. Critics of such programs have seen them as helping to perpetuate stratification in society, channeling the children of the affluent into programs that lead them into high-status occupations while directing poorer children into programs that prepare them for less skilled positions. For example, after manual training was introduced into many high schools, it was criticized by some labor groups and others as limiting the horizons and opportunities of low-income youth.

Debate about the desirability of schools having varied curricula continues, often centering on the practice of "tracking" in high schools.[8] Some educators contend that providing different programs for students with different skill levels and interests makes teaching more effective and helps to maintain all students' interest in their schoolwork. In addition, some commentators believe that if schools pressure all students to pursue academic courses, they neglect the training and welfare of those students who do not want to go to college.

Critics of tracking in the schools argue that students who are channeled into nonacademic tracks are stigmatized as inferior and provided with an inferior education. Because the "lower" tracks do not prepare students for college, they say, students in those tracks are consigned to lower-status, lower-paying occupations. Moreover, critics of tracking point to the fact that poor and minority students are more likely than others to be in noncollege tracks.

In addition to controversies about the types of courses and programs that schools offer, different views have been put forth concerning the type of knowledge and skills that students should learn in any particular course. Some have argued that schools need to "return to basics" and emphasize the teaching of important information and basic skills (such as historical facts, grammar, and computations.) Others advocate greater attention to developing students' skills of conceptual thinking and problem solving.[9]

Some of the issues regarding what schools should teach center on differences of values and priorities that cannot be resolved by evidence. But there is much evidence, especially concerning the effects of different curricula and programs on student achievement, that can help us to make judgments about these questions. Chapter 2, "The Curriculum," discusses issues of curriculum and reviews research evidence bearing on these issues.

HOW SHOULD TEACHERS TEACH AND MANAGE THEIR CLASSES?

Throughout the history of American schools, there have been changes and controversies not only concerning what is taught but also about *how* the subject matter is taught—that is, about the style and methods of teaching. Teachers in early schools generally relied on methods of rote learning, with students repeating and hopefully remembering what the teacher and the textbook said. A mechanistic model of teaching was taken to its extreme in the "monitorial" public schools of the early nineteenth century; in such schools each lesson was divided into very small bits, to be transmitted by a more advanced pupil to the memory of a less advanced pupil.

Those in the progressive education movement of the late nineteenth century and the first half of the twentieth century advocated and practiced a new approach to education in which the child's interests and enthusiasms would be engaged. Rather than being a passive listener and memorizer, the child would participate actively in deciding the subjects and methods of his or her own learning, with the teacher as more of a guide than a dictator.

By the 1940s, progressive education ideas were dominant among educational leaders, although actual practice in the schools varied. However, by the 1950s, progressive education came under increasing attack as having allowed school discipline to become lax and academic standards to decline. Thereafter, the pendulum has swung back and forth between a renewed focus on maintaining rigorous standards by placing control firmly in teachers' hands and renewed concern about engaging student motivation and involvement by providing more flexibility in teaching methods and more choices for students. Debate continues about which emphasis is better, although some observers have proposed policies that combine elements of each approach.[10]

The question of whether to group students in classes according to their ability or skill also has aroused controversy. Those favoring ability grouping have viewed it as a way to make instruction easier for teachers and more effective for students. Others see the practice as stigmatizing students with lower skills and providing them with an inferior education.

Recently the role of computers in teaching has been a subject of discussion and sometimes of dispute. Some enthusiasts see the use of computers as providing an exciting expansion of learning. Others are more skeptical, saying that the educational rationales for computer use often are weak and their advantages often exaggerated.

Chapter 3, "Teachers and Students in the Classroom," reviews evidence concerning these and other issues centering on the classroom. Research and ideas concerning learning activities, instructional methods, grouping of students, classroom management, and the use of computers are among the specific topics considered. The aim is to see how classrooms may be organized and run in order to motivate students most strongly and produce the greatest learning.

HOW SHOULD SCHOOLS BE ORGANIZED AND RUN?

As in other organizations, the success of schools is affected by the ways in which they structure their programs and the working relationships among their staff members. Both the academic programs and the administration of schools have aroused discussion and debate.[11]

ACADEMIC PROGRAMS

One controversial academic program is bilingual education. Advocates of bilingual programs maintain that teaching non-native students in their home language, at least for a time, is necessary for them to learn both

English and school subjects. Many supporters, including especially those of
Hispanic background, also believe that it is important for children to maintain ties to the language and culture of their heritage. Opponents of bilingual programs argue that such programs often keep children from learning
English well, thereby impeding their success in school and later in occupations. Some opponents also see dual-language programs as threatening
America's cultural unity.[12]

Other aspects of schools' academic programs have aroused less public
controversy than bilingual education but are subjects of frequent discussion
and of disagreements or uncertainty. While most schools adhere to the traditional time schedule of six or seven periods, each one 50 minutes long,
many schools have adopted "block scheduling," under which there are
fewer periods of longer length each day (such as four 90-minute periods).
Opinions vary about whether block scheduling increases teaching effectiveness, student motivation, and learning.

A number of other school-level programs and policies that may affect the
motivation of students (and teachers) also elicit different opinions and
approaches. For example, to what extent and in what ways should schools
emphasize strict discipline for students? Does the great attention given in
many schools to nonacademic activities, especially to sports, detract from
academic effort and learning? What can a school do to encourage students
to give as much admiration to the scholar as to the athlete?

These and other issues are discussed in Chapter 4, "The Academic
Program." In that chapter, I review the results of research that relates features of a school's academic program to the motivation and learning of its
students.

Staff Relationships

The way in which decisions are made in schools has varied in different
eras and locations. In the late nineteenth and early twentieth centuries, as
schools grew in number and size, school districts generally adopted more
standardized procedures, increased the number of administrators, and centralized much decision making to a level above the individual school. Some
see centralized control as necessary in order for schools to operate in a uniform and coordinated way. Critics of centralized bureaucracy complain that
it leads schools to be inflexible as circumstances change, to long delays in
action, to one-way (top-down) communication, and to feelings of power-
lessness and apathy among school staff.

In some school districts much decision-making power has been moved
away from central bureaucracies and down to local school staffs and communities. Proponents of such plans see decentralized control as leading to
more effective schools, but some have questioned its results.

In addition to their possible participation in school decisions, other
aspects of teachers' positions have been seen as affecting the quality of edu-

cation. Some states and districts have adopted programs, such as "merit pay" to reward good teachers, or "career ladders" to try to provide greater incentives for teachers to upgrade their skills. Such programs often have met resistance from teachers who question the accuracy and fairness of teacher evaluations and who see such plans as fostering competition among teachers that is ultimately harmful to school effectiveness.

The relationships among teachers in a school have been highlighted by some observers as important to school success. The traditional pattern in most schools has been for each teacher to be generally isolated in his or her own classroom and to have little interaction with other teachers. Many recent discussions of school life have emphasized that collaboration among teachers can contribute greatly to better instructional methods and to higher morale among the faculty. However, promoting such fruitful cooperative relationships among teachers often is difficult.

In order to organize schools more effectively, we need to look at available evidence about what types of organization have been most effective in producing good outcomes for teachers and students. In Chapter 5, "Teachers and Administrators," I discuss alternative patterns of decision making in schools; varying compensation and career arrangements for teachers; the role of teacher unions in schools; and factors that lead to collaborative relations among teachers. Chapter 5 highlights the ways in which different types of school organization affect teachers' motivation and skills and also the school's instructional program.

HOW SHOULD THE STUDENT BODY OF A SCHOOL BE COMPOSED?

The size of a school and the makeup of the student body, especially in terms of race/ethnicity and social class, also have been seen by many as affecting the quality of education the school provides.

From the one-room schoolhouses of an earlier era, schools expanded in size, through population growth and consolidation, and high schools with several thousand students became common in many American cities. Some educators and others have favored large schools as being more economically efficient and offering more programs, courses, activities, and services than small schools can offer. Others say that a small school is better because it promotes more personal interaction between students and faculty and more cohesive relationships among the school staff.[13]

The racial composition of schools has been a subject of national attention since 1954, when official school segregation in the South was ruled unconstitutional and de facto racial segregation in much of the rest of the country was challenged. Civil rights organizations, led by the National Association for the Advancement of Colored People, along with many liberal white allies, have long advocated programs, including busing of children, that will produce a mix of black students and white students in each school.

Where they have been put into effect, by court order or by administrative decision, plans that bus students in order to achieve "racial balance" have been fiercely controversial. Advocates believe that racial mixing is necessary in order for minority children to get an equal education. Critics of such plans, including many minority parents, point to their costs (in student travel time as well as in dollars) and question whether black and other minority students need to attend racially mixed schools in order to get a good education.[14]

What information do we have on these issues of student body composition? In Chapter 6, "School Characteristics," I review the evidence on the effects of different school size (and of varying class size) on schools and on student learning. That chapter also discusses extensive research on the effects of the racial composition, as well as the social class composition, of schools on student achievement. In addition, Chapter 6 considers the impact of differences in school spending on school effectiveness.

HOW SHOULD STUDENTS AND
SCHOOLS BE ASSESSED?

In reaction to concerns by business groups and others that many students are receiving an inadequate education, many local districts, states, and the federal government as well have mandated more testing of students. Most states already do, or will soon, require that all students pass a state competency test in order to graduate from high school. Many states have established assessment programs for schools that require each school to test its students' knowledge in basic subjects and reward and/or penalize schools on the basis of the performance of their students. The federal government added its considerable weight to the movement for more testing with the No Child Left Behind Act, which was adopted in 2001. This law mandates that states (if they are to continue receiving federal aid) test students annually in grades 3 through 8, take steps to improve schools that the tests show to be below par and permit parents to transfer their children out of failing schools.

The rationale for having extensive testing in schools, and for having consequences for test performance, is straightforward. Unless students are forced to demonstrate competence in basic subjects and skills, testing advocates say, schools will permit many students who are barely literate to slip through the system. Requiring each student to demonstrate basic information and skills in order to graduate will, they say, force schools to offer all students the education they need and force students to apply themselves to take advantage of what is provided.

Requiring schools to provide data on the overall test performance of their students is, testing advocates say, the best way to make each school accountable. Making information about the performance of each school public informs the staff of each school about how well its school is doing compared to other schools. Publicity about its school performance, plus rewards and penalties contingent on school performance, provide added incentives for principals and teachers to improve their educational program.

However, the recent emphasis on testing in the schools has aroused a backlash of criticism and resistance. Parents of minority children and organizations representing minorities have protested that large numbers of minority children are being denied high school diplomas because of proficiency tests. Many other parents protest that their children are spending too much time taking tests and feeling too much pressure because of testing. Many parents, and many educators as well, charge that widespread use of standardized tests has led schools and teachers to narrow the curriculum and instruction to what is contained on the tests. The tests themselves have been criticized as focusing on rote memorization of disconnected, often trivial, information. Some educators have proposed, and some have used, alternative types of assessments that encourage student thinking and creativity.[15]

The accuracy and fairness of evaluating schools on the basis of their students' test results also have been questioned. Critics have pointed especially to the difficulty of comparing schools whose students come from very different home backgrounds, with respect to parents' education, race, and other characteristics.[16] Whether the assessments of schools, based on test results, leads to improvements in the schools also has been debated.

Given the lively, often heated, controversies about testing in schools, it is important to examine the relevant evidence as objectively as possible. What effects have testing programs of different sorts had on student motivation and student achievement? How have they affected schools' curricula and the instructional methods that teachers use?

Chapter 7, "Assessing Students and Schools," first discusses alternative methods of assessing student learning and their effects on students' motivation, learning, and completion of school. The chapter next describes programs that have been used to assess school performance and discusses the effects of such programs on curricula, teaching, and other aspects of school programs.

WHAT ARE THE EFFECTS OF GIVING PARENTS A CHOICE AMONG SCHOOLS?

The common, or public, school became widespread in the United States in the nineteenth century. Public schools were given the tasks of giving young people the skills they needed in an industrializing economy,

"Americanizing" large numbers of immigrants, and preparing youth to be good citizens. While some students attended religious (mostly Catholic) schools and a small number went to private schools, most children of all backgrounds attended the public schools together. Public schools generally were seen as a cornerstone of American society.

In recent decades, however, some people have contended that improvement of education is impeded by the public school system's monopoly on free education. This monopoly, they say, gives parents little or no choice among schools. Giving each family a choice among schools—both among different types of public schools and between public and private schools— would, these critics say, permit parents to match a school's program with their own values and needs. Moreover, they argue, giving families a choice among schools would force schools to be accountable to their "customers" and to improve if the customers were not satisfied. School choice plans, including charter schools and vouchers for private schools, have been advocated especially by conservatives who believe in free markets and by some advocates for poor minority students, who are receiving inadequate educations in some public schools.

Opposition to school choice programs, especially to vouchers and tax credits for use in private schools, has come from teacher unions and other educators and also from political liberals, including some representatives of minority groups. Advocates of the traditional common school fear that school choice programs will lead to a division of American youth into a variety of separate groups, based in part on ethnicity, economic status, religion, and other social characteristics. They also predict that, rather than leading to improvement of public schools, choice programs will weaken public schools by draining money, the best students, and the most engaged parents away from them.

Much of the debate on this subject has centered on differences of opinion, rather than on evidence. Also, discussion of school choice often has not distinguished enough among various types of choice programs—those administered by a public school district (such as alternative schools, magnet schools, and open enrollment plans), charter schools (publicly funded but autonomous), and voucher programs that give parents money to be used for private schooling.[17]

With many states now encouraging charter schools to operate and with the U.S. Supreme Court recently (in 2002) clearing away the federal constitutional barrier to voucher programs, it is important for legislators, educators, parents, and other citizens to consider the available evidence on outcomes of school choice programs. Chapter 8, "Family Choice Among Schools," reviews and discusses the relevant evidence. It looks at the effects that choice programs of different types have had on parents' and students' satisfaction, on school programs, on student achievement, on clustering of students of similar ethnicity, and on traditional neighborhood public schools.

WHY IS THERE AN ACHIEVEMENT GAP BETWEEN MINORITY AND OTHER STUDENTS?

While the need to improve education is a general one, the problem is most acute for African-American students, Hispanic-American students, and some other ethnic minorities. On average, minority students (other than those of Asian descent) complete less education and, among those at the same grade level, are less proficient in academic subjects. The educational gaps among racial/ethnic groups makes it difficult for our society to achieve economic and social equality.

In the 1950s and 1960s many civil rights advocates expected that an end to racial segregation in the schools, better funding of schools attended by blacks, and a reduction of poverty among blacks would quickly narrow the gaps in school achievement. But even in racially mixed schools, in schools with funding equal to that of most other schools, and among those from relatively affluent families, achievement scores of minority students are substantially below those of non-Hispanic white students.[18]

Many explanations of the continuing disparity in achievement scores between whites and blacks and other minorities have been advanced.[19] Some, including many teachers, focus their explanations of poor school performance on students' families and home situations. They point to problems of poor nutrition, family turmoil, child abuse and neglect, low parent involvement in schooling, and bad neighborhood influences (such as gangs). Some observers speak of a "culture of poverty" that undermines student aspirations and school effort.

Others, including many representatives of minority organizations, blame the low achievement of minority students primarily on deficiencies of the schools. They cite cases of schools that are run-down and that lack sufficient resources; low standards for student performance; lax discipline; poorly trained teachers; and curricula that do not engage students' interest.

Another type of explanation, put forward by some educators and some academics, focuses on the attitudes and behaviors of minority students. Minority students sometimes have been described as apathetic or hostile to schooling. Some writers have described an "oppositional culture" among minority students that rejects the values and rules of schools. Minority students also have been said to hang back from serious effort and success in school for fear of being labeled as "acting white" by their peers.

Any or all of these types of explanations of the ethnic achievement gap may have some validity. But if we are to gain a good understanding of this problem and get some direction for improving the situation, we must assess the relevant evidence carefully. We need to see which factors contribute to racial/ethnic gaps in school achievement, the relative importance of these determinants, and how the various contributing factors relate to each other.

In Chapter 9, "The Education Gap Between Minority Students and White Students," I discuss research evidence that explores the extent and ways in which racial/ethnic differences in school achievement are related to students' home background, to the school situation, and to students' own attitudes and behavior. Some ideas about ways to reduce the achievement gap also are presented in Chapter 9.

OVERVIEW OF DETERMINANTS OF STUDENTS' LEARNING

The issues discussed in the preceding sections should not be considered in isolation from each other. What goes on in the classroom, the way in which student learning is assessed, the characteristics and organization of the school, and societal structuring of the school system all are interrelated.

Figure 1-1 presents an overview of the determinants of student learning. Starting at the right side of the diagram, the final result of schooling is the amount of student learning that has occurred. Student motivation, which is closely related to student learning, and assessments of learning are shown in the same box in the figure.

Figure 1-1 shows that student motivation and learning are affected most directly by students' experiences in the classroom and also are affected directly by features of the school as a whole and by the broader society. More specifically, Figure 1-1 shows the following factors to have a direct influence on students' motivation and learning.

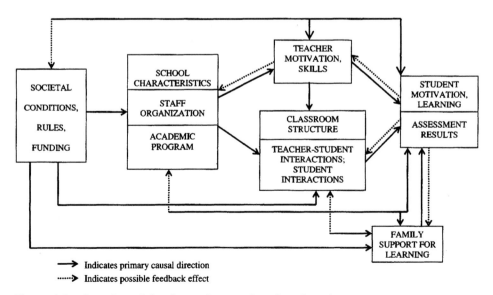

Figure 1-1   Overview of the determinants of student learning.

1. Organization of the classroom (e.g, the types of activities and the grouping of students) and the instructional methods used by teachers.
2. Teacher motivation and skills.
3. The curriculum of the school and other aspects of its academic program (e.g., time blocks for classes, programs for students with limited English proficiency, and incentives for students).
4. Characteristics of the school, such as its size and the ethnic and social class composition of its student body.
5. Pressures and incentives created by governments and other agencies outside the student's own school, such as mandated tests for high school graduation and school choice programs.
6. Support for learning from the student's family.

These factors that affect student motivation and learning are not independent of each other, as Figure 1-1 also shows. What happens in classrooms is affected by characteristics of the school (e.g., when most students come from poor minority families, teachers are less likely to give assignments that require problem-solving); by the school organization (e.g., whether team teaching is encouraged); and by the school's academic program (e.g., whether it has the longer class periods provided by block scheduling).

The motivation and skills of teachers, which are so important in the classroom, are influenced by the organizational context in which teachers work. For example, teachers are more likely to feel a sense of personal responsibility for the learning of all students when a school is small; they are more likely to improve their instructional methods when they are involved in collaborative activities with other faculty members. Circumstances in the larger society, such as state regulations for teaching certification and the content of teacher education programs, also impact teacher characteristics and skills.

The characteristics and organization of schools are affected by decisions of administrators, lawmakers, and others outside the individual school. For example, state legislatures may mandate certain curricula and testing programs for schools; and laws that permit new charter schools to be created lead some existing schools to create new programs in order to compete with the new charter schools.

Family support for student learning may be affected by features of the school, especially by whether its academic program includes efforts to actively involve parents. Broader societal conditions, such as the affordability of a college education, also may affect family support.

Student learning is, of course, usually assessed by tests, with grades, and in other ways. As Figure 1-1 shows, these assessments may have "feedback" effects on individual students, on teachers and classrooms, on schools, and on educational and government bodies. How well students do on tests may affect their motivation (e.g., a student who repeatedly fails may stop trying); on classroom activities (e.g., if students do poorly on standardized math tests, teachers may spend more time drilling them on test-related computations); on a school's academic program (e.g., the adoption of specific learning goals); and on societal regulation (e.g., a requirement of standard competency exams).

What goes on in classrooms may "feed back" to affect the features of schools and the decisions of regulatory bodies. For example, if teacher skills are weak, a school is more likely to adopt a program of peer mentoring and states may change their rules for teacher certification.

Feedback effects receive the most attention in Chapter 7, "Assessing Students and Schools," where the effects of assessment on students and schools are discussed. Feedback effects receive less attention in other chapters, where the focus is on factors that affect student learning.

An understanding of how the various factors shown in Figure 1-1 affect student motivation and learning, both directly and indirectly, is important for addressing the seven questions raised earlier in this chapter. For example, to answer the question "How should schools be organized and run?", we need to know how school characteristics (such as size and student body composition) and school organization (such as teacher meetings) affect students, either directly or through their impact on classroom life.

Chapters 2 through 8 discuss various factors shown in Figure 1-1 and their direct and indirect influences on student learning. Chapter 9 considers the persistent gap in academic achievement among students of different racial and ethnic backgrounds in the context of the various influences on learning discussed in earlier chapters. Chapter 10 summarizes the findings of the book, draws conclusions from these findings, and suggests ways in which schools can be more effective.

NOTES

1. Quoted in G. Bracey, *The War Against America's Public Schools.* Boston: Allyn & Bacon, 2002, p. 5.
2. D. Berliner and B. Biddle, *The Manufactured Crisis: Myths, Fraud, and the Attack on America's Public Schools.* Reading, MA: Addison-Wesley, 1995, p. 6.
3. National Center for Education Statistics, *Digest of Education Statistics.* Washington, DC: 2002.
4. See J. Spring, *Conflicts of Interests: The Politics of American Education.* Boston: McGraw-Hill, 2002.
5. See H. Button and E. Provenzo, Jr., *History of Education and Culture in America.* 2nd edition. Englewood Cliffs, NJ: Prentice-Hall, 1989.
6. A. Powell, E. Farrar, and D. Cohen, *The Shopping Mall High School.* Boston: Houghton Mifflin, 1985.
7. See D. Tyack and L. Cuban, *Tinkering Toward Utopia: A Century of Public School Reform.* Cambridge, MA: Harvard University Press, 1995.

8. See M. Hallinan, Tracking: From Theory to Practice. *Sociology of Education, 67,* 1994, 79–84; J. Oakes, More Than Misapplied Technology: A Normative and Political Response to Hallinan on Tracking. *Sociology of Education, 67,* 1994, 84–89.

9. For one view, see H. Erickson, *Concept-Based Curriculum and Instruction: Teaching Beyond the Facts.* Thousand Oaks, CA: Corwin Press, 1998. For another view, see E. Hirsch, Jr., *Cultural Literacy: What Every American Needs to Know.* Boston: Houghton Mifflin, 1987.

10. See, for example, J. Chall, *The Academic Achievement Challenge.* New York: Guilford Press, 2000.

11. J. Murphy and K. Louis, eds., *Handbook of Research on Educational Administration,* 2nd edition. San Francisco: Jossey-Bass, 1999.

12. See R. Rothstein, Bilingual Education: The Controversy. *Phi Delta Kappan, 79,* 1998, 672–678.

13. See V. Lee, School Size and the Organization of Secondary Schools. In M. Hallinan, ed., *Handbook of the Sociology of Education.* New York: Kluwer, 2000, 327-344.

14. For evidence on public opinion about school busing, see H. Schuman, C. Steeh, and L. Bobo, *Racial Attitudes in America.* Cambridge, MA: Harvard University Press, 1985.

15. For some different views on testing in schools, see section on High Stakes Testing. *Phi Delta Kappan, 84,* 2003, 502-520; K. Marshall, A Principal Looks Back: Standards Matter. In D. Gordon, ed., *A National Reformed.* Cambridge, MA: Harvard Education Press, 2003, 53–68.

16. See H. Ladd, ed., *Holding Schools Accountable.* Washington, DC: Brookings Institution Press, 1996.

17. For one discussion of the history of debate on this subject, see T. Good and J. Braden, *The Great School Debate: Choice, Vouchers, and Charters.* Mahwah, NJ: Lawrence Erlbaum, 2000.

18. See C. Jencks and M. Phillips, eds., *The Black-White Test Score Gap.* Washington, DC: Brookings Institution Press, 1998.

19. See M. Hallinan, Sociological Perspectives on Black-White Inequalities in American Schooling. *Sociology of Education,* Extra Issue, 2001, 50–70.

Chapter Two

THE CURRICULUM: WHAT
SHOULD STUDENTS BE TAUGHT?

What kinds of information, understanding, and skills should schools provide to their students? Should all students be given the same kind of knowledge or should the kinds of subjects, information, and abilities that are taught be varied according to the differing abilities and interests of the students?

Views on these questions differ and have sometimes led to lively controversies about what schools are or should be teaching (see Chapter 1). Differences of viewpoint about desirable curricula stem partly from differences of preference and values concerning what types of knowledge and skills are important for students to have. But different curriculum choices also derive in part from different expectations about how particular kinds of curricula affect outcomes for students, including their motivation in school, their achievement, and their staying in school. Thus, evidence about such outcomes is important in making curriculum choices.

This chapter focuses on the ways that different school curricula affect student learning. I consider the impacts of the subjects taught; interdisciplinary approaches; whether the curriculum focuses on facts and basic skills or on thinking skills; and the organization of subject content. In addition, a substantial portion of the chapter considers the practice of curriculum tracking and its impact on students. (For a discussion of curriculum standards, see Chapter 7, which deals with this topic in the context of testing programs and school accountability.)

SELECTING SUBJECTS

Educators, parents, and others often propose the inclusion or expansion of particular subject matter in the school curriculum—for example, music, geography, foreign languages, domestic arts, or drug education. Some have advocated a multicultural curriculum in which students devote much of their time to studying the history and culture of their own ethnic and racial groups. All of these ideas, and others, concerning inclusion or expansion of particular subjects have their advocates and often their opponents.

Underlying disagreements about the inclusion of particular subjects in school curricula are different views about the most important purposes of education. There is widespread support for at least three ways in which the young should be prepared to live successful lives: (1) preparation for earning a living; (2) preparation for participation in the civic life of the society; and (3) preparation for living satisfying and healthy personal lives.[1] However, although most people see all of these objectives as desirable, they disagree on the priority that should be given to each and the ways in which they should be reached.

Disagreement on educational priorities has led to controversy about the extent to which education should focus on academic subjects as opposed to "practical" subjects or subjects closely related to the interests and personal development of students. In the 1920s and 1930s, as larger proportions of the nation's youth attended high school, enrollments in academic subjects, including foreign languages, mathematics, and science, declined while enrollments in "personal development" courses such as health, physical education, and driver's education increased.[2] "Progressive" educators throughout the first half of the twentieth century advocated matching the school curriculum to the interests and life experiences of students. For example, the educator Norville Smith wrote in 1945: "A core curriculum represents the sum total of personal youth problems and the problems of social significance encountered in youth. It exists without relation to subject lines and is organized around problems."[3]

A renewed emphasis on academic disciplines, especially on mathematics and the sciences, came in the 1950s as a result of widespread concern that the United States might be falling behind in the technological-military race with the Soviet Union. Since that time the pendulum has swung back and forth between emphasis on a "rigorous" curriculum centered on academic disciplines versus a curriculum that meets the different needs and interests of varied groups of students.

In the 1970s, attention was focused on "equity" in education, specifically on better serving the needs and interests of racial and ethnic minorities, females, and the handicapped. Academic excellence received less emphasis; less time was devoted to basic academic courses, and the "general" track became predominant in high schools.[4]

Concerns about declining achievement scores and "dilution" of the curriculum led many state legislatures to mandate that the number of required courses in basic academic subjects—such as English, math, and science—be increased. In recent decades the "core curriculum" of most American schools (i.e., the subjects deemed essential for all students) has been built around a set of academic disciplines—most often mathematics, science, English, and social studies.[5]

SUBJECTS STUDIED AND STUDENT ACHIEVEMENT

Much of the variation in students' achievement appears to be due simply to the types of courses that they take and the amount of time they spend on particular subjects. Evidence supporting this not surprising but important conclusion comes from a number of types of studies: historical trends; comparisons of students with different course-taking patterns; comparisons of Catholic schools and public schools; and comparisons of the achievement of students in different nations.

Between 1963 and 1976 the average verbal and mathematics achievement scores of students who took the Scholastic Aptitude Tests (those planning to go to college) declined substantially. Some investigators studying this trend found that the decline in average SAT scores paralleled, and could be explained by, the erosion of standards in high schools' academic tracks— that is, to fewer required courses and less extensive coverage of topics.[6] In a study of the courses that students take in high school, William Schmidt found that students who attend the same school may "by their own choice or through the influence of counselors, be exposed to radically different curricula." He concluded that "the more courses and time spent in a given curricula area, the better the resulting achievement in that area."[7]

Students attending Catholic schools have been found to attain higher average scores on standardized tests of achievement than those attending public schools. This advantage occurs even when background factors, such as race and socioeconomic status, are taken into account. The better performance of students in the Catholic schools appears to be due to their taking more courses in core academic subjects, such as mathematics and science.[8] Among public schools, differences in curriculum also affect achievement. Studies of schools that succeed in producing high-achievement students, including schools serving low-income minority students, have found that a focus on academic learning is one of the keys to their success.[9]

Comparisons among nations with respect to student achievement also indicate the importance of the time devoted to particular subjects. For example, the higher average mathematics scores of Taiwanese elementary students compared to American students at the same level appears to be related to the fact that the Taiwanese students had both more instructional time and more homework time devoted to this subject.[10] International comparisons indicate that factors other than time devoted to a subject also affect student achievement. For example, a lower level of math content, rather than less time on math, was associated with lower average math scores for American eighth graders compared to their German and Japanese counterparts.[11]

An extensive cross-national study recently has been conducted that relates differences in the mathematics and science curricula of each of 29 nations to achievement gains of their students.[12] Students in all these nations were given the same tests as part of the Third International

Mathematics and Science Study. Each nation's math and science curricula, including the specific topics in their content standards, the amount of instructional time spent on each topic, and the textbook coverage of various topics, also were assessed.

The researchers found that differences in the learning gains in math and science that were achieved by students in the various countries were significantly related to curriculum differences among the countries. For almost every topic in math and science, student learning was higher in countries in which content standards gave greater attention to that topic, and/or textbooks gave greater coverage to the topic, and/or teachers devoted more instructional time to the topic. Usually at least two, and often all three, of these aspects of curriculum contributed directly or indirectly to greater student learning. The researchers also looked at variations in learning for students in different schools *within* each country and found that these achievement differences also were related to differences in curricula.

After reviewing much of the evidence, Diane Ravitch comments:

> The international assessments demonstrate that students tend to learn what they have studied and that they cannot learn what they have not studied. If this point seems obvious, it nonetheless is important advice in a nation where many youngsters choose whether or not to study basic academic courses; where many students are "tracked" into programs that deny them access to courses necessary either for college or a technical career; where students in many schools are taught arithmetic again and again until high school years, instead of being introduced to higher-order mathematical thinking drawn from statistics, probability, geometry, algebra, and other areas.[13]

The curriculum that students follow in high school also affects the likelihood that they will eventually complete college. A large national study of American high school students found that taking advanced academic courses in high school—especially a high level of mathematics—is a better predictor of whether a student will later get a college degree than is the student's race or socioeconomic status.[14]

During the 1980s and 1990s, the decline in enrollments in academic courses in America's high schools was reversed. Most states increased their requirements for graduation from high school, adding courses in core academic subjects, especially in math and science. By the early 1990s, students of all racial and ethnic groups and both boys and girls were taking more academic courses than they were a decade earlier. Enrollments in foreign languages, as well as in math and science, rose considerably. Enrollments in advanced courses in these subjects also rose substantially during this period.[15]

However, increasing the number of required courses in a subject does not necessarily result in all students covering advanced content in that subject area. Schools often respond to the requirement for more courses in a subject such as mathematics by offering more basic or remedial courses in that subject. For example, after the state of Maryland required an additional credit in mathematics (plus one added credit in a fine arts or practical arts course), minority students and girls were likely to achieve equity with white boys in the number of math credits earned. However, many took remedial or lower-level math courses. Moreover, despite the new graduation requirements, students in the nonacademic tracks continued to earn fewer credits and take more practical arts courses than students in the academic program.[16] Thus, while strengthening graduation requirements is likely to raise the achievement of students who have been performing most poorly, it does not, in itself, expose all students to the same level of curriculum.

INTERDISCIPLINARY CURRICULA

The real world is not divided neatly into phenomena that correspond to separate academic disciplines. To understand the working of the environment, we may need to bring to bear knowledge from geology, biology, zoology, chemistry, and other fields. To understand the changes in the American family, we may need to combine knowledge from a number of disciplines, such as history, psychology, sociology, and economics.

Yet, each of the specific subjects that is part of the curriculum may be taught in isolation from the material in other subjects. This "fragmentation" of the curriculum has been seen by some observers as one of the current problems of education, especially at the high school level. Thus, writing of the major criticisms that are being made of American high schools, Kenneth Tewel refers to "a curriculum, that is fragmented, thereby rendering students unable to make important connections to real-world phenomena."[17]

Efforts to relate various separate subjects to each other, and to common problems, go back at least to the early twentieth century. Advocates of social efficiency called for interpreting academic and vocational knowledge to deal with real-life problems. Many of those concerned with child development favored project-centered learning that drew from a variety of disciplines. And social reformers proposed integrating knowledge from many fields in order to solve pressing social problems.[18]

Recently, there has been renewed interest in reducing the isolation of different disciplines in the curriculum, so that students can see how knowledge from each may relate to knowledge from the others. However, the role of traditional disciplines in an "integrated" curriculum remains controversial. For those who favor the full integration of different subjects, traditional academic disciplines are of secondary importance; they are used only in the context of the themes that are the focus of learning. Other analysts of curricula think that, even while bringing the knowledge of various academic disciplines together, it is important to maintain the study of each discipline.

In her book titled *Concept-Based Curriculum and Instruction*, H. Lynn Erickson stresses the use of "unit themes" (such as the environment, or conflict, or living in the future) as focal points for learning to which several disciplines participating in the unit will contribute. But each discipline is studied in depth, preserving its integrity; ". . . it is not a little art, a little mathematics, a little history, and so forth."[19] She argues that, in bringing disciplines to bear on themes, we should do so in a way that ensures "integrity of instruction through the grades related to the key concepts and principles that form the foundation of each discipline."[20] A number of other writers view learning separate disciplines as a prerequisite to competent interdisciplinary work.[21]

While there is disagreement about the extent and manner in which academic disciplines should be related to each other, there is much wider agreement that subjects should not be taught in isolation. Moreover, there is evidence that interdisciplinary curricula and instruction tend to have positive effects on academic outcomes. For example, several studies found that, compared to students who took traditional courses, students who completed interdisciplinary programs in middle school or junior high school made equal or better grades in high school. In his review of relevant research, Gordon Vars says: "More than 100 studies conducted over a sixty-year period point to the same conclusion: Almost without exception, students in innovative interdisciplinary programs do as well as, and often better than, students in so-called conventional programs."[22]

Planning a curriculum that relates different subjects to each other in a meaningful way often faces obstacles. Many teachers, administrators, and parents are accustomed to the traditional system of separate subjects, and some school personnel have a vested interest in maintaining this arrangement. Moreover, cross-disciplinary, multidisciplinary, or fully integrated curricula usually require teachers to spend extra time in planning activities, finding resources, and sometimes meeting together. However, a curriculum that encourages students to learn about and apply a number of disciplines in order to learn about issues and problems of interest in their world can lead to an increased level of motivation and learning.

SUBJECT CONTENT

Deciding which subjects are to be included is only the first step in developing a curriculum. What is to be taught in each subject—what topics, what information, what concepts, what skills, and so on—must be specified also.

BASIC SKILLS VERSUS THINKING SKILLS

Before the twentieth century, the main aims of schools were to teach: (1) a few basic skills such as reading, writing, and spelling in English and adding and dividing in mathematics; and (2) a body of important facts—about history, geography, science, and a few other subjects. More recently, educators (and many others) have increasingly thought that schools and teachers should focus not on the rote learning of facts and basic skills but, instead, on teaching students how to think and to solve problems.

Critics of an education that emphasizes memorizing information argue that such an education does not adequately prepare young people for a technologically complex and changing world of work, in which they will need to have sophisticated understandings, solve problems, and adapt to new situations. Furthermore, critics of "strictly the basics" learning maintain that, in order to be responsible citizens in a democracy and to live satisfying personal lives, young people must learn to think and reason effectively.

They also point to a greater emphasis on critical thinking skills in other countries. For example, Donald Chalker and Richard Haynes, in their book *World Class Schools*, comment, "While the Japanese teacher focuses on teaching an understanding of process and reasoning, the American teacher frequently feeds the expectations of parents and children by giving worksheets that students quickly finish so the child can be given another worksheet. The American student prepares for a test with memorization and short-term cramming; the Asian child prepares to demonstrate an understanding of the process, not just the answer."[23]

However, when American schools have focused on encouraging students to be independent and creative thinkers, as happened especially in the late 1960s and early 1970s, many observers complained that children were not learning important basic information and important basic skills. Stories emerged about high school graduates who could barely read and who did not know the most elementary facts of history and geography. Stung by such criticism, and sometimes pushed by irate parents and employers, some schools returned to emphasizing basic information and basic skills. Over time, the pendulum has swung back and forth between an emphasis on teaching students "the basics" and teaching higher-level understanding (of concepts, principles, etc.) and higher-level thinking skills (such as analysis, synthesis, forming and testing hypotheses and applying knowledge to solve new problems).

Some guidance on this issue is offered by research that deals with concept formation and which compares the learning outcomes of different types of instruction.

DEVELOPING CONCEPTUAL FRAMEWORKS

Drawing on the findings of cognitive research, many curriculum specialists and other educators have pointed out that a set of disconnected facts usually is not meaningful to students nor long remembered.[24] Studies of cognition show that people develop mental frameworks that organize the information they get. Incoming information often is interpreted and modified to fit with existing mental frameworks of concepts and relationships. Information that does not fit into some organizing framework is not meaningful and is easily forgotten.[25]

As children become older, they are able to understand more complex concepts and abstractions. For example, while children in the early primary school grades (age 6 to 8) can group objects on the basis of one particular feature (such as size, shape, or texture), those in higher primary grades (age 8 to 10) are more able to categorize by several dimensions at once (e.g., a blue square can share membership with other blue objects and with other square objects at the same time). As students move to the middle school level and then to the high school level, they are increasingly capable of moving from concrete examples to abstract ideas (such as justice, freedom, and specific gravity), to use logic, to analyze ideas, and to solve problems. Cognitive scientists believe that, as children grow older, there is a natural development of their cognitive capabilities. However, such abilities will develop fully only if students are stimulated and encouraged to use them.

A number of writers on curriculum say that schools need to give more attention to helping students form conceptual frameworks for the information they get in order to promote meaningful learning. H. Lynn Erickson writes:

> National and state frameworks consistently have a standard that says, 'Students will understand the concepts and principles of [science, social studies, mathematics, etc.]'. The traditional and prevalent models of curriculum design list a myriad of topics and facts to be learned (covered), but they fail to emphasize key concepts and principles. This omission creates a missing link in the curriculum and implementation designs of some national standards and most state and district standards.[26]

Erickson calls for a curriculum that emphasizes "essential understandings"—that is, the key principles and generalizations that develop from the fact base.

DEVELOPING THINKING SKILLS

In addition to emphasizing that students should learn concepts and generalizations, rather than facts alone, curriculum analysts also have seen several other types of learning as important. These include learning how to solve problems of specific types, general strategies to investigate and solve problems, and ways to evaluate information received and the significance of conclusions reached. There is some evidence that students make the greatest gains in learning if they are given the chance to collect data, discuss ideas, test hypotheses, and draw conclusions.[27]

Evidence that is important to engage students in reasoning and problem solving comes from the Third International Mathematics and Science Study. In countries where instruction challenged students' thinking most, achievement gains were greatest. For example, for some math topics, countries in which teachers spent more class time on writing equations, achievement gains were larger than in countries where teachers spent more time emphasizing computational skills.[28] The researchers conclude:

> We found evidence that the quantity of coverage associated with a topic is not all that contributes to the learning it produces. . . . The quality of that coverage is also important, both in terms of the level of cognitive demands expected of students and in terms of the types of instructional activities the teacher uses. The data seem clearly suggestive that drill and practice does not appear to be adequate for the level of attainment sought for most students in most countries, and neither is concentrating only on absorbing knowledge and learning to perform routine processes.[29]

Additional evidence of the learning advantages of curricula that involve students in reasoning and problem solving comes from studies of inquiry-based science programs. In such programs, students actively "do" science—preparing questions, designing experiments, organizing data, and developing conclusions.[30] Studies in Wisconsin and California have compared the performance on state and district tests of elementary school students who experienced inquiry-based science instruction and those who followed traditional text-based science programs. Students who had been in the inquiry science programs not only scored higher in science but also did better in math, reading, and writing. Researchers in the California study believe that skills of reading and math are strengthened when students use them while engaged in the high-interest activities of inquiry-based science.[31]

Whether more traditional curricula (focused on teaching basic information and skills) or more innovative curricula (emphasizing thinking skills) produces better-educated students depends on the *kind* of learning that one values. Decker Walker and Jon Schaffarzick reviewed 23 experimental studies that were designed to compare the subject matter achievement of students using innovative curricula with that of students using traditional curricula.[32] They found that students who had studied more innovative curricula generally did better on tests that assessed the kind of content and skills that they had studied—such as application of ideas to new situations. Students studying the more traditional curricula tended to do better on certain other kinds of tests, especially those assessing knowledge of the particular material they had studied and skills they had practiced. For example, students in English courses that focused on grammar did better on grammar, while those whose curriculum focused on the development of themes in writing scored higher on writing assessments. The author of the review concluded that "different curricula are associated with different patterns of achievement.[33]

In recent years, there has been widespread acceptance among educators and others of the idea that young people should learn thinking skills. In some schools, this rhetorical acceptance has been translated into practice. For example, Central Park East High School in New York City encourages students to evaluate (among other questions) how good the evidence is ("How do we know what we know?"), what the viewpoint and possible bias of a communicator is ("Who's speaking?"), and what the significance of a subject or conclusion is ("Who cares?").[34]

However, while most educators give rhetorical support to developing students' thinking skills, in their actual curriculum and teaching practices many schools continue to focus on providing information that students must memorize and give back on tests. Thus, Arthur Applebee writes:

> Progressives and conservatives alike have argued that students should be taught to arrive at new understandings, to think for themselves, to become independent knowers and doers. This in turn will produce flexible lifelong learners able to adapt to changing conditions in the workplace, the home, and the global community. But these goals are rarely attained. Commentators in subjects as diverse as science, math, history, and English . . . have lamented the extent to which learning becomes a matter of memorization and recitation, where the teacher is seen as a provider of knowledge that the student is expected to replicate.[35]

Some attempt to implement programs to promote thinking skills appear to be occurring in many schools—at least at the high school level. A national survey of all accredited high schools in the United States (both public and private), conducted in 1993, asked principals to what extent their schools had implemented programs that promote thinking skills. Almost one-third of the schools said that they had fully implemented thinking skills programs, and about half said they had partially implemented such programs. (They were somewhat more likely to be reported as present in private schools than in public schools.[36]) Such programs undoubtedly vary widely in their comprehensiveness and quality.

FACTS AND THINKING

A curriculum that emphasizes learning specific information and one that emphasizes conceptual understanding and creativity have sometimes been seen as antithetical. At times an extreme and perhaps distorted focus on one aspect of learning has, in fact, led to neglect of other aspects of learning. Thus, a single-minded emphasis on student creativity sometimes has led educators to neglect teaching students important facts and basic skills. Conversely, a single-minded devotion to teaching "the basics" sometimes has led educators to have students memorize isolated fragments of information that do not lead to real understanding.

Rather than being alternatives, learning basic information and learning thinking skills actually are complementary. As many contemporary educators point out, learning facts and simple skills is an essential prerequisite to forming meaningful concepts and generalizations. Concepts, ideas, and principles must be derived from specific facts and from activities using specific skills (such as those of mathematics). H. Lynn Erickson notes: "Idea-centered curricula focus on deeper, conceptual ideas and use facts to support the understandings. Facts are viewed not only as critical for building content knowledge but also as tools for gaining insight into the conceptual ideas that transfer across time and cultures."[37] Conversely, more general ideas and understandings (concepts, theories, etc.) can be useful in finding new facts and showing the connections between facts.

ORGANIZATION OF CONTENT

An effective curriculum must not only teach students an appropriate set of facts, concepts, generalizations, and skills. It also must organize the content in an effective sequence so that (1) students' later experiences build upon their earlier ones, and (2) students can see meaningful relations among specific pieces of knowledge and among specific skills.

Sequence

Sometimes students are taught about the same topics in different grades. For example, such repetition may occur in history or other social studies courses where students may learn about, say, the American Revolution or the Civil War in several grades. Covering the same material—for example, long division—also has been common in mathematics courses.[38]

Covering the same subject matter at different points in a student's education may have some advantages—for example, if the subject is taught again briefly as a "refresher" or with increasing degrees of complexity and sophistication in later grades.[39] However, coverage of the same material often is mostly redundant. Clearly, it is important for curriculum planners to plan the specific content of subjects taught to students across the grades so that time and interest is not wasted with unnecessary repetition.

Curriculum planners and teachers also face the problem of how best to sequence material on a particular topic. A variety of ways to arrange materials in a meaningful sequence have been proposed and used—for example, from concrete to abstract, from whole to part, from general ideas to detailed ones, in chronological order, and in terms of the logical dependency of ideas. Research on this topic suggests that there is no single or simple answer regarding the general importance of sequencing and regarding the most effective types of sequencing. Results appear to depend on the type of material being taught and on the kinds of learning outcomes examined.

A general-to-detailed sequence in which general and inclusive ideas are presented first, followed by related ideas of greater specificity, has been found to be effective when used for highly conceptual, verbal types of content, such as social sciences. On the other hand, in the learning of intellectual *skills*, it appears better to teach simpler component skills before more complex combinations of these parts.[40] An example of such a "learning hierarchy" from the subject of physics is provided by Robert Gagne. In order to learn to calculate the components of force using vector diagrams, the student must have previously learned a number of other skills, such as using trigonometric rules to represent the relationships in a right triangle.[41] While knowledge about effective sequencing of material is limited, educators need to think about what sequences are likely to be most useful in presenting various materials, and to try out and compare the effectiveness of different orders.

Synthesizing Content

For learning to be most meaningful and retained best, facts and ideas must be related to each other. As C. M. Reigeluth says, relating and integrating individual bits of learning can provide students with valuable knowledge (about those relationships), produce a deeper understanding of the individual ideas, increase the meaningfulness and motivational effect of new knowledge, and increase retention.[42] A number of methods have been introduced to help students to integrate content material. One of the most promising is the synthesizing strategy proposed by Reigeluth and his colleagues. A "synthesizer" is a chart that depicts visually the relationships among concepts, procedures, or phenomena (e.g., types of government or parts of an essay); a theoretical structure (e.g., the relationships among concepts used in studying electricity, such as power, current, and resistance); or a procedural structure (e.g., successive steps in the statistical analysis of differences between samples). Both a lesson synthesizer, showing the relationships among ideas within a single lesson, and a set synthesizer, showing the relationship among ideas across many lessons, have been used. While research on the use of this method is limited, the available studies suggest that the use of the synthesizer, and of some related methods, can help students to understand better the relationships among ideas presented in a given subject.[43]

DIFFERENT CURRICULA: TRACKING

One of the main issues of curriculum design is whether all young people should learn the same things or whether there should be different courses of study for those with different interests, abilities, and aspirations.

Before the twentieth century, only a very small percentage of young people attended high schools, which generally offered traditional academic programs. As a more technologically advanced economy required workers with greater skills, and as the use of child labor by industry was restricted, high schools were asked to teach a much larger proportion of the nation's youth, including large numbers of immigrants' children.

Some educators and others maintained that all students should be given rigorous academic training. But the most influential view of the time was that schools should try to meet what many educators saw as the different needs of different students. Schools were responding in part to the pressures they were feeling to try to interest students with varied backgrounds and preparation. David Tyack and Larry Cuban suggest that, in creating a variety of new courses and tracks, educators were "trying to provide something sufficiently practical and engaging to persuade adolescents to stay in school."[44] Moreover, employers encouraged the creation of vocational programs that would give workers the skills needed in business and industry.

Many educators in the early part of the twentieth century saw a varied curriculum as making the schools more democratic. Elwood Cubberly wrote: "As the children of these new classes have crowded into our public schools, our school systems have been compelled to direct their attention less exclusively to satisfying the needs of the well-to-do classes. Education has in consequence recently turned away still more from its aristocratic nature, and has become more and more democratic in character."[45]

While offering a number of different types of curricula made high schools more inclusive, and in this sense more democratic, it also tended to stratify students into a higher-status group in the academic programs and larger lower-status groups in vocational and general programs.

In the United States today, as in most other countries, there is considerable variation in the subjects and materials studied by different students in the same school districts. At the elementary school level, these curriculum differences are relatively small. All students tend to study the same subjects. However, students are often grouped by ability (between classes, within classes, or for specific subjects) and the specific topics covered by those in high-ability versus low-ability groups may differ appreciably.[46] (See Chapter 3 for further discussion of ability grouping.)

As students move into middle school (usually grades 6 to 8) and especially when they enter high school, their programs of study tend to vary much more. In some cases, students attend a specialized vocational school or a school that specializes in certain subjects (the arts, drama, science, etc.). A much larger number of students attend a "comprehensive" high school in which students within the same school often take different programs of courses.

Sometimes students are formally enrolled in separate programs, such as an academic (college preparatory) program; a vocational program (offering broad or specialized preparation for jobs), or a general program (some mix of different types of courses). In many cases, curriculum programs are more informal; students choose elective courses that will prepare them for college, for work after high school, or for no particular life path.

Even when students take the same subject, because it is required of all or because they choose it, they may study somewhat different material. These variations in curriculum may result from ability grouping—for example, into groups assigned to work at accelerated, average, and slower paces. Alternatively, requirements in particular broad subjects may be met by taking a number of different courses; for example, a math requirement may be met by taking calculus, algebra, or basic math.[47]

ENTRY INTO TRACKS

How do students end up taking a particular program of studies? Most students choose their own programs or "tracks." However, students usually follow the recommendations of teachers and counselors.

Studies of the placement of students into different tracks show that students' prior performance, as indicated especially by grades and scores on standardized tests, is the strongest predictor of their placement in a particular track.[48] But factors other than students' prior performance also affect track placement.[49]

With prior school performance held constant, students from poorer, less well-educated families are less likely than others to be in a college-preparatory track. Girls have an advantage over boys in being placed in a college track, other things equal. The effects of race and ethnicity are more complex. On the one hand, when students in a large number of schools are studied, minorities do *not* appear to be disadvantaged. Hispanic students are enrolled in college-preparatory programs in proportions consistent with their prior school performance and other characteristics. African-American students appear to have a *better* chance than white students of being placed in a college-preparatory program (after controlling for prior achievement). This racial difference probably occurs because black students generally attend schools in which the average achievement score is lower than that in other schools; therefore, those at the high end of the score distribution have a better chance of being in the "high-achieving" group than they would have elsewhere.

On the other hand, several studies of the placement of students within the *same schools* have found that low-income black students tend to be put in lower tracks than white schoolmates with equal records of achievement.[50] These effects of social background within the same school appear to result in part from greater intervention by higher-income and white parents, who sometimes lobby school administrators to place their children in higher tracks. Upper-income and white parents also may place pressure on their children to apply for higher tracks. In addition, class or race stereotypes may lead teachers and counselors to give less encouragement to low-income and minority students to enter the "higher" tracks. Overall, the effects of race and ethnicity and of social class on student placement into different tracks appear to be small.

However, while students' backgrounds have only small effects on track placement when their prior school performance is equal, the prior achievement of minorities and of low-income students tends to be below that of non-Hispanic whites (and of Asians). Thus, minorities and low-SES students are much more likely to be placed in low-ability, low-track courses and programs, based on their prior school performance.

How permanent are initial track assignments? In a review of research on tracking, Maureen Hallinan says that "track assignments tend to be less permanent than is commonly believed. It is not uncommon for a student to change tracks during the school year and from one school year to the next."[51]

The flexibility of track assignments varies by subject, by grade level, and by school. One study found much more change of tracks in math than in English among high school freshmen.[52] Track assignments also tend to become more permanent as students' school careers progress. Placements of sixth graders into different tracks, mainly on the basis of prior school performance, tend to continue into middle school and beyond.[53] By the time students get well into their high school years, opportunities for change may diminish.

In his study of schools in 13 American communities, John Goodlad was often told that switching from a vocational program to an academic program could be difficult after completion of the 10th (sophomore) grade and impossible at the end of the 11th (junior) grade without substantially increasing the time spent in high school. He comments: "With two years yet to go, then, the two worlds of secondary education appeared quite far apart in those schools that I visited."[54]

EFFECTS ON ACHIEVEMENT

A central issue in the evaluation of tracking is its effect on student achievement. Views differ regarding whether tracking, and the ability grouping that it usually involves, helps or hinders student achievement. The opposing views are summarized by Robert Slavin:

> In essence, the argument in favor of ability grouping is that it will allow teachers to adapt instruction to the needs of a diverse student body and give them an opportunity to provide more difficult material to high achievers and more support to low achievers. The challenge and stimulation of other high achievers are believed to be beneficial to high achievers. Arguments opposed to ability grouping focus primarily on the perceived damage to low achievers who

receive a slower pace and lower quality of instruction, have teachers who are less experienced or able and who do not want to teach low-track classes, face low expectations for performance, and have few positive behavioral models.[55]

Two types of relevant studies have been done in secondary schools. The first set of studies looks at students who were similar in IQ, prior achievement, and other measures but who were assigned either to tracks or to heterogeneous classes. The later achievement of these groups of initially similar students is then compared. The second set of studies focuses on students who are following different tracks in secondary school but who generally differed in their academic performance prior to entering their particular tracks. The achievement *gains* of students in the different tracks are compared.

Effects of Tracking on Initially Matched Groups

Studies that use initially matched groups of students are intended to see the effects of tracking, and of the ability grouping it entails, on student achievement independent of any initial differences among students who enter the various tracks. Robert Slavin found 29 studies in secondary schools (both high schools and middle schools) in which initially similar groups of students were assigned either to tracks or to heterogeneous groups and compared with respect to later achievement. Overall, he found no effect of ability grouping on student achievement, either in the high-ability or low-ability groups.[56] (For the effects of ability grouping *within* each class, see Chapter 3.)

Frederick Mosteller and his colleagues noted inconsistencies in previous studies and even in previous reviews of studies. They selected for review only the best studies—those that compared groups of initially matched students who were randomly assigned to either skill-level groups or to heterogeneous groups.[57] They found 10 such experimental studies, primarily in middle schools and senior high schools.

Results from five of these studies showed skill grouping to have a positive effect on students' learning, but three of the studies favored heterogeneous grouping, and two studies showed essentially no effect of skill grouping on achievement. These studies (like other studies) generally found that skill grouping tended to have slightly positive effects for high-skill students and slightly negative effects for medium to low-skill students. But the effects of grouping were weak at all skill levels. Marsteller and his colleagues conclude: "Overall, results of the ten studies suggest that XYZ grouping, [i.e., grouping by several skill levels] on average, does not have much effect on achievement."[58]

Evidence from these experimental studies does suggest a possible tendency for students grouped by skill to be more satisfied with their schooling experience (their school, their class placement, and the difficulty of schoolwork) than students of similar skill in heterogeneous classes. Among six experiments that included measures of student satisfaction, four of the six studies found no difference between skill groups and mixed groups. In the two studies that found a difference, students in skill-grouped classes were more satisfied than those in heterogeneous classes.[59]

Effects of Tracking on Initially Different Students

Studies that have compared achievement gains for students assigned by normal placement procedures to different tracks or class levels often have found greater effects on achievement than have the experimental studies, which compared initially similar students placed either in homogeneous or in heterogeneous ability groups. Students who follow "higher" tracks, especially the academic track, usually enter these programs with higher IQ scores, higher scores on prior tests, and higher socioeconomic status than those of students who enter "lower" tracks, such as the general or vocational track. But even after controlling for such prior differences, many studies have found that students in high tracks gain significantly more in achievement than do students in low tracks.[60]

For example, using data from a national sample of high school students, a carefully done study compared growth in math achievement for students in college-preparatory tracks to that of students in other tracks, from their sophomore to senior years in high school.[61] About 80 percent of the difference between those in different tracks was explained by initial differences, primarily in math achievement as sophomores, between those in the different tracks. But about 20 percent of the difference was due to the effect of the tracks themselves; most notably, the higher the students' math achievement as sophomores, the more gain they experienced in college tracks.

Why, under normal tracking practices, do students in higher tracks gain more in achievement than those in lower tracks? One possible reason is a phenomenon known as "fan spread," which is a general tendency, regardless of circumstances, for high achievers to gain more per year than do low achievers;[62] because of this phenomenon, the gap between the groups tends to grow over time.

Another possible reason for the varying gains in achievement in different tracks is that students in academic tracks usually take more courses, or more advanced courses, than do students in other tracks, such as the general or vocational tracks. (Such track differences in course-taking were minimal in the experimental studies of tracking, in which students were initially matched.) However, there is only limited and mixed evidence that differences in course-taking account for the greater achievement gains made by students in higher tracks.[63] For example, one study found that the fact that students in academic tracks take more, and more advanced, courses in math and science partially explained their greater achievement gains in these subjects; however, differences in course-taking did not explain track differences in achievement gains in a number of other subjects, such as reading and civics.[64]

In addition to the "fan spread" phenomenon and differences in course-taking, variations in teaching and classroom experiences may help to account for differences in average achievement gains.

Classroom Differences Across Tracks

Grouping students by level of skill has been seen by many educators as a way of facilitating instruction. Teachers overwhelmingly prefer skill grouping, with many teachers saying that grouping makes it easier for them to plan to teach a curriculum.[65]

However, critics of ability grouping and tracking charge that these practices often reduce the quality of teaching. Teachers of high-ability classes may be better qualified than those who teach lower-track classes. Thus, in secondary schools, teachers of lower-level science and math classes tend to have less experience, are less likely to be certified in math or science, and tend to have fewer degrees in these subjects.[66]

Students in higher-level tracks are likely to cover a larger amount of content in a given subject; this occurs partly because teachers in the higher-level classes spend a larger proportion of class time on learning, versus administrative or disciplinary matters. Also, teachers in higher-level classes are more likely to emphasize thinking, problem solving, and creativity, while teachers of lower-level classes are more likely to focus on facts and drills.[67]

In his large-scale study of 38 schools in 13 communities throughout the United States, John Goodlad describes some of the differences between classes from different track levels as follows:

> High track classes spent a larger proportion of class time on instruction, and their teachers expected students to spend more time learning at home than was the case in the low tracks. High track classes devoted more time to relatively high level cognitive processes—making judgments, drawing inferences, effecting syntheses, using symbolism, and so on. Low track classes devoted a much larger share of instructional time to rote learning and the application of knowledge and skills. Again, the middle track classes were much more like the upper than the lower track classes. . . .
>
> Teachers in the upper track classes definitely expressed more clearly their expectations for students, and they were perceived by students to be more enthusiastic in their teaching. . . . Students in high track classes saw their teachers as more concerned about them and less punitive toward them than did other students. Teachers in these classes spent less time dealing with student behavior and discipline.[68]

When classes in higher-level and lower-level tracks are compared, as they are in Goodlad's and other studies, a picture of higher-track classes as more interesting, stimulating, and pleasant for students generally emerges.

Variations in Track Effects on Achievement

The effects of tracking on learning may vary considerably in different circumstances. Relevant circumstances include teaching methods, course content, and certain characteristics of the schools.

Slavin suggests that the small effect of ability grouping in secondary schools may be due to the use of the same traditional teaching methods at all ability levels. He writes: "The lesson to be drawn from research on ability grouping may be that unless teaching methods are systematically changed, school organization has little impact on student achievement . . . if teachers continue to use some form of lecture-discussion/seatwork/quiz, then it may matter very little in the aggregate which or how many students the teachers are facing."[69] He points out that in elementary schools, where teaching methods varied more, certain kinds of ability grouping seemed to be generally helpful to learning. Similarly, Kulik and Kulik stress that benefits of grouping students by skill level will be unlikely to occur if teachers cover the standard curriculum in the same way at all skill levels.[70]

Besides differences in teaching practices, tracks at equivalent levels (low, average, or high) but in different schools, may differ in a variety of other ways. The criteria for assigning students to different tracks may vary. Some schools rely only on objective measures of achievement, such as prior grades and scores on standardized tests; other schools also use other criteria, such as teacher judgments, parental or student choice, and sometimes race or gender in order to have students with different characteristics represented in a given track, such as an honors math track. Schools also vary in the number and size of their tracks; the size of classes within each track; the ease of transferring across tracks; and, perhaps most important, the kinds of courses available, and the content of courses taught, to students in each track.

With so much possible variation across schools, it is not too surprising that a study in the middle and secondary schools of two midwestern cities found that the effect of students' tracks on their achievement varies in different schools (even when holding other variables, including race and social class, constant.)[71] Students in the upper tracks did better in English and in math in some schools than in others. Similarly, lower-track students performed better in some schools than in others.

In reporting that study, Maureen Hallinan, does not specify the differences in tracking procedures across schools that affect their success. But in other writing, she suggests a number of ways in which the negative consequences that often accompany tracking can be reduced or eliminated, while retaining its benefits.[72] These approaches include using rewards that recognize the accomplishments of low-track students (in order to keep their motivation high); keeping tracks homogeneous so that teachers can fit instruction to students' skill levels; flexibility in reassigning students so that they are in an appropriate track; and improving instruction, especially by making subjects interesting for students. However, critics of tracking argue that a tracking system is inherently flawed—that no matter how it is arranged, tracking students into different courses or skill levels produces status differences, stereotypes, and different life chances.[73]

Overall, the evidence suggests that tracking students by ability, interests, and skill level can have either positive or negative effects on their achievement. When tracking is used, administrators and teachers need to try to create conditions (such as those mentioned previously) that will maximize its possible positive benefits and avoid conditions that lead to negative outcomes. (See the Summary and Conclusions section at the end of this chapter for more discussion of this issue.)

EFFECTS ON FURTHER SCHOOLING AND CAREERS

Early educators who planned varied high school programs for students with different skill levels and interests hoped that such choices would help keep young people in school. However, American students in non-college tracks are somewhat less likely to graduate from high school than are other students. Graduation rates for students in the college track have been found to be about 10 percentage points higher than for those in non-college tracks.[74]

This difference occurs in part because students in nonacademic tracks generally come from families of lower socioeconomic status and have lower achievement scores, compared to students in the college track. Some studies conducted in Ireland and Israel suggest that, even with these factors held constant, providing more varied programs (such as vocational education) has not helped to keep students in school longer than they would otherwise attend.[75] However, some recent programs in the United States that try to integrate academic studies with workplace experiences have reduced dropout rates, especially among those considered to be at high risk of not graduating.[76]

With regard to college attendance, it is, of course, not surprising that students in college-preparatory programs will be more likely than other students to go to college. This expected difference has been found repeatedly. What is more interesting is that even among students with similar records of performance in high school, academic-track students are more likely to aspire to and actually enroll in college (and, if enrolled, to graduate from college).[77] These differences between those with similar high school records probably reflect differences in parental aspirations, students' own aspirations early in high school, income differences (making college more or less affordable), courses taken to prepare for college, and perhaps other qualifications for college (especially scores on SAT tests). In addition, students in nonacademic programs probably receive less encouragement from teachers and from peers to attend college.

The existence of separate ability tracks does not necessarily lead to more educational inequality. A study of the effects of ability grouping in junior high schools in Taiwan found that placement in high-ability classes led to higher educational aspirations among students of lower social class background, as well as among other students.[78] The author of this study concludes that, on balance, ability grouping contributes to greater equality of educational outcomes for those of different social class backgrounds in Taiwan.

Do vocational programs in the high schools increase the occupational success of those students who take such programs? The outcomes of job-oriented programs have varied. Some studies have found that students who participate in vocational programs have not had enhanced chances for being employed or getting higher wages. Data from California, in fact, have shown high school dropouts doing as well at work as graduates of vocational programs. Participation in vocational programs has been found to be least helpful for the work outcomes of poor and minority students.[79]

However, recent studies of "school-to-work" programs indicate that some types of vocationally oriented programs can have more positive outcomes.[80] These federally funded programs, intended to link academic and work-based learning, vary in content in specific locations; the most common activities for students are visits to work sites and job shadowing. Students in school-to-work programs have better attendance and are less likely to drop out of school than are comparable students who are not in such programs. They also believe that their experiences in exploring careers were helpful in clarifying their own career goals. There is some evidence that, once they enter the labor market, participants in such programs are more likely to be employed, to be in meaningful career paths, and to earn higher wages than comparable nonparticipants. In some other countries, such as Germany, programs of vocational education in high school have been quite successful in training students who are not planning to attend college for skilled occupations and placing them in relatively high-paying jobs.[81]

Clearly, not all work-oriented programs are equally effective. Among the characteristics that seem to contribute to their success are: (1) Rather than downplaying academic subjects, such as science and mathematics, they give students substantial amounts of work in academic subjects, while linking this knowledge to success in careers that are attractive to students. Thus, students are motivated to acquire knowledge and skills that will prepare them for high-skill jobs. (2) Close and supportive contact between students and adults, who serve as mentors in school and as workplace supervisors, contributes to student involvement and success in school-to-work programs. (3) Good career-oriented programs are flexible enough so that students are not locked into a specific career at an early age and also are able to attend college if they decide to do so.

MAGNET SCHOOLS

Students usually follow different tracks (formal or informal) within the same comprehensive high schools. Another way in which some school districts have designed curricula to serve the interests and abilities of particular groups of students is by developing separate "magnet schools" for students with different interests. Magnet schools are schools with specialized curricula designed to attract students from throughout a school district. (Many actually occupy only part of a school building and thus are "schools within schools".)

At the elementary and middle school levels, magnet schools include (among others) schools that focus on basic skills; on foreign languages; on science, math, and/or computers; on visual, performance, and/or creative arts; and on gifted and talented students. At the high school level, where the focus is more likely to be career-oriented, magnet programs include (among others) those giving special emphasis to science, aviation, engineering, and/or computers; vocational career preparation; business and marketing; creative and performing arts; medical careers; and college preparation.[82] A national study in 1994 found that over half of secondary magnet schools and about a quarter of elementary schools have some kind of admission test.[83]

Many magnet schools were created as a way to decrease racial segregation in the schools by bringing together students from an area larger than that served by the traditional (and often segregated) neighborhood school. In many cases, assignment to a magnet school is voluntary; in other cases, it has been mandatory.

What effects have magnet schools had on student motivation and achievement? A number of studies have found that students in magnet schools have average scores on standardized tests in reading and mathematics that are above the average scores of students in other schools in their districts. Even when students in magnet schools are compared to those with similar characteristics (such as earlier academic achievement, race, and socioeconomic status), the magnet school students have significantly higher scores on tests in a variety of subjects. Students in magnet schools also have been found to have fewer behavior problems, more on-task behavior, and better attendance than students in regular schools. They also are less likely to drop out of high school than are students of similar background in regular schools.[84]

The higher achievement of students in magnet schools, compared to those in regular schools, is not explained by differences in courses taken.[85] It may be that students in schools that have a special curriculum or pedagogical focus form a stronger bond with their school than do students in other schools. Also, there is some evidence that teachers in magnet schools may be more highly motivated and have higher expectations for students than do their peers in regular schools.[86] (A fuller discussion of magnet schools is presented in Chapter 8.)

SUMMARY AND CONCLUSIONS

Evidence from American schools and from international comparisons shows that much of the variation in student achievement is due to the types of courses that students take and the amount of time they spend on particular subjects. In addition, the level of the subject content—for example, the type of mathematics taught—also makes a difference; students who study more advanced content do better. These results, while not surprising, suggest the importance of schools having curricula that provide their students with sufficient coverage of important academic subjects. Also, programs that apply several academic disciplines to the same practical problems tend to improve learning.

Most states in the United States recently have increased the number of academic courses, especially in math and science, that students must complete in order to graduate from high school. These new requirements have resulted in students taking more courses in basic academic subjects. However, many students take lower-level or remedial courses (e.g., remedial math) to fulfill these requirements. Schools may need to give greater attention to the content of such required courses in order to be sure that the content is at an appropriate level.

Other aspects of the content of courses in a particular subject also are important. There has been recurring controversy about whether school curricula should focus on imparting basic information and skills or on more general ideas and problem solving. Students who study traditional curricula tend to do well on tests of the specific information that these curricula cover. However, students make greater gains in learning when the curriculum challenges their thinking (e.g., in testing hypotheses and establishing relationships), rather than concentrating on providing information and having students perform routine processes. Moreover, curricula that challenge students to reason and solve problems tend to involve students more in their learning and such involvement generally promotes higher interest and motivation.

Research on cognitive processes shows that disconnected facts usually are not very meaningful to students nor long remembered. Effective curricula must provide organizing concepts and frameworks that make concrete information meaningful. While official statements on curricula usually cite the importance of students understanding the key concepts and principles of given subjects, in practice an emphasis on such broad understandings often is lacking.

A curriculum that emphasizes learning specific information and skills and one that emphasizes conceptual understanding, problem solving, and even creativity are not necessarily antithetical. Facts and basic skills are essential prerequisites to forming meaningful concepts and generalizations. Conversely, general concepts and understandings are useful in discovering new information and new connections between facts. Both types of knowledge need to be taught together.

As students move into higher grades, especially into high school, most follow (either formally or informally) separate curriculum programs. Most often these are college-preparatory, vocational, or "general" programs. Ethnicity and social class, in themselves, have only small and inconsistent effects on student placement into different tracks. However, because blacks, Hispanics, and low-income students tend to have poorer performance records in lower grades, students from these groups are overrepresented in non-college-preparatory tracks. As students progress into the later years of high school, change from one curriculum track to another becomes difficult.

Students in academic (college-preparatory) tracks have been found to make greater gains in achievement than the gains made by other students. This advantage of students in the "higher" tracks does *not* appear to be due to any effects of ability grouping *per se*. Some of the difference in achievement gains may be due to the general tendency for initially higher achievers to have higher rates of learning over time, regardless of circumstances. The advantage of students in academic tracks also is explained partly (although far from completely) by the fact that they take more, and more advanced, courses in subjects such as science and math. In addition, the teaching and class experiences of students often are different in higher tracks than in lower tracks. Teachers of high-ability classes tend to be better qualified than those who teach lower-ability classes. Teachers in higher-track classes spend a larger part of class time on instruction and less time on discipline; they also devote more time to encouraging student thinking and problem solving and less time on rote learning than do teachers of lower track classes.

The effects of tracking on student achievement vary among schools; for example, lower-track students have performed better in some schools than in others. Also, the outcomes of vocational programs vary widely. Many vocational programs in the United States and in several other countries have not been very successful in influencing students to complete high school or in preparing students for good jobs. However, some well-designed vocational programs that integrate academic studies and work experience have raised students' school attendance, reduced dropouts, and placed students on paths to good careers.

An approach to curriculum differentiation that has generally worked well is the magnet school. Each magnet school usually emphasizes a particular subject area. Students in magnet schools generally score higher on standardized achievement tests than do comparable students in regular schools in their districts. Magnet school students also have better attendance, fewer behavior problems, and fewer dropouts than do students at regular schools.

Overall, having separate curriculum programs for students of different skill levels and different interests has both potential advantages and potential disadvantages. In order for the practice of curriculum tracking to provide net benefits to students—especially to those who have not done very well earlier in school—separate curriculum programs must provide, and be seen by students as providing, opportunities for them to pursue their interests and to reach their goals. Courses in "lower" level programs need to include solid academic content, to have able teachers, and to be taught with as much (or more) energy and creativity as courses for students who start with stronger academic skills. Expectations and standards of performance for students need to be high in every program and students in every program should be helped to experience success in their schoolwork and to be rewarded for doing so. In addition, the location of students in tracks needs to be flexible so that students can switch from one program to another without difficulty and all students can choose to take courses that prepare them for college if and when they wish to do so.

NOTES

1. For a discussion of the widely shared purposes of education, see H. Gardner, *The Disciplined Mind: What All Students Should Understand.* New York: Simon & Schuster 1999.

2. D. Angus and J. Mirel, Rhetoric and Reality: The High School Curriculum. In D. Ravitch and M. Vinovskis, eds., *Learning from the Past.* Baltimore: Johns Hopkins University Press, 1995.

3. N. Smith. The Core Program. *Social Studies, 36,* 1945, 164–168.

4. D. Ravitch. *National Standards in American Education: A Citizen's Guide.* Washington, D.C.: The Brookings Institution, 1995, Chapters 2 and 3.

5. J. Goodlad and Z. Su, Organization of the Curriculum. In P. Jackson, ed., *Handbook of Research on Curriculum.* New York: Macmillan, 1992, pp. 327–344.

6. Ravitch, *National Standards,* Chapter 3.

7. W. Schmidt, High School Course-Taking: Its Relationship to Achievement. *Journal of Curriculum Studies, 15,* 1983, 167–182.

8. J. Coleman, T. Hoffer, and S. Kilgore, *High School Achievement: Public, Catholic, and Private Schools Compared.* New York: Basic Books, 1982; S. Morgan and A. Sorensen, Parental Networks, Social Closure, and Mathematics Learning: A Test of Coleman's Social Capital Explanation of School Effects. *American Sociological Review, 64,* 1999, 661–681.

9. L. Schorr, *Common Purpose.* New York: Anchor Books, Doubleday, 1997, pp. 251–253.

10. J. Stigler, S. Lee, G. Lucker, and H. Stevenson, Curriculum and Achievement in Mathematics: A Study of Elementary School Children in Japan, Taiwan, and the United States. *Journal of Educational Psychology, 74,* 1982, 315–322.

11. L. Peck, *Pursuing Excellence: A Study of U.S. Eighth-Grade Mathematics and Science Teaching, Learning, Curriculum, and Achievement in International Context.*

Washington DC: National Center for Educational Statistics, U.S. Department of Education, November 1996.

12. W. Schmidt and Others, *Why Schools Matter: A Cross-National Comparison of Curriculum and Learning.* San Francisco: Jossey-Bass, 2001.

13. Ravitch, *National Standards*, p. 88.

14. C. Adelman, *Answers in the Toolbox: Academic Intensity, Attendance Patterns, and Bachelor's Degree Attainment.* Washington, DC: U.S. Department of Education, 1999.

15. Ravitch, *National Standards*, Chapter 3.

16. G. Rossman, *Pathways Through High School: Translating the Effects of New Graduation Requirements.* Annapolis, MD: Maryland Department of Education, 1987.

17. K. Tewel, *New Schools for a New Century.* Delray Beach, FL: St. Lucie Press, 1995, p. 2.

18. J. Beane, *Curriculum Integration.* New York: Teachers College Press, 1997, Chapter 2.

19. H. Erickson, *Concept-Based Curriculum and Instruction.* Thousand Oaks, CA: Corwin Press, 1998, p. 65.

20. Erickson, *Concept-Based Curriculum*, p. 45.

21. See, for example, Gardner, *The Disciplined Mind*, pp. 53–54.

22. G. Vars, The Effects of Interdisciplinary Curriculum and Instruction. In P. Hlebowitsch and W. Wraga, eds., *Annual Review of Research for School Leaders.* New York: Scholastic, 1996, p. 148.

23. D. Chalker and R. Haynes, *World Class Schools: New Standards for Education.* Lancaster, PA: Technomic Publishing, 1994, p. 136.

24. See, for example, C. Bereiter and M. Scardamalia, Cognition and Curriculum. In P. Jackson, ed., *Handbook of Research on Curriculum.* New York: Macmillan, 1992, pp. 486–516.

25. See J. Byrnes, *Cognitive Development and Learning in Instructional Contexts.* Boston: Allyn & Bacon, 1996.

26. H. Erickson, *Concept-Based Curriculum and Instruction.* Thousand Oaks, CA: Corwin Press, 1998, p. 50.

27. L. Lowery, *Thinking and Learning: Matching Development Stages with Curriculum and Instruction.* Kent, WA: Books for Educators, Inc., 1989.

28. Schmidt and Others, *Why Schools Matter.*

29. Schmidt and Others, Ibid., pp. 356–357.

30. O. Jorgenson and R. Vanosdall, The Death of Science? *Phi Delta Kappan, 83,* 2002, 601–605.

31. M. Klentschy, L. Garrison, and O. Ameral, Valle Imperial Project in Science. *Journal of Research in Science Teaching* (In Press).

32. D. Walker and J. Schaffarzick, Comparing Curricula. *Review of Educational Research, 44,* 1974, 83–111.

33. Walker and Schafferzick, Ibid., p. 97.

34. D. Meier, *The Power of Their Ideas: Lessons for America from a Small School in Harlem.* Boston: Beacon Press, 1995.

35. A. Applebee, *Curriculum as Conversation: Transforming Traditions of Teaching and Learning.* Chicago: University of Chicago Press, 1996, p. 21

36. G. Cawetti, *High School Restructuring: A National Study.* Arlington, VA: Educational Research Service, 1994.

37. Erickson, *Concept-Based Curriculum*, p. 51.
38. J. McNeil, *Curriculum: A Comprehensive Introduction*, 5th edition. New York: HarperCollins, 1996, pp. 359–363.
39. J. Bruner, *The Culture of Education*. Cambridge, MA: Harvard University Press, 1996.
40. J. Van Patten, C. Chao and C. Reigeluth, A Review of Strategies for Sequencing and Synthesizing Instruction. *Review of Educational Research, 56,* 1986, 437–471.
41. R. Gagne, *The Conditions of Learning*, 3rd edition. New York: Holt, Rinehart and Winston, 1977, p. 143.
42. C. Reigeluth and F. Stein, The Elaboration Theory of Instruction. In C. Reigeluth, ed., *Instructional Design Theories and Models*. Hillsdale, NJ: Lawrence Erlbaum, 1983.
43. Van Patten and others, *A Review of Strategies.*
44. D. Tyack and L. Cuban, *Tinkering Towards Utopia: A Century of Public School Reform*. Cambridge, MA: Harvard University Press, 1995, p. 52.
45. E. Cubberly, *Public Education in the United States*. Boston: Houghton Mifflin, 1919, revised 1947, p. 505.
46. See J. Oakes, A. Gamoran, and R. Page, Curriculum Differentiation. In P. Jackson, ed., *Handbook of Research on Curriculum*, 1992, pp. 570–608.
47. See Oakes and Others, *Curriculum Differentiation.*
48. A. Gamoran and R. Mare, Secondary School Tracking and Educational Inequality. *American Journal of Sociology, 94,* 1989, 1146–1183; S. Dauber, K. Alexander, and D. Entwistle, Tracking and Transitions through the Middle Grades. *Sociology of Education, 69,* 1996, 290–307.
49. Gamoran and Mare, Secondary School Tracking.
50. Oakes and Others, *Curriculum Differentiation*; Dauber and Others, *Tracking and Transitions.*
51. M. Hallinan, Tracking: From Theory to Practice. *Sociology of Education, 67,* 1994, 79–84.
52. M. Hallinan, School Differences in Tracking Effects on Achievement. *Social Forces, 72,* 1994, 799–820.
53. Dauber and Others, *Tracking and Transitions.*
54. Goodlad, *A Place Called School*. New York: McGraw-Hill, 1984, p. 145.
55. R. Slavin, Achievement Effects of Ability Grouping in Secondary Schools: A Best-Evidence Synthesis. *Review of Educational Research, 60,* 1990, 471–499; quote from p. 473.
56. Slavin, Ibid.
57. F. Mosteller, R. Light, and J. Sachs, Sustained Inquiry in Education: Lessons from Skill Grouping and Class Size. *Harvard Educational Review, 66,* 1996, 797–842.
58. Mosteller and others, Ibid., p. 807.
59. Mosteller and others, *Sustained Inquiry in Education.*
60. A. Gamoran and M. Berends, The Effects of Stratification in Secondary Schools. *Review of Educational Research, 57,* 1987, 415–435.
61. Gamoran and Mare, *Secondary School Tracking and Educational Inequality.*
62. J. Coleman and N. Karweit, *Information Systems and Performance Measures in Schools*. Englewood Cliffs, NJ: Educational Technology Publications, 1972.
63. Slavin, *Achievement Effects of Ability Grouping.*

64. A. Gamoran, The Stratification of High School Learning Opportunities. *Sociology of Education, 60,* 1987, 135–155.

65. Mosteller and others, *Sustained Inquiry in Education.*

66. J. Oakes, *Multiplying Inequalities: The Effects of Race, Social Class, and Tracking on Opportunities to Learn Math and Science.* Santa Monica, CA: RAND Corporation, 1990.

67. Goodlad, *A Place Called School.*

68. Goodlad, Ibid., 154–155.

69. Slavin, *Achievement Effects of Ability Grouping,* pp. 491–492.

70. C. Kulik and J. Kulik, Effects of Ability Grouping on Secondary School Students: A Meta-analysis of Evaluation Findings. *American Educational Research Journal, 19,* 1982, 415–428.

71. Hallinan, *School Differences in Tracking.*

72. Hallinan, *Tracking: From Theory to Practice.*

73. For one statement of this view, see J. Oakes, More Than Misapplied Technology: A Normative and Political Response to Hallinan on Tracking. *Sociology of Education, 67,* 1994, 84–89.

74. Gamoran and Mare, *Secondary School Tracking.*

75. D. Hannan, S*chooling Decisions: The Origins and Consequences of Selection and Streaming in Irish Post-Primary Schools.* Dublin: Economic and Social Research Institute, 1987; Y. Shavit and R. Williams, Ability Grouping and Contextual Determinants of Educational Expectations in Israel. *American Sociological Review, 50,* 1985, 62–73.

76. K. Hughes, T. Bailey, and M. Karp, School-to-Work: Making a Difference in Education. *Phi Delta Kappan, 84,* 2002, 272–279.

77. Oakes, *Curriculum Differentiation.*

78. C. Broaded, The Limits and Possibilities of Tracking: Some Evidence from Taiwan. *Sociology of Education, 70,* 1997, 36–53.

79. Oakes, *Curriculum Differentiation.*

80. Hughes and Others, *School-to-Work.*

81. D. Stern and D. Wagner, *International Perspectives on the School-to-Work Transition.* Cresskill, NJ: Hampton Press, 1999.

82. N. Estes, D. Levine, and D. Waldrip, eds., *Magnet Schools: Recent Developments and Perspectives.* Austin, TX: Morgan, 1990; C. Smrekar and E. Goldring, School Choice in Urban America. New York: Teachers College Press, 1999.

83. J. Nathan, *Charter Schools.* San Francisco: Jossey-Bass, 1996, p. 7.

84. See, for example, M. Raywid, The Accomplishment of Schools of Choice. In Estes et al., *Magnet Schools,* pp. 31–47; A. Gamoran, Student Achievement in Public Magnet, Public Comprehensive, and Private City High Schools. *Educational Evaluation and Policy Analysis, 18,* 1996, 1–18.

85. Gamoran, Student Achievement, Ibid.

86. P. Fleming, R. Blank, R. Dentler, and D. Baltzell, *Survey of Magnet Schools.* Washington, D.C.: James Lowry and Associates, 1982.

Chapter Three

TEACHERS AND STUDENTS
IN THE CLASSROOM

The focal point of the educational system is the classroom. Here is where most learning does or does not take place.

A great deal has been written about what goes on in the classroom, based on the experiences of teachers, observations of classrooms, and systematic research. What generalizations can we derive from this large amount of material? What seem to be the key elements in the classroom that influence student learning?

In this chapter, I consider the way in which the classroom is organized—the learning activities in which students are engaged; the grouping of students (especially ability groups and cooperative learning groups); standards for evaluating students; and the rules and incentives that help shape student behavior. We will see how variations in classroom organization may affect student learning.

I also examine the interactions that occur between teachers and students (and among students as well) in the classroom. We will want to see especially what kinds of teacher behaviors and what kinds of teacher–student interactions contribute most to student learning.

Both the organization of the classroom and the kinds of interactions that occur in the classroom affect not only the opportunities that students have to learn but also their motivation to do so. I trace some of the connections between students' classroom experiences and their perceptions and motivation.

Finally, the role of computers in the classroom, and the effects they may have on learning, is discussed. The chapter closes with a schematic overview of how various factors in the classroom affect student learning and a section that summarizes the material presented and draws some conclusions.

ACTIVITIES IN THE CLASSROOM

Life in the classroom, for both students and teachers, consists primarily of a series of activities. How much and how well students learn depends to a considerable extent on the kinds of activities in which they are involved. Phillip Schlechty comments: "The key questions for schools to focus on concern what students are expected to do in order to learn whatever it is expected they will learn."[1]

TEACHER-CENTERED AND STUDENT-CENTERED ACTIVITIES

One important question concerns the relative advantages of "teacher-centered" versus "student-centered" activities. In the traditional teacher-centered classroom, all or most activities focus on the teacher. The teacher presents information, gives demonstrations, asks questions of students in "recitation" periods, and conducts class discussions.

The instructional methods used in teacher-centered classrooms have some advantages. By lecturing and by making other direct presentations, the teacher can communicate much information in a short time. She can control the pace, content, and organization of the material. And the same facts and ideas can be presented to all students. H. J. Freiberg and Amy Driscoll state: "The lecture method has survived over 2000 years because it is both efficient and familiar."[2]

However, the traditional method of teachers lecturing to students (often somewhat derisively referred to as "talk and chalk") has come under severe attack. "Talking at" students may make them passive and leave them bored. Lectures often emphasize lower-level cognitive skills of memorizing facts, rather than higher-level skills such as analysis, synthesis, and problem solving. Students may be unchallenged and unmotivated to actively engage in their own learning. Critics of such teacher-centered methods of instruction argue instead for instruction in which students can actively and somewhat independently pursue their own learning. In more "student-centered" classrooms, students spend a large part of their time actively engaged in individual or small-group activities, such as gathering information, writing papers, preparing reports, or conducting experiments.

The effectiveness of teacher-centered instructional methods have been compared in research studies to the effectiveness of student-centered instruction.[3] In general, these studies indicate that more traditional, more direct teaching results in greater student learning of specific knowledge and skills—for example, in reading and in math—than does less direct instruction. Several studies in grades 4 through 8 found that effective mathematics teachers spent twice as much time in lecture, demonstration, and discussion as less effective math teachers. Effective teachers used this additional presentation time to give many explanations, to use many examples, and to check for student understanding; students were then able to do independent "seatwork" with less difficulty. Other support for the value of traditional instructional methods comes from a "meta-analysis" of about 800 studies of teacher effectiveness conducted by H. J. Walberg.[4] Walberg found that explicit and direct teaching was among the factors that contributed to higher student achievement.

Teacher-centered methods, using direct instruction to whole classes, are more advantageous in some circumstances than in others. Such methods are most effective in early school grades and for students of lower ability or skill levels.[5] Moreover, direct instruction appears to be most applicable to a well-structured body of knowledge (e.g., the periodic table of elements in chemistry or the formal structure of the U.S. government) and less applicable for content that is less well structured or where skills do not follow explicit steps (such as analyses of literature or discussion of social issues or concepts).[6] Lectures may be especially useful to introduce and explain new concepts, to show how specific pieces of information fit into logical structures, and to review and summarize information.

While teacher-centered instruction is often effective in communicating specific information and skills to students, instruction that involves students more actively in their learning appears more effective in engaging students' interest in their schoolwork. In a longitudinal study of both elementary and high school students in 33 schools across the United States, students gave responses during the course of each day about their level of engagement in given classes—that is, whether they were attentive to their lessons or were thinking about other matters. Students were found to be most attentive to their lessons when they worked in groups or in labs and least attentive during lectures or while watching television or a video in school. Their engagement was at an intermediate level during class discussion, individual work, and student presentations.[7]

Active participation by students in classroom activities also may help students gain a deeper understanding of the subject matter. Young children learn concepts of shape and color better when they are asked to sort objects according to their similarities and differences than when they are merely told about shape and color concepts. A study of students' knowledge about science found that when students are given a more active role in discovering and constructing knowledge, they showed greater understanding, were better at problem solving, and displayed more creativity. Another study of 11,000 students in 820 high schools found that schools that reorganized their academic programs around active learning had significantly higher achievement gains in all subjects (math, reading, social studies, and science) than did other schools. Similar results were found in several studies of elementary and middle schools.[8]

Overall, the evidence indicates that teacher-centered instruction and student-centered instruction each have advantages. Presentations of a teacher to a whole class, as in lectures, are an efficient way of communicating the same material to many students in a short period of time; it appears especially effective in teaching specific information. However, instructional methods that engage students more actively in gathering information and formulating ideas are more likely to interest and motivate students in the subject they are studying. Active, student-centered instruction also is more likely than teacher-centered methods to stimulate students' conceptual thinking, problem solving, and creativity.

Teacher-centered, direct instruction and student-centered methods that emphasize independent activity by students need not be mutually exclusive. A teacher may combine the two approaches, for example, by using lectures to introduce and to summarize a topic and having students carry out independent (or group) investigations of some aspect of the topic. Also, lectures can be made more effective by getting the student more actively involved in the material. J. S. Cangelosi found that "for students to be engaged in lecture-type learning activity, they must attentively listen to what the teacher is saying . . . such engagement requires the student to be cognitively active, while physically inactive."[9]

A number of techniques have been used to increase the extent to which students are actively listening to a lecture. These techniques include setting a purpose for listening (e.g., to learn how to set up an electrical circuit), teaching students how to take notes, and asking students to summarize the key points of the lecture (as well as their questions about it) for each other. In addition, the teacher can check students' understanding of the lecture material by interrupting at various points to ask questions about the material. Also, the teacher may follow lecture segments with questions that are intended to promote discussion and critical thinking about the lecture material. Preferably, the teacher would alert students that such critical discussion will follow the lecture. Such procedures are likely to increase the extent to which students are "cognitively active," rather than passive, when listening to lectures.[10]

In addition, direct instruction may be used to help the student develop her own independent cognitive skills. By describing and modeling processes of reasoning, analysis, synthesis and problem solving, the teacher can provide a "support structure" or "scaffold" for the student to develop her own higher-level cognitive skills. The teacher can use more directive teaching initially and then gradually transfer greater responsibility to the student for independent inquiry.[11]

CHARACTERISTICS OF ACTIVITIES

The effectiveness of a classroom activity (whether teacher-centered or student-centered) depends on a number of its characteristics. These include: (1) the cognitive processes required of the student; (2) the value of the activity to the student; (3) the difficulty of the activity; and (4) how much autonomy the student has in carrying out the activity.

Depending on such characteristics of activities assigned, students may perceive themselves as more or less competent to do the work, as having more or less control over their success, as caring more or less about completing tasks, and as having greater or lesser expectancy of being successful. As a result, their motivation and effort may be affected. Because of these variations, and of the different cognitive demands of various activities, students may learn more or less of certain kinds of knowledge and skills. Next we consider the characteristics of student activities in somewhat greater detail.

Cognitive Processes Required

Activities assigned to students vary with respect to the types of cognitive processes they require. Activities may involve students in learning and recalling facts, forming concepts, relating facts and concepts to each other (e.g., with regard to their causal order), applying concepts or principles to specific cases, solving problems, and so forth.[12]

In order for students to successfully accomplish tasks that require higher-order thinking (analysis and synthesis of information, hypothesis formation, problem solving, etc.), they must first accomplish the lower-level tasks that require acquisition of information. Discussing the importance of such a sequence of types of activities, James Byrnes remarks:

> ". . . it is not a problem if preschool or early elementary teachers focus mainly on lower-level skills. The problem is that teachers of older students never go beyond fact-learning."[13]

The phenomenon of (some) teachers having students engage in activities—such as classroom drills and seatwork—that focus almost exclusively on memorization of facts and use of simple skills, appears to occur most often when students come from racial minorities and/or from families of low education and income.[14] Teachers may use low-level activities that require only low-level skills for a variety of reasons—because they think that their students cannot do higher-level work, because they think such activities will help with problems of class management, or because of pressures from administrators to raise students' scores on standardized tests. Whatever the reasons, a failure to move beyond teaching information and basic skills to activities that promote skills of analysis and problem-solving leaves many minority and low-income students, as well as some other students, with an inferior preparation for attaining further education or good jobs.

Value of Activity to Student

In a review of research concerning motivational influences on students' academic performance, Kathryn Wentzel and Allan Wigfeld note that "students' purposes for an activity are central to their decisions about how avidly they pursue an activity."[15] They assert that the value of a task to a student depends on its interest value (how much she likes or is interested in the activity) and the utility value of the activity (its perceived usefulness).

In one study, students in elementary, middle, and high schools across the United States were asked these questions about specific activities in their classes: "Was this activity important to you?" and "How important was it in relation to your future goals?" The more a student perceived a specific activity to be relevant to him (based on these two questions), the more attentive he was to the class lesson.[16]

An activity may appear interesting or useful to students for a variety of reasons. The activity may interest students because they see it as relevant to their own lives and experiences. For example, in a memoir Frank McCourt tells of the positive transformation that occurred in the efforts of a previously lethargic high school class when he introduced a writing activity that drew on the wartime letters of the students' relatives and neighbors.[17] Similarly, if the subject of an activity (e.g., reducing violent crime) seems to students to be important to their community—and thus, indirectly, to them—their interest in the activity is likely to increase.

An activity also may be valued by students because they believe the knowledge gained will be useful in their own personal lives (e.g., in learning to drive a car or in avoiding sexually transmitted diseases). Finally, activities that are novel and those that are game-like are likely to engage students' interest.

When students see school activities as dull and having little relevance to their own lives, they are apt to exert little effort and may become inattentive or even disruptive. Such problems may occur especially among students from racial and ethnic minorities and those from families of low socioeconomic status. Writing about African-American students, Jabari Mahari says that students of color often see themselves as being forced to learn things in which they have no interest.[18] Mahari argues that teachers should try to connect school knowledge to the culture and personal experiences of students. As an example of such connection, he describes a program in which African-American students were asked to analyze rap music in terms of various themes, such as identity, values, male-female relationships, and violence. Students became very interested in the activity, which was used to develop both their writing and thinking skills.

Level of Difficulty

In order for students to learn well, the activities they are assigned must be at an appropriate level of difficulty. Tasks need to be neither too easy nor too difficult for students to do well. Achievement motivation has been found to be highest when tasks are of moderate difficulty.[19]

Having students engage in activities that are very easy for them, given their abilities and prior preparation, is likely to leave them bored. A national study found that the more students find class activities challenging, the greater their concentration in class. Moreover, activities that are very easy for students are not likely to develop much their knowledge and their capacities for critical thinking and problem solving. Some writers have criticized American schools for downgrading the difficulty of their courses and textbooks.[20]

While tasks that are too easy can be unmotivating and produce too little learning, activities that are too difficult for students also may not be conducive to learning. High motivation and achievement has been found to be related to students' sense of personal competence and their perceptions of a high probability of success in their work. An activity that is very difficult for a student is likely to lead him to feel incompetent, to doubt that he can succeed, and therefore to stop trying very hard. Similarly, when students are not given adequate time to complete a task, they are likely to feel less involved in their work.[21]

Tasks of high difficulty also are likely to raise fears of failure, especially among those whose general fear of failure (based on past experiences) is high. Such perceptions and fears of likely failure often lead students to withdraw (psychologically or even physically) and/or to engage in disruptive behavior. In their review of research on the relation of teacher behavior to student achievement, Jere Brophy and Thomas Good summarize findings that indicate that teachers need to plan activities of appropriate difficulty that lead to success experiences for students. This body of research indicates that teachers must balance the need to cover enough content with the aim of enabling students to move "through small steps with high (or at least moderate) rates of success and minimal confusion or frustration."[22]

Brophy and Good emphasize that trying to produce high rates of success does not mean having students do low-level "busywork." Rather, they state that students need to practice new learning until they have mastered it thoroughly and, where necessary, learn to integrate the new learning with other concepts and skills and apply it to problem situations. They comment: "Thus, the high success rates result from effort and thought, not mere automatic application of already overlearned algorithms."[23]

The appropriate level of difficulty for student activities will vary with the type of students and the type of material involved. Continuous progress at high rates of success has been found to be especially important in early grades and where students are learning basic knowledge and skills that will be applied later in higher-level activities (e.g., doing simple mathematical operations of addition, subtraction, and division, prior to solving math problems). Students from lower socioeconomic backgrounds and low-achieving students require smaller steps and higher success rates than do higher-achieving students, who tend to be more highly motivated by challenging activities.[24] It is important that teachers diagnose the learning needs and abilities of their students so that the activities they assign are at a level of difficulty that provides challenge without discouraging students.

Autonomy for Students

Another important aspect of classroom activities that affects students' motivation and learning is the extent to which they are given control and responsibility over what to do and how to do it.

Most school administrators, teachers, and parents believe that the experience and knowledge of educators qualify them to make decisions in the school and classroom. However, in the tradition of progressive education, some contemporary education reformers maintain that students learn best if they choose what, when, and how they want to learn.

A number of experimental programs that gave great autonomy to students have had only limited success. While some self-directed students responded positively to their independence, many students drifted without direction, feeling bewildered and frustrated. In general, relevant research finds that most students do less well academically when they are free to choose the subjects, methods, and pace of their own learning.[25]

While it seems best for administrators and teachers usually to maintain general control over student activities in the classroom, there are important advantages to giving students some autonomy and some participation in decisions about their activities. First, where teachers exercise strict control of students' behavior, students may become resentful and, in some circumstances, rebellious. For example, the nonconformist group of "streetwise" boys in the high school studied by Jay McCleod hated having teachers tell them what to do. One boy said, "I hate the teachers. I don't like someone always telling me what . . . to do."[26] Some of these boys did more schoolwork when placed in the class of a teacher who had firm goal requirements but who permitted his students to do the work in their own way at their own pace.

Giving students some measure of control over, and responsibility for, their activities also can help raise their motivation to do their school tasks well. One of the conditions under which a person's achievement motivation is aroused is that she have some control over her performance.[27] If someone else, such as a teacher, is telling the student exactly what to do and exactly how to do it, then successful completion of the task is not much of an achievement for her.

The results from general research, which shows achievement motivation to be related to autonomy, are paralleled by results from studies of students' motivation in schools. The more students believe that they have control over success in their school activities, the greater their persistence and effort, as well as their achievement. The more teachers are disposed to give some autonomy to students, the higher the task motivation of the students.[28]

The effect of student autonomy on student motivation is illustrated in a study of 134 middle school (seventh grade) classrooms drawn from 12 school districts in Michigan.[29] The researchers found that most students expressed a wish for more decision-making opportunities in math classes (helping decide what math work they do during class, what the class rules are, etc.) than they had experienced before in grade school (sixth grade). However, the middle school students generally experienced a *decrease* in opportunities for participation in classroom participation, compared to such opportunities in their grade school math classes. Thus, there was generally a mismatch between student desires for greater autonomy and the reality of reduced autonomy in the middle school. The more students saw their present middle school as putting greater constraints on their participation in classroom decisions than was true in their elementary classes, the larger the declines in the students' interest in math between the sixth and seventh grades.

Other research also has found that democratic teaching styles, in contrast to authoritarian teaching styles, contribute to high academic motivation among students. When students have the opportunity to participate in decision making and to take some responsibility for their own learning, they tend to be more highly involved in their tasks.[30] Allowing students greater participation in decisions also has been found to improve student attitudes toward the teacher and the subject matter. Positive student attitudes have been related to teachers' use of student ideas, willingness to listen to students, and respect for their contributions.[31]

Just as an appropriate level of task difficulty will vary with different types of students, so too will an appropriate level of student autonomy vary. Students who have the ability, motivation, and self-discipline to work independently will benefit most from a considerable amount of autonomy and participation in decisions concerning their activities. Students who have lower levels of ability or preparation, and those with less self-discipline or initial motivation, generally will need to have procedures for their activities laid out more completely.[32] However, even for less able and initially less well motivated students, giving students as much opportunity as feasible to decide on the specifics of what they will do and how they will do it is likely to increase their task motivation and ultimately their achievement.

LEARNING ACTIVITIES AND CLASSROOM ORDER

In order for teacher and student activities to result in learning, they must take place in a context of order in the classroom. Students' behavior must be directed toward accomplishing the tasks assigned, rather than in wandering around, in trying to find out what to do next, or in casual conversation or "horseplay" with peers. Most teachers are often, sometimes continuously, concerned with maintaining order in their classrooms—that is, with keeping students' cooperation in learning activities.

Management of classroom activities becomes more difficult with certain patterns of activities than with others. When instruction is differentiated for various students—that is, different individual students or groups of students have different assignments, or work at different paces on the same assignment—the teacher has a harder job of guiding, monitoring, and assisting students than when all students work together at about the same pace. For example, in classes in which mastery learning programs were used, delays sometimes occurred because some students finished their work successfully while other students were still attempting to do so.[33] In addition, activities in which students have greater choice of their specific behaviors and greater physical mobility in the classroom (e.g., role-playing exercises) create greater problems of supervision, control, and coordination for teachers than do activities in which students have fewer choices and move around less.

There is another important way in which the types of activities used affect classroom order. A given activity may or may not engage the attention, the interest, and the motivation of students. For example, student involvement tends to be high in teacher-led small groups and in mastery-learning activities; student involvement tends to be low in "seatwork" activities.[34] When student involvement is high, problems of order are reduced. Students do not have to be closely monitored to see that they are not "goofing off" or misbehaving. Classroom order arises out of the engagement of students in their work.

Often the activities that present the greatest technical problems of class management—for example, individual assignments or group projects—are also those that produce the greatest student engagement in their work and thus promote an order based on student involvement. Conversely, activities that present the fewest technical problems of class management—for example, lectures or seatwork—often result in low student engagement and thus create management problems stemming from inattention or off-task behaviors.

Sometimes teachers may choose to use—or use most often—activities that make it easiest to maintain classroom order, even though the particular activities may not promote the types of learning that are most desirable. Some studies have found that many teachers emphasize easily managed procedures, such as students completing worksheets, without much concern about whether students are attaining a full understanding of the materials. As Walter Doyle notes, "Lessons can move along quite smoothly without high-quality engagement with the content.[35]

In choosing class activities—for a single lesson or over a longer period of time—teachers are faced with the problem of balancing the need for smooth management and good order with the need for promoting the fullest learning. Without smooth management and good order, little learning can take place. On the other hand, good order should not be an end in itself. Moreover, activities that engage student interest can help to promote good order as well as learning.

STUDENTS' WORK AND TEACHER ACTIONS

The characteristics of the activities assigned to students have important effects on their motivation and learning. But what the teacher does after the student begins work on a task also is important. The teacher must monitor the student's progress, give help where needed, provide feedback to the student about his progress, and finally evaluate the student's performance. If this sequence of events proceeds effectively, the student's task motivation will be maintained and he will complete the task successfully.

MONITORING, HELPING, AND PROVIDING FEEDBACK

After assigning tasks to students, the teacher needs to monitor their performance to see whether they are doing the work correctly and at a proper pace. Monitoring student progress in their work has been found to be especially important with students who have been low achievers and when students are engaged in challenging tasks and/or working independently, for example, in seatwork.[36] However, the teacher should not monitor students' work so closely that students perceive that they lack any real control over their own work. Excessively close monitoring is likely to undermine students' intrinsic task motivation.[37] A proper balance between necessary guidance and stifling student autonomy will depend on the student's ability level and the difficulty of the task.

As the teacher monitors students' responses and work, he needs to give them feedback on how they are doing and help as needed. For example, as the first-grade student reads aloud, the teacher corrects mistakes and helps the student to pair sound with letters; when students respond to the teacher's questions during recitation period, he indicates whether their answers are correct and clarifies matters that they may have misunderstood; when the high school student has outlined a research paper, the teacher tells the student if the topics included are appropriate and may suggest another important topic that the student should cover.

In his analysis of about 800 studies on the relation between teaching methods and student achievement, H. J. Walberg found that corrective feedback by teachers was among the methods that makes a large positive contribution to student achievement.[38] Similarly, in their extensive review of research on teaching methods, Jere Brophy and Thomas Good find that feedback from teachers to students about their performance, including their homework, is one of the strongest contributors to high student achievement. They say: "Students should know what work they are accountable for, how to get help when they need it, and what to do when they finish. Performance should be monitored for completion and accuracy, and students should receive timely and specific feedback. . . . Where performance is poor, teachers should provide not only feedback but re-teaching and follow-up assignments to make sure that the material is mastered."[39]

EVALUATION

In the course of monitoring students' work and providing feedback to them, teachers usually will give students some informal indication of how they evaluate the students' work. At various points, and especially when students complete an assignment or are tested, teachers provide more formal evaluations. How a student is evaluated is likely to influence the student's perceptions of her competence and her motivation and effort in future work.[40]

There is evidence that giving frequent tests or quizzes generally contributes to high student achievement.[41] However, the frequency of tests may not be as crucial as the standards for evaluation. First, it is important that teachers provide clear standards of excellence.[42] For example, when a teacher is grading math work, students should know how much weight she will give to using the correct method for solving the problem, to getting the correct answer, to showing all the steps of the work, and to neatness. General research and theory on achievement motivation indicates that a clear standard of excellence is one of the conditions necessary for stimulating high achievement motivation.[43]

An important aspect of standards for evaluation is the extent to which each student's performance is judged by some absolute criterion (e.g., what percentage of her answers are correct) versus being judged by her performance relative to that of other students. Grading students "on a curve" (i.e., in terms of their relative performance) guarantees that some students will get low grades. Usually the same students consistently will have low rankings relative to their peers (even if they are doing well by some absolute criterion); thus, they will experience repeatedly low evaluations of their work. Often such students will come to adopt "ego-protective" strategies, such as downgrading the importance of academic work, that undermine their motivation and achievement.[44]

In classrooms that are oriented to student mastery of the material, rather than their ranking relative to peers, every student who tries and who performs well can experience the success of getting a good grade. Students in such settings have been found, more than students in different types of settings, to focus on self-improvement rather than on social comparison, to see themselves as able, and to have high expectations for success.[45] Other research suggests also that students' intrinsic motivation to do their schoolwork (their engagement in the work itself) is higher when schools and teachers base their evaluation on students' mastery of their work rather than on comparisons to peers.[46]

TEACHER EXPECTATIONS

The reactions that teachers exhibit toward students' schoolwork—their standards of evaluation, the amount and kinds of help and feedback they give to students, and so on—is influenced greatly by the teachers' expectations about student performance.

Teachers generally perceive some students as having more academic ability and as likely to perform better than others. In forming their expectations, teachers tend to rely on students' records (test scores and grades), on the reports of other teachers, and on their own classroom experiences with students. However, teacher expectations are sometimes influenced also by the students' social class and race; they may have higher expectations of middle- or upper-class students than of lower-class students and higher expectations of non-Hispanic whites than of blacks or Hispanics.[47]

The expectations that teachers have for students' academic performance affect their behavior toward their students. When they have low expectations of students, they tend, for example, to call on them less often to answer questions; give them the answers to questions more often, rather than helping them to find the right answers themselves; criticize them more often when they fail at a task; praise them less often when they succeed; place fewer academic demands on them; and pay less overall attention to them. Some studies have found that teachers give black students less positive feedback and more negative feedback than white students, although this has not always been found to be true.[48]

The expectations that teachers have of their students do appear to affect the students' academic performance. Low teacher expectations tend to lower students' performance, while high expectations tend to raise performance. These effects undoubtedly occur in part because of the links between teacher expectations and teacher behavior. Teacher expectations may also have an impact on students' performance because they affect students' own expectations. Students become aware of their teacher's expectations for them and they tend to have expectations for themselves that are similar to those of their teachers.[49]

While teacher expectations appear to have some effect on students' performance in school, this effect is not large for individual students. Brophy concludes from his own research, and that of others, that a typical student's academic performance is lowered or raised 5 to 10 percent as a result of teacher expectations.[50]

However, teacher expectations, and those of school administrators as well, do not affect only individual students. They also may affect the programs and the atmosphere of the entire school. Especially in schools that enroll mostly low-income minority students, the teaching staff and administrators may have basically given up on providing a good education. Their low expectations are reflected in the few demands placed on their students.

TEACHER PRAISE AND OTHER REWARDS

Students in the classroom, like people anywhere, are more likely to continue effort on a task when their behavior is rewarded. The process by which teachers give feedback about, and evaluation of, students' work involves at least implicit rewards (and/or punishments) in the form of appraisals of the student's work. Praise by teachers can have a substantial impact on students.

An analysis of 96 experimental studies found that verbal praise leads to an increase in students' intrinsic task motivation.[51] Explicit praise, as merited, also may be important for maintaining and improving student performance. There are a number of reasons why praise may increase motivation and performance. Praise of student's work raises the student's perception of her competence to do the task, raises her expectancy of further success on this and related tasks, and thus increases her motivation to perform the task. Praise also conveys information to the student about the teacher's expectations and about what good work is. In addition, the positive experiences of praise connected to an activity may increase the value of the activity for the student, further increasing her intrinsic task motivation.

Praise is especially likely to be effective when used with students from low socioeconomic backgrounds or with dependent or anxious students.[52] These types of students are more likely than others to lack confidence in their competence and therefore require more reinforcement when they do well.

Praise by a teacher is most likely to be effective when it is specific rather than general (e.g., given for solving a specific set of problems correctly rather than for "doing well in the subject").[53] Specific praise communicates to the student just what kind of behavior is desirable and thus encourages him to repeat it.

Praise for a student's effort may strengthen his task motivation.[54] However, in an analysis of 96 experimental studies concerning the relation of rewards to task motivation, Judy Cameron and W. D. Pierce conclude that rewards can have a *negative* effect on task motivation when they are given to people just for doing a task, without consideration of how well they are performing.[55] Thus, while some praise for students' effort is desirable, the reactions of a teacher to each student's work should ultimately depend on how well the student meets standards of performance.

Additional research shows the importance of making it clear to students that their performance reflects their current skills and effort, not their innate intelligence; otherwise, current high-performers may see effort as unnecessary and current low-performers may see effort as ineffective.[56]

Whether praise by a teacher increases students' effort and achievement also may be affected by whether students see the praise as *deserved*. A study of elementary school students gathered information about whether the students saw teachers' praise as deserved. Praise seen as deserved led to greater student participation in classroom discussions. More classroom participation was, in turn, related to higher achievement in reading, even after initial reading ability was controlled.[57]

Overall, praise by teachers appears to be most effective in raising student motivation and performance when it is given for specific behaviors; when it recognizes effort but does not ignore performance; when it focuses on the student's current behaviors and *not* on her supposed innate abilities; and when it is seen by the student as deserved.

External Rewards

Rewards other than praise may, of course, also be given to students by teachers. Grades may be an important reward for a number of reasons. Good grades may signify personal success to the student and may bring approval from parents and others. In addition, various kinds of other extrinsic rewards—such as gold stars, extra recess time, or candy treats—sometimes are used to encourage student effort and performance.

Some theorists have cautioned against the use of tangible rewards on the grounds that, while they may increase present effort, such tangible rewards may reduce later motivation to work on the task out of intrinsic interest. Edward Deci and his colleagues have summarized the results of over 100 studies concerning the effects of tangible rewards (such as money, prizes, trophies, and awards) on students' intrinsic motivation (as indicated by their self-reported interest or by their later free choice of the activity).[58] They found that when tangible rewards were offered for engaging in a task, for completing the task, or for performing the task well, intrinsic motivation to do that task generally was lower than it was among students not offered tangible rewards.

Deci and his colleagues assert, with some supporting evidence, that tangible rewards are less likely to depress intrinsic motivation when they do not undermine students' self-determination and when they maintain or increase students' perception of their own competence. Thus, if teachers offer tangible rewards to encourage students to engage in a task, they should do so in a way that is supportive, rather than controlling or pressuring, and in a way that preserves the self-perceived competence of many students (e.g., by giving rewards to most or all students, not only to a few who excel in a task).

DEALING WITH UNDESIRABLE STUDENT BEHAVIOR

When students work on assigned tasks, their efforts and accomplishments can be encouraged and rewarded. But what should teachers do when students behave in ways that interfere with their own or with other students' learning activities? The most common such behaviors include being late for class; cutting class; not bringing necessary books or supplies; inattentiveness; talking that is disruptive; mild verbal or physical aggression (such as calling another student names or pushing him); cheating; and failure to do homework. Students also may commit more serious transgressions, such as using or selling drugs, extortion, theft, or assault.[59]

To deal with behaviors that interfere with learning, teachers and school administrators may use a number of approaches, including managing classes in ways that keep students engaged in activities; developing and communicating effective rules; and imposing penalties for violations of rules.

Class Management

Inappropriate or disruptive behavior by students is more likely to occur when students are not engaged—physically and psychologically—in classroom activities. When there are excessive delays in the flow of classroom events or when activities are not well-defined, well-structured, and interesting for students, their attention and actions are likely to wander from the task.[60]

The close connection between classroom activities and undesirable behavior by students is illustrated in a study of 242 black inner-city elementary school classrooms.[61] The researchers saw children getting out of their seats, wandering around the room, opening drawers, rattling papers, leaning across the table, talking with other children, calling out to get the teacher's attention, and turning toward or touching another child. Commenting on these results, Jacqueline Irvine notes: "These minor student disruptions, which were associated with the teacher's lack of management skills, occurred when students were unoccupied, when they made transitions to other periods, and when they became bored with drawn-out recitation sessions; they did not occur because the children were uncontrollable, incapable, or unwilling to learn."[62]

Rules

Another way to help discourage inappropriate or off-task behavior by students is for school administrators and teachers to formulate appropriate, enforceable rules of behavior and communicate these rules clearly to students.[63] Rules are most likely to be effective if they are few, simple, clear, and stated in terms of what positive behaviors are desirable, rather than what behaviors are prohibited.[64] A system of rules that is overly restrictive, unclear, or inconsistent may cause students to feel frustrated and resentful and thus interfere with learning. In other words, rules should facilitate learning; they should not put a student in a straitjacket.

If rules are to be maximally effective in guiding students' behavior, students have to believe that they are reasonable and appropriate. Administrators and teachers must explain and justify the rules, so that students can see them as fair and necessary for their own education. Students are most likely to accept and to follow school and classroom rules if they participate in shaping them.

Paula Short, Rick Short, and Charlie Blanton discuss their experiences in many schools with regard to improving student discipline. They state that one of the critical components for strengthening discipline is student involvement in the development of school-wide expectations for behavior.[65] For example, involvement was one of the elements in a Discipline Management Program carried out in a secondary school in a large midwestern metropolitan area. This program was successful in sharply reducing fighting, disrespectful actions toward teachers, and disruptive noise at the school.[66]

There is much evidence from research in a variety of organizations that people tend to support what they help to create.[67] These findings, as well as some experience directly in schools, suggests that giving students a role in helping to formulate the rules they must live under tends to increase their conformity to the rules.

Penalties

While the frequency of undesirable behavior by students can be reduced by better class management, by getting students more motivated in their schoolwork, and by a clear set of rules, some transgressions of the rules are bound to occur. In order for rules to be effective, there must be some penalties for breaking them, and students must know clearly, and in advance of any transgressions, what the possible penalties are.

There has been much controversy about the use and effectiveness of punishment in changing behavior. It is clear that punishment and threats of punishment often inhibit undesired behavior—at least in the short run and while the punisher is watching.[68] There is evidence that various penalties and threatened penalties applied to students for misbehaving in school—being kept late, getting a poor grade, even being paddled—sometimes have inhibited behaviors that teachers and administrators would like stopped.[69]

However, it also is clear that punishment often may be ineffective or even stimulate further undesirable behavior. The person punished may feel angry and resentful at this treatment. He may seek to "get even" with the punisher—although perhaps waiting until he is not being watched and/or the punisher is less able to act.[70] Thus, frequent use of corporal punishment in schools has been found to be associated with school vandalism.[71] Also, use of punishment, especially corporal punishment, as a primary method of discipline is associated with delinquency among youth.[72] Frequent use of punishments in schools makes students' attitudes toward their teachers and toward school subjects more negative.

Punishment is more likely to be effective under some conditions than under other conditions. In the short run, penalties (or threats of penalties) are most likely to be effective if they are speedy (rather than delayed in time), certain (rather than unlikely or uncertain), relevant to something the student cares about, and of sufficient magnitude.[73] Thus, for example, if a teacher reacts to every instance of a student initiating a fight by immediately and substantially reducing the offender's recess time for that day, and students care about having recess time, the frequency of fighting is likely to drop considerably. Related to the need for punishment to be relatively certain, there is considerable evidence that when punishment is consistent, it is more likely to be effective.[74]

For punishment to be most effective, it needs to be seen by the (potential) target of the punishment not only as sure, quick, and sufficiently unpleasant, but also as legitimate. Punishment that is consistent makes it seem not only more likely (when a transgression occurs) but also more fair. Otherwise, the student may reasonably ask "Why did you punish me now but not when I did the same thing last month?" The problem of consistency becomes particularly important if inconsistency seems to reflect favoritism. Then the student's question becomes "Why punish me and not him for a similar offense?" Perceived favoritism may become an especially important issue if several racial or ethnic groups are present in the school.[75]

Penalties are more likely to be seen as legitimate, and thus be resented less, if they are proportionate to and, if possible, logically linked to the offending behavior. For example, as Paula Short and her colleagues note, if the student has not finished her work on time, a logically linked penalty would be to require her to use other "free" time to complete the unfinished work.[76]

Acceptance of penalties as fair and legitimate by students also is likely to be increased by student participation in school and class decision making. It was noted previously that students are more likely to accept rules of behavior when they have a part in formulating such rules. Similarly, students are more likely to accept penalties for violating the rules as legitimate if they have helped to create these rules, especially if they also have helped to mold guidelines for penalties for various kinds of offenses.

Finally, punishment for undesirable behavior is much more likely to be effective if it is *combined with reward* for positive behaviors. Students, like others, are much more likely to switch from prohibited behaviors (which usually are giving them rewards of some kind) to approved behaviors when the net balance of rewards and penalties tilts clearly in favor of the approved behavior. This is most likely to happen when the rewards of constructive academic activity—intrinsic interest, success in schoolwork, teacher approval, parental approval, extra privileges, and so forth—are increased at the same time that penalties for nonacademic behaviors increase.

Discipline and Class Activities

While rules of student behavior and penalties for breaking rules are necessary, too much emphasis on discipline can be harmful to students' learning. The essential purpose of discipline in the classroom is to keep students working on academic tasks, but class time spent on discipline is time taken away from learning; moreover, disciplinary interventions by the teacher disrupts the flow of class activities.

Successful teachers reduce the amount of time spent on enforcing order by trying to catch potentially disruptive behavior early and by making brief and unobtrusive interventions. For example, direct eye contact with an offender, moving closer, very short verbal desist statements such as "Shh" or "No" may be used. By making interventions early, short, and in a form that does not invite comment or discussion by the student, the flow of class activity is only minimally disturbed.[77]

There are, of course, situations in which student misbehavior is difficult to control with brief and unobtrusive actions and thus where teachers need to intervene more forcefully to enforce class order. However, experience and research on class management make it clear that teachers cannot rely primarily on discipline, especially in the form of penalties, to get students to engage in learning activities. Order in the classroom must derive primarily from involving students in a well-structured set of activities that manage to engage their motivation in some way. Discipline, in the form of rules and penalties for breaking rules, can help to keep students on-task, but it cannot itself get students fully engaged in their schoolwork.

OVERALL QUALITY OF STUDENT–TEACHER RELATIONS

The overall quality of relations between students and their teachers has been found to be linked to a number of student attitudes and behaviors. Positive student attitudes toward the teacher, the subject matter, and the class have been found to increase as teachers display greater warmth and more willingness to listen to students. Furthermore, when students perceive that teachers are supportive and care about them, they are more likely both to follow classroom rules and to be motivated to master the subjects they are studying. Also, democratic teaching styles have been found to increase students' academic motivation.[78]

It is not necessary for teachers to relax their standards and "go easy" on students in order to be seen in positive ways by their students. Students who describe their teachers as supportive and caring also tend to describe these teachers as consistent in setting rules and as having high, although attainable, standards for performance. These teachers are, in addition, seen as being concerned for their students' well-being and as being fair to all students.

When students' academic efforts are given warm support by teachers, they are likely to value success in doing their work, in part because they value the approval of the teacher. Students in such a supportive atmosphere also are likely to have their sense of competence raised, along with their confidence that they can do required tasks successfully. In addition, when teachers are well liked by their students, norms among students tend to shift in the direction of supporting achievement among their peers. When teachers are unpopular, peer norms are more likely to oppose achievement.[79]

Several studies have found a general decline in the warmth of student-teacher relationships as students move out of elementary school and into higher grades.[80] In one such study, Jacquelynne Eccles and her colleagues investigated students' attitudes toward mathematics in 12 school districts in Michigan.[81] They found that students who moved from highly supportive math teachers in the sixth grade to less supportive seventh-grade math teachers (based on students' ratings of their teachers' friendliness and fairness) showed a decline in their ratings of the intrinsic value, usefulness and importance of math. Low-achieving students showed the most negative change in their attitudes toward the subject when they saw their present teachers as less supportive than their previous teachers.

These studies suggest that schools and teachers need to try to preserve the close student–teacher relationship that tends to be most common in lower grades, even as students mature and move into grades where they have a different teacher for each subject. A number of organizational devices, including small school size or creating smaller-size "schools" and programs within schools, can be helpful in promoting close relations between students and teachers (see Chapter 6).

ORGANIZING CLASSES: INDIVIDUALS, WHOLE CLASS, OR GROUPS?

An important aspect of classrooms is whether activities take place for the class as a whole, for subgroups, or for individuals.

INDIVIDUAL WORK

Much of American students' time in classrooms is spent working alone. For example, each student may be given a worksheet and asked to do a set of division problems or to answer questions about a brief story. Such individual activities may engage each student in recalling, practicing, or applying the information, concepts, and skills that the teacher has presented to the whole class or that is contained in their textbooks. (Students also may work individually with computers. This kind of individual activity is discussed separately later in this chapter.)

Individual work by students has been seen by some as desirable because it may permit each student to work at her own pace. However, while activities for individual students sometimes are necessary or useful, there is considerable evidence that working alone often is detrimental to students' motivation and achievement. Unless independent "seatwork" by students is continuously monitored by teachers, students' engagement in their work and their achievement often are lower than they are for either whole-class or group activities.[82] Such negative effects of individual "seatwork" are particularly apparent in classes of 20 students or more. In classes of this size, the teacher has little time for giving feedback and guidance to each student.

Studies comparing American students to students in Asian school have found that American students are more likely to work alone. Researchers have found that the emphasis in the United States on individual work at an individual pace has led many American students to feel lonely. Moreover, American children are less likely than Asian students to say that they like school.[83] Commenting on this research, Jeanne Chall says: "It is ironic that the ideal in the United States of individualizing instruction, originally thought to bring greater desire for learning and higher achievement, is seen by [these researchers] as contributing to U.S. students' lack of enthusiasm for school and their lower academic achievement."[84]

Advocates of "progressive" education have argued that students will become highly motivated in their work when they are given sufficient autonomy—choosing their own goals, their own activities, their own methods, their own pace, and so on—with teachers functioning only as resource persons and guides. A few plans for such independent learning by students—for example, the Dalton Plan, used in many schools in the 1920s and 1930s—have been tried. Such independent learning has worked well for some students with initially high motivation, high skills, and high self-discipline. But most students exposed to arrangements calling for them to take substantial responsibility for their own education responded with frustration and/or idleness. Moreover, for teachers, the task of coordinating, monitoring, and assessing the disparate activities of a large number of students working independently left most teachers exhausted.[85]

Overall, the evidence of past experience and research indicates that, while some autonomy and some independent work by students is desirable, students benefit by the greater interaction with teachers (and with other students) that they usually get in groups. Such interaction with others provides greater input, help, and feedback from others than typically occurs in independent work. Interaction with others may occur in a single group constituted by the whole class or in subgroups of the class.

WHOLE-CLASS ACTIVITIES

Activities in which the class participates as a whole usually involve lectures by the teacher; recitations by students (that is, students responding to questions posed by the teacher); discussions among students (with the teacher as initiator and moderator); or some combination of these activities. The class as a whole also may listen to (and perhaps discuss) presentations by members of the class or watch and/or listen to audiovisual materials (television programs, videos, audiotapes, etc.).

Whole-class activities have some important advantages. Lectures and demonstrations by the teacher, as well as other activities for the whole class, provide all students with the same body of necessary information and ideas. Because all students in the class are learning the same materials at the same pace, the teacher's job of preparing lessons, running the class smoothly, and assessing students' work is less difficult and stressful than it is when students work at different activities and/or at different paces.

Teaching students in a whole-class format also has some important problems and limitations. One problem is that students usually differ in their ability or skill level. Therefore, the optimal level of difficulty of material presented or assignments given, as well as the optimal pace of the learning, may vary for different students. For some students, the material may be too easy and the pace too slow; for others, the material may be too hard and the pace too fast.

As part of a class that learns the same material at the same pace, students also tend to have little autonomy in their work and to be fairly passive. The focus of the class is on the teacher—certainly during lectures, to a large extent during recitations, and to a considerable extent in other whole-class activities (such as discussions) as well. Students have relatively little interaction with each other and do not stimulate or help each other much in their schoolwork.

ABILITY GROUPS

To tailor teaching to different student ability and skill levels, classes often are divided into subgroups of students. (Grouping of students into *separate classes or tracks*, based on ability level, is discussed in Chapter 2.)

Within-class ability groups are most often created for reading and mathematics in elementary schools. For example, a third-grade teacher may create three groups of students, based on their skill levels in arithmetic. The teacher may give short lessons to each subgroup separately, while students in the other groups work by themselves on other arithmetic assignments. Students combine again into one class for some other subjects (e.g., social studies or music).

Ability groups within classes are rarely, if ever, used in high schools and are much less common in middle school classes than in elementary schools. There have been a few studies of ability grouping in middle school and junior high school classes. These studies have found no achievement differences between students taught in ability groups and those in heterogeneous classes.[86]

However, research in elementary schools—where grouping within classes is widely used—indicates that such grouping generally raises the achievement of students at all ability levels. Robert Slavin selected eight especially well-designed studies of ability grouping in elementary schools. These studies compared initially similar students who were assigned either to heterogeneous classes or to ability groups within classes. All of these studies examined students' achievement in math, and one study included achievement in reading and spelling as well. In all eight of these studies, students in homogeneous groups did better on standardized tests of achievement in math than did comparable students in heterogeneous classes. The positive effect of skill grouping was present for students at various skill levels.[87]

Slavin summarizes the findings as follows: "Research on the use of math groups consistently supports this practice in the upper elementary grades. There is no evidence to suggest that achievement gains due to within-class ability grouping in mathematics are achieved at the expense of low-achievers; if anything, the evidence indicates the greatest gain for this subgroup."[88]

Grouping students within a class for some subjects may be beneficial for several reasons. Besides the obvious advantage that the content and pace of the lesson can be tailored to fit students at different skill levels, such arrangements may permit the teacher to have more intimate contact with students in the smaller subgroups and may encourage more interaction and mutual help and encouragement among students in the smaller, more homogeneous groups.

However, there are some problems with, and drawbacks to, the use of ability subgroups within classes.[89] The teacher is required to do more planning, and may have more difficulty coordinating student activities, when dealing with several subgroups rather than one larger class. Also, when moving between groups, the teacher spends less time with any given student than she would in a whole-class setting.

The most important problem that arises with ability grouping within classes (as it does with differentiating whole classes by ability) is a result of the major advantage of grouping—namely, the opportunity to vary the content and pace of learning among groups. Because students in a high-skill group are likely to be taught more, and/or at a higher level of complexity, than those in a low-skill group, the initial gap in achievement between the groups is likely to increase (even if all students do better than they would in one heterogeneous class). Students who are initially placed in low-skill groups, sometimes with insufficient reason, may find themselves falling farther and farther behind their peers in the higher-skill groups. Therefore, ability grouping within classes may require making a trade-off between (1) raising the average achievement of all students and (2) increasing the differences among students and constraining the mobility of students in the lower-skill groups.

To be most useful, ability grouping within classes is best used in certain circumstances and in certain ways. It is most useful in subjects, such as reading or math, where students acquire skills in a progressive fashion, building learning at each stage on the foundation of learning acquired earlier. In such cases, the skill level already achieved by students at the start of a lesson or segment of the course will be important in determining what and how they are taught next. Ability grouping also is most helpful when the range of skill levels within a class is great and when grouping will reduce considerably the heterogeneity within each group.

Research evidence suggests that if ability grouping is to improve learning, teachers must vary their teaching methods to suit the varying needs of students at each ability level.[90] Also, it is important that grouping be flexible, so that students can be moved into higher (or lower) groups as their performance changes or is more fully evaluated.

One type of flexible within-class ability grouping is group-paced mastery learning.[91] In this plan, students are grouped after each lesson into "masters" and "nonmasters" groups on the basis of a test. Students who are nonmasters receive further instruction, while those who have mastered the material do enrichment activities. The composition of masters and nonmasters groups changes after each lesson or unit of work is completed.

COOPERATIVE LEARNING GROUPS

Another widely used alternative to teaching all students together is to divide a class into groups of students who cooperate in learning together.[92] While there a number of specific variants of cooperative learning, a common feature of these methods is that students work together to learn and are responsible for each other's learning. To help make this ideal a reality, rewards (e.g., grades, awards, privileges) are given for good team performance and, at the same time, individual students are held accountable for their own performance. Thus, for example, after students in a group have discussed subject material and helped each other to understand it, each student may take a quiz and the team score will be the sum of all individual scores.

To give each student, regardless of ability, an equal chance to contribute to the total team score, his individual score may be computed on the basis of how much he has improved from his previous performance. Another technique sometimes used to ensure that every student is able to contribute to team success is the "jigsaw" method, by which each student must master a different part of the total task that the group must complete. Thus, while each individual is accountable for her own learning, all the members of the group depend on each other for group success. Rewards (e.g., grades) are given according to some combination of group and individual success.

Cooperative learning groups have been used at all grade levels (grades 2 to 12) and in all major subjects. Some forms of cooperative learning are very general and some have been developed for specific subjects, such as mathematics. These methods are intended to make students more active and more motivated in their learning and to take more advantage of their potential to help each other. (Peer tutoring also has been used as a way of getting students to help one another.) In addition, cooperative learning has been seen as a way to teach students to collaborate on shared tasks and as a way to improve relations among students, especially those from different ethnic groups.

What effect does cooperative learning have on achievement? A large amount of relevant research has been done, both concerning the effects of cooperation on achievement generally and concerning the effects of cooperative learning in schools specifically.

In a research review of cooperative learning methods in schools,[93] Robert Slavin found 67 high-quality studies that compared the achievement of students who experienced cooperative learning with those taught in more traditional ways in whole-class groups and/or with individual activities. Teachers and classes were otherwise comparable, having been randomly assigned to either cooperative or to control conditions or matched on prior achievement and other factors.

Forty-one of the 67 studies (61%) found achievement to be higher in cooperative classes than in control classes, 25 studies (37%) found no difference among the conditions, and in only one study the control group performed better than the cooperative group. When examining more closely those studies where cooperative learning was *not* superior to other methods, it turned out that some of the crucial elements for successful cooperative learning were missing; in particular, the less effective cooperative learning groups often lacked either group goals or individual accountability. When these elements were both present, students in cooperative learning situations outperformed comparable students in 37 of 44 studies (84%).

In discussing the importance of both group goals and individual accountability for cooperative learning, Slavin comments: ". . . when the group's task is to ensure that every group member *learns* something, it is in the interest of every group member to spend time explaining concepts to his or her groupmates."[94]

The school studies reviewed by Slavin also showed that cooperative learning methods were effective among many types of students and in a wide variety of settings. Cooperative learning was beneficial for learning among both boys and girls; at a variety of grade levels (although fewer studies were done in high schools than in elementary schools); in urban, rural, and suburban schools; for students of all ability levels; and among various ethnic groups, but especially among black students. Studies of cooperative learning done after Slavin's review of research generally continue to show this method to have positive effects on student achievement.[95]

Most cooperative learning programs have used groups of students who are heterogeneous with respect to skill level. Sometimes such diversity in skill level has been seen as an intrinsic feature of cooperative programs, partly on the grounds that more skilled students will be best able to help peers with lesser skills. However, the question arises as to whether students, particularly those of higher ability, will achieve more in homogeneous cooperative groups than they will in cooperative groups of mixed ability.

There have been more than a dozen studies that address this issue. These studies generally show that low-ability students learn best in collaborative groups that include high-ability peers. Below-average students appear to benefit from interaction (asking questions, discussions, etc.) with students who have more skills.[96]

However, high-ability students tend to achieve more in homogeneous groups (i.e., with other students of high ability) than in mixed-ability groups. For example, one study found that high-ability grade school students who worked on math problems in homogeneous pairs worked more collaboratively, engaged in more cognitive conflict and resolution, and produced superior work than high-ability students in mixed-ability dyads.[97] Students of medium ability also tend to learn more in homogeneous groups than in heterogeneous groups.

Noreen Webb and her colleagues suggest that the results of their study (and of other studies) pose a dilemma. They assert: "The performance of high- and low-ability students cannot be optimized at the same time."[98] However, these researchers also say that heterogeneous cooperative groups provide a greater benefit for below-average students than they impose a disadvantage on high-ability students. Thus, they argue that heterogeneous cooperative groups will, on average, lead to greater student achievement than will homogeneous groups.

In addition to promoting greater student achievement, cooperative learning groups have been found to have other positive benefits. Students in cooperative groups like school more, develop peer norms that favor doing well academically, and spend more time on their academic tasks. They have greater feelings of control over their own fate in school, have higher self-esteem, and—not surprisingly—are more cooperative and altruistic in their attitudes than students in other learning settings.[99]

One of the most important advantages of cooperative learning groups is that they consistently result in more friendliness and greater liking among students. This positive effect on student harmony has been found to occur when students come from different racial and ethnic backgrounds as well as among students from the same ethnic groups. Thus, cooperative learning groups can be an important tool for promoting positive relations among different ethnic groups in school.

While the potential benefits of cooperative learning groups are great, they are not automatic. As David Johnson and his colleagues note: "Simply placing students in groups and telling them to work together does not mean that they know how to cooperate or that they will do so even if they know."[100] First, students may not be motivated to perform the task assigned and even may discourage each other from doing so; they may prefer to talk about other things. Thus, it is important that there be rewards for group (and individual) success on the task that are meaningful to the students. Sometimes competition with other groups may help to raise students' task motivation. So too may some degree of autonomy for group members to choose specific activities that interest them, as well as to choose ways to accomplish the task.

A second possible problem is that students may not participate in, or contribute equally, to the work of the group. Some studies have found that low-achieving students, in particular, may be passive and not focus on the group's work.[101] Students who do contribute more may feel overburdened and resentful. To try to reduce such problems, it is important, as noted earlier, that each student should be held accountable for his own work. This means concretely that each student's work should be assessed and usually that his outcomes (such as grades) should depend on his own performance as well as on that of the group. In addition, structuring the group's task in ways that require unique contributions from each member and assessing groups on the basis of how much each member has *improved* also helps to reduce resentments caused by unequal contributions.

In their extensive discussion of cooperative methods in the classroom, Johnson, Johnson, and Holubec emphasize the importance of teaching students how to work together effectively.[102] Such skills include asking for ideas and opinions from others, asking for help or clarification, encouraging everyone to participate, expressing support and acceptance, and criticizing ideas without criticizing people. Johnson, Johnson,, and Holubec also recommend that teachers award group points and group rewards partly on the basis of social skills exhibited by the group and that students assess their own group processes at the end of their work periods, discussing how to improve them if necessary.

Teachers' Role

For learning in cooperative groups to take place effectively, the teacher has an important role to play.[103] Specifically, the teacher needs to carry out the following set of activities:

1. Setting up the cooperative groups. Deciding on the size of the groups, assigning students to groups, arranging the room, and assigning roles (e.g., recorder, materials handler) to group members.
2. Preparing the group for this task. Preparation includes teaching students any material they should know; explaining the objectives and procedures for the group activity; explaining the goals and joint rewards of the group; explaining the ways in which individual students will be accountable; and teaching collaborative skills.
3. Monitoring and helping. While students are working in their groups, the teacher should circulate to see if students understand the material and the assignment and are doing their tasks successfully. The teacher can give feedback to the students, praise where appropriate, and help when needed—both with respect to the task and with respect to the process of working together.
4. Evaluating students' work. The teacher must evaluate the work of the group and of individuals within the group on academic tasks, as well as with respect to their collaboration. Evaluations should be discussed with the groups and with individuals, including discussion of how students' performance can be improved in the future.

Clearly, the teacher needs to be busy when classes are engaged in cooperative learning activities, just as they are when using other teaching methods. Many of the activities that teachers carry out when students learn in groups are the same general activities that teachers perform when students learn as individuals or in a whole-class setting, including preparing students to carry out tasks, monitoring their work, helping, giving feedback, and evaluating the students' performance.

COMPUTERS IN THE CLASSROOM

The activities of teachers in the classroom often are supplemented by technological devices. Videotapes and audiotapes can present information and ideas to students. Most notably, computers now are widely available as an instructional medium. Some people see providing computers to students as a way to bring rapid growth in their learning.

Computers have helped students in two major ways: as a teacher and as an assistant to the student.[104]

THE COMPUTER AS TEACHER

A computer can be a surrogate, or substitute, for a teacher in a number of ways. Computer programs can present and demonstrate information and ideas (e.g., how electrical circuits work or the geography of Africa), perhaps along with pictures, maps, graphs, and other visual aids. They can provide students with drill and practice, perhaps substituting for worksheets, leading the student through a series of practice exercises to help him to memorize and rehearse information and simple skills (spelling of words, arithmetic computations, scientific terms, historical facts, etc.). They can provide tutorials to individual students (e.g., in reading or in arithmetic), presenting content, asking questions, analyzing the student's responses, and giving appropriate feedback until the learner demonstrates a certain level of competence.

The types of computer programs just mentioned (presentations, drill and practice, tutorials) reflect directive methods of teaching, in which information is provided to and memorized by students. Other computer programs provide activities that are more consistent with student-centered methods of instruction, in which the student plays a more active role in learning. Programs in which the student is more actively involved include those for simulations, instructional games, and other problem-solving applications.

THE COMPUTER AS ASSISTANT TO STUDENT

Computers also can help students to do a variety of tasks that contribute to their learning. Word processors make it easier for students to do a variety of types of writing, such as papers, stories, and records of experiments or projects. Using the word processor makes it easier and faster for students to create a draft, edit the material, and produce a new product than it would be without computer assistance.

Computer programs provide access to many databases. Access to these databases makes it possible for students to find extensive information on a wide range of topics to an extent never before possible.

Spreadsheets provide a way for students to electronically represent a set of numbers. Using such spreadsheets, students can make various kinds of calculations on these numbers in ways that would not be feasible without the aid of a computer. For example, in a biology (or social studies) class, students might use a spreadsheet that shows birth rates, death rates, and population growth for a given geographic area at different times. They would then explore the effects of changes in birth rates and death rates on amount of population growth. Students can use spreadsheets for a number of other purposes, including creating charts and graphs.

In addition to learning from the computer as a teacher and getting assistance from the computer in doing their schoolwork, students may learn from instructing or programming the computer to accomplish some task (e.g., to create geometric designs or to produce a report of a certain type). Such activities, where the student "teaches" the computer, can help the student develop skills of logical thinking and problem solving.[105]

While computer activities usually are designed for individuals, computers are often used for cooperative activities as well. For example, many instructional games involve groups of students, and in cooperative research projects students can research a problem on the computer, either individually or in groups.

POSSIBLE ADVANTAGES OF COMPUTERS

The availability of computer programs for learning has generated great enthusiasm among many people both in and out of school systems. They see the use of computers as a key way in which "our youngsters' minds and lives will be enriched, society will benefit, and education will be permanently changed for the better."[106] Computers, as compared to other media, such as texts, or to human teachers, have been seen as having some important advantages. These presumed advantages include: ability to interact with many individuals simultaneously; raising student motivation; unique instructional capabilities; and greater efficiency for the work of students and teachers.

Unlike a human teacher, computer programs can interact separately with many individuals simultaneously, adjusting the level of difficulty and pace to the learner. Also, computers are able to stimulate and appeal to the student's senses—with color, graphics, text highlighting, and so on—in ways that may keep students' attention and get and keep them engaged.

Computers have some unique capabilities, such as manipulating multiple variables, searching quickly over a wide range of data sources, expanding or contracting the effects of time, and introducing chance as one determinant of outcomes. Such special capabilities of the computer provide support for, and sometimes make it more feasible for, human teachers to use certain instructional approaches, such as having students perform a series of experiments in a short time, gather a large amount of information on a topic, or simulate the operation of a complex system.

Teachers also may use computers to help perform a variety of their tasks. such as planning lessons, keeping records, preparing instructional materials (such as graphs), and marking and analyzing scores on tests. Some people have suggested that computers also can make schools more efficient by permitting them to optimize the use of scarce resources, especially a limited number of teachers.[107]

CONCERNS ABOUT COMPUTER USE

Some voices have been raised to express skepticism or concern about the use of computers in schools. Critics have suggested ways in which computer activities may promote learning that is superficial or limited. For example, the fact that computer programs force the student to choose among predetermined responses may limit original thought.[108] Some "drill and practice" programs have been described as "a new way to do busywork."[109] Students who use the spell-check feature of word processors may not learn to spell themselves. Regular computer users may read few, if any, books. Students may present computer-packaged information "dressed up" to look like research, without doing the real thinking that should go into research.[110] And students who spend long periods of time at computers may get little stimulation for learning from teachers and peers.[111]

The most serious problem raised by critics, and by some people basically supportive of computer use, is the danger that the attractive technology of computers will overshadow the purpose of education. Stephen Kerr writes: "Technology itself, rather than the particular goals and ends we wish students to achieve by using it, often seems to have the priority."[112] For example, in schools that have used "Integrated Learning Systems" (ILS), based on computer technology, some teachers are concerned that the ILS curriculum may drive the school's curriculum, rather than the reverse."[113] M. D. Roblyer and Jack Edwards note that technology in education is especially prone to the "glitz" factor and that flashy products with thin educational rationales may be too readily adopted.[114] Other observers comment that, in the excitement about connecting schools to the Internet, some people forget that a wealth of raw information has little value to students if they lack the ability to analyze, interpret, and place it in some context.[115]

EFFECTS OF COMPUTERS ON LEARNING

Given the impressive capabilities of computer programs and the great advantages that have been claimed for them, as well as the concerns about computers that have been expressed by some, what effects have computers actually had on students' learning? And how have computers affected teachers?

There is some evidence that the visual and interactive features of computers often focus students' attention and engage them in the computer activities.[116] Moreover, computer-based learning sometimes has been found to improve students' learning. For example, one study examined the effect of teaching algebra to high school freshmen with the use of computers. Students who were taught by computer in 21 classes in three high schools were compared to comparable students in math courses taught in standard ways. The computer-taught students scored somewhat higher on standardized tests.[117]

However, while a few studies have indicated that students using computers for learning had slightly higher achievement than students learning with traditional methods,[118] most of the evidence to date does not show that the use of computers generally improves student achievement. One study of Minnesota elementary school children even found that students using computers performed less well in math, reading, and language arts than those taught by traditional methods.[119]

Reviews of relevant studies show mixed, sometimes contradictory, results. One research review concluded that computer-based instruction "usually produces positive effects on students."[120] However, other reviewers reach different conclusions. A review of studies that compare achievement scores of students who had access to a variety of media (using "hypermedia" computer software) with those who used paper media, such as books, found no overall difference in achievement on either simple or complex tasks.[121] Another review of studies that compared students who used computer simulation for science learning with students who were taught by expository methods (such as lecture) found no difference in achievement.[122] Several more general reviews of studies that compared students using various computer technologies with those in more traditional learning environments also have found no overall differences in achievement.[123] The use of word processors in classrooms does often result in longer and better-quality student writing, but these positive effects are not consistent.[124]

In their book on educational technology, Roblyer and Edwards write: "Although technology (especially computers) has been in use in education since the 1950s, research results have not made a strong case for its impact on teaching and learning."[125] Other writers on the subject speak of the "unfulfilled expectations of educational technology."[126]

Under what conditions have computers been found to be most helpful? And how can the potential benefits of computers for learning be realized more?

Computers appear to have been most helpful for students when they have been used for relatively simple processes, such as in drill and practice programs, and for assisting students in obtaining information and in preparing compositions and reports. Computer programs generally have had more limited success in promoting complex learning. In their review of studies bearing on the effectiveness of computer hypermedia technology, Andrew Dillon and Ralph Gabbard conclude: ". . . the weight of evidence points to hypermedia being suitable mainly for a limited range of tasks involving substantial searching or manipulation and comparison of visual detail where overlaying of images is important. In short, the evidence does not support the use of most hypermedia applications where the goal is to increase learner comprehension (however measured)."[127]

An evaluation of software products that were intended to support acquisition by students of critical thinking skills found that few of these products used effective methods to accomplish this purpose.[128] Sometimes computer programs do not assess students' real learning adequately. A study of integrated learning systems found some inconsistency between computers' evaluations of students' answers and students' actual understanding; the student might be scored as correct without an understanding of the material or might be scored as incorrect when he did understand the material.[129]

Another problem is that students may have difficulty in successfully carrying out the activities required by the computer program. For example, many students using computer simulation for science "discovery" learning were found to have great difficulty in generating hypotheses, designing experiments, and interpreting the data.[130]

Several studies indicate that less able students often have trouble in working successfully with the computer and may become frustrated in trying to do so.[131] Students in general, but weaker students in particular, need more structure to guide their efforts than many computer programs provide.

The reactions of teachers to computers, and the way in which they use computers, vary greatly and may help determine how effectively they are used. A study in 13 elementary schools in Kentucky[132] found that some teachers felt antagonistic toward the use of computers and distanced themselves from computers, while others embraced the technology.

Teachers who were antagonistic toward computers sometimes had experienced problems with their use—for example, students being confused by unfamiliar terminology in the software. Teachers sometimes had to spend time on mechanical or technical problems of computer use at the cost of instructional time. More generally, some teachers thought that computers were diminishing their role by fixing students' attention on the machines rather than on them. Thus, some teachers came to resent computers.

Teachers who distanced themselves from computers devoted less time than the "embracers" to preparation for using computers (e.g., in specifying their objectives and in previewing programs); they also were less likely than the other teachers to monitor students' work at the computer, for example, making suggestions and clarifying points that were unclear to the student; instead they let students work unsupervised at computers while the teachers caught up on other work. Teachers who were antagonistic to computer use also were less likely to integrate work on the computer into their overall lesson plan than were those who were more favorable to computers. Overall, computers contributed much more to student learning in the classes of those teachers who were more favorable to their use.

The material discussed in this section indicates both the promise of computers in the classroom and some of the limits of their contribution to date. Commenting on the use of computers in education, Jane Healy says: "I believe success is possible, but it is not automatic, inexpensive, or attained without a great deal of thought and effort."[133]

A key to the successful use of computers in schools is to use programs that fit with the educational purposes of schools and teachers. Alison Armstrong and Charles Casement comment: "Students did not benefit from using computers more often, but from using them in particular ways."[134] As an example, they note a study in which eighth-grade students who learned higher-order thinking skills through computer simulations had higher math scores than students who used drill-and-practice computer programs. However, drill-and-practice programs may be useful where teachers wish to teach some basic information and skills to young or low-achieving students as a foundation for their acquiring higher-level skills later.

One necessary line of work is to improve educational software, particularly programs that are intended to promote higher-level thinking and problem solving. After reviewing studies that show (computer) hypermedia programs to be ineffective in increasing learner comprehension, Dillon and Gabbard point to "a particularly limited knowledge base in terms of how best to organize information in a digital form that exploits the cognitive capabilities of learners to link and organize new information."[135]

Studies of computer simulation applications have shown that programs can be modified in ways that facilitate student learning. For example, one study found that providing specific information at the time it is needed by the learner is more effective than giving her all the necessary information at the start of the simulation.[136] More generally, computer applications need to be guided by an understanding—both theoretical and empirical—of good learning and higher-order thinking and how they are developed. This important point is emphasized by Gabriel Salomon and David Perkins, who outline some key ideas about learning and cognition and give examples of computer programs that are consistent with these principles.[137]

FITTING COMPUTERS WITH TEACHERS

With the increasing use of computers in schools, what is the role of the teacher in this new technological environment? First, research on the effects of computers indicates that assistance by teachers often is needed if students are to use computers effectively. For example, while the computer gives students access to extensive databases, they often have difficulty formulating appropriate questions and making correctly targeted searches and they have difficulty in interpreting results. Teachers can help guide students through this process.[138] More generally, teachers facilitate students' computer work by monitoring their progress, giving feedback, and making suggestions.

Teachers also play an important role in other aspects of computer use. They may decide what computer activities will be assigned to students, giving consideration to the kinds of cognitive activities involved, the level of difficulty, the amount of control students have, and so on. They may provide feedback, help for, and evaluation of the students' overall work on a computer activity or activities. Moreover, they can provide the encouragement and support for students' efforts that machines cannot provide in the same way.

While teachers continue to play an important role in computer-based activities, their role in the classroom is changed when computer activities are used. Teachers are less the focus of attention, and less the primary provider of knowledge, than they were in traditional classes. Even more than in some other kinds of activities, such as cooperative learning groups, the teacher assumes the role of guide and coach when students work with computers. Teachers also are more likely to work with individual students than they would in other activities.

However, computer activities are usually not, and probably should not be, the sole, or even primary, type of activity in the classroom. Other activities, including short presentations by the teacher, discussions in a whole-class or small-group format, and cooperative group learning (which may use the computer but is not limited to it) may provide students with perspectives, and with interchange of their ideas with those of others, that are difficult to get in computer work. Computer activities need to be integrated with other types of activities and integrated also with the overall curriculum and overall teaching plans.[139]

OVERVIEW OF LEARNING IN CLASSROOM

In this chapter, we have looked at many aspects of the classroom situation—learning activities, rules, incentives, teacher–student interactions, interaction among students, student perceptions, and others—that may affect student learning. It is useful now to try to get an overview of how these aspects of the classroom situation may relate to each other and may combine in their effects. Figure 3-1 presents such an overview.

The far left side of Figure 3-1 shows several aspects of classroom structure including learning activities, grouping of students, rules for student behavior, incentives for students (rewards and penalties), and standards for evaluating student performance.

Classroom structure has direct effects on students' learning. For example, activities that are at a moderate level of difficulty (challenging but "doable") and that give students some autonomy generally increase the amount of learning that occurs.

The classroom structure also has (as Figure 3-1 shows) some important indirect effects on student learning. First, class structure affects the amount and types of interactions that occur between teachers and students. For example, whole-class activities, as compared to individualized activities for students, will lead each student to spend more total time with the teacher, but to have fewer personal exchanges involving help, feedback, and so forth, with the teacher. Second, class structure affects the amount and types of interaction among students. For example, cooperative group activities may enhance the amount of mutual help among students.

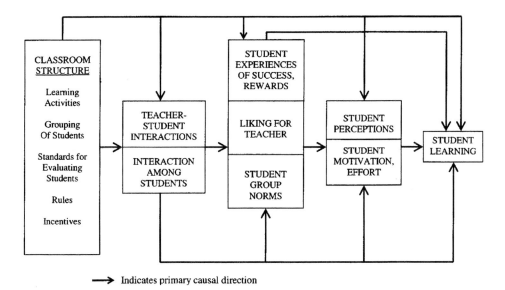

Indicates primary causal direction

Figure 3-1 Factors in the classroom affecting student learning.

Classroom structure also affects student experiences of success (e.g., activities that are not overly difficult make success more likely); liking for the teacher (e.g., arbitrary rules may lead to dislike of the teacher); and student group norms (e.g., cooperative activities tend to promote group norms that support good academic work).

Finally, the structure of the classroom affects students perceptions about their learning situation—most importantly, about the value of their school activities, the value of succeeding in their school work, the likelihood that effort will lead to success, and their control over their own school outcomes. For example, the more assigned activities are relevant to students' own lives, the more likely these activities are to be seen as intrinsically valuable; the more standards of evaluation permit every student to succeed, the better chance students will see for effort to lead to success. These student perceptions, in turn, affect students' motivation and effort in their learning activities.

In addition to the major influences of classroom structure, the interaction between teacher and students also has important effects on learning (see Figure 3-1). Some of these effects are direct. For example, the more a teacher provides help and feedback to the student, and the more the teacher praises student accomplishment (where deserved), the more the student generally learns.

In addition to the direct effect of teacher–student interaction, Figure 3-1 shows some important indirect effects on learning that may result from this interaction. When interaction with the teacher results in positive evaluations from the teacher, the student will experience success and have a sense of competence, and thus a high expectancy of success in further activities.

These perceptions will tend to increase his motivation and effort in learning activities.

Positive interactions with the teacher (e.g., help, praise) also will tend to increase liking for the teacher. The more the student likes the teacher, the more she values approval from the teacher and perhaps even wants to be like the teacher. Such feelings will make the student value success in her schoolwork more and thus will tend to increase her motivation and effort.

An additional way in which teacher–student interaction may indirectly affect student learning is by its possible impact on student group norms. When the teacher and students have frequent positive contacts, students will tend to encourage each other to support learning goals; they will be less likely than otherwise to pressure each other to resist the teacher's efforts. A pro-learning norm among students will increase the value to them of success in their schoolwork.

While interaction between teacher and students is always of great importance, interaction among students also can have both direct and indirect effects on learning (as Figure 3-1 indicates). The more students help one another in their school activities, as happens most notably in cooperative learning groups, the greater their learning. In addition, the amount and type of interaction among students may affect student norms about schoolwork. The more contact students have with each other—in and outside of class—the more likely they are to develop shared ideas (norms) about how much effort they should devote to schoolwork. The more students work together cooperatively toward shared goals, the more likely it is that the norms they develop will favor accomplishment of school goals.

Overall, then, student learning in the classroom is shaped most basically by:

1. The classroom structure, especially the types of learning activities, grouping, rules, incentives, and standards of evaluation.
2. The amount and types of interaction between teacher and students, and secondarily among students. (These interactions are influenced by, but not completely determined by, classroom structure.)

Both classroom structure and classroom interactions have direct effects on what students learn. They also affect learning indirectly by influencing the likelihood that students will experience success, their liking for their teacher, their group norms, their perceptions, and ultimately their motivation and effort.

Factors outside the classroom—especially the influences of parents—also have effects on student learning, of course. These effects are considered elsewhere in this book (see especially Chapters 4 and 9).

This general overview of factors in the classroom that affect student learning, and how they are related to each other, suggests the importance of knowing what type of classroom structure (activities, grouping of students, etc.) and what types of interactions (especially between teacher and students) are most likely to promote learning. The preceding sections of this chapter have discussed many of these specifics. The section to follow reviews the major conclusions of the chapter about what types of classroom structure and teacher–student interactions appear to be most useful for learning.

SUMMARY AND CONCLUSIONS

Student learning in the classroom is shaped by the ways in which the classroom is organized (the activities, the grouping of students, etc.) and by the types of interaction between teachers and students and among students.

Traditionally, classroom activities center around the teacher, who lectures and leads students in "recitations." Presentations by teachers often are an efficient way of transmitting specific information to many students in a short time. Direct instruction by teachers is most effective in the early grades, for students with low skills, and when teaching a well-structured body of knowledge.

However, instructional methods that actively engage students in gathering information and formulating ideas are more likely to interest and motivate students in the subjects they are studying. Active, student-centered instruction also is more likely than teacher-centered methods to stimulate students' analytical thinking, problem solving, and creativity. In many situations, teachers can combine some direct instruction with related activities that actively engage students for the most effective results.

Activities that are most conducive to good student learning have the following characteristics:

1. They go beyond teaching information and basic skills and promote also skills of analysis and problem solving.
2. The activity is valued by the student because it interests her or is seen as useful in her own life.
3. The task is of moderate difficulty—hard enough to be challenging but not so hard as to discourage effort or prevent success. Students from poverty backgrounds and low-achieving students usually require smaller steps and a higher success ratio than do other students.
4. While it is generally best for teachers to maintain general control over the activity, students should have some autonomy or participation in decisions about carrying out the activity.

As students engage in learning activities, the interaction of the teacher with the student is important in maintaining students' motivation and promoting success experiences for them. Monitoring students' progress in their work is helpful, especially for low-achievers, for students who are doing challenging tasks, and for those working independently. But teachers should not monitor students' work so closely that students perceive that they lack any real control.

Corrective feedback from teachers to students about their performance, including homework, is one of the strongest contributors to high student achievement. Evaluation of student performance on the basis of how successfully each student masters a given body of material, rather than on how she ranks compared to other students, helps to raise most students' motivation and achievement.

Praise from teachers for student work leads students to have greater intrinsic task motivation and to perform better. Praise is especially effective when used with students from low socioeconomic backgrounds or with dependent or anxious students—all of whom may lack confidence and require more reinforcement than others. Praise works best when it is linked to specific behaviors of both effort and performance (not general ability) and when it is seen by students as deserved.

To discourage off-task and other undesirable behaviors by students, teachers need to manage their classrooms in ways that keep students engaged, physically and psychologically, in learning activities. Punishments for students who break rules often may be necessary and sometimes are effective in discouraging undesirable behavior. But punishment may, instead, produce anger, rebellion, and the desire to "get even" with the punisher. Punishment is most likely to be effective when it is consistent, is seen as legitimate, and is combined with reward for positive behavior. Order in the classroom derives primarily not from punishment but from engaging students' interest in learning activities.

To tailor teaching to different ability or skill levels, classes often are divided into subgroups based on skill, especially for math or reading in elementary school. Students assigned to homogeneous ability groups in math have been found consistently to achieve better than those in heterogeneous ability groups. Both high-skill and low-skill students have been found to do better in groups of student with similar skill levels. However, the initial gap in achievement between the high-skill and low-skill students is likely to increase when students are taught in homogeneous groups. Ability grouping is most useful for subjects, such as reading and math, in which students build later skills on the foundation of skills acquired earlier; when the range of skills within a class is great; when teachers vary their methods to suit the needs of different ability levels; and when the grouping plan is flexible, so that students can be readily moved to a different group as their performance changes.

Another widely used alternative to teaching all students together is to divide a class into groups of students who cooperate in their learning, earning rewards for their group as well as for individual work. Of the large number of studies that have compared students in cooperative learning groups to those in more traditional settings, the great majority find student learning to be better in the cooperative groups. Cooperative learning methods have been found to be effective for many different types of students and at a variety of grade levels.

To make cooperative learning groups effective in promoting learning, it is helpful to structure the group's task in ways that require unique contributions from each member; to make outcomes (such as grades) for each student depend on his own work, as well as that of the group; and to teach students the skills necessary to work together effectively.

Computers can contribute to student learning in many ways. They can interact with many individuals simultaneously and can provide some unique instructional capabilities. However, the high expectations of some regarding the benefits of computers in the classroom have been largely unfulfilled to date. Studies that have compared the learning of students using various computer technologies with those in traditional learning environments generally have found no overall differences in achievement. Computer applications need to be improved, guided by an understanding of good learning and higher-order thinking and how they are developed. Teachers continue to play an important, although somewhat changed, role in classrooms when computers are used.

An overview of the classroom shows that the ways in which it is organized (activities, grouping of students, rules, incentives, and standards of evaluation) affect the amount and types of interaction between teacher and students and among students. Both classroom organization and classroom interactions have a direct effect on learning. They also affect student learning indirectly—by giving students experiences of academic success, by shaping positive attitudes toward the teacher, by stimulating students to help each other's learning, and by leading them to be highly motivated to do well in their schoolwork.

NOTES

1. P. Schlechty, *Shaking Up the Schoolhouse: How to Support and Sustain Educational Innovation.* San Francisco: Jossey-Bass, 2001, p. 53.
2. H. Frieberg and A. Driscoll, *Universal Teaching Strategies*, 3rd edition. Boston: Allyn & Bacon, 2000, p. 177.
3. See Freiberg and Driscoll, Ibid.; J. Chall, *The Academic Achievement Challenge.* New York: Guilford Press, 2000; J. Brophy and T. Good, Teacher Behavior and Student Achievement. In M. Wittrock, ed., *Handbook of Research on Teaching*, 3rd edition. New York: Macmillan, 1986.
4. H. Walberg, Productive Teaching and Instruction. *Phi Delta Kappan, 71,* 1990, 470–478.
5. Chall, *The Academic Achievement Challenge.*
6. B. Rosenshine, Explicit Teaching. In B. Berliner and B. Rosenshine, eds., *Talks to Teachers.* New York: Random House, 1987, pp. 75–92.

7. G. Yair, Educational Battlefields in America: Students' Engagement with Instruction. *Sociology of Education, 73*, 2000, 247–269.
8. See C. Glickman, *Revolutionizing America's Schools.* San Francisco: Jossey-Bass, 1998, pp. 27–36.
9. J.S. Cangelosi, *Classroom Management Strategies*, 2nd edition. New York: Longman, 1993, p. 156.
10. Frieberg and Driscoll, *Universal Teaching Strategies*, Chapter 7.
11. Chall, *The Academic Achievement Challenge*; P. Blumenthal, R. Marx, H. Patrick, J. Krajcik, and E. Soloway, Teaching for Understanding. In R. Biddle, et al., eds., *International Handbook of Teachers and Teaching.* Boston: Kluwer Academic, 1997, pp. 819–879.
12. See B. Joyce and M. Weil, *Models of Teaching*, 4th edition. Boston: Allyn & Bacon, 1992; Freiberg and Driscoll, *Universal Teaching Strategies.*
13. J. Byrnes, *Cognitive Development and Learning in Instructional Contexts.* Boston: Allyn & Bacon, 1996, p. 79.
14. See, for example, Chall, *The Academic Achievement Challenge*; Brophy and Good, *Teacher Behavior and Student Achievement.*
15. K. Wentzel and A. Wigfield, Academic and Social Motivational Influences on Students' Academic Performance. *Educational Psychology Review, 10*, 1998, 158.
16. Yair, *Educational Battlefields in America.*
17. F. McCourt, *T'is: A Memoir.* New York: Scribner, 1999.
18. J. Mahiri, *Shooting for Excellence: African American and Youth Culture in New Century Schools.* New York: Teachers College Press, 1998.
19. J. Atkinson and N. Feather, eds., *A Theory of Achievement Motivation.* New York: John Wiley, 1966.
20. See, for example, D. Ravitch, *National Standards in American Education.* Washington, DC: Brookings Institution Press, 1995.
21. See Wentzel and Wigfield, *Academic and Social Motivational Influences*; C. Spaulding, *Motivation in the Classroom.* New York: McGraw-Hill, 1992.
22. Brophy and Good, *Teacher Behavior and Student Achievement*, p. 360.
23. Brophy and Good, Ibid., p. 361.
24. Brophy and Good, Ibid.
25. See Chall, *The Academic Achievement Challenge*, p. 117.
26. J. MacLeod, *Ain't Making It: Aspirations and Attainment in a Low-Income Neighborhood.* Boulder, CO: Westview, 1995, p. 108.
27. See M. Patchen, *Participation, Achievement, and Involvement on the Job.* Englewood Cliffs, NJ: Prentice-Hall, 1970.
28. See Spaulding, *Motivation in the Classroom.*
29. J. Eccles and Others, Negative Effects of Traditional Middle Schools on Students' Motivation. *Elementary School Journal, 93*, 1993, 553–574.
30. Wentzel and Wigfield, *Academic and Social Motivational Influences.*
31. Brophy and Good, *Teacher Behavior and Student Achievement.*
32. Brophy and Good, Ibid.; Chall, *The Academic Achievement Challenge.*
33. W. Doyle, Classroom Organization and Management. In M. Wittrock, *Handbook of Research on Teaching*, pp. 392–431.
34. Doyle, Ibid.
35. Doyle, Ibid., p. 417.
36. Brophy and Good, *Teacher Behavior and Student Achievement.*

37. Spaulding, *Motivation in the Classroom.*

38. Walberg, *Productive Teaching and Instruction.*

39. Brophy and Good, *Teacher Behavior and Student Achievement,* p. 364.

40. Wentzel and Wigfield, *Academic and Social Motivational Influences.*

41. Walberg, *Productive Teaching and Instruction.*

42. Brophy and Good, *Teacher Behavior and Student Achievement.*

43. Atkinson and Feather, *A Theory of Achievement Motivation.*

44. M. Covington, *Making the Grade: A Self-Worth Perspective on School Reform.* New York: Cambridge University Press, 1992.

45. J. Nicholls, Achievement Motivation: Conceptions of Ability, Subjective Experience, Task Choice, and Performance. *Psychological Review, 91,* 1984, 328–346.

46. Wentzel and Wigfield, Academic and Social Motivational Influences; Spaulding, *Motivation in the Classroom.*

47. See, for example, L. Miller, *An American Imperative: Accelerating Minority Educational Advancement.* New Haven, CT: Yale University Press, 1995.

48. J. Irvine, *Black Students and School Failure.* New York: Greenwood Press, 1990.

49. Miller, *An American Imperative.*

50. J. Brophy, Research on the Self-Fulfilling Prophecy and Teacher Expectations. *Journal of Educational Psychology, 75,* 1983, 327–346.

51. J. Cameron and W. Pierce, Reinforcement, Reward, and Intrinsic Motivation: A Meta-Analysis. *Review of Educational Research, 64,* 1994, 363–423.

52. Brophy and Good, *Teacher Behavior and Student Achievement.*

53. Brophy and Good, Ibid.

54. C. Ames, Classrooms: Goals, Structures and Student Motivation. *Journal of Educational Psychology, 84,* 1992, 261–271.

55. Cameron and Pierce, *Reinforcement, Reward, and Intrinsic Motivation.*

56. C. Dweck, Messages That Motivate. In J. Aronson, ed., *Improving Academic Achievement.* San Diego: Academic Press, 2002, pp. 38–61.

57. G. Morine-Dershimer, Pupil Perceptions of Teacher Praise. *Elementary School Journal, 82,* 1982. 421–434.

58. E. Deci, R. Koestner, and R. Ryan, Extrinsic Rewards and Intrinsic Motivation in Education: Reconsidered Once Again. *Review of Educational Research, 71,* 2001, 1–27.

59. Doyle, Classroom Organization and Management; P. Short, R. Short, and C. Blanton, *Rethinking Student Discipline.* Thousand Oaks, CA: Corwin, 1994.

60. Doyle, Ibid.

61. H. Gouldner, *Teachers' Pets, Troublemakers, and Nobodies: Black Children in Elementary School.* Westport, CT: Greenwood, 1978.

62. J. Irvine, *Black Students and School Failure,* p. 18.

63. See Short, et al., *Rethinking Student Discipline.*

64. See, for example, Short, et al., Ibid.; Doyle, *Classroom Organization.*

65. Short, et al., *Rethinking Student Discipline.*

66. Short, et al., Ibid., pp. 15–17

67. See, for example, E. Williams, ed., *Participative Management: Theory and Practice.* Atlanta: Georgia State University Press, 1976.

68. See G. Walters and J. Gruzec, *Punishment.* San Francisco: W. H. Freeman, 1977.

69. E. Wynne, Improving Pupil Discipline and Character. In O. Moles, ed., *Student Discipline Strategies*. Albany: State University of New York Press, 1990, pp. 167–190.

70. Walters and Grusec, *Punishment*.

71. W. Doyle, Classroom Management Techniques. In Moles, *Student Discipline Strategies*.

72. Wynne, *Improving Pupil Discipline*.

73. Walters and Grusec, *Punishment*.

74. Doyle, *Classroom Management Techniques*.

75. See M. Patchen, *Black-White Contact in Schools*. Lafayette, IN: Purdue University Press, 1982.

76. Short, et al., *Rethinking Student Discipline*.

77. Doyle, *Classroom Organization and Management*.

78. See Brophy and Good, Teacher Behavior and Student Achievement; Eccles, et al., *Negative Effects of Traditional Middle Schools*; Wentzel and Wigfield, Academic and Social Motivational Influences.

79. B. Bank, Peer Cultures and Their Challenge for Teaching. In B. Biddle, et al., *International Handbook of Teachers and Teaching*, pp. 879–937.

80. Wentzel and Wigfield, *Academic and Social Motivational Influences*.

81. Eccles, et al., *Negative Effects of Traditional Middle Schools*.

82. Brophy and Good, *Teacher Behavior and Student Achievement*.

83. H. Stevenson and J. Stigler, *The Learning Gap: Why Our Schools Are Failing and What We Can Learn from Japanese and Chinese Education*. New York: Simon & Schuster, 1992.

84. Chall, *The Academic Achievement Challenge*, p. 89.

85. See, for example, D. Tyack and L. Cuban, *Tinkering Toward Utopia: A Century of Public School Reform*. Cambridge, MA: Harvard University Press, 1995.

86. R. Slavin, Achievement Effects of Ability Grouping in Secondary Schools. *Review of Educational Research, 60*, 1990, 471–499.

87. R. Slavin, Ability Grouping and Student Achievement in Elementary Schools. *Review of Educational Research, 57*, 1987, 293–336; See also F. Mosteller, R. Light, and J. Sachs, Sustained Inquiry in Education: Lessons from Skill Grouping and Class Size. *Harvard Educational Review, 66*, 1996, 797–841.

88. Slavin, *Ability Grouping and Student Achievement*, p. 320.

89. See Slavin, Ibid.; J. Kulik, *An Analysis of the Research on Ability Grouping*. Ann Arbor: University of Michigan Press, 1992; A. Pallas, et al., Ability-Group Effects: Instructional, Social, or Institutional? *Sociology of Education, 67*, 1994, 27–46.

90. Slavin, Ibid.; Kulik, Ibid.; Y. Lou, et al., Within-Class Grouping: A Meta-Analysis. *Review of Educational Research, 66*, 1996, 423–458.

91. J. Block and L. Anderson, *Mastering Learning in Classroom Instruction*. New York: Macmillan, 1975.

92. See R. Slavin, Synthesis of Research on Cooperative Learning. *Educational Leadership*, February 1991, 71–94; D. Johnson, R. Johnson and E. Holubec, *Cooperation in the Classroom*, revised edition. Edina, MN: Interaction Books, 1991.

93. Slavin, *Synthesis of Research on Cooperative Learning*.

94. Slavin, Ibid., p. 77

95. See, for example, J. Lampe, G. Rooze, and M. Tallent-Runnels, Effects of Cooperative Learning Among Hispanic Students in Elementary Social Studies. *Journal of Educational Research, 89,* 1996, 187–191.

96. N. Webb, K. Nemer, A. Chizlik, and B. Sugru, Equity Issues in Collaborative Group Assessment: Group Composition and Performance. *American Educational Research Journal, 35,* 1998, 607–651.

97. L. Fuchs, D. Fuchs, C. Hamlett, and K. Karns, High-Achieving Students' Interactions and Performance on Complex Mathematical Tasks as a Function of Homogeneous and Heterogeneous Pairings. *American Educational Research Journal, 35,* 1998, 227–267.

98. N. Webb, et al., *Equity Issues,* p. 643.

99. Johnson, Johnson, and Holubec, *Cooperation in the Classroom;* Slavin, *Synthesis of Research on Cooperative Learning.*

100. D. Johnson, et al., Ibid., p. I.7.

101. V. Randall, Cooperative Learning: Abused and Overused? *Gifted Child Today, 122,* 1999, 14–16; C. Mulryan, Student Passivity During Cooperative Small Groups in Mathematics. *Journal of Educational Research, 85,* 1992, 261–273.

102. D. Johnson, et al., *Cooperation in the Classroom.*

103. D. Johnson, et al., Ibid.

104. See T. Newby, D. Stepich, J. Lehman, and J. Russell, *Instructional Technology for Teaching and Learning,* 2nd edition. Upper Saddle River, NJ: Merrill, 2000; M. Roblyer and J. Edwards, *Integrating Educational Technology into Teaching,* 2nd edition. Upper Saddle River, NJ: Merrill, 2000.

105. See, for example, A. diSessa, *Changing Minds: Computers, Learning and Literacy.* Cambridge, MA: MIT Press, 2000.

106. J. Healy, *Failure to Connect: How Computers Affect Our Children's Minds—For Better of Worse.* New York: Simon & Schuster, 1998; Excerpts, p. 1.

107. Roblyer and Edwards, *Integrating Educational Technology.*

108. S. Kerr, Visions of Sugarplums: The Fate of Technological Education and the School. In S. Kerr, ed., *Technology and the Future of Schooling.* Chicago: University of Chicago Press, 1996, pp. 1–27.

109. Newby, et al., *Instructional Technology.*

110. Healy, *Failure to Connect.*

111. A. Armstrong and C. Casement, *The Child Machine: How Computers Put Our Children's Education at Risk.* Beltsville, MD: Robins Lane Press, 2000.

112. Kerr, *Visions of Sugarplums,* p. 4.

113. Newby, *Instructional Technology,* p. 170.

114. Roblyer and Edwards, *Integrating Educational Technology,* p. 10.

115. diSessa, *Changing Minds.*

116. Roblyer and Edwards, Ibid., pp. 12–13.

117. F. Bennett, The Future of Computer Technology in K–12 Education. *Phi Beta Kappan, 83,* 2002, 621–625.

118. Newby, et al., *Instructional Technology,* p. 164.

119. Armstrong and Casement, *The Child Machine,* p. 65.

120. C. Kulik and J. Kulik, Effectiveness of Computer-Based Instruction. *Computers in Human Behavior, 7,* 1991, 75–94.

121. A. Dillon and R. Gabbard, Hypermedia as an Educational Technology. *Review of Educational Research, 68,* 1998, 322–349.

122. T. deJong and W. vanJoolingen, Scientific Discovery Learning with Computer Simulations of Conceptual Domains. *Review of Educational Research, 68,* 1998, 179–201.

123. Kerr, Visions of Sugarplums, p. 11; Roblyer and Edwards, *Integrating Educational Technology,* p. 12; M. Evans-Andriss, A*n Apple for the Teacher: Computers and Work in Elementary Schools.* Thousand Oaks, CA: Corwin, 1996.

124. Newby, et al., *Instructional Technology,* p. 174.

125. Roblyer and Evans, *Integrating Educational Technology,* p. 12

126. N. Hatira and A. Lesgold, Situational Effects in Classroom Technology Implementations. In Kerr, *Technology and the Future of Schooling,* pp. 131–171; quotation on p. 133.

127. Dillon and Gabbard, Hypermedia, p. 334.

128. Roblyer and Edwards, *Integrating Educational Technology,* pp. 166–167.

129. Hativa and Lesgold, Situational Effects.

130. DeJong and VanJoolingen, Scientific Discovery Learning.

131. DeJong and vanJoolingen, Ibid.; Dillon and Gabbard, Hypermedia; Hativa and Lesgold, Situational Effects.

132. Evans-Andriss, *An Apple for the Teacher.*

133. Healy, *Failure to Connect,* Excerpts, p. 4.

134. Armstrong and Casement, *The Child Machine,* p. 69.

135. Dillon and Gabbard, Hypermedia, p. 334.

136. D. Berry and D. Broadbent, Explanation and Verbalization in a Computer-Assisted Search Task. *Quarterly Journal of Experimental Psychology, 39A,* 1987, 585–609.

137. G. Salomon and D. Perkins, Learning in Wonderland: What Do Computers Really Offer Education? In Kerr, *Technology and Future of Education.*

138. See Newby, et al., Instructional Technology; Hativa and Lesgold, Situational Effects.

139. See C. Morton, The Modern Land of Laputa: Where Computers Are Used in Education. *Phi Delta Kappan, 77,* 1996, 416–419.

Chapter 4

THE SCHOOL'S ACADEMIC PROGRAM: PROMOTING LEARNING

What goes on in each teacher's classroom is affected by the situation that exists in the school as a whole. School policies and programs influence classroom instruction and the motivation and effort of students.

In this chapter, I discuss a number of ways in which schools have tried to improve their students' learning: (1) by setting academic goals; (2) by stimulating student effort with rewards and penalties; (3) by organizing the school day into fewer but longer blocks of time; (4) by providing special programs to students with limited proficiency in English; (5) by involving parents in their children's education; and (6) by assessing the school's progress in reaching its academic goals. (The effects of curriculum on learning are discussed in Chapter 2.)

The sections of this chapter discuss, in turn, each of these aspects of a school's academic program. The chapter closes with an overview and with a summary and some conclusions about which types of academic programs have contributed most to students' learning.

SETTING SCHOOL GOALS

To be effective, schools must have clear goals. Stewart Purkey and Marshall Smith explain: "Common sense, if nothing else, indicates that a clearly defined purpose is necessary for any endeavor hoping for success. Within the limits imposed by the common public school philosophy, schools need to focus on those tasks they deem most important."[1]

School officials often declare goals that command wide acceptance but that are very general—for example, providing an "excellent education" or teaching students to "use their minds well" or aiming to make sure that "every student reaches his or her potential." Such goals, while laudable, provide little in the way of concrete objectives.

Sometimes the professed primary goal of a school—student learning—is displaced in reality by a secondary objective. In particular, in some inner-city schools, disciplinary problems become the main focus of attention. The goal of maintaining order becomes *de facto* the primary goal of the school, in place of the official goal of student learning. In such settings, the competent administrator or teacher is seen to be the one who can maintain order among students.[2]

One of the key features that distinguishes effective schools from less effective schools is the presence of clear and specific goals concerning the basic information and skills that students should acquire. In addition, in the most effective schools, there is agreement between administrators and teachers about the importance of these goals and shared plans for reaching the goals.[3] As an example of the concrete and specific nature of goals in effective schools, some inner-city elementary schools specified that 60 percent of their students should read at grade level or above.[4] Of course, specific school goals may go beyond high student performance on standardized tests to include such other goals as developing students' abilities to write clear, reasoned essays or to successfully carry out research projects and experiments.

Along with clear and specific goals for student learning, principals and teachers in effective schools have been found consistently to have high expectations for student performance. In many cases, the school principal helps to stimulate these high expectations. Susan Rosenholtz says: ". . . from the ineffective principal's viewpoint, it may make no sense to set academic goals if teachers or students seem incapable of reaching them. In contrast, effective principals convey certainty that teachers can improve student performance and that students themselves are capable of learning."[5]

When a school's staff shares specific goals for student achievement and has high expectations about reaching these goals, they have a basis for action. The goals help to direct their behavior (regarding curriculum, instruction, assessment, etc.), serve to motivate them, and suggest criteria for evaluating progress. Studies in elementary, junior high, and high schools also indicate that the greater the agreement within the faculty regarding school goals, the higher the commitment of teachers to their jobs—as indicated, for example, by fewer teacher absences.[6]

Having explicit school goals also has been found important in research on school reform efforts. Reviewing studies pointing to the importance of clear goals, Kenneth Tewel writes: "People need a clear and simple 'promised land' to which they can travel . . . the easiest way to accomplish clarity of purpose is with an energizing, inspiring vision as the key to mobilizing support. This vision is the picture that drives all action. It includes both deeply felt values and a picture of the school's strategic focus."[7]

How does a school come to have a clear vision and specific goals for student learning? In many cases, school principals have taken the lead in formulating goals and have provided the driving forces of vision and commitment (and often pressure) to make progress toward the goals. However, a principal who tries to impose goals that he or she has decided alone on the entire school faculty may be unsuccessful in gaining acceptance of the announced goals. Agreement among teachers and other staff members on goals, and their commitment to work toward such goals, is essential if these goals are to be realized. A large body of research shows that participation of teachers in decision making can contribute greatly to school success. As Purkey and Smith comment: "Schools by their nature may not prove amenable to command structure approaches, especially given the vested interests of the various groups of relatively autonomous professionals involved in the day-to-day operations of a school."[8]

Leadership by a principal usually is important in helping a school's staff to formulate specific learning objectives.[9] But effective leadership can be shared with other staff members, and participation in setting objectives widened, so that widespread agreement and commitment to school goals can occur.[10]

In sum, the effectiveness of a school in promoting its students' learning is enhanced when the school's staff forms a consensus on clear and specific goals. Having such shared goals helps to motivate and focus the teachers' efforts and leads to higher student achievement.

STIMULATING STUDENT EFFORT

By offering a rich curriculum and having clear goals and high expectations for students, a school's staff can create some of the conditions for effective learning to occur. But for such learning to actually take place, students must participate in their own learning. They must attend regularly, not be disruptive, pay attention, do their homework, and generally try their best. Students who are more engaged in their school work have higher achievement.[11] One writer comments: "The most immediate and persisting issue for students and teachers is not low achievement, but student disengagement. The most obviously disengaged students disrupt classes, skip them, or fail to complete assignments. More typically, disengaged students behave well in school. They attend class and complete the work, but with little indication of excitement, commitment, or pride in mastery of the curriculum."[12]

DISCIPLINE

There is much evidence that students learn more in schools that are orderly and have clear and effectively enforced rules.[13] Much of this evidence comes from the studies that have examined characteristics of schools that were unusually effective in producing high academic achievement with predominantly low-income minority students. Reviewing some of the research on effective schools, Stewart Purkey and Marshall Smith comment:

"The seriousness and purpose with which the school approaches its task is communicated by the order and discipline it maintains in its building. Again, common sense alone suggests that students cannot learn in an environment that is noisy, distracting, or unsafe."[14] In the most effective schools, rules were clear and consistent and there also was clarity in who should enforce the rules and how this should be done.

Further evidence indicating the importance of effective discipline comes from research that compares academic achievement in public schools and in Catholic schools. Achievement generally has been higher in Catholic schools, even when background characteristics of students (such as family income and ethnicity) are held constant. One of the reasons for the better outcomes in Catholic schools appears to be that their discipline is more effective. School administrators in Catholic schools describe rules in their schools as more strictly enforced, and students in Catholic schools see discipline as more effective (as well as more fair) than do their counterparts in public schools. Moreover, the higher level of rule-violation in public schools (absenteeism, cutting class, fighting, threatening teachers) accounts for a substantial proportion of the difference in achievement between students in Catholic schools versus public schools.[15]

One of the important ways in which effective discipline in schools affects education is through its impact on teachers. Where schools are orderly and rules regarding student conduct are effectively enforced, teachers are more likely to believe that they can be successful, are more motivated, and are more committed to their jobs. One relevant study looked at how the job-related attitudes of over 1,200 teachers in 78 elementary schools in Tennessee were related to characteristics of their schools.[16] One of the school characteristics that affected teacher attitudes was the extent to which the school managed student behaviors effectively (especially by having explicit, consistent rules and enforcing the rules). The more teachers saw their school as managing student behavior effectively, the more they reported enthusiasm for their teaching, the less often they felt disillusioned about teaching, and the more committed they were to their jobs. The extent to which the school had effective discipline was especially important in influencing the morale of beginning teachers.

Another relevant study is a national survey conducted with about 8,500 teachers in 354 high schools.[17] This study, like the study of elementary school teachers in Tennessee, investigated the links between teacher attitudes and characteristics of their schools. The measure of teacher attitudes focused on their feelings of efficacy (e.g., "I sometimes feel it is a waste of time to try to do my best as a teacher.")

Among the school characteristics about which teachers were asked was the amount of disorderly student behavior (e.g., noise, horseplay, fighting, drug or alcohol use, tardiness, and class cutting) and the extent to which such behaviors interfere with their teaching. The more teachers in a school reported a high level of disorderly student behavior in their school, the lower their feelings of efficacy in their teaching.

Overall, these studies and other studies show that ineffective discipline in a school tends to make teachers disheartened and unmotivated in their work. Additional research suggests that frequent disciplinary problems in a school also contribute to high rates of absence and turnover among teachers.[18]

While rules about student behavior in a school need to be clear, consistent, and well-enforced, this does not mean that school administrators and teachers should be authoritarian or that they should maximize restrictions on students. In the most effective schools, while students are orderly, they also "acquire a sense of control over their environment."[19] Overly restrictive rules and arbitrary or unnecessarily harsh penalties are likely to lead to strong resentment and at least passive resistance among many students.

We have noted earlier (in Chapter 3) that for discipline to be most effective, rules should be applied only to behaviors that really affect learning; that the nature and magnitude of punishments should be appropriate to offenses; and, most important, that the rules and their enforcement should be seen by students (and others) as legitimate and fair. One of the best ways to ensure that students see the disciplinary system as fair is to involve the students in developing and enforcing the rules.[20]

There is a danger that satisfactory discipline in school may become an end in itself.[21] An intensive study of 15 high schools in locations throughout the United States found that many teachers explicitly or implicitly made "treaties" with their students under which the teacher demands little effort by students in return for students giving at least minimal compliance to school rules. The researchers state: "Teachers sometimes offer a passing grade in return for the students 'just sitting there.' In one class, the fact that passing was contingent only on orderly attendance was publicly stated. Even when the terms are not quite as explicit, students actively try to find out what the deal is and participate as much as possible in the negotiation."[22] In such settings, there is the appearance, but not the reality, of learning.

LEARNING AND REWARDS IN SCHOOL

For students to learn well, they must feel that engaging and succeeding in academic activities is important to them. Learning and success in school is likely to be valued by students when it brings them rewards—psychological, practical, or social.

Immediate Satisfactions from Learning

For some students, successful learning is valued for itself. Such students may find pleasure in reading English literature, be intrigued by the events of history, or be excited by the process of carrying out an experiment in chemistry. Doing well in school—getting good grades and positive evaluations by teachers—also may bring students positive feelings of achievement and high self-esteem. (Chapter 3 discusses the classroom conditions and teacher reactions to students that make success for students in their school work meaningful, likely, and rewarding.)

Learning as a Means to Success

Students may value learning because they think it will bring them practical benefits. They may believe that certain information and skills will help them in their personal lives or in their careers—for example, that information about personal hygiene will help them to remain healthy and that knowing math will help them in a career. (Evidence that students are more engaged when school activities are important to them is noted in Chapter 3.)

Some students are motivated to try for good grades and high test scores because they think that this kind of record will make it possible for them to get into college and eventually lead to the kind of career and lifestyle to which they aspire. However, while getting into the "right" college undoubtedly helps to motivate some students, admission to some college is not difficult for the great majority of students. Arthur Powell and his colleagues comment: "The impact of what used to be called 'higher' education on student incentives has diminished, in part because post-secondary education has become nearly as much an entitlement . . . as high school itself."[23] Moreover, any incentives that college admission or adult career and income may provide are too remote in time to affect the daily behavior of many students throughout most of their long school careers, especially in elementary school.[24]

Recognition by School

Students are likely to value academic achievement more highly when the school recognizes and rewards this achievement. Such recognition and reward may take a variety of forms. For example, students who do well in their studies may receive formal certificates of commendation; the names of those on the honor roll may be publicized; special ceremonies of recognition and plaques in prominent locations may honor academic "stars"; small tangible rewards, such as appealing books, may be given; and teachers and administrators may praise and show their respect for good students.

In presenting a "portrait of an effective school," reflecting their summary of extensive research, Stewart Purkey and Marshall Smith list "schoolwide recognition of academic success" as one of the conditions for school effectiveness. They state: "A school's culture is partially reflected in its ceremonies, its symbols, and the accomplishments it chooses to recognize officially. Schools that make a point of publicly honoring academic achievement and stressing its importance through the appropriate use of symbols, ceremonies, and the like encourage students to adopt similar norms and values."[25] Additional research indicates that one of the characteristics of principals of high-achieving schools is that they recognize the accomplishments of students.[26]

However, in many schools, recognition and honor tend to go most often to nonacademic accomplishment. Commenting on studies that find many schools to be undemanding of academic excellence, Barbara Bank says: ". . . official school cultures often fail to develop themselves as contexts in which academic striving is expected, commonplace, and praised. There are many reasons for such failures . . . but their likelihood is probably increased by the heavy emphasis in the official cultures of many schools, especially in the United States, on extracurricular activities that contribute little to the academic mission of the school, and may even undermine it."[27]

Approval by Others

For many—perhaps most—students, the most important reason to care about (or *not* care about) their level of academic success is the effect it may have on the approval and respect they get from others.

One important source of approval, especially for younger students, is their parents. When mothers and fathers show interest in their children's learning, encourage them to do well in school, and reward successful achievement (with approval, affection, treats, etc.), students will be motivated to do well in school in order to win their parents' approval.[28] Students, especially at younger ages, also may be motivated to try hard when they have warm relationships with teachers who encourage and reward effort and success.[29]

For a great many students, the strongest social influence, especially as they get older, is that of their peers—that is, their friends and the informal groups with which they have frequent contact. Peer influence has been found to have a strong and consistent effect on many educational outcomes, including academic achievement and occupational aspirations for both elementary and high school students. Peer influences are substantial for both elementary and high school students, but they become stronger as students grow older.[30]

The nature of the influence that peer groups exert on students varies somewhat with such factors as social class, gender, race, and the interests of students. There are some peer groups whose members support and encourage each other to study, learn the subject content, and get good grades.[31] However, many studies of peer cultures in schools have found that students commonly put little emphasis on, and place relatively little value on, academic ability and academic success. Rather, they give high value and respect to other qualities and accomplishments—physical attractiveness, social skills and popularity, clothes, family status, being in "the leading crowd," being a leader in school activities, and—most important (especially for boys)—being a good athlete.

Students who are academically oriented often are derided with such terms as "brains," "grinds," or "nerds."[32] One study of adolescent culture found that brilliant studious nonathletes were judged by their high school schoolmates as least socially acceptable.[33] Another major study found that, as students progressed through high school, their desire to be seen as an outstanding student decreased.[34]

Students who succeed in sports enjoy especially high respect from their peers. Barbara Bank notes: "One of the best established findings in studies of peer cultures is the importance they assign to athletics."[35] This emphasis has been found as early as the third grade of elementary school and grows stronger as students progress into middle school and high school.[36] Students who participate in athletics do not necessarily do more poorly academically than other students; the evidence is inconsistent.[37] However, a general atmosphere in which athletic success is emphasized tends to deemphasize the importance of academic achievement.

The way in which a student's athletic success may be celebrated, regardless of his academic success, is illustrated in the comments of a teacher who described a football rally at which "the whole student body stood up and cheered the captain of the football team for *five minutes*. And I know that kid. He can't read! But that's the way this place is."[38]

Why should students who excel in sports receive the admiration of their peers much more often than those who excel academically? First, as some research in high schools has documented, those who are outstanding athletes are more visible and better known to their peers than are outstanding scholars.[39] Considerable publicity—within the schools and outside the school as well—is given to athletic success; much less publicity is given to success in academic endeavors.

Second, good athletes are admired because they are seen as working hard for their fellow students, struggling to win victory and prestige for the school, and thereby to all its students, in competitions with other schools. On the other hand, smart and studious students may be seen as causing difficulties for their fellow students by raising the competitive standards for academic performance and grades. They may be viewed, therefore, as selfish—striving to raise their own academic accomplishments at the expense of others. After reviewing evidence that high school students had the greatest respect for nonstudious athletes and the least respect for studious nonathletes, James Coleman comments: "School forces a scholar to choose between being *selfish* by studying hard, and being *unselfish* by working for the glory of the school in its interscholastic games."[40]

Some researchers have suggested that the same principles that explain why athletic success brings prestige may be applied to make scholastic success more prestigious among students. They point out that visible contributions to reaching group goals may be made in academic as well as in athletic competitions.

At the classroom level, activities such as peer tutoring and cooperative learning provide opportunities for students who are academically able and hardworking to make contributions to the success of others as well as themselves. Thus, the student in a cooperative learning group who can contribute relevant ideas and correct answers to his group will be respected and liked because he is helping the group to do well and thus all of its members to get good grades.[41] Competition between groups can be introduced in the classroom to make the value of contributions to the group even greater. Political games and management games in which teams represent different political parties, or union and management, or competing firms, or nations, have been used successfully with students; such games arouse high levels of student engagement and motivation.[42]

Competitive group activities can be used both within a school and between schools. In competitions between schools, greater emphasis can be placed on activities that are scholastic or that focus on the arts. Debates, group science or technology competitions, group math tournaments, musical group contests, and drama contests are examples of such activities. Competition between schools in academic or artistic activities can be especially useful in providing visibility and importance to such activities, similar to that accorded to sports. Where this occurs, students who are outstanding scholars or who have other outstanding nonathletic talents will be given admiration and esteem by their peers.

The status system that exists in many schools, whereby students admire athletes and ignore or look down on outstanding scholars, is not an inevitable one. In his classic study, *Adolescent Society*, James Coleman wrote: "The norms of the student social system are created in large part by the activities to which it is subject. And it is the adult community that fixes the activities of the adolescent community. It does so by fixing the activities of the *school*—for example, by using high-school sports as community entertainment, and as contests between communities. . . ."[43] By placing greater emphasis on academic achievement, by rewarding such achievement, and by arranging for group activities in which students with academic abilities can contribute to the success of their group or school, schools can shift the social norms of students toward support of academic achievement.

CLASS TIME SCHEDULES

To be most effective in promoting learning, schools must make the best use not only of their physical resources (such as their libraries and computers) and human resources (teachers' and students' efforts and talents) but also of their resource of time.

Traditionally, the day in American high schools and middle schools is divided into about eight periods. Each period is about 50 minutes long, with about 10 minutes for students to move from one class to another. Each student has classes in five to six subjects (e.g., English, mathematics, science, a foreign language, history, and physical education) plus a lunch period and perhaps a study period. Each teacher is assigned to teach about five to six separate classes each day (and uses the other periods for lunch, class preparations, and other school duties). Each course—especially those in core subjects, such as English or math—continues from one semester to the next during the academic year. Thus, for example, freshman English spans both the fall semester and the spring semester of the student's first year in high school.

This traditional way or organizing time in high schools has been criticized by many educators.[44] Critics have argued, first, that the pattern of many short periods wastes time used for frequent movement by students between classrooms and also requires extra time for teachers to get each class organized to begin and to wrap up the period. A more serious problem alleged is that, because of their relative brevity, classes of less than an hour tend to encourage teachers to lecture in order to cover the material of the day; thus, teachers will emphasize passive learning, especially memorization, rather than active learning by students.

Furthermore, critics of the traditional schedule say that having many classes in a single day is not optimal either for good learning or for good teaching. The student may have her time, attention, and thought processes divided among five or six subjects and be unable to focus her attention sufficiently on any of them. The teacher must prepare for five to six classes every day for about 10 months. He must interact with, evaluate, and mark the work of about 120 to 180 students. For both the student, trying to keep up with five academic subjects at the same time, and the teacher, having to deal with many classes and a large number of students every day, stress is likely to be high. Thus, effective teaching and effective learning may be compromised.

Block scheduling is an alternative way of dividing time during the school day so that most classes meet for longer periods than the traditional 50 minutes or so.[45] One common pattern (the "4 x 4") is to have four blocks of 90-minute periods each day (with additional time being used for other activities, such as remediation or enhancement activities). Each course lasts for one semester. Each student takes three or four courses each semester and a different group of courses the next semester. Because class periods are longer, each course is completed in one semester, rather than two semesters. Teachers usually teach no more than three classes each semester and devote one of the four basic time blocks to preparation (and perhaps to other duties as well).

A second frequently used pattern also has four major time blocks (usually about 90 minutes each) each day, but students take different courses on alternate days, while teachers teach a different set of classes on alternate days. For example, a student might take English, math, and history on Monday; then take French, science, physical education, and music on Tuesday; return to his first set of courses on Wednesday; and so on.

Other specific types of class schedules, employing the central idea of substantial time blocks for some or all classes, also have been used. By the mid 1990s, 40 percent of American high schools were using some form of block scheduling.[46] About 10 to 20 percent of middle and junior high schools also had changed in this direction.[47]

EFFECTS ON TEACHERS AND STUDENTS

Research on the use of block scheduling has found that it generally has benefits for instruction and for learning.[48] Compared to teachers following traditional schedules, those in block schedule classes have been found to spend less time on classroom management; spend less time in reviewing class lessons; have more time for planning; and make more use of performance-based assessments. Some research has found a more relaxed atmosphere, and students receiving more individual attention from teachers, in block schedule classes.

There also is evidence of more positive outcomes for students attending block schedule classes. Discipline problems tend to be fewer, attendance better, and graduation rates higher. Students tend to be more engaged in their studies. In addition, there is some evidence that a block schedule tends to improve student achievement, although the evidence for positive effects on achievement is not consistent. Several studies have found little or no difference in test scores between students following block schedules as compared to those with traditional time schedules. However, several other studies found students following block schedules to have higher achievement than other students—as indicated by teacher judgments, grades, or standardized tests.[49]

After experiencing a block schedule, teachers, students, and parents all generally like this type of time schedule and prefer it to the traditional schedule. In one study, a high school principal reported: "Last year, 98 percent of my teachers stated on our anonymous survey that they would not want to return to traditional scheduling.[50]

While block time schedules appear often to have benefits, there are some problems that may arise with their use. When the 4 x 4 type of schedule (students taking a small number of different subjects each semester) is used, there may be a loss of continuity between sequential courses in the same subject (most notably in a foreign language) and students may not retain information well from one course in a subject sequence to the next. When an alternate-days block schedule is used, such problems of continuity and retention are reduced. However, a drawback to the alternating day schedule is that the number of courses that each student takes every semester, and the total number of courses and students for which each teacher is responsible each semester, is no fewer than in a traditional schedule.

Whatever the specific type of block schedule used, it will have benefits only if teachers take advantage of the longer time periods by using more and different instructional methods and actively engaging students' interest and effort. Some teachers do not use the full time afforded by a long—say, 90-minute—period for instruction. Instead, they may use part of the long period—say, 30 minutes—for other purposes (such as letting students study while the teacher marks papers). While some teachers with block schedules use varied instructional methods (some combination of lecture, discussion, cooperative group activities, games, problem-solving exercises, experiments, etc.), other teachers do not go beyond the "chalk and talk" methods of traditional classes.

One study found that teachers relied heavily on lectures in 30 percent of block classes. David Hottenstein describes the tendency of many teachers to continue to rely on lectures when their school changes to a block schedule. "My social studies department was one of the most enthusiastic about the move to intensive scheduling. In fact, they were disappointed that the blocks were only 85 minutes long. They went through the training, marched into the classroom, and lectured extensively!"[51]

Several additional studies have found that teachers in block schedule classes do not use their instructional time differently than teachers in traditional-length classes.[52] In one of these studies, instructional activities used by teachers in 26 block schedule (4 x 4) classes and 26 traditional high school classes were observed. The researchers found that teachers were using slightly more interactive instruction in traditional shorter classes than were teachers in the longer, block schedule classes. A similar but larger study found that, regardless of the particular type of block schedule format, teachers in block schedule classes and those in traditional classes did not generally differ significantly in their instructional strategies.

In a review of research on block scheduling, J. Allen Queen comments: "It is important to note that merely changing the amount of time students spend in class through block scheduling does not guarantee school success. Appropriate changes in instructional practices and the effective use of class time have been found to be essential to the success of block scheduling."[53] To promote such appropriate changes in instructional practices, some schools have used training programs to help prepare teachers to make effective use of the longer class periods in block schedule programs.[54]

To summarize our discussion of school time schedules: Block schedules, under which students study fewer subjects in longer class periods each day, are intended to focus the efforts of both students and teachers and to permit the use of more varied instructional methods. When compared to traditional schedules, block schedules generally have been found to be liked more by both teachers and students; to aid teachers in managing class activities; and to promote some positive student outcomes (such as fewer disciplinary problems and absences). However, for block scheduling to be most effective, schools need to encourage and train their teachers to take advantage of the longer class periods to employ varied and interactive methods of instruction.

PROGRAMS FOR STUDENTS WITH LIMITED ENGLISH

An important issue facing many schools is that many of their students have grown up using a language other than English and are not fully proficient at communicating in English. By the last decade of the twentieth century, well over 5 million children from 5 to 17 years old in the United States (or 13% of the school-age population) spoke a language other than English at home. Of these, over two-thirds were Spanish speakers, about 10 percent spoke other European languages, and 14 percent spoke Asian languages. (The rest spoke other languages.)[55] With increased levels of immigration in recent years, the number of children from non-English-speaking homes has continued to increase.

Some children growing up in a home where Spanish or Chinese or some other non-English language is spoken are able to learn a good deal of English anyway (from friends, television, and other sources). But many students from such backgrounds have only limited proficiency in English when they enter school. If English is the predominant, or only, language of instruction, these students may have difficulty in learning. This problem is especially salient in areas that have high proportions of recent immigrants in their population. For example, one analysis of students in Los Angeles County found that about half were not fully proficient in English.[56]

Public policy concerning the use of non-English languages in the schools has varied over time. In the early nineteenth century public schools sometimes used a non-English language of the local population (e.g., German). However, by the early twentieth century, English was adopted as the sole language of instruction in most states. Schools followed a "sink or swim" policy toward students with limited English, assuming that once immersed in an all-English setting, they would quickly pick up the language skills they needed. Among the children of European immigrants (Italians, Germans, Russian Jews, and others) early in the twentieth century, some foreign-language speakers did learn quickly to "swim" in English-language classrooms, but many others tended to "sink" for at least a time, falling behind their age-appropriate grade level.[57] Among public school students of Spanish-speaking backgrounds in the mid-twentieth century, evidence from five southwestern states showed that average educational achievement was far behind that of students from English-speaking backgrounds.[58]

To try to help students who spoke little English, some communities created programs that used the children's native language (usually Spanish) as well as English. In 1968, the U.S. Congress passed the Bilingual Education Act, which made money available to poor school districts for bilingual education. These programs promoted the use of students' home language to begin their instruction, while the students also learned English. English was to be used later in instruction. The federal legislation specified that the goal of the bilingual program was to make students proficient in English.

Many states followed the federal initiative by passing laws that created bilingual education programs. Court decisions and actions by the U.S. Office of Civil Rights also promoted wider use of bilingual programs in the 1970s and in the years following. By the early 1990s, 60 percent of state and locally funded programs for students with limited English proficiency were labeled bilingual education.[59]

DEBATE ABOUT BILINGUAL EDUCATION

The widespread use of bilingual education programs has generated a considerable amount of opposition and criticism. Some of the opposition has come from those who see the increasing use of other languages as a threat to the preeminent position of English in the United States and, more broadly, as a threat to traditional American culture. Criticism of bilingual programs also has come from some people, including some educators, who question their educational effectiveness. A backlash against bilingual education in California led to a severe curtailment of these programs in a 1998 referendum.

Many of those who support bilingual education argue, first, that such programs are necessary to help students from other language backgrounds learn English well. They draw on "facilitation theory,"[60] which asserts that children who reach a high level of competence in reading and writing in their first language will eventually reach a higher level of competence in a second language (English) than those who are taught entirely in the second language. Advocates of bilingual programs also maintain that learning in the language of their own original culture, under the tutelage of teachers of their own background, raises students' self-esteem and gives them role models for learning. They point to evidence they believe shows that students' use of their home language in school enhances both their learning of English and their achievement in academic subjects. Furthermore, they argue that, in an increasingly global economy, both students and American society benefit when school graduates have extensive knowledge of more than one language and culture.[61]

Opponents of bilingual education dispute almost all of the claims of its advocates. They state that, rather than helping students to make a transition to English, bilingual programs often continue to teach students in Spanish for most or all of their elementary school years. They say that there is no good evidence to support the theory that learning to read and write in one's first language facilitates better learning of a second language.[62] The results of bilingual programs, they assert, are that students do not learn English well and that this deficit is an obstacle to their educational and occupational success.

Critics of bilingual programs also argue that these programs result in lower academic achievement for students and that most Hispanic parents prefer that their children's academic courses be taught in English.[63] Finally, critics point to what they see as serious social and practical problems with such programs, including the "segregation" of students from non-English-speaking backgrounds.

The debate about bilingual education often has aroused strong feelings among those on both sides of the issue. Proponents and opponents make conflicting claims about the evidence concerning the effectiveness of bilingual education. A recent review of relevant research notes: "This field is so ideologically charged that no one is immune from ideological bias or preconceived notions."[64]

EFFECTS OF BILINGUAL PROGRAMS

Given this "minefield" of conflicting perspectives and claims, what can we conclude about the effectiveness of bilingual education? As a first step, one must distinguish among various types of bilingual programs and among alternatives to bilingual education.[65] Almost all bilingual education programs teach students to read and write in their home language first and only later in English. Programs differ with respect to how soon and to what extent students will experience a transition from home language to the use of English. The majority of elementary school programs have as a goal that students leave the program and join a "mainstream" class after three years. But many students are allowed to stay in these programs longer (sometimes through elementary school or even beyond). Some bilingual programs are designed to continue for seven years (a time period endorsed by several theorists of bilingual education).

Bilingual education programs also differ in their goals. Most aim to teach English, as well as academic content, to their students. Some programs, while sharing those goals, also aim to develop literacy in and use of the students' first (non-English) language, thus producing fully bilingual, bicultural persons.

The major alternatives to bilingual education programs for teaching students who lack English language proficiency are: (1) "submersion" in mainstream classes; (2) English as a Second Language (ESL) programs; and (3) structured immersion programs.[66]

The "submersion" method of instruction simply places children with limited English proficiency in a regular classroom with English-speaking children. They are given no special help beyond that normally given to students. Educators in these circumstances hope that the children from non-English-speaking backgrounds will soon "pick up" the English language skills they need.

In ESL programs, students who lack proficiency in English participate in regular classrooms, with native English speakers, for most of the day. They are removed from class for a number of periods during each week for lessons in English and then return to their classes.

In structured immersion programs, students are in class with other students from their own (non-English-speaking) background. Instruction is primarily in English but the level of English is geared to the students' level of proficiency. Furthermore, the teacher is able to speak the students' first language and uses that language to clarify or supplement the instruction in English. Teachers use English for 70 to 90 percent of instructional time, averaged over the first three years of instruction. Students learn English and subject matter content at the same time.

A careful review of studies that compare outcomes for students in bilingual education programs (teaching students in their home language first) with outcomes for similar students in other situations (submersion, ESL, and structured immersion) has been made by Christine Rossell and Keith Baker.[67] From among 300 evaluations of bilingual programs, they selected 72 studies that adequately matched students assigned to bilingual and other types of classes and that were methodologically sound in other ways as well. Each of these studies compared students in a bilingual program with students in another type of program with respect to their average scores on tests (in English) of reading, language (understanding of grammar), and math.

The largest differences in achievement were found in the studies that compared bilingual education to a structured immersion program (instruction primarily but not entirely in English). Of 12 studies that compared these types of programs with respect to achievement in reading, 10 found that students in structured immersion scored higher than bilingual education students and two studies found no difference. Of eight studies that compared bilingual and structured immersion programs with respect to students' achievement in math, three found those in structured immersion programs to score higher, while five studies found no difference between the two programs. Of 21 studies that compared bilingual education students and structured immersion students with respect to some measure of achievement, *no* study found bilingual education students to achieve better.

Overall, the review of research by Rossel and Baker finds that, as measured by tests in the English language, students in bilingual education programs tend to achieve less well than students in submersion situations, less well than those in ESL programs, and especially less well than those in structured immersion programs.

However, it is useful to distinguish between the effects of bilingual programs that are geared toward moving students into mainstream classes relatively quickly and those that plan to keep students in the bilingual program for longer periods. A notable study compared achievement gains in math, language, and reading through grade 3 for students in "early-exit" bilingual programs (which aim to put students into mainstream classes after about three years); "late-exit" bilingual programs (which aim to continue students in bilingual education for seven years); and structured immersion programs (described above).[68] Little difference in achievement scores on any of the tests was found between students in the bilingual early-exit program and students in structured immersion. But students in late-exit bilingual programs did more poorly on all three tests (math, language, and reading) than did students in either the early-exit bilingual or the structured immersion programs.

While the best research evidence indicates that bilingual education programs (especially late-exit programs) lead to poorer achievement for students than do other programs, this does not mean that it is a good idea to immediately place students who do not speak much English into classes where only English is spoken. After reviewing a wide variety of evidence, Rossell and Baker assert that bilingual education has a positive effect on students' learning at the very beginning of the acquisition of English. Early use of the child's home language may aid communication between teacher and students, make the child feel more comfortable, and prevent the child from feeling bewildered and inadequate. However, these researchers say, as students' knowledge of English increases, they benefit from moving as quickly as possible to instruction primarily or entirely in English.

Based on their review of the evidence, Rossell and Baker suggest the following hypothesis (to be tested against further research): "Native tongue instruction should be minimal and used only in the beginning when a LEP [limited English proficiency] student's English knowledge is very low. The time period for the superiority of or need for native tongue instruction may be a matter of *months.*"[69]

Any judgment about the merits of bilingual education programs, as compared to those of alternative programs, must be made in the context of the programs' goals. If the goal of the educational program is to produce students who are truly bilingual—not only in conversation but also in reading and writing in more than one language—then bilingual education programs may be more effective than programs that focus on getting students with limited English proficiency to learn and use English. Moreover, from a perspective that gives equal value to different languages, some supporters of bilingual programs argue that measuring achievement only with English-language tests may be misleading.

However, if the goals of bilingual education programs are to help students to learn English well and to use English to learn other academic subjects—as envisioned in the Bilingual Education Act—then long-term bilingual programs that stretch out over most or all of the elementary school years do not appear to be effective. Rather, programs (such as briefer bilingual and structured immersion programs) that provide students with some home-language help at the start of school but move them fairly quickly to all-English instruction, appear to be superior.

NON-LANGUAGE PROBLEMS

The problems of providing a good education for students whose home language is not English are not restricted to problems of language. The low academic achievement and high dropout rates that characterize many such students—such as those of Spanish-language background—also are affected by a variety of economic, cultural, and social factors.[70] For example, student achievement may be lowered when families move often, leading to poor school attendance; when parents place little emphasis on education; when students are not well motivated because they see little opportunity to attain good careers; and when teachers are unable to relate well to students because they are not familiar with their culturally based style of behavior.

While some of the factors that affect the learning of non-native-English students (e.g., moving by families) are beyond the control of the school, there are some ways—in addition to dealing with language problems—that the school can help.[71] Schools can reach out to students' parents (in their own language) to acquaint them with the school's programs and enlist whatever support the parents can provide. Schools can familiarize teachers with the customs and typical behaviors of people from non-Anglo cultures—for example, how children are taught to act with adults and whether they are used to working individually or in groups. Schools can include in their curricula (e.g., stories read in English classes and material covered in history classes) some content of particular relevance to those from particular cultural backgrounds. Some researchers have suggested that class size should be reduced more than usual and/or the school day should be lengthened for students whose first language is not English and therefore face greater challenges in learning.[72] In sum, providing a good education for students from non-English-speaking backgrounds requires that schools try to deal with students' language problems and take whatever other actions they can to promote their learning. (The education of language-minority students, along with that of other minority students, is discussed further in Chapter 9.)

INVOLVING PARENTS

To be most effective, schools must coordinate their efforts with what goes on in students' homes.

PARENTS' INFLUENCE ON STUDENTS

Parents affect their children's school learning in a number of ways. First, parents may prepare a child to learn by helping to develop her cognitive capacities before she starts school.[73] The influence of family milieu on a child's learning continues after she is enrolled in school. When parents provide what has been termed an academically enriching environment—for example, parent-child discussion of current events, and reading magazines at home—the academic achievement of their children tends to rise.[74]

Parents' actions also may affect their children's school achievement more directly. First, parents may communicate to a child their expectations about the amount of education he will attain and about his current level of school performance. For example, fourth- and fifth-grade students in a suburban school district in northern California were asked about how much education they expect their child to obtain and how they would feel if their child brought home certain grades (e.g., a D). Holding constant parents' education and income, the more education parents expected their child to attain, the higher the child's actual grades were (particularly among European-American and Asian-American children). The more upset parents said they would be with a child's grade of D (or, for Asian-American parents, even with a grade of B), the higher their child's actual grades were.[75]

More parental support and encouragement for their children's school efforts also contributes to more positive school attitudes and higher achievement for students at all grade levels.[76] In addition, the amount of support from families can affect the entry of their children into particular tracks in high school. One study conducted in six San Francisco Bay area high schools found that, with students' prior achievement held constant, their choice of a high school track was influenced by the amount of encouragement, praise, and offers to help given by their parents.[77]

In addition to giving emotional support and encouragement, parents also may contribute to their children's achievement by aiding the specific instructional objectives of their children's teachers. For example, a study of students in grades 3 and 5 found that when teachers involved parents in reading activities with their children at home, the students' reading achievement scores rose more during the school year.[78]

There is some evidence, too, that when parents give more importance to knowing about their children's activities, including what they are doing at school, their children do better in school. Perhaps reflecting the importance of parents' interest in what goes on at school, more involvement by parents in school activities, such as parent-teacher conferences and the parent-teacher organization, also is related positively to their children's school achievement.[79]

Because parents play a significant role in the education of their children, schools can increase their effectiveness by working together cooperatively with parents. James Comer and Norris Haynes comment: "Meaningful parent participation is essential for effective schooling. The best results are achieved only when these two institutions work together."[80]

SCHOOLS' EFFECTS ON PARENT INVOLVEMENT

The extent to which parents become involved in their children's education—at home, in contacts with school staff, or by assisting in school—depends in part on the parents' social and personal characteristics.[81] However, school programs and teacher practices also have an important influence on parent involvement. Joyce Epstein comments: "At the elementary, middle, and high school levels, surveys of teachers, principals, and students reveal that if schools invest in practices to involve families, then parents respond . . . including many parents who might not have otherwise become involved on their own."[82]

The characteristics and organization of the school, the beliefs and attitudes of school staff, and specific school programs all play a role. First, the level of the school—elementary school versus middle school or high school—matters. As children move from elementary school to middle school or high school, their parents' contacts with teachers and the school drop considerably.[83] In part, this may indicate that parents feel less need to (and are less able to) keep close tabs on their children as they grow older. However, much of the decline in parent involvement appears to be due to the characteristics of schools at different levels.

Compared to elementary schools, middle schools and especially high schools are likely to be larger and a longer distance from parents' homes. Moreover, because students have different teachers for different subjects, there is less contact between particular teachers and both students and their families. Jacquelynne Eccles and Rena Harold comment: "Parents who are involved in their neighborhood elementary schools may see this involvement as part of their connection with their community and friends . . . parents and teachers get to know each other over the years their children are in the school . . . as children leave their home schools . . . the sense of belonging and investment may decrease, and as a result, parents may feel less able and less inclined either to be involved or to try to effect change in the educational experiences of their children."[84]

Involvement of parents also is influenced by the attitudes of teachers toward such involvement. Administrators, teachers, and other school staff sometimes are reluctant to involve parents in their children's schooling. They may see most parents as disinterested, ignorant, unreasonable, or meddlesome.[85] Such negative perceptions of parents are especially likely in low-income and minority neighborhoods, where, as Eccles and Harold note, "parents may be seen as part of the problem in educating their children, rather than as a resource."[86] School staff who hold such beliefs have been found to discourage involvement by parents in their children's classroom or school.

PROGRAMS TO INVOLVE PARENTS

Schools can take a variety of actions to increase parental involvement in their children's education. These actions include:

1. Establishing stronger connections with parents—for example, by a call from the child's teacher in which the teacher invites the parents to contact her anytime with questions. In describing the conditions that help to involve parents in schools, Rebecca Burns says "[Schools] must communicate that parents are partners and that their involvement is needed and valued."[87]

2. Keeping parents well-informed about school programs and about their own child's progress. For example, the school can assign a contact person for each family to make sure parents are getting ample information.

3. Involving parents in learning activities at home. For example, schools may provide information on learning goals and ways in which parents can help to achieve these goals.

4. Providing opportunities for parents to assist with activities at the school. Parents may be asked to assist the school in a variety of ways, such as tutoring, teaching special skills, and helping to supervise activities during and after school.

Parents also may play a role in decision making about the program and policies of the school. For example, schools that have adopted "site-based management" often include parents (along with teachers and others) in councils that help plan curriculum, student services, and other programs (see Chapter 5).

One widely known program to involve parents meaningfully in schools, and to make each school part of a broader community, has been developed by James Comer and his colleagues.[88] In a school that follows this program, parents participate in one or more of three ways. First, a small group of parents (usually five or six) serve along with school staff on a team that plans and manages the school's academic and social programs. These parent representatives are elected by their peers. Second, some parents participate in the ongoing day-to-day activities of the classroom and school and in a parent organization. Third, a larger proportion of parents attend various activities (such as performances and holiday programs) at the school in which their children are involved. Thus, parents are integrated in several ways, and at several levels of responsibility and involvement, into the life of the school.

A substantial number of schools (over 100) throughout the United States have implemented a Comer-type program. There is some evidence that adoption of the Comer program has led to improvements in parental participation, student test scores, and attendance by both students and teachers.[89]

In the 1990s, the Utah Center for Families in Education carried out a five-year study on the involvement of families and community with schools. The study covered eight elementary schools, two middle schools, and two high schools, selected to ensure as much diversity as possible with regard to parents' education, income, and ethnic background. Each school participating in the study established seven committees, each chaired by a teacher and a parent. Each committee was charged with promoting cooperation between the school and others in its area of responsibility (e.g., involvement at school by parents; involvement in learning activities at home; and involvement in decision making, governance, and advocacy by parents). An evaluation of this program indicates that students have improved their academic performance in the majority of the participating schools.[90]

ASSESSING PROGRESS TOWARD GOALS

In order for a school to maintain or improve the effectiveness of its academic program, it must have good information about how well it is reaching its goals. To get such information, it must have a system for assessing student learning and other important school outcomes.

Describing the "feedback mechanism" of the effective school, Susan Rosenholtz writes: "Obtaining information on the outputs of teaching, comparing those outputs against the standards prescribed by goals, detecting significant departures from the standards, and issuing technical assistance and directives back to the technical core to improve on the quality of outputs suggest a taut system where teacher uncertainty is minimized."[91]

A variety of "outputs" of a school's programs may be assessed. These include attendance rates, numbers of disciplinary actions, graduation rates, and student academic achievement, as well as other indicators of student motivation and learning. Student achievement usually has been measured by standardized tests, but tests of performance—such as writing an essay or carrying out a research project—also are often used.

Studies of schools that are unusually effective in educating students in low-income areas have found that a system for monitoring student progress in learning is present in most of these effective schools.[92] Other evidence indicating that an "output-driven" system tends to improve student learning comes from a study of gains in math and science between the 8th and 10th grades among a large nationally representative sample of students.[93] Achievement gains in both math and science were greater in schools that sent students' test results to parents than in schools where parents did not receive such test results. Collecting and publicizing such measures of learning outcomes may raise the motivation of a school's staff to improve their school's effectiveness.

While assessing student learning is—in principle and often in practice—an important element in creating an effective school, there are a number of important problems that may arise in carrying out such assessments. One basic issue—especially relevant to assessing student achievement—is the type of measures that are used. There is considerable evidence that the type of tests used to assess student learning affects what is taught in the classroom.[94] If achievement tests require only memorization of isolated facts, teachers are likely to cover and adjust their teaching styles to such content. On the other hand, when students are assessed with regard to broader understandings and their ability to solve problems, curriculum and instruction are likely to emphasize such understanding. Both types of learning—of facts and basic skills and of abstract ideas and thinking abilities—are useful. Schools need to be careful that a system of assessment helps to reach educational goals that are set prior to, and independently of, tests, and that having students do well on available tests does not become the goal in itself.

Use of rigorous tests, with high standards for performance, may present a daunting challenge to some students and lead to higher dropout rates. To counter such negative effects, and to make tests an aid to further learning, it is desirable to use tests to pinpoint areas of strength and weakness for individual students so that problems can be remediated.[95]

A system for assessing learning outcomes will help a school to reach its goals for student learning only to the extent that ongoing assessments lead the school to improve its curriculum, its teaching methods, its organization, or other aspects of its operation. However, educators often use performance data mostly for purposes of compliance with administrative or legal mandates, rather than to improve practice.[96] It is important for schools to link their measures of student learning to their overall goals, to specific curriculum objectives, and to instructional activities and methods. The U.S. Office of Educational Research and Improvement has stated: "Accountability is a blunt tool unless policymakers, educators, and the public have information that allows them to determine the likely sources of a problem and find clues about how to fix it. Consequently, accountability systems should do more than simply collect testing data. They should provide an integrated picture of the schooling environment. . . ."[97]

In order for assessments of school outcomes to lead to school improvements, people in the school—teachers and students, along with administrators—must be motivated to improve their results. Discussing the concept of output-driven schools, James Coleman has argued that teachers, students, and parents often have few incentives to improve students' performance. He suggests that greater attention be given to providing incentives (especially rewards but also penalties) linked to school performance.[98] For example, in schools for which there is evidence of high student achievement, teachers might be given public recognition and financial bonuses; students might be given opportunities to take part in enjoyable activities (such as trips to amusement parks). Coleman suggests that an "output-driven school" provide yearly rewards to teachers, students, and parents for a high level of performance and for performance gains. Coleman also sees incentives for high performance as contributing to the formation of norms among students and staff that encourage high academic achievement. For teachers and other school staff, motivation for improving the school and reaching learning goals is likely to come not only from personal incentives but also from active involvement in a school community that has jointly set goals and made decisions about how to reach them. (See Chapter 7 for a fuller discussion of how programs for standards, testing, and school accountability affect students' learning.)

OVERVIEW: EFFECTS OF
ACADEMIC PROGRAM

Figure 4-1 presents an overview of ways in which the academic program of a school affects outcomes for students.

A number of aspects of the academic program discussed in this chapter are listed at the left of the figure. Also included in this list is the school's curriculum, which was discussed in the previous chapter.

The figure shows, first, that the academic program affects the activities and the instructional methods used in the classroom. For example, specific goals set for math learning—such as that students should be able to apply general algorithms to specific problems—will affect the kinds of activities a teacher introduces in a specific math class; having this math class on a block schedule will give the teacher more opportunity to vary the teaching methods she uses during class; and programs for assessing student learning may lead the teacher to change procedures that are not producing adequate results in this class.

The academic program also affects the motivation and the norms of teachers. For example, the motivation of a teacher is likely to be raised when the school staff has agreed on a set of specific learning goals for her students (e.g., that at least 80% should be reading at grade level) and when the disciplinary system creates an orderly atmosphere that permits her to concentrate on student learning. The teacher and her colleagues also are

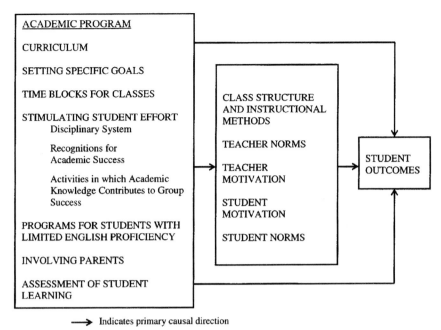

Figure 4-1 Effect of school's academic program on teachers, students, and learning.

likely to encourage each other to overcome problems when the staff agrees on specific goals and when there is a system to assess progress toward those goals.

The academic program also influences the motivation and the norms of students. For example, students may be bored by a history curriculum that emphasizes a set of names and dates but excited by a history curriculum that tells a dramatic story and highlights still-important issues; a student may be motivated to try his best (and his peers may encourage him to try hard) when the school holds a technology tournament in which the student's group competes with other groups; the student who speaks little English may be discouraged from trying hard (or even from attending school) if the school has no adequate program for teaching him English when he begins school.

By its effects on classroom activities, on teachers, and on students, the school's academic program indirectly affects student outcomes—including learning, attendance, completion of school, and going on to higher education. The academic program also has some direct effects on outcomes for students, independent of its effects on classroom activities, teacher motivation, and student motivation. For example, the content of the curriculum will directly affect what students learn; a disciplinary system that expels students who have a number of serious offenses may directly affect the school's graduation rates; and "early-exit" bilingual programs may directly affect learning.

SUMMARY AND CONCLUSIONS

Schools produce good outcomes for students when they complement a good curriculum with academic procedures and programs that energize teachers, engage students in their studies, and facilitate effective classroom instruction.

School effectiveness is enhanced when the school's staff agrees on clear and specific goals for their students' education. Having shared goals helps to focus and to motivate teachers' efforts and leads to higher student achievement.

Schools must try to engage students in their own learning and motivate them to put forth the needed effort. Creating an orderly atmosphere in which rules for student conduct are clear, consistent, and enforced is a necessary first step. But even greater emphasis must be put on creating positive incentives for students to learn and to do well in their schoolwork. Making studies as interesting and stimulating as possible, providing opportunities for success experiences, and making clear the relevance of their studies to students' own lives, will help to engage many students. Recognition of high-achieving students by the school often will be helpful. Probably the strongest influence on most students is the approval and esteem of others and especially that of their peers. Greatest respect from peers usually has gone to those who succeed in nonacademic activities, such as sports. By structuring group activities and competitions around academic goals, schools can increase the approval and esteem that go to those who excel in learning.

The effectiveness of a school's academic program is also affected by the way in which it organizes available time. Under traditional school schedules, time for both students and teachers is divided into seven or eight periods each day. Block schedules have fewer but longer class periods. They are intended to permit both students and teachers to focus their attention and effort on fewer classes each day and to permit teachers to use more varied methods of instruction.

Compared to traditional schedules, block schedules generally are liked more by both students and teachers; they make it easier for teachers to manage class activities; and they lead to more positive student behaviors, such as fewer disciplinary problems and fewer absences among students. However, the instructional methods used by teachers under block schedules generally do not differ much from methods used by teachers under traditional schedules. For block scheduling to be most effective, schools need to encourage and train their teachers to take full advantage of longer class periods by using more varied and interactive methods of instruction.

Many students in U.S. schools have limited English proficiency (LEP). To facilitate learning for such LEP students, many schools have programs that primarily use the home language of the students at the start of their schooling, as they also learn English.

Research studies have compared the effectiveness of bilingual education programs to several alternatives: (1) "submersion" of LEP students into regular English-speaking classes; (2) teaching English as a second language, as a "pullout" program for LEP students in regular classes; (3) "structured immersion" programs that use English as the main language of instruction, but supplement it with some use of LEP students' home language. The best research evidence shows that, when compared on tests of achievement in English and in math, students in bilingual programs generally do less well than those "submerged" in regular classes, less well than those taking English as a second language, and most clearly less well than those in structured immersion programs. "Early- exit" bilingual programs, in which students move relatively quickly to regular classes, appear to be more effective for learning than "late-exit" bilingual programs.

Overall, if a school's goals are to help students learn English well and use English to learn other academic subjects, then programs that give students some home-language help at the start of school but move them fairly quickly to all-English instruction appear to be most effective.

For schools to be most effective, they need to enlist the cooperation of parents. Parents have a marked influence on their children's attitudes and achievement in school. When parents are interested in their children's school activities, encourage their learning, and participate themselves in school activities, students generally do better in school.

Some schools have increased parental involvement by establishing more personal contacts between the parents and school personnel; by establishing effective channels to keep parents well-informed; by providing opportunities for parents to assist in school activities; and sometimes by having parent representatives help plan school programs and policies. Several programs that have increased parental involvement by such means have had positive effects on student achievement.

In order for a school to maintain or improve the effectiveness of its academic program, it must have a good system for assessing outcomes for students. Measures of student achievement should be tailored to prior instructional objectives, so that high test scores do not become an end in themselves. Measures of student achievement, both for individuals and for the school, should be used in combination with other information that makes the assessments a tool for improvement. School staff and students can be motivated to improve school effectiveness by linking personal rewards to measures of school outcomes.

An overview of the topics discussed in this chapter shows that the various aspects of a school's academic program impact student outcomes in several ways: by influencing the activities and instructional methods in classes, by affecting the norms and motivation of teachers, and by affecting the motivation and norms of students.

NOTES

1. S. Purkey and M. Smith, Effective Schools: A Review. E*lementary School Journal, 83*, 1983, 445.
2. S. Rosenholtz, Effective Schools: Interpreting the Evidence. *American Journal of Education, 93*, 1985, 352–388.
3. Rosenholtz, Ibid.; Purkey and Smith, Effective Schools.
4. R. Venezky and L. Winfield, *Schools That Succeed Beyond Expectations in Reading.* Studies on Education Technical Report, No. 1. Newark, DE: University of Delaware, 1979.
5. Rosenholtz, Effective Schools, p. 360.
6. See, for example, D. Spuck, Reward Structures in the Public High School. *Educational Administration Quarterly, 10,* 1974, 18–34.
7. K. Tewel, *New Schools for a New Century.* Delray Beach, FL: St. Lucie Press, 1995, p. 207.
8. Purkey and Smith, Effective Schools, p. 441.
9. Purkey and Smith, Ibid.; K. Louis, J. Toole, and A. Hargreave, Rethinking School Improvement. In J. Murphy and K. Louis, eds., *Handbook of Research on Educational Administration*, 2nd edition. San Francisco: Jossey-Bass, 1999, pp. 251–276.
10. Purkey and Smith, Effective Schools.
11. F. Newman, G. Wehlage, and S. Lamborn, The Significance and Sources of Student Engagement. In F. Newmann, ed., *Student Engagement and Achievement in American Secondary Schools.* New York: Teachers College Press, 1992, Chapter 1.
12. Newman et al., Ibid., p. 2.
13. T. Good and J. Brophy, School Effects. In M. Wittrock, ed., *Handbook of Research on Teaching,* 3rd edition. New York: Macmillan, 1986, pp. 502–602; Purkey and Smith, Effective Schools.
14. Purkey and Smith, Ibid., p. 445.
15. J. Coleman, T. Hoffer, and S. Kilgore, *High School Achievement: Public, Catholic, and Private Schools Compared.* New York: Basic Books, 1982.
16. S. Rosenholtz and C. Simpson, Workplace Conditions and the Rise and Fall of Teachers' Commitment. *Sociology of Education, 63,* 1990, 241–257.
17. V. Lee, R. Dedrick, and J. Smith, The Effect of the Social Organization of Schools on Teachers' Efficacy and Satisfaction. *Sociology of Education, 64,* 1991, 190–208.
18. Rosenholtz, Effective Schools, p. 372.
19. W. Brookover, C. Beady, P. Flood, J. Schweitzer, and J. Wisenbaker, *School Social Systems and Student Achievement.* New York: Praeger, 1979, p. 243.
20. See P. Short, R. Short, and C. Blanton, *Rethinking Student Discipline.* Thousand Oaks, CA: Corwin Press, 1994.
21. Rosenholtz, Effective Schools.
22. A. Powell, E. Farrar, and D. Cohen, *The Shopping Mall High School.* Boston: Houghton Mifflin, 1985.
23. Powell, et al., Ibid., p. 68.
24. Powell, et al., Ibid., p. 107
25. Purkey and Smith, Effective Schools, p. 444.

26. R. Heck and G. Marcoulides, Principal Leadership Behaviors and School Achievement. *NASSP Bulletin, 77,* 1993, 20-28; Newmann, *Student Engagement.*

27. B. Bank, Peer Cultures and Their Challenge for Teaching. In B. Biddle, et al., eds., *International Handbook of Teachers and Teaching.* Boston: Kluwer Academic, 1997, p. 903.

28. S. Lamborn, B. Brown, N. Mounts, and L. Steinberg, Putting School in Perspective. In Newmann, *Student Engagement,* pp. 153–181.

29. R. Goddard, S. Sweetland, and W. Hoy, Academic Emphasis of Urban Elementary Schools and Student Achievement in Reading and Mathematics. *Educational Administration Quarterly, 36,* 2000, 683–702.

30. Bank, Peer Cultures, p. 918.

31. Bank, Ibid.; Coleman, *The Adolescent Society.* Glencoe, IL: Free Press, 1961.

32. Bank, Ibid.; Coleman, Ibid.

33. A. Tannenbaum, Adolescents' Attitudes Toward Academic Brilliance. Ph.D. Dissertation, New York University, 1960.

34. Coleman, *Adolescent Society,* Chapter 10.

35. Bank, Peer Cultures, p. 904.

36. Bank, Ibid.

37. T. Eitle and D. Eitle, Race, Cultural Capital, and the Educational Effects of Participation in Sports. S*ociology of Education, 75,* 2002, 123–146; B. Broh, Linking Extracurricular Programming to Academic Achievement. *Sociology of Education, 75,* 2002, 69–95.

38. P. Cusick, *Inside High School: The Student's World.* New York: Holt, Rinehart and Winston, 1973, p. 30; italics in original.

39. Coleman, *Adolescent Society,* Chapter 10.

40. Coleman, Ibid., p. 310; italics in original.

41. Bank, Peer Cultures.

42. Coleman, *Adolescent Society.*

43. Coleman, Ibid., p. 350; Italics in original.

44. J. Queen, Block Scheduling Revisited. *Phi Delta Kappan, 82,* 2000, 214–222.

45. See D. Hottenstein, *Intensive Scheduling: Restructuring America's Secondary Schools Through Time Management.* Thousand Oaks, CA: Corwin Press, 1998.

46. Queen, Block Scheduling Revisited.

47. Hottenstein, *Intensive Scheduling.*

48. Hottenstein, Ibid.; J. Queen and K. Isenhour, *The 4 x 4 Block Schedule.* Princeton, NJ: Eye on Education, Inc., 1998; E. Seifer and J. Beck, Relationships Between Task Time and Learning Gains in Secondary Schools. *Journal of Educational Research, 7,* 1994, 5–10; R. Canady and M Rettig, *Block Scheduling: A Catalyst for Change in High Schools.* Princeton, NJ: Eye on Education, Inc., 1995; S. Skrobarcek, Collaboration for Instructional Improvement: Analyzing the Academic Impact of a Block Scheduling Plan. *NASSP Bulletin, 81,* 1997, 104–111.

49. Queen, Block Scheduling Revisited; Hottenstein, *Intensive Scheduling.*

50. Hottenstein, Ibid., p. 39.

51. Hottenstein, Ibid., p. 46.

52. W. Hart, A Comparison of the Use of Instructional Time in Block Schedules High School Classrooms. Ph.D. Dissertation, University of North Carolina, Charlotte, 2000; E. Jenkins, A Comparative Study of Teaching Strategies

Reported by North Carolina High School Teachers in Block and Traditional Schedule Schools. Ph.D. Dissertation, University of North Carolina, 2000.

53. Queen, Block Scheduling Revisited, p. 218.

54. Hottenstein, *Intensive Scheduling.*

55. M. Brisk, *Bilingual Education.* Mahwah, NJ: Lawrence Erlbaum, 1998, Chapter 1.

56. Council of Chief State School Officers. School Success for Limited English Proficient Students. Washington, DC: Author, 1990.

57. Brisk, *Bilingual Education*, Chapter 1; R. Rothstein, Bilingual Education: The Controversy. *Phi Delta Kappan, 79*, 1998, 672-678.

58. U.S. Commission on Civil Rights, Report II. *The Unfinished Education: Outcomes for Minorities in the Five Southwestern States.* Washington, DC: Government Printing Office, 1971.

59. American Legislative Exchange Council, *The Cost of Bilingual Education in the United States, 1991–1992.* Washington, DC: Author, 1994.

60. See J. Cummins, Educational Implications of Mother Tongue Maintenance in Minority Language Groups. *Canadian Modern Language Review, 34,* 1978, 395–416.

61. See Brisk, *Bilingual Education*, Chapter 1.

62. See C. Rossell and K. Baker, The Educational Effectiveness of Bilingual Education. *Research in the Teaching of English, 30,* 1996, 7–74; R. Gersten, The Changing Face of Bilingual Education. *Educational Leadership, 56,* 1999, 41–45.

63. L. Chavez and J. Amselle, Bilingual Education Theory and Practice: Its Effectiveness and Parental Opinions. *NAASP Bulletin, 18,* 1997, 101–106.

64. Rossell and Baker, Educational Effectiveness of Bilingual Education, p. 26.

65. See Brisk, *Bilingual Education*, Chapter 1, for a description of various bilingual and other programs for students with limited English proficiency.

66. See Rossell and Baker, Educational Effectiveness of Bilingual Programs; K. Baker, Structured English Immersion. *Phi Delta Kappan, 79,* 1998, 199–204.

67. Rossell and Baker, Ibid.

68. K. Baker, et al., Misled by Bad Theory. *Bilingual Research Journal, 16,* 192, 63–90.

69. Rossell and Baker, Educational Effectiveness of Bilingual Education, p. 40.

70. See Brisk, *Bilingual Education*, Chapter 2.

71. See Brisk, Ibid., Chapters 3-5.

72. Baker, Structured English Immersion.

73. See, for example, M. Phillips, et al., Family Background, Parenting Practices, and the Black-White Test Score Gap. In C. Jencks and M. Phillips, eds., *The Black-White Test Score Gap.* Washington, DC: Brookings Institution Press, 1998, pp. 103–145.

74. See L. Okagaki and P. Frensch, Parenting and Children's School Achievement: A Multiethnic Perspective. *American Educational Research Journal, 35,* 1998, 123–144.

75. Okagaki and Frensch, Ibid.

76. See K. Bierman, Family-School Links: An Overview. In A. Booth and J. Dunn, eds., *Family-School Links: How Do they Affect Educational Outcomes?* Mahwah, NJ: Lawrence Erlbaum, 1996, pp. 275-287.

77. S. Dornbusch and K. Glasgow, The Structural Context of Family-School Relations. In Booth and Dunn, *Family-School Links*, pp. 35–44.

78. J. Epstein, School and Family Connections. In D. Unger and M. Sussman, eds., *Families in Community Settings: Interdisciplinary Perspectives*. New York: Haworth Press, 1990, pp. 99–126.

79. Okagaki and Frensch, Parenting and Children's School Achievement; Bierman, Family-School Links; D. Stevenson and D. Baker, The Family-School Relation and the Child's School Performance. *Child Development, 58*, 1987, 1348–1357.

80. J. Comer and N. Haynes, Parent Involvement in Schools: An Ecological Approach. *Elementary School Journal, 91*, 1991, 276.

81. See K. Hoover-Dempsey and H. Sandler, Why Do Parents Become Involved in Their Children's Education? *Review of Educational Research, 67*, 1997, 3–42.

82. J. Epstein, Perspectives and Previews on Research and Policy for School, Family, and Community Partnerships. In Booth and Dunn, *Family-School Links*, p. 217.

83. J. Eccles and R. Harold, Parent-School Involvement During the Early Adolescent Years. *Teachers College Record, 94*, 1993, 568–587.

84. Eccles and Harold, Ibid., p. 577.

85. R. Burns, *Parents and Schools: From Visitors to Partners*. Washington, DC: NEA Professional Library, 1993.

86. Eccles and Harold, Parent-School Involvement, p. 577.

87. Burns, *Parents and Schools*, p. 18; Comer and Haynes, Parental Involvement in Schools.

88. C. Payne, The Comer Intervention Model and School Reform in Chicago. *Urban Education, 26*, 1991, 8–24.

89. G. Lloyd, Research and Practical Application for School, Family, and Community Partnerships. In Booth and Dunn, *Family-School Links*.

90. Lloyd, Ibid.

91. Rosenholtz, Effective Schools, p. 370.

92. Rosenholtz, Ibid.; Good and Brophy, School Effects; Purkey and Smith, Effective Schools.

93. S. Plank, H. Wang, and B. Schneider, Reconsidering Roles and Incentives in Schools. In J. Coleman, B. Schneider, S. Plank, K. Schiller, R. Shouse, and H. Wang, *Redesigning American Education*. Boulder, CO: Westview, 1997, pp. 87–118.

94. See J. Adams and M. Kirst, New Demands and Concepts for Educational Accountability. In Murphy and Louis, *Handbook of Research on Educational Administration*, pp. 463–489.

95. T. Hoffer, Accountability in Education. In M. Hallinan, *Handbook of the Sociology of Education*. New York: Kluwer Academic, 2000, pp. 529–543.

96. Adams and Kirst, New Demands and Concepts.

97. Office of Educational Research and Improvement, *Creating Responsible and Responsive Accountability Systems*. Washington, DC: U.S. Department of Education, 1988.

98. J. Coleman, Output-Driven Schools: Principles of Design. In Coleman, et al., *Redesigning American Education*, pp. 13–38.

Chapter 5

TEACHERS AND ADMINISTRATORS: DECISION MAKING AND COMMUNITY

We have examined (in Chapter 3) the ways in which outcomes for students are shaped by activities in the classroom and by interactions between teachers and students. We have looked also (in Chapters 2 and 4) at how activities in the classrooms are affected by the academic organization of the school (its curriculum, time schedules, learning goals, etc.). Now we trace the chain of events in schools back a step further. Who makes decisions about the academic organization of the school? And how are the motivations and the skills that teachers bring to the classroom affected by the kinds of relationships they have with their colleagues and with school administrators?

This chapter begins with a discussion of alternative ways of running schools: centralization versus decentralization (community control and site-based management). The impact of these alternative arrangements on schools, and especially on teachers, is examined.

Next I consider alternative ways, such as merit pay and career ladders, that have been used to try to improve the quality of teaching. Have these plans raised the motivation, the skills, and the effectiveness of teachers? This discussion is followed by consideration of the types of relationships that exist among teachers and other staff members in a school. My focus is on organizational arrangements that lead to feelings of "community" among teachers (and other staff members) and the consequences that such staff communities have for school effectiveness.

Finally, the role that teacher unions play in schools is discussed. The chapter closes with an overview of school organization, a summary, and some conclusions.

AUTHORITY AND DECISION MAKING

The presence of a great many different units and of people doing many different types of jobs throughout a school district creates some problems that are common in organizations.[1] Schools, like other organizations, need to coordinate the work of different units and specialists so that their efforts are consistent and mutually supportive. This means, for example, having curricula in different grades and different courses that are cumulative and mutually reinforcing, rather than overlapping or unrelated. It means having school personnel apply similar standards of conduct for students; use textbooks and other materials in one grade or course that are consistent with those used in the next grade or course; and use methods and standards for evaluating students that are reasonably consistent.

Schools, like other organizations, also need effective communication among their members. Members need information in order to do their own jobs most effectively. For example, a classroom teacher needs to get timely information about her students (their past performance, their performance in other classes, and their performance in school activities); about any change in schooltime schedules; about professional training opportunities; and about many other topics. Full and timely communication also is necessary for each person and unit in order to coordinate their actions with those of others in the school. For example, the more a teacher knows about what other teachers are doing (the content they are covering, the teaching methods they are using, etc.), the more she will be able to coordinate her own efforts with theirs.

For teachers and staff specialists to do their jobs well, and to coordinate their work effectively with that of others, they must be not only well informed, but also well motivated. Thus, schools need to be organized in a way that maximizes the motivation of their staff.

To deal with the organizational problems they face, schools, like other organizations, may use one of two main alternative strategies. The first is to centralize the decision-making process. The second is to decentralize this process. Let us consider the use of these alternative decision-making processes in schools and their consequences.

CENTRALIZATION OF AUTHORITY

One approach to running an organization, especially a large one, is to follow the bureaucratic model. Theorists of bureaucracy have seen it as a rational system whose features include among others: (1) specialization of jobs, with each person having a limited set of tasks; (2) clear lines of hierarchical authority, whereby orders are passed down a "chain of command"; and (3) decision making based on rules, in order to guarantee consistency of action.[2]

Schools generally are bureaucratic in some aspects of their organization. Decisions about curriculum, testing, texts, and other matters often are made by school boards or district administrators and passed down to principals, department heads, and teachers. School personnel often are subject to standard rules concerning disciplinary procedures, promotion policies, testing, time schedules, salary schedules, and other matters. Staff members are specialized with respect to the subject matter or the grade level they teach or their specific areas of expertise (special education, guidance, media, etc.); the work of each type of personnel may be done in relative isolation from the work of others.[3]

However, decisions are not always, or even usually, made at the highest level of formal authority. A nationally representative survey of schoolteachers and administrators in secondary schools[4] found that principals generally reported having a great deal of influence (and more influence than school boards or teachers) over hiring new teachers, setting school discipline policy, and establishing school curricula. Teachers generally reported having little control over school-level decisions, such as those concerning grouping students by ability, faculty in-service programs, school discipline policy, and the school curriculum. In most schools, however, teachers reported having a great deal of influence about some classroom decisions, particularly regarding teaching techniques and amounts of homework.

Pluses and Minuses of Bureaucracy

Bureaucratic organization in schools, with centralization of authority, can have definite advantages. Research on effective schools—especially in schools that are unusually successful with low-income students—finds that the curriculum and the instructional program in such schools are tightly linked. School goals, grade level and classroom instructional objectives, instructional content and activities, and measures of pupil performance are all aligned; students are exposed to a well-ordered and focused curriculum; and the instructional efforts of teachers and other instructional staff are consistent and cumulative.[5] Reviewing these findings, Michael Cohen asserts: ". . . this description of articulation among goals, curricular content, and performance measures suggests an image of schools that conforms fairly closely to classical models of bureaucratic organization: goal-oriented organizations with technical and management structures in which decisions regarding work activities, resource allocations, and adjustments of organizational performance are made on the basis of clear and agreed-upon goals and feedback regarding goal attainment."[6]

In reviewing the literature relevant to decision making in schools, Daniel Brown notes that when classical (i.e., bureaucratic) management theory is disregarded, there may be confusion over authority in school districts. He says: "It is not always obvious who reports to whom, who is enabled to do what, and whose clearance is needed to accomplish whatever. It also appears that staff and line roles are mixed, that authority does not coincide with responsibility. . . ."[7]

While centralized control does sometimes help schools to operate in a coordinated way, the bureaucratic model of organization often has serious drawbacks. Where there are rules handed down from above about most aspects of school operations, teachers tend to feel powerless and often become apathetic. Valerie Lee and her colleagues note: ". . . in a highly bureaucratized school environment, expressions of 'Just tell me what you want me to do' are a reasonable response . . . such behaviors on the part of teachers are counter-productive to advancing good teaching and good schooling."[8] Furthermore, when rules must always be followed, the behavior of administrators, teachers, and others becomes inflexible and they are not able to adapt to different or changing circumstances.

In bureaucratic organizations, communication generally flows one way, from top to bottom. Robert Rothstein states: "Several studies indicate that communication patterns in schools are often one-sided. In a steady flow of messages from above, memos, reports, orders, instructions, and data are placed in teachers' mailboxes, while very little information flows the other way. Such communication is often stifled by the submissiveness of teachers behaving as bureaucrats, thus depriving administrators of information they need to do their work effectively."[9]

Centralized systems also often result in long, frustrating difficulties and delays for principals and teachers in getting resources they need. For example, school principals in one Canadian province expressed great dissatisfaction about their inability to get supplies, textbooks, custodial services, and needed maintenance.[10]

The very serious problems that can develop in bureaucratic school organizations, especially in large cities, are detailed in a description of the New York City school system administration as it was in the 1960s. David Rogers writes: "The New York City school system is typical of what social scientists call a 'sick bureaucracy'—a term for organizations whose traditions, structure, and operations subvert their stated missions and prevent any flexible accommodation to changing client demands."[11]

DECENTRALIZATION OF AUTHORITY

Experience with the serious problems often found in bureaucracies has led many organizations to distribute decision-making authority more widely. For example, some business firms have established small self-managing production units, each of which makes decisions about its budget, its personnel, and other resources.[12]

Many observers of schools have advocated moving authority from large districts to districts covering only a few schools or down to each individual school. Two types of decentralized governance that have been tried in schools are: (1) community control and (2) site-based management.[13]

Community Control

In some large cities, a perceived lack of responsiveness by the central school bureaucracy to problems of low-achieving minority students led to demands that local communities be given control of the schools. Some scholars and activists argued that if the local community were "empowered" to control the schools, it would see to it that the schools did a more effective job of educating their children. With the support of parents, community activists, officials and legislators, foundations, and business leaders, "community control" of the school system has been tried in a number of cities—most notably in New York City, Detroit, and Chicago.[14]

The state of New York in 1969 passed a law that put control of New York City's elementary and junior high schools in the hands of 31 local school boards, elected by people in each local community. At about the same time, Detroit adopted a school decentralization plan that divided the city into eight regions, in each of which schools were to be run by an elected board of community residents. In Chicago in 1988, control of each individual school was transferred primarily to parents and community members.

Community control of schools has met with a number of serious problems. A study of local school councils in Chicago found that parents often lacked both the time and the skills to deal effectively with problems of school reform. School council meetings often did not focus on central issues of curriculum and instruction. In New York City and Detroit, local school boards were accused (sometimes with supporting evidence) of being centers of patronage and sometimes corruption. In both New York City and Detroit, efforts by community boards to hire, fire, and transfer teachers and administrators—sometimes on the basis of their race—led to confrontations with teacher unions that shut down the schools for extended periods. In New York, teacher unions came to dominate some local boards.[15]

Evidence concerning the impact of community control on student learning is mixed. Some researchers found improvements in reading and math scores in New York City in the decade following school decentralization,[16] but others concluded that decentralization did not improve the schools either in New York or in Detroit.[17] In Chicago, reading and math scores rose after the start of community control. However, in 118 of Chicago's 460 elementary schools, there were fewer students at or above national norms in reading in 1996 than at the start of community control in 1988.[18] In Chicago high schools, student test scores showed very little improvement during this period.[19]

After reviewing the evidence on the "empowerment" of parents through community control of schools, Dan Lewis and Kathryn Nakagawa state: "We question when and how this most radical of decentralization policies will ignite into fundamental change.[20]

Moving Away from Community Control

Community control of schools was short-lived in Detroit. After a decade, almost every major interest group in that city declared that decentralization had failed to improve the quality of education. Detroit residents voted by a four-to-one margin to recentralize the school system.[21] In New York City, continued dissatisfaction with the education provided by city schools led the state legislature in 2002, at the request of New York City's mayor, to abolish the 32 local community boards that governed the schools; authority was recentralized in one school board dominated by appointees of the mayor. Other cities as well—including Philadelphia, Boston, and Cleveland—recently have moved to greater centralization of authority over the schools, with city mayors often exercising ultimate control.

Writing of a general trend toward recentralizing school governance in the mid to late 1990s, Larry Cuban and Michael Usdan observe: "Centralizing authority on school matters into the hands of district superintendents and aligning the different elements of school operations became a familiar recipe for improving district management and students' academic performance."[22] At the same time, a belief that effective top management is the key to school improvement led some big cities to hire business executives and retired generals as their school superintendents.

However, recentralization of decision making and strong top managers appear to be no panaceas for school effectiveness. Reviewing evidence on the impact of recent changes in school governance on student test scores and on the gap between white students' scores and minority students' scores in six cities, Cuban and Usdan state: "Except for slight to moderate improvements in elementary students' test scores across the cities, little improvement emerges for secondary school students and the gap in achievement scores remains largely as it was prior to initiatives taken by the urban school leaders since the mid-1990s."[23]

The main reason that "top-down" reform efforts show scant evidence of success to date, Cuban and Usdan conclude, is that administrators have not enlisted the active cooperation of teachers and parents and thus have not succeeded in changing classroom practice in the ways intended. They observe: "Based on the history of classroom innovations, without parent endorsement and active teacher cooperation in putting the changes into practice, urban school reformers again will be disappointed."[24]

For over 100 years, American public schools have tended to move from a largely decentralized system, to a centralized system, back to decentralization, and then back to centralization. Each has advantages and disadvantages, as discussed previously. Neither system, in its purest form, appears to be capable of producing effective schools consistently.

This history, and the mixed experiences both with centralization and with decentralization, have led some observers to propose a system of school governance that: (1) engages the knowledge, ideas, and enthusiasm of those (teachers, principals, and parents) most directly involved with students; and also (2) provides needed coordination among individual schools and enough oversight and assistance to these schools so that they are effectively performing their jobs. In other words, some combination of local decision making, as occurs with community control (or with site-based management), and centralized oversight may be most effective.

Such a system of school governance that combines considerable local community control with accountability of local groups to a central school authority has been tried in Chicago and in New York City (prior to New York's ending community control). Writing about such efforts, G. Alfred Hess, Jr. comments ". . . local control of schools has been balanced with centralized authority to monitor the performance of individual schools and to intervene when performance standards are not being met."[25]

We do not have much evidence about how successful this "balanced" approach to school governance can be in helping schools to provide effective learning to their students. But since neither top-down control alone nor bottom-up control alone appears to be effective, a more balanced approach, which combines the advantages of each approach while reducing the disadvantages of each, seems to hold some promise.

Site-Based Management

While efforts to establish community control have focused on giving greater power to local communities (especially parents), programs of site-based management (SBM) focus on giving greater authority to those (especially school staff) who are most directly responsible for running each individual school. SBM takes a variety of forms.[26] Typically, a good deal of authority is exercised by a council that consists of various stakeholders in the school. Which specific groups are included on the council, and the size of their representation, varies among SBM programs. Councils almost always include a number of teachers and one or more administrators. Often representatives of parents and/or the community are included; sometimes student representatives also are present. School personnel (teachers, administrators, and others) usually constitute a clear majority of council members.

The scope of authority exercised by school councils also varies. For example, a given council may or may not control the school budget or the hiring of new teachers. Usually subcommittees are formed to deal with those areas—such as instructional materials, staffing, budget, curriculum, planning, student services, and professional development—over which the school council has full or partial control. Each subcommittee then reports back to the full council.

School-based management does not mean that all decisions are made at the local school level. Some decisions, such as those concerning overall budget allocations and general curriculum guidelines, may be made by central school boards and administrators. Legal requirements regarding health, safety, racial discrimination, and other matters constrain the actions of local schools. And some matters, such as salary scales, are established by agreements between unions and a district-wide board. Still, site-based management often gives the local school much wider autonomy than is enjoyed by schools in a more centralized system.

One example of a program to decentralize much of decision making to the local school is the SBM program begun by the Memphis, Tennessee, school system in 1989.[27] In each of seven schools included in the program, a local school council was formed to set school policy. This council was composed of seven or eight members, including the principal, three teachers at the school, two parents of students currently in the school, one community member living within the school attendance zone, and one student representative. All members, except the principal, were elected by the groups they represented.

The local school councils had some responsibility for decisions on a variety of matters—such as instructional programs, hiring of personnel, and budget—although the extent to which each school's council was able to exercise authority in particular areas varied. The teacher union in Memphis supported the SBM program, modifying its prior contractual agreements to facilitate changed teacher roles.

Outcomes of Site-Based Management

There is some evidence that teachers and others involved in schools react positively to having a greater role in the management of their schools.[28] Teachers, especially those who participate actively in school decision making, establish more collegial relationships with other teachers than is generally true in non-SBM schools. Participation in governance activities at SBM schools also increases teachers' sense that they can promote positive changes in their schools. In addition, satisfaction among teachers generally increases when meaningful SBM is implemented in schools, especially in its early stages. There is some evidence of higher satisfaction among parents and students in SBM schools as well.[29]

On the key question of how SBM affects students' outcomes, there is less evidence to support a positive link. In a few school districts (e.g, one in California), introduction of SBM was followed by rises in student test scores. In Dade County, Florida, student attendance improved and student dropouts were fewer following introduction of SBM.[30] However, a number of studies—including ones in Louisiana, Kentucky, Chicago, and Dade County, Florida—have found that greater self-governance for schools did not improve learning outcomes for students. A number of reviewers of the literature on SBM agree that, overall, the evidence of links between SBM and improved student performance is not encouraging.[31] For example, Priscilla

Wohlstetter and Susan Mohrman write: "While school-based management continues to be a priority in state and district reform efforts across the country, there is scant evidence linking SBM to improved school performance."[32]

The frequent failure of SBM to improve student learning appears to be a result of a common failure of decentralized decision making to improve classroom practice in significant ways. There are some schools in which giving teachers and other "stakeholders" more involvement in running the school has led to important changes in instructional methods, curriculum, assessment systems, and other practices that directly affect student learning in the classroom. But in most cases SBM has not resulted in substantial changes in classroom practice.[33] Thus, one review of research states: "There are few, if any, indications that early movement toward SBM has been associated with substantial change in instructional delivery."[34]

A large-scale study by Priscilla Wohlstetter and Susan Mohrman, funded by the U.S. Department of Education, investigated the circumstances under which SBM in schools does lead to active restructuring of curriculum and instructional methods.[35] The study was conducted in 44 schools (both elementary and high schools) located in 13 school districts in the United States, Canada, and Australia. All of these schools had been using SBM for a number of years. Some of the schools had made substantial changes intended to improve classroom practice. Other schools had done much less to try to improve curriculum and instruction. In each school, the investigators interviewed administrators, teachers, parents, and students in order to learn what distinguished SBM schools that had restructured their classroom practices (which they called "successful" schools) from those SBM schools that had not done so.

The investigators found that the "successful" SBM schools were different from the less successful ones in several ways:

1. The way in which the decision-making bodies were organized and run was important. In schools where SBM led to transformed instruction, a broad range of people within (and outside) the school were involved in multiple teacher-led teams, each of which focused on specific tasks having to do with such matters as curriculum, school material selection, assessment, and professional development. A school council served to coordinate the activities of various decision groups. Such broad involvement reduced the workload on particular individuals and broadened the commitment to reform.

2. Principals in successful SBM schools were supportive of innovation but delegated responsibilities to committees, thus sharing leadership.

3. Information about what was happening in the school, and about innovations at other schools, was widely shared among those inside the school and with parents and the community.

4. Those working to achieve school objectives often were rewarded, sometimes financially for their extra time or extra responsibilities, but more often with recognition and signs of appreciation.

In all of these ways, schools in which SBM resulted in transformed instruction had created a decision-making process that drew on the energies and ideas of a wide range of people and actually changed the ways in which school decisions were made. In those SBM schools where little change in classroom practice occurred, SBM was usually a less vital process, involving just a small number of people, with little participation or interaction among teachers. As Wohlstetter and Mohrman note, effective SBM is a time-consuming and complicated process. Thus, it cannot be done successfully as a low-effort "add-on" to usual school activities.

In addition to the ways in which they organized their SBM, there are two other important ways in which effective SBM schools differed from less effective SBM schools: (1) attention to improvements in classroom practices, and (2) attention to the professional development of teachers. In less successful SBM schools, decision-making councils often gave most of their attention to issues other than how to improve learning in the classroom—including issues of power, such as who can attend meetings and who can vote. Other research has found that meetings in SBM schools often focused on the working conditions of school personnel—for example, parking spaces and hall and playground duties. Successful SBM schools focused on improving student learning, often using district, state, or national guidelines for standards, curriculum, and assessment systems as frameworks within which they developed their own plans for improvement.

Successful SBM schools also gave high priority to the professional development of their staff. Often the council or other decision-making group assessed the development needs of staff and planned regular training activities tied to the school's reform objectives.

The central importance of improvements in teacher's knowledge and skill in making reform efforts successful has been emphasized in recent studies by Richard Elmore, Penelope Peterson, and Sarah McCarthey.[36] These studies found that changes in school structure (including increasing the role of teachers in decision making) do not necessarily result in changes in teachers' instructional methods in the classroom. They state: "Changing practice is primarily a problem of learning, not a problem of organization."[37] However, they point out that changes in school structure can provide new opportunities for teachers to learn new practices. Thus, school-based management can, if carried out effectively, create a school climate of information flow, collegial interaction, and learning activities that enhances the knowledge and skills of teachers.

LEADERSHIP BY THE PRINCIPAL

The successful management of a school is, of course, influenced by the leadership provided by its principal. Strong leadership by the school's principal has been found to contribute to better learning by students, in part by the principal's selecting effective teachers.[38] The principal's leadership also is a key to successful efforts to improve a school.[39]

The principal can contribute to the school's effectiveness in a number of ways. He can help to establish a general vision, and more concrete learning goals, for the school and its students; help secure resources for the school and its staff; monitor classroom activities; help teachers to develop their skills; and "buffer" teachers from distractions and stresses in the classroom (e.g., by establishing clear disciplinary rules for students.)[40]

Most significantly, the principal's actions are likely to have important effects on the patterns of decision making and on collegiality among teachers. Principals may involve teachers in a variety of planning and problem-solving activities regarding learning goals, curriculum, student evaluation, scheduling, professional development, and a host of other issues affecting teachers and students. They can arrange time and opportunities for teachers to meet and to work with each other in such cooperative activities. Cooperative work by teachers is likely to promote a spirit of collegiality among teachers, which, in turn, promotes better teaching (see section "Relationships Among Teachers" later in this chapter). Susan Rosenholtz has noted: "Norms of collegiality do not simply happen. . . . Rather, they are carefully engineered by structuring the workplace with frequent exposure to contact and frequent opportunities for interaction. . . . Such social engineering in schools is the most likely product of direct principal intervention."[41]

The importance of leadership by the principal does not mean that the most effective principal is one who tells everyone what they should do and how to do it. The effective leader encourages, stimulates, and sometimes inspires others to work together effectively. Karen Louis and her colleagues state: "A key leadership skill now is how to unleash intelligence, creativity, insight, and self-initiated activity throughout the organization."[42]

The most effective leadership style varies with different school situations.[43] However, in general, the most effective principal will not be one who emphasizes her own authority and the exercise of control. Rather, the most effective leader generally is one who acts as a catalyst, a person who facilitates and helps to coordinate the work of many people toward common goals. Moreover, while the principal can and should exercise significant leadership, leadership can be shared by many people in the school; that is, teachers and others in the school also can propose, initiate, and help to coordinate cooperative activities toward common goals.[44]

PAY AND OTHER TEACHER INCENTIVES

Another important aspect of a school's organization is the way in which it pays teachers and structures their roles. Like people in any occupation, teachers put greater effort into their work when they have strong incentives. Teachers consistently rate the intrinsic rewards they get from their work— for example, "knowing that I have reached students and they have learned" — as stronger motivators than extrinsic rewards such as money. Pride in their craft and satisfying relationships with other school staff also are strong motivators for teachers, contributing, for example, to their remaining in their jobs.[45]

Although the intrinsic rewards of their work are important to most teachers, teachers are, of course, also concerned about their salaries. Since the 1940s, salaries for teachers in American public schools usually have been determined by each teacher's level of academic preparation and her years of experience. This system was supported by most teachers because they saw it as removing favoritism in setting of salaries.

However, as concern about the quality of education grew in the 1980s and later, some people have proposed that teachers be given greater financial and career incentives to do a good job of educating their students. They have urged that salaries and other rewards for teachers should be linked more closely to evidence of student learning.[46] Many states have, in fact, implemented programs intended to reward good teachers.[47]

The major ideas that have been proposed, and often implemented, include: (1) merit pay; (2) pay based on knowledge and skills; (3) creating "career ladders" for teachers; and (4) providing financial incentives for teachers based on the performance of their school.

MERIT PAY

A "merit pay" plan bases teachers' salaries in part on some criterion (such as their students' scores on achievement tests) intended to assess the teachers' effectiveness; alternatively, some teachers may receive a monetary bonus based on some indicator of their teaching effectiveness.

Merit pay plans, where adopted, generally have not appeared to provide genuine incentives for most teachers. Teachers have widely seen such merit systems as unfair, as based on flawed measures of teaching effectiveness, and as open to favoritism. Many teachers see a linking of pay to results on standardized tests as pushing them to abandon well-rounded instruction in order to "teach to the test." Moreover, many teachers dislike the competitiveness that merit pay plans may introduce and see the collegiality they value being undermined. There is little evidence that merit pay plans have improved teaching or learning. Moreover, most of the merit pay programs begun have not lasted long.[48]

In one relevant study, teachers were interviewed in a New Hampshire school district that had adopted a "Performance-Based Salary Program." That program, provided "recognition for excellence" by rewards of money, as well as by other means. Most teachers saw the performance-based salary program as having led to a reduction in trust between teachers and the school administration. Teachers also tended to see a lower level of cooperation among teachers as a consequence of the program. Overwhelmingly, they believed that the performance-based salary program had hurt teacher morale. The main concern of the teachers was with the system of evaluating teachers—that is, with the competence and fairness of evaluations and the bases on which evaluations were made. Some teachers were demoralized when, after striving to do their best all year, they were rated as average or below average in an evaluation process that they saw as questionable.[49]

PAYING FOR KNOWLEDGE AND SKILLS

In recent years, the idea of linking teacher compensation to the knowledge and skills of teachers has gained some prominence.[50] Many states and districts are encouraging teachers to upgrade their knowledge and skills so that they can be certified by the National Board for Professional Teaching Standards; many school districts are paying higher salaries to board-certified teachers.

In a parallel development, some districts are implementing pay systems based on the use of recently developed tools, including peer review, to assess teacher competence. An advocate of this approach, Allan Odden, suggests that tying teacher pay to "higher levels of relevant knowledge, skills, and professional expertise" could have "positive benefits for students, teachers, and the education system."[51] Although there is some evidence from other types of organizations that linking pay to competence can improve both morale and organizational performance,[52] there is little relevant evidence on this approach from schools to date.

CAREER LADDERS AND
EXPANDED TEACHER ROLES

Another strategy for providing incentives to teachers—both to improve their skills and performance, and to stay in the profession—is to create opportunities for teachers to rise in professional status and responsibility.[53] The "career ladder" is a strategy used by many states and districts to provide such opportunities. Beginning teachers are at the first rung of the ladder, perhaps as probationary teachers in their first year. They then have the opportunity to move up a number of steps (e.g., five steps in Tennessee) to levels of higher status (perhaps "master teacher") at the top. At each higher level, teachers earn more and may have greater professional responsibility—for example, in assisting new teachers or in curriculum development.

Teachers are evaluated at each step of the ladder to judge whether they qualify for advancement to a higher level. The bases and processes of such evaluations vary considerably across states and across school districts.

A related approach to provide greater incentives for teachers is provided by programs that create mentor teachers. Mentor teachers usually supervise and help train new or struggling teachers and often have other expanded duties, such as aiding in curriculum development. They are paid more for their extra responsibilities. Mentor teachers usually are chosen on the basis of outstanding teaching. Under one plan used in California, mentor teachers have been nominated by committees that include a majority of teachers. Mentor teachers serve for varying periods—sometimes a few years, sometimes longer—in different districts.

Evidence about the success of career ladder or mentor teaching programs is limited. However, experience with such programs in some states indicates that, at least in certain circumstances, they may not have their intended effects on teachers' motivation and performance.

In Texas, most teachers had negative views about a career ladder system instituted in the 1980s. For example, teachers in Austin saw the career ladder program, which was open there to only one-third of the teachers, as fostering competition and division among teachers. Throughout that state, teachers were dubious about the validity and fairness of evaluations that would place a teacher at a given step of the career ladder. Writing about this program, Thomas Timar notes that dissatisfaction by teachers is a "sign of trouble for a program intended to be an incentive to teachers to work harder and stay in teaching."[54]

In Utah, a career ladder program for teachers also met "the active opposition and hostile indifference" of a large number of teachers, which "threatened the success of the program."[55] In assessing the Utah program, Timar asserts that in order for the career ladder program to succeed, it must be implemented so that it is (1) connected to school improvement, and (2) connected to teachers' professional growth and development. He writes:

> The career ladder components serve as a system of rewards and incentives to teachers if teachers perceive them as real opportunities for expanding their job responsibilities, improving the quality of their teaching, and developing and improving curriculum and teaching materials. Teachers will resist participation in incentive pay and career ladder schemes if they perceive themselves as 'jumping through hoops' for a few extra dollars. Under those conditions, teacher reform strategies demoralize, rather than inspire, teachers.[56]

Mentor teacher programs also have been met at times with considerable opposition from teachers. Like negative reactions to career ladders and to merit pay, much of the opposition among teachers has stemmed from skepticism about methods for evaluating teacher performance. Also, in

California, many school districts did not have clear plans about how to use those given the status of mentor as instructional leaders. Timar asserts that, to act as a true incentive, a mentor teacher program—like a career ladder program—must be seen by teachers as an opportunity for challenging work, professional growth, and prestige.

AWARDS FOR SCHOOL PERFORMANCE

Some states and school districts have adopted incentive programs that base rewards on the performance of the whole school. Rewards, including monetary bonuses, sometimes are shared among individual members; sometimes rewards (money for educational uses; plaques or flags; exemption from some state or district rules, etc.) are given to the school as a whole; and sometimes rewards are given both to schools and to individual teachers in those schools.

Schools may compete against each other for awards, usually on the basis of standardized test scores. For example, in South Carolina. schools have been grouped by the socioeconomic status of their students and awards given to the top 25 percent of schools in each group. Alternatively, awards may be given to a school for meeting a fixed level of performance (e.g., having a certain proportion of its students score as proficient on standardized tests).

A number of studies have examined the impact on teachers' motivation of programs that give money to individual teachers based on their school's performance. Allan Odden summarizes the findings as follows: "Briefly, this research has found that school-based performance programs have the potential to work. However, the ones currently in place have weak motivational impact."[57] The impact of the programs sometimes has been limited by the small size of bonuses offered and by teachers' uncertainty that bonuses would actually be awarded if goals were met. Collective incentive systems also must address a number of difficult issues, including what criteria should be measured and rewarded, what comparisons among schools should be used, and at what organizational level incentives should be established.[58]

Despite these difficulties, research conducted in business organizations indicates that collective incentives can have important positive outcomes. Incentive programs that permit employees to share in the financial benefits of better organizational performance have typically led to higher individual motivation and greater unit effectiveness. These kinds of incentive programs are most likely to be successful when employees participate in decision making about their work. Where the benefits of success are shared, people are more likely to cooperate to do the work well.[59] Such results from business firms suggest that it is worthwhile to continue efforts to apply to schools the principle of rewards based on collective success.

EVALUATION OF TEACHERS

Our review of evidence concerning programs that provide higher pay and other incentives for effective teachers has indicated that teachers often have concerns about the way in which they are evaluated. But teachers often are disturbed also by a lack of evaluation and feedback from supervisors about their work. Teachers do not want to feel that no one cares about their efforts. In one study, a teacher commented: "If I were to drop dead, the only way they could find out would be the smell after a few days.[60]

Teachers who say they are evaluated frequently by their principals are more likely to say that the principals are helpful in their acquiring more skills. Moreover, more frequent evaluation of teachers is strongly correlated with teacher satisfaction.[61]

Studies of effective schools indicate that principals or their assistants in these schools make vigorous efforts to monitor what goes on in classrooms. Such monitoring often results in help to teachers to enable them to improve their teaching skills and classroom management. Feedback and help to teachers also make teachers feel more confident in their work. A study of 52 urban elementary schools found that frequent observational feedback from administrators or colleagues, combined with teacher confidence that they could improve student learning, accounted for 30 percent of the variation in student achievement among schools (holding constant the socioeconomic status of students and the experience of teachers in each school).

Overall, the evidence indicates that monitoring of a teacher's classroom activities by others, plus constructive feedback to the teacher, often results in more effective teaching and better learning.[62] Such positive effects are more likely to occur when teachers see such feedback as competent, fair, and contributing to their professional growth.

RELATIONSHIPS AMONG TEACHERS: ISOLATES OR COMMUNITY?

The attitudes of teachers toward their work, and the way they perform in the classroom, are greatly affected by the kinds of relationships that they have with other teachers.

Traditionally, in American schools, each teacher has been alone in her individual classroom throughout most of each school day, having little professional or social interaction with other teachers. In recent years, many observers have argued that this traditional pattern of teachers' isolation, each one in her own classroom, is not the most effective pattern for good teaching and learning. They describe, as a desirable alternative, a school where teachers constitute a "community" of like-minded professionals who work together and who learn from each other.[63]

These conceptions of community among teachers (and, more broadly, among the entire school staff) include several components. First, staff members have frequent interaction with each other—in formal and informal meetings, discussions, and work activities (e.g., in curriculum planning sessions). Second, the interaction is of a friendly and cooperative kind in which staff members consult with, collaborate with, and encourage and support each other in their work. They may, for example, share ideas about teaching strategies or even work cooperatively in team teaching.

Third, staff members share beliefs, values, and goals that are important to their work. For example, they may share the belief that all children in their school are capable of mastering the basic material, they may think it important that all students learn these "basics," and they may share specific learning goals—for example, that at least 85 percent of the students read and compute at grade level in the coming year. The sharing of such beliefs, values, and goals is not mere coincidence but, rather, a result of norms that grow out of frequent and positive interactions.

A fourth component of the concept of "community"—closely related to the others—is that staff members are committed to the school as an entity. Each teacher thinks of himself not only as an English teacher or as a fifth grade teacher, but as a member of (say) Theodore Roosevelt School. Each is concerned not only about his own personal well-being and accomplishments but also about positive outcomes for the school as a whole. And each staff member devotes energy to helping to reach school goals.

The preceding description of a school community represents an ideal and seldom is realized fully. But there are some schools that approximate this ideal. For example, in his book, *Among School Teachers*, Joel Westheimer describes two California middle schools that have many features of a community.[64] In one of these schools, teachers often exchange ideas and advice and there is some collaborative planning. Teachers offer and expect support from their colleagues. While some disagreements and tensions exist among faculty in this school, Westheimer describes the general atmosphere there as follows: "Teachers at Brandeis are part of a professional community characterized by an ethic of individual professionalism within a caring, supportive, and largely harmonious community."[65] Several studies of Catholic schools indicate that these schools are more likely than others to have important elements of community—including shared educational goals and commitment to school goals among their faculty.[66]

EFFECTS OF COLLEGIAL RELATIONSHIPS

Does the type of relationships that exist among teachers affect the educational process? There is considerable evidence that whether teachers have close collegial relationships, rather than doing their jobs as generally isolated individuals, makes a difference for their teaching methods, their attendance on the job, their attitudes about their work, and ultimately for student outcomes.

Teachers who frequently discuss their work and mutual problems with their peers are more apt to change their teaching methods than those who have little interaction with their peers.[67] Through discussion and collaboration, teachers learn about what others are doing and what works or does not work for their peers. Such professional communication helps individual teachers to further develop their expertise in managing students, choosing classroom activities, interacting with students, evaluating students, and other skills of classroom instruction. Links with teachers in other schools, through professional networks, also help to expand teachers' information about useful instructional practices. However, in order for teachers' own practices to change, it often is necessary for teachers to be exposed not only to new information but also to seeing how new practices look when carried out in a classroom.[68]

When there is a great deal of collegial interaction among teachers, there tends also to be consistency in the instructional practices used by individual teachers.[69] Such consistency in practice may arise in part from teachers sharing information about what works in their classes. In addition, a group of closely interacting colleagues may develop norms that certain practices are desirable and exert social pressures (especially of approval or disapproval) for the use of particular instructional methods. (As noted below, consistency in teacher practices may or may not contribute to student achievement.)

Teacher's relationships with their peers also affect their attitudes and behavior in a variety of ways.[70] When teachers have close collegial relationships with their colleagues, they feel less isolated and less alienated or disengaged from their work, more enthusiastic about and committed to their work, and less likely to feel "burnt out." They also are more likely to think that they can be effective in their teaching and make a difference for their students.

One of a number of studies that have investigated the relationship between teacher collegiality and teacher attitudes is a large-scale study of about 8,500 teachers in 354 public and Catholic high schools.[71] The researchers focused on trying to explain variations in teacher morale. Their measure of teacher morale was based on responses to four items: (1) How successful do you feel in educating students? (2) I look forward to working everyday; (3) I sometimes feel it is a waste of time to do my best as a teacher; and (4) How much of the time do you feel satisfied with your job in this school? (Each teacher was asked to choose from among several responses to each question or statement.)

The researchers also obtained information about characteristics of each school that might affect the morale of teachers in that school. Among these school characteristics was "sense of community," which was assessed by the average responses of teachers in each school to the following five items: (1) You can count on most staff members to help out anywhere, anytime—even though it may not be part of their official assignment; (2) Most of my colleagues share my beliefs and values about what the central mission of the school should be; (3) I feel accepted and respected as a colleague by most staff members; (4) There is a great deal of cooperative effort among staff members; and (5) This school seems like a big family; everyone is so close and cordial.

The researchers found that the stronger the sense of community among teachers in a school, the higher their morale. This relationship was apparent even after a number of other school characteristics that may affect teacher morale (socioeconomic status of students, size of school, concerns about student disorder, etc.) were held constant. Other research is consistent with this study in showing that the more teachers share common beliefs, help each other, and have friendly cooperative relations, the higher their satisfaction, commitment, and effort.[72]

The evidence that stronger teacher collegiality leads to higher teacher motivation and to innovations in their teaching methods suggests that the end result of a stronger teacher community should be better outcomes for students. Available evidence indicates that this indeed is the case. Where community among teachers is stronger, student test scores have been found to be higher and dropout rates among students have been lower.[73]

However, while the effects of teacher community usually are positive for students, this is not always the case. Jeffrey Yasumoto and his colleagues obtained information on achievement gains in math and science for students in a national sample of 52 public high schools.[74] They also got detailed information about the instructional practices and the cohesiveness of teachers in each department of each school. The researchers found that, in general, when a cohesive group of teachers was consistent in their use of instructional practices, student achievement was raised. The researchers comment: "These results indicate the positive consequences for achievement growth of a high rate of collegial interaction when it reinforces consistent practice."[75]

However, in some instances a cohesive group of teachers was consistent in using an *ineffective* practice; in these cases, the negative effect of such practices was intensified. Yasumoto and his colleagues observe: "Here, we may be observing the results of error or conservatism, probably reinforced by cumulative exposure. Members of collegial groups are not inerrant problem solvers."[76] In sum, then, sharing of information and ideas generally will lead teachers to share methods that are useful for facilitating student achievement. However, groups of teachers—like other groups—can be wrong and, when this occurs, the negative effects of certain ineffective practices may be intensified by their consistent use within the faculty.

DETERMINANTS OF COMMUNITY AMONG TEACHERS

Under what circumstances do close collegial relationships and feelings of community come to exist among teachers? First, participation by teachers in making school decisions that affect their own lives and those of their students helps to create a professional teacher community. The impact of such participation in decision making on teacher collegiality and sense of community is shown especially by the research on site-based management (see section on this topic earlier in this chapter). When teachers take part in making decisions about a variety of matters affecting them and their classrooms—curriculum, evaluation, hiring, budget, scheduling, and so on— they are likely to have a higher level of commitment to the school and to their colleagues than when they are the passive recipients of decisions made only by administrators. Greater participation by teachers in decisions made at the school (or department or grade) level necessarily leads each teacher to have more contact with other staff members. Such interaction, focused on making joint decisions, also tends to produce, or reinforce, shared beliefs and common goals that are an important aspect of community.

In addition to participation in decision making on a school level, other collaborative activities also are important in strengthening collegial relationships. The more teachers meet and work together to share ideas, discuss teaching strategies, and plan common, complementary, or joint activities (e.g., in team teaching or planning curricula together), the more friendly their relations and the greater their sense of common purpose. Joel Westheimer comments: "Social bonds form among teachers when they are engaged professionally in a common mission."[77]

The engagement of teachers in common activities is shaped to a considerable extent by the school organization. By scheduling meetings for discussion, planning, or program evaluation, school administrators can arrange to bring teachers together to talk about professional matters. They can arrange for, or facilitate, some team teaching.[78] They can define the role of a teacher in a way that broadens her activities beyond those concerned only with her particular classes to those that are part of a range of school activities.[79]

In describing the operation of her own school, Deborah Meier provides some examples of the ways in which the school can structure a broad range of interactions among faculty members. She writes:

Each team of teachers that works with the same students and the same curriculum also teaches at the same time and are "off" together. The school's structure, from the placement of rooms to the scheduling of the day, is organized to enable teachers to visit each other's classes, to reflect on their own and their colleagues' practice, and give each other feedback and support. Curricular teams who teach the same division of students the same agreed-upon topics, for example, have a full morning each week outside the classroom to critique student work and each other's plans, and occasional full days to work on standards and long-range expectations. For the same reason, those who teach the same eighty kids—the faculty of each house—have an hour-and-a-half extended lunch together every week. The entire staff meets from 3:00 to 5:00 P.M. every Monday and from 1:30 to 3:00 P.M. on Fridays to make collective school-wide decisions, discuss ideas, and work out both curricular and graduation standards, issues that overlap all ages and divisions.[80]

There are some impediments to creating bonds of a professional community among teachers. A high rate of staff turnover may reduce the average strength of bonds among teachers. Moreover, some teachers may prefer to work separately and autonomously. They may not want to spend the time and effort required to work with, and adjust to the ideas of, other staff members. Such preference for "splendid isolation" may stem from, or be reinforced by, norms of traditional school practice. In addition, there may be competition among teachers—for material resources, class assignments, status, influence, and promotion—that reduces friendly bonds among teachers.[81]

Strong bonds of collegiality are more likely to develop among teachers in some types of schools than in others. Bonds of community generally are stronger in small schools than in large schools; teachers in small schools have more interaction with the total faculty and generally participate more in the overall activities of the school than do teachers in large schools.[82]

Building bonds of collegiality may be easier in magnet schools—that is, schools that emphasize particular subject fields or particular pedagogies—than elsewhere. Teachers who are attracted to magnet schools are more likely than teachers in general to share common beliefs regarding the important methods and goals of learning.[83]

Bonds of community also have been found to be stronger in Catholic schools than in public schools. For example, teachers in Catholic schools have been found more likely to cooperate with colleagues, to spend time planning with other teachers, and to report consensus on their beliefs and values. Anthony Bryk, Valerie Lee, and Peter Holland, who compared Catholic and public schools, attribute the stronger bonds in Catholic schools at least partly to the tradition of these schools, which emphasizes the ideal of schools as communities of people working together for a common good.[84]

While building strong collegial relationships among teachers may be easier in some settings than in others, and while some impediments to building teacher community exist in all schools, the basic factors that lead to a strong professional community can operate anywhere. When people are required to work together in cooperative activities toward common goals, they tend strongly to develop friendly cohesive relations. This has been found true in a wide variety of settings[85] and is true of teacher relations in schools as well.

TEACHER UNIONS

Most teachers in the United States belong to a teacher union.[86] The type of relationship that exists between a teacher union and school officials, at the district and at the school levels, may have an important impact on teachers' morale, on teachers' professional development, on the instructional program of the school, and on the school's overall effectiveness.

Teacher unions were formed, and continue to command widespread teacher support, because they help to protect some important interests of teachers—including adequate salaries, equitable treatment, reasonable demands on their time, and protection against abuse. However, most teachers prefer to have a professional relationship, rather than a "labor-management" relationship, with school administrators. They usually also have allegiances to their school and their students, in addition to (and sometimes more strongly than) whatever allegiance they may have to their union.[87]

What effects have teacher unions had on the quality of education? Some scholars have contended that teacher unions have been detrimental to school effectiveness. They argue, for example, that union contracts have limited teachers' activities in the school (e.g., time devoted to meetings or to after-school activities), blocked the transfer of teachers to positions where they were most needed, and prevented schools from dismissing incompetent teachers.[88]

Several studies have attempted to assess through quantitative measures the effect of teacher unionization on students' academic achievement. One study related the growth of teacher unions from 1960 to 1992 to trends in student achievement. The study concluded that teacher unionization was a significant contributor to the decline in student achievement.[89] Another study found that increased spending for education was associated with gains in student achievement before 1960 but not after, and points out that increases in spending since 1962 have served mainly to raise teacher salaries and to reduce class size. [Other research finds that there is little correlation between teacher salaries and student achievement and that the link between class size and achievement is weak (see Chapter 6).] Unionization also appears to be associated with a higher dropout rate for students. Reviewing evidence concerning the educational impact of unionization, Caroline Hoxby concludes that "their overall effect on student achievement is negative."[90]

However, relationships between teacher unions and school administrators vary widely and so, therefore, do the effects of unions on school effectiveness. One study of teacher unions found that some relationships between unions and school administrators are contentious; others are cooperative and collaborative. While union contracts in some districts had detrimental effects on school effectiveness, in other cases union agreements affected schools favorably (e.g., by introducing more order and equity into decisions and by promoting staff participation in school policy making).[91]

A study of union contracts in districts scattered throughout the United States found that some contracts reflect what has been called "industrial unionism" while others reflect "reform unionism."[92] Industrial unionism is adversarial; it focuses on advancing the interests of teachers as workers against those of management with regard to compensation, job protection, assignments, working conditions, and related issues. Reform unionism, while also trying to protect teachers' rights, goes beyond concern with teachers' interests as employees to advance their interests as professionals. Unions with a reform perspective try to work collaboratively with school administrators to promote teachers' professional development and to improve the instructional program of the school.

In recent years, many local teacher unions, as well as national teacher unions, have put greater emphasis on working collaboratively with administrators to improve teaching and learning in the schools.[93] Teacher unions have collaborated in such joint activities as developing peer review of teaching quality and mentor teacher programs. Unions have taken part in school decision-making groups that plan curriculum, budgeting, staffing, and other important school matters. Sometimes unions have provided waivers from their contracts with school districts in order to allow individual schools flexibility in changing their procedures.

An example of a union–management relationship that changed from an adversarial, industrial type to one of collaboration between "partners" (as they called themselves) is that of "East Port," described in a recent study.[94] The union contract in that school district included provisions for a professional development center, a mentor teacher program administered by a joint labor-management committee, and another joint committee to study student discipline. In addition, school site councils were established, providing shared teacher-administrator control over curriculum design, budget, and staffing. Individual schools were given flexibility to decide how to allocate time during the school day.

In a school district described in another study, in which relations between union and administration changed from adversarial to cooperative, the union president observed: "We really got down to what the problems were. . . . And out of that came some agreements about how we would behave toward each other and an agreement to try to conclude the next round of negotiations on a win-win basis.[95]

A number of scholars who have studied teacher unions have urged that unions and administrators should enlarge the role of collective bargaining so that the two parties work together effectively to improve education.[96] For this to happen more widely, both teacher unions and school administrators must be willing to go beyond a purely labor-management relationship. In advocating a broader, more collaborative relationship, Nina Bascia urges unions to look beyond their traditional function of protecting teacher interests and help teachers to be more involved in a broader range of school issues that affect their professional lives. But these kinds of collaborative activities can only happen if administrators are willing to give teachers a meaningful role in decision making. Bascia notes: "To the extent that administrators are unable or unwilling to share power with teachers, the old dynamics will remain in place and teachers' traditional concerns will continue to be salient."[97]

OVERVIEW: THE ORGANIZATION OF THE SCHOOL

Figure 5-1 presents a schematic overview of how the organization of a school's staff affects the school's academic program and the performance of its teachers. This diagram is intended to show how the aspects of school life discussed in this chapter are related to each other.

Figure 5-1 shows, first, that the organization of the school staff affects the academic program of the school. Some of this effect is direct; for example, who is involved in decisions (about school goals, curriculum time schedules, discipline, etc.) will help to shape the nature of the academic program. In addition, school organization impacts the academic program indirectly through its effects on staff interactions. For example, when teachers work together on school issues, they are more likely than otherwise to coordinate the subject content covered in their classes.

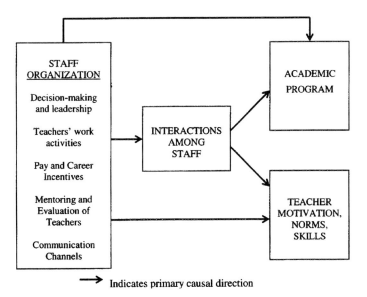

Figure 5-1   Some effects of staff organization.

Figure 5-1 also indicates that the organization of the school staff has important effects on teachers—their satisfaction, motivation, skill development, and norms. Some of these effects are direct. For example, participation in school decisions tends to increase teachers' job satisfaction, and career incentives may raise teacher motivation. By affecting the frequency and nature of interaction among school staff, especially among teachers, staff organization also has important indirect effects on teachers. Frequent and cooperative interactions among teachers—that is, the creation of a collegial community—lead to higher teacher satisfaction and motivation, better teacher skills, and teacher norms that support school improvement.

While Figure 5-1 shows the effects of school organization, it does not indicate the determinants of school organization. In this chapter, I discussed one such determinant, the kinds of agreements reached between school management and teacher unions. For example, any salary incentives for teachers often will be affected by union contracts. In subsequent chapters, the ways in which the organization of school staff is influenced by school characteristics, such as school size, and by some other factors outside the school, are discussed.

SUMMARY AND CONCLUSIONS

This chapter has focused on how the organization of members of a school's staff impacts the school's effectiveness, especially by affecting the interactions, attitudes and work of teachers.

A major aspect of school organization is the extent to which its decision-making process is bureaucratic (based mainly on standard rules and a chain of command) or more decentralized (with wider participation of staff and more flexibility). While bureaucracy has some advantages, it also has important disadvantages, including inflexibility, little upward communication, and apathy among school staff members.

Frustration with the rigidity and ineffectiveness of school bureaucracies led some large cities to transfer control of schools to elected representatives (parents and others) in each local community. However, many local school councils have not functioned effectively, and there is little evidence that community control of schools generally has improved student learning.

Continued dissatisfaction with low student achievement has led many cities to move back to greater centralization of school authority. However, recentralization also has not produced consistent improvement in urban schools. One important reason is that, where important decisions have been made at the top, the active cooperation of teachers and parents often has not been forthcoming.

Thus, neither centralization nor community control of large urban school systems has been able consistently to improve classroom practice and student learning. The advantages of each system are often offset by its disadvantages. A possible solution to this seeming dilemma is to balance local control of schools with an oversight body that monitors and assists schools to be sure that they meet high standards of performance.

In addition to community control, a widespread approach to decentralizing school decision-making is site-based management (SBM). Site-based management moves many important decisions down to the individual school and particularly to school staff. Teachers, along with the school principal, usually have major decision-making responsibility, although others (parents, community members, students) also may participate.

Where SBM has been used, it usually has had some positive effects on teachers: higher teacher satisfaction, more collegiality among teachers, and a greater perception among teachers that they can promote positive change in their schools. However, there is little evidence that SBM generally improves the classroom practices of teachers or leads to better learning outcomes for students.

Site-based management has been found to have its intended effect of changing a school's classroom practices only when certain conditions are present. These conditions for an effective SBM program include: the participation in decision making of a broad range of people in the school; wide sharing of information about events in the school; and a focus by decision-making groups on improvements in classroom practices and the professional development of teachers (rather than on other subjects, such as the working conditions of school personnel). If carried out effectively, SBM can lead to teachers (and others) feeling more involved in the school and to improvements in school effectiveness.

A second aspect of school organization is the set of incentives that are provided for teachers. The major types of incentive programs that have been proposed and implemented include: (1) merit pay, linking teacher salaries or bonuses to some measure of teacher effectiveness; (2) linking teacher pay to measures of their knowledge and skills; (3) career ladders and mentor teacher programs that provide opportunities for teachers to rise in professional status and responsibility; and 4) awards for school performance that give financial or other rewards for effective performance to schools and/or to their individual members.

Research on teacher incentive programs generally has found them to have very limited effects on teacher motivation and performance or on student learning. The evidence indicates that, to be successful, incentive programs must overcome a number of potential problems. First, any program for judging the worthiness of particular teachers (and schools) to receive rewards must use methods of evaluation that are accepted by teachers as valid and fair. Teachers are more likely to accept a system for evaluating them if they have a role in developing the system and if they are judged, at least in part, by their peers.

Second, a teacher incentive program is more likely to be successful if it avoids promoting an ethic of competition among teachers. A competitive atmosphere is destructive of teacher morale and of the collegial collaboration that contributes to teaching effectiveness. For this reason, incentive programs that offer potential rewards to all teachers who meet some criteria of excellence seem preferable to those that reward only a select number. Linking pay to demonstrated skills and knowledge, providing career ladders, and giving collective rewards to teachers in an effective school are all approaches that make rewards for excellence available, in time, to all teachers.

Finally, to be most effective, programs intended to provide incentives for teachers need to be part of a broader plan to provide professional growth for teachers and better learning for students. Teachers need to be helped to improve their skills—through constructive feedback, mentoring, workshops, encouragement to take relevant courses, and so forth—and teaching effectiveness needs to be judged in the context of school goals and programs to improve student learning.

The attitudes of teachers toward their work and the way in which they do their jobs are affected greatly by their relationships with other teachers. When teachers often share information and ideas about their work, and when they also share a commitment to the school and its learning goals, they may be said to be a professional community. The more teachers are a professional community, the greater their satisfaction, commitment, and effort. Where a strong professional community exists, teachers also are likely to use information and ideas from their colleagues to improve their teaching methods. The end result of greater teacher collaboration is that academic achievement among students generally improves.

A strong professional community grows out of cooperative activities in which teachers and others work toward common goals. Participation in decision-making groups to plan aspects of the school program (curriculum, standards, learning goals, after-school activities, etc.) brings staff members together in a common purpose and leads to more collegial relationships. Team teaching, arranging for visits by teachers to each other's classes, and meetings of teachers to discuss students they teach in common are other examples of cooperative activities that may contribute to a strong teacher community.

Teacher unions often play a role in shaping the organization of a school, such as the school's decision-making processes, teachers' work activities, and pay and career policies. Thus, unions may affect teachers' morale and professional development and the instructional program of the school. Historically, unions may have had a somewhat negative effect on school effectiveness. However, the relationship between a teacher union and school administrators varies widely; some are contentious, some are cooperative. Union contracts appear to have a detrimental impact on school effectiveness in some instances; in other cases, union agreements have affected schools favorably.

In many school districts, unions are moving away from a sole focus on protecting teachers' welfare to concern with a broader range of school issues that affect their members' professional lives. Many teacher unions are collaborating with administrators to improve schools' instructional programs, through such means as teacher participation in decision making, peer review of teaching, and mentor teacher programs. Such collaboration requires both a willingness by unions to broaden their traditional concerns and a willingness by administrators to share power with teachers.

The chapter concluded with presentation of a schematic representation that showed the connections between the organization of a school and the work of its teachers in the classroom.

NOTES

1. For a general discussion of problems of organizations, see, for example, J. Gibson, J. Ivancevich, and J. Donnelly, Jr., *Organizations*. Homewood, IL: Irwin, 1991.

2. See R. Stark, *Sociology*. Belmont, CA: Wadsworth, 1998, Chapter 20, The Organizational Age.

3. See S. Rothstein, *Schools and Society*. Englewood Cliffs, NJ: Merrill, 1996, Chapter 6, The School as a Bureaucracy.

4. R. Ingersoll, Organizational Control in Secondary Schools. *Harvard Educational Review, 64*, 1994, 150–173.

5. M. Cohen, Instructional, Management, and Social Conditions in Effective Schools. In A. Odden and L. Webb., eds., *School Finance and School Improvement*. Cambridge, MA: Ballinger, 1983, pp. 17–50.

6. Cohen, Ibid., p. 31.

7. D. Brown, *Decentralization and School-Based Management*. London: Falmer Press, 1990, p. 58.

8. V. Lee, A. Bryk, and J. Smith, The Organization of Effective Secondary Schools. In L. Darling-Hammond, ed., *Review of Research in Education, 19*, 1993, p. 206.

9. Rothstein, *Schools and Society*, p. 97.

10. Brown, *Decentralization and School-Based Management*, Chapter 1.

11. D. Rogers, *110 Livingston Street: Politics and Bureaucracy in the New York City School System*. New York: Vintage Books, 1969, p. 267.

12. See E. Lawler, *High-Involvement Management*. San Francisco: Jossey-Bass, 1986.

13. Community control sometimes involves management of individual school sites. However, most site-based management groups are composed mainly of school personnel, rather than community members or parents.

14. D. Lewis and K. Nakagawa, *Race and Education Reform in the American Metropolis: A Study of School Decentralization*. Albany: State University of New York Press, 1995.

15. Lewis and Nakagawa, Ibid.

16. D. Rogers and N. Chung, *110 Livingston Street Revisited: Decentralization in Action*. New York: New York University Press, 1983.

17. D. Ravitch and W. Grant, *School Decentralization in New York City 1975 [and] Detroit's Experience with School Decentralization*. Washington, DC: Center for Governmental Studies, 1975.

18. G. Hess, Understanding Achievement (and Other) Changes Under Chicago School Reform. *Educational Evaluation and Policy Analysis, 21*, 1999, 67–83.

19. S. Grosskopf and C. Moutray, Evaluating Performance in Chicago Public High Schools in the Wake of Decentralization. *Economics of Education Review, 20*, 2001, 1–14.

20. Lewis and Nakagawa, *Race and Education Reform*, p. 148.

21. J. Mirel, *Rise and Fall of an Urban School System: Detroit 1907—81*. Ann Arbor: University of Michigan Press, 1993.

22. L. Cuban and M. Usdan, What Happened in the Six Cities? In L. Cuban and M. Usdan, eds., *Powerful Reforms with Shallow Roots: Improving America's Urban Schools*. New York: Teachers College Press, 2003, p. 152.

23. Cuban and Usdan, Ibid., p. 155.

24. Cuban and Usdan, Ibid., p. 160.

25. Hess, Understanding Achievement (and Other) Changes Under Chicago School Reform, p. 223.

26. S. Mohrman and P. Wohlstetter, eds., *School-Based Management*. San Francisco: Jossey-Bass, 1994.

27. C. Etheridge and Associates, *Challenge to Change: The Memphis Experience with School-Based Decision Making*. Washington, DC: National Education Association, 1994.

28. See L. Beck and J. Murphy, *The Four Imperatives of a Successful School*. Thousand Oaks, CA: Corwin Press, 1996, p. 7.

29. Brown, *Decentralization and School-Based Management*.

30. R. Ogawa and P. White, School-Based Management: An Overview. In Mohrman and Wohlstetter, *School-Based Management*.

31. Reviewers who have reached this conclusion include Ogawa and White, School-Based Management; Beck and Murphy, The Four Imperatives; and P. Wohlstetter and S. Mohrman, *Assessment of School-Based Management*. Washington, DC: U.S. Department of Education, 1996.

32. Wohlstetter and Mohrman, Ibid., p. 32.

33. Beck and Murphy, *The Four Imperatives*.

34. D. Levine and E. Eubanks, Site-Based Management. In J. Lane and E. Epps, eds., *Restructuring the Schools*. Berkeley, CA: McCutchan, 1992, pp. 61–62.

35. Wohlstetter and Mohrman, Assessment of School-Based Management.

36. R. Elmore, P. Peterson, and S. McCarthey, *Restructuring in the Classroom*. San Francisco: Jossey-Bass, 1996; P. Peterson, S. McCarthey, and R. Elmore, Learning from School Restructuring. *American Educational Research Journal, 33*, 1996, 119–153.

37. Peterson, et al., Ibid., p. 148.

38. S. Rosenholtz, Effective Schools: Interpreting the Evidence. *American Journal of Education, 93*, 1985, 352–388; D. Brewer, Principals and Student Outcomes: Evidence from U.S. High Schools. *Economics of Education Review, 12*, 1993, 281–292.

39. M. Leighton, *The Role of Leadership in Sustaining School Reform*. Washington, DC: U.S. Department of Education, 1996.

40. K. Louis, J. Toole, and A. Hargreave, Rethinking School Improvement. In J. Murphy and K. Louis, eds., *Handbook of Research on Educational Administration*,

2nd edition. San Francisco: Jossey-Bass, 1999, pp. 251–276; V. Lee, A. Bryk, and J. Smith, The Organization of Effective Secondary Schools. In L. Darling-Hammond, ed., *Review of Educational Research, 19.* Washington, DC: American Educational Research Association, 1993, pp. 171–268.

41. Rosenholtz, Effective Schools, p. 367.
42. Louis, et al., Rethinking School Improvement, p. 267.
43. L. Evans and C. Teddlie, Facilitating Change in Schools: Is There One Best Style? *School Effectiveness and School Improvement, 6,* 1995, 1–22.
44. See, for example, M. Heller and W. Firestone, Who's in Charge Here? Sources of Leadership for Change in Eight Schools. *Elementary School Journal, 96,* 1995, 65–86.
45. L. Frase, The Effects of Financial and Non-financial Rewards. In L. Frase, ed., *Teacher Compensation and Motivation.* Lancaster, PA: Technomic Publishing, 1992, pp. 217–238.
46. See T. Timar, Incentive Pay for Teachers and School Reform. In Frase, *Teacher Compensation and Motivation,* pp. 27–60.
47. Timar, Ibid.
48. R. Murname and D. Cohen, Merit Pay and the Evaluation Problem. *Harvard Educational Review, 56,* 1986, 1–17; W. Firestone, Redesigning Teacher Salary Systems for Educational Reform. *American Educational Research Journal, 31,* 1994, 549–574; Timar, Incentive Pay; Frase, Effects of Financial and Non-financial Rewards.
49. R. Schwab and E. Iwanicki, Can Performance-Based Salary Programs Motivate Teachers? Insights from a Case Study. In Frase, *Teacher Compensation and Motivation,* pp. 151–185.
50. A. Odden, New and Better Forms of Teacher Compensation Are Possible. *Phi Delta Kappan, 81,* 2000, 351–366.
51. Odden, New and Better Forms of Teacher Compensation, Ibid., pp. 365–366.
52. R. Heneman and G. Ledford, Jr., Competency Pay for Professionals and Managers in Business: A Review and Implications for Teachers. *Journal of Personnel Evaluation in Education, 12,* 1998, 103–121.
53. Timar, Incentive Pay for Teachers and School Reform; Firestone, Redesigning Teacher Salary Systems.
54. Timar, Ibid., p. 41.
55. Timar, Ibid., p. 45.
56. Timar, Ibid.; Firestone, Redesigning Teacher Salary Systems.
57. Odden, New and Better Forms of Teacher Compensation.
58. Firestone, Redesigning Teacher Salary Systems.
59. Firestone, Ibid., Odden, New and Better Forms of Teacher Compensation.
60. G. Natriello and S. Dornbusch, Pitfalls in the Evaluation of Teachers by Principals. *Administrators Notebook, 29,* Nos. 6–7, 1980–1981.
61. Rosenholtz, *Effective Schools.*
62. Rosenholtz, Ibid.
63. See, for example, J. Westheimer, *Among School Teachers.* New York: Teachers College Press, 1998; T. Sergiovanni, *Building Community in Schools.* San Francisco: Jossey-Bass, 1994.
64. Westheimer, *Among School Teachers.*
65. Westheimer, Ibid., p. 63.

66. A. Bryk, V. Lee, and P. Holland, *Catholic Schools and the Common Good.* Cambridge, MA: Harvard University Press, 1993.

67. C. Bidwell, K. Frank, and P. Quiroz, Teacher Types, Workplace Controls, and the Organization of Schools. *Sociology of Education, 70,* 1997, 285–307; J. Yasumoto, K. Uekawa, and C. Bidwell, The Collegial Focus and High School Students' Achievement. *Sociology of Education, 74,* 2001, 181–209.

68. Elmore, et al., *Restructuring in the Classroom.*

69. Yasumoto, et al., The Collegial Focus.

70. See, for example, V. Lee, R. Dedrick, and J. Smith, The Effect of the Social Organization of Schools on Teachers' Efficacy and Satisfaction. *Sociology of Education, 64,* 1991, 190–208; S. Raudenbush, B. Rowan, and Y. Cheong, Contextual Effects on the Self-Perceived Efficacy of High School Teachers. *Sociology of Education, 65,* 1992, 150–167; Bryk, et al., *Catholic Schools and the Common Good*; Westheimer, *Among School Teachers.*

71. Lee, et al., The Effect of School Organization.

72. Lee, et al., The Organization of Effective Secondary Schools.

73. Westheimer, *Among School Teachers*, p. 140.

74. Yasumoto, et al., The Collegial Focus.

75. Yasumoto, et al., Ibid., p. 196.

76. Yasumoto, et al., Ibid., p. 201.

77. Westheimer, *Among School Teachers*, p. 117.

78. Sergiovanni, *Building Community in Schools.*

79. Bryk, et al., *Catholic Schools and the Common Good.*

80. D. Meier, *The Power of Their Ideas.* Boston: Beacon Press, 1995, p. 56.

81. Westheimer, *Among School Teachers.*

82. Bryk, et al., *Catholic Schools and the Common Good.*

83. Westheimer, *Among School Teachers.*

84. Bryk, et al., *Catholic Schools and the Common Good.*

85. D. Johnson and R. Johnson, *Cooperation and Competition: Theory and Research.* Edina, MN: Interaction Books, 1989.

86. N. Bascia, *Unions in Teachers' Professional Lives.* New York: Teachers College Press, 1994.

87. Bascia, Ibid.

88. See, for example, M. Lieberman, *The Teachers Unions.* New York: Free Press, 1997.

89. S. Peltzman, The Political Economy of the Decline of American Public Education. *Journal of Law and Economics, 36,* 1993, 331–370.

90. C. Hoxby, How Teachers Unions Affect Education Production. *Quarterly Journal of Economics, 111,* 1996, 671–718; p. 707.

91. S. Johnson, *Teacher Unions in Schools.* Philadelphia: Temple University Press, 1984.

92. S. Johnson and S. Kardos, Reform Bargaining and Its Promise for School Improvement. In T. Loveless, ed., *Conflicting Missions? Teachers Unions and Educational Reform.* Washington, DC: Brookings Institution Press, 2000, pp. 7–46.

93. Bascia, *Unions in Teachers' Professional Lives.*

94. Johnson and Kardos, Reform Bargaining.

95. Bascia, *Unions in Teachers' Professional Lives*, p. 55.

96. For example, see Johnson and Kardos, Reform Bargaining; C. Kerchner, J. Koppoch, and J. Weeres, *Taking Charge of Schools: How Teachers and Unions Can Revitalize Schools.* San Francisco: Jossey-Bass, 1998.
97. Bascia, *Unions in Teachers' Professional Lives*, p. 99.

Chapter 6

SCHOOL CHARACTERISTICS:
THE "GIVENS" SHAPING A SCHOOL

In previous chapters, we have looked at how outcomes for students—their motivation, their learning, and so forth—are shaped by what goes on in classrooms, by the curriculum and other parts of a school's academic program, and by the organization of the school staff. Now we consider the ways in which all of these aspects of the school's activities are, in turn, influenced by some basic features of schools that are to a large extent "givens" for them—that is, conditions under which the schools must operate. Such features include: (1) the size of the school, (2) the size of classes, (3) the social class and ethnic composition of the student body, and (4) the amount of money available to the school. To what extent are the activities and experiences of teachers and students, and outcomes for students, affected by these characteristics of schools? The following sections discuss, in turn, each of these school characteristics.

SIZE OF SCHOOL

The question of how large a school should be has been debated for many decades. Some have favored large schools on the grounds that they are more economically efficient and that they permit schools to offer a wide array of programs, courses, activities, and services that small schools cannot offer. Others have argued that a small school is better because it promotes more personal, caring relations between students and school staff and more cohesive relations among staff members. A number of recent books and reports on school reform, including a report issued by the National Association of Secondary School principals (NASSP),[1] have recommended that high schools should be, or be broken into subunits that are, fairly small.

However, one of the foremost researchers on the issue of school size recently asserted: "The fact is that reformers are out in front of researchers on the issue of high school size . . . there is little empirical evidence to support the decisions that are being made."[2]

154

Let us, then, look at the available evidence. In discussing the effects of school size, we may consider how size affects: (1) efficiency, (2) the curriculum, (3) relations among staff members, (4) relations between students and teachers, (5) student involvement, and (6) student achievement.

EFFICIENCY

Organizations, including schools, may be able to achieve certain savings as their size increases. They can make larger purchases of supplies and materials (e.g, books and paper) at a relatively low unit cost; they can maintain other costs (such as lighting and heat) at a relatively flat level regardless of numbers served; they may be able to substitute one person (e.g., one principal or one librarian) for several people who fill the same roles at several smaller schools.[3]

However, the savings forecast by advocates of larger or consolidated schools have not materialized.[4] Like other organizations, as schools become larger, they expand their administrative and support staffs (assistant principals, clerical people, etc.) to handle the greater demands of communication and coordination. Moreover, additional costs, such as those of transporting students from a wider area, also tend to be borne by larger schools. Overall, the case for larger size as a means to greater efficiency does not appear to be supported.

THE CURRICULUM

The larger the school, the more it can differentiate its curriculum. Instead of teaching only a few basic science courses, it can offer courses in other science areas—for example, earth science and astronomy—as well. Rather than offer only Spanish, French, and German as foreign languages, it can teach Chinese, Japanese, or Russian to interested students. More specialized and more advanced courses in every subject can be made available to students. Increasing school size tends to lead not only to a greater variety of courses but also to more specialized programs.[5]

While a greater variety of courses and programs provides students with more choices, some observers have suggested that more specialized curriculums are not necessarily desirable. They may lead to greater differences in students' academic experiences and thus promote social stratification.[6]

Some small high schools (especially Catholic schools) provide a fairly uniform, mostly academic program of study to almost all of their students. Such a policy has been found to result both in higher academic achievement and in achievement that is more equally distributed among students than is true in most larger high schools.[7]

Some small high schools have tried, despite their size, to offer a diverse curriculum, like that of a comprehensive high school. Valerie Lee and her colleagues describe the curriculum in several such small schools as "constituted of unusual and illogical course sequences"[8] and thus as generally inadequate. Rather than attempting to provide a diverse curriculum with their own limited resources, some small schools have combined with other schools to offer specialized courses or have arranged for students to get special educational experiences at other institutions (e.g., at universities or museums).

RELATIONS AMONG STAFF

As schools become larger, the professional and personal ties among school staff tend to weaken. Much of the communication among administrators, teachers, and support staff becomes more formal and indirect. Teachers' loyalties often focus on subunits, such as departments, rather than on the school as a whole. Also, as the size of a school's faculty grows, it becomes more difficult for teachers to participate directly in decisions about school policies regarding curriculum, disciplinary practices, scheduling, and many other topics.[9]

Deborah Meier, writing of her experiences in New York City schools, says:

> Only in a small school can deep ongoing discussion take place in ways that produce change and involve the entire faculty. . . . For teachers to start thinking through the task before them, collectively and collaboratively, schools must be so small that grievance does not become the topic of discussion but issues of education do, so small that the faculty as a whole becomes the decision-making body on questions of teaching and learning.[10]

In another passage, Meier goes on to say: "This continuing dialogue, face to face, over and over, is a powerful educative force. It is our primary form of staff development."[11]

In small schools, teachers are more likely to feel a sense of personal responsibility for the learning of students in the whole school. A recent study conducted with 4,494 teachers in 264 Chicago elementary schools investigated the relationship between school size and teachers' perceptions of their colleagues' feelings of responsibility for learning outcomes in their school.[12] (Examples of questions asked of teachers: "How many teachers feel responsible when students in the school fail? . . . feel responsible to help each other do their best?") Schools were grouped into three size categories: less than 400 students; 400 to 749 students; and 750 or more students. As the size of the school increased, teachers were less likely to say that their colleagues felt responsible for the learning of students in their school. This effect of school size on reported teacher attitudes was large and occurred when characteristics of the student body (percentage low-income; percentage black; percentage Hispanic) were held constant.

Such feelings of collective responsibility among teachers have been found to affect student learning. In high schools where teachers had greater feelings of collective responsibility, and where there was greater consistency among teachers in such attitudes, students made greater gains in achievement in a variety of subjects.[13]

RELATIONSHIPS BETWEEN STUDENTS AND TEACHERS

As schools become larger, students and teachers may know each other less well. Personalized and intimate relationships between teachers and students have been found to be more common in small than in larger high schools.[14] Such close contacts between students and staff make it more likely that students will share the norms and "academic culture" of the school faculty, rather than being immersed solely in a peer culture that may not support learning.[15]

However, the relationships between students and teachers may not always be closely related to school size. A study of 41 elementary schools in a large suburban district found no significant relationship between school size and measures of "school climate" that included students' feelings of a close relationship to their teachers. The same study found that school climate tended to become more negative as class size increased.[16] Thus, factors other than the size of the school also may affect student–teacher relationships.

STUDENT PARTICIPATION AND ENGAGEMENT

Large schools can offer not only a greater variety of courses but also a wider choice of extracurricular activities to appeal to the interests of different students. On the other hand, as the number of students increases, there is less chance for students to compete successfully for selective positions, such as places on athletic teams, editors of publications, elected student representatives, and performers in plays. Moreover, despite the wider choice of some activities, overall student participation in school activities tends to decrease as school size increases.[17]

Students in large schools also tend to be less engaged in their schoolwork than those in smaller schools. A large national study, using data from a sample of almost 12,000 students in 830 American high schools, included measures of the academic engagement of students.[18] Students were asked how often they "work hard" in each of four basic subject classes (math, English, history, and science). They also were asked how often they "feel challenged" in each of these classes. A measure of academic engagement, based on answers to these questions, was computed for each student.

As the size of a school increased, there was a significant, although modest, decline in the average academic engagement of students. This negative relationship was found even when a number of other characteristics of each school including average socioeconomic status (SES) of students, minority percentages, religious affiliation (Catholic vs. other), and academic emphasis of the school were controlled.

STUDENT ACHIEVEMENT

The most central question regarding school size is its effect on student achievement. Available evidence has been consistent in showing that, in general, as the size of a school increases, student achievement declines.[19] However, the relationship is not a simple one. The fullest picture of the relationship between school size and student achievement has been presented by Valerie Lee and her colleagues.[20] They used data from a nationally representative sample of almost 10,000 students who attended 789 public, Catholic, and private high schools. Change in achievement scores from the eighth grade to the end of high school were assessed for each student who had remained in the same high school. Schools were divided into eight size categories, ranging from 300 or fewer students to more than 2,100 students.

The relationship between school size and student gains both in reading and in math was curvilinear (see Figure 6-1). The greatest average gain in achievement in both subjects was made by students in high schools having between 600 and 900 students. Students in schools having between 900 and 1,200 students also made relatively large gains. Students in schools with fewer than 600 students (especially those in schools below 300) and students in schools with more than 1,200 students (especially the very largest schools, having over 2,100 students) had lower gains in achievement than those in schools of medium size. (The effects of school size were controlled for other major school characteristics.)

The effects of school size on achievement gain were similar for students in high schools whose students were generally from lower-income backgrounds and schools whose students came from higher-income families. Size effects also were similar for schools with high and low proportions of minority students. In other words, regardless of the social backgrounds of their student bodies, high schools of medium size showed larger achievement gains than did either smaller or larger schools.

However, the effect of school size was greatest among schools whose students came from low socioeconomic backgrounds; students in low-SES schools benefited more than students in high-SES schools from going to schools of medium size. Moreover, the gap in average achievement gain between low-SES and high-SES high schools was less when schools were of medium size than it was when schools were either very small or very large.

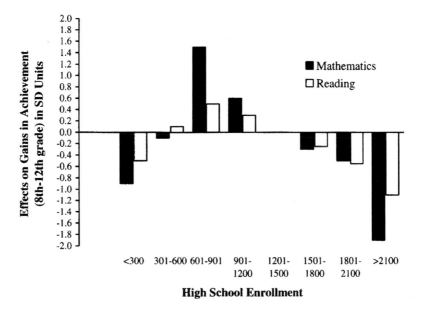

Figure 6-1 Effects of high school size on achievement gains in mathematics and reading (high school size of 1,201 to 1,500 was used as the comparison category). *Source:* V. Lee, using Hierarchical Linear Modeling to Study Social Contexts: The Case of School Effects. *Educational Psychologist,* 35, 2000, p. 132.

Overall, then, medium-sized high schools seem to benefit the academic achievement of all students but especially that of those students who are most at-risk academically.

Additional evidence comes from a study of 264 elementary schools in Chicago that compared gains in mathematics learning among students attending schools in three size categories: small (fewer than 400 students); medium (400–749 students) and large (750 or more students).[21] (The effects of income level and racial and ethnic composition on learning were controlled.) Students in small schools learned substantially more math than did those in medium-sized schools. Students in small elementary schools also made more gain in math than did those in large schools, although this difference was not statistically significant. The effects of school size on learning did not differ for schools with different socioeconomic or racial and ethnic compositions.

Note that these findings from elementary schools (in one city) show the most learning taking place in the smallest schools (under 400 students), while the results from the national study of high schools found that students in medium-sized schools (600–900) learned most. High school students require a greater variety of courses, facilities, services, and activities than do students in elementary schools. Therefore, the disadvantages of very small schools may be more salient at the high school level than at the elementary school level.

OPTIMAL SCHOOL SIZE

Both small size and large size have advantage for schools, as we have seen. Those in schools of one size often long for the benefits that a different size might bring. Valerie Lee and her colleagues interviewed staff members (principals, teachers, and guidance counselors) in five small high schools (less than 500 students) and four relatively large schools (more than 1,500 students) in a Midwestern state.[22] They found that almost all those in small schools wanted their schools to be larger. Having more pupils means getting more money, which they thought was important to strengthen their school programs. On the other hand, many of those in the large schools preferred their schools to be smaller. They were concerned about too much specialization and a lack of close personal relationships in their schools.

A number of researchers have suggested that school size should be such as to balance the advantages of bigness and of smallness. Schools should be big enough to have good facilities and to offer enough courses and services to their students; they should be small enough to maximize participation by staff and by students, as well as close personal relationships among and between teachers and students.

A variety of more specific school sizes have been proposed by various commentators.[23] The evidence on student achievement presented by Lee indicates that a range of about 600 to 1,000 students may be optimal for most high schools and that a student body of less than 400 may be best for most elementary schools. Further research will be needed to confirm or to modify these findings.

However, optimal size for a school may vary with circumstances. Deborah Meier asserts that the advantages of small schools—especially in facilitating development of its staff—can be realized only if the school enjoys substantial autonomy.[24] Lisbeth Schorr states that some large schools (e.g., high schools of science or the performing arts) have been effective in promoting learning when they are organized around a clear and widely shared purpose.[25] In such cases, she suggests, there may be less need for close interpersonal relationships than there is in most schools.

Schools may be able to overcome at least to some extent, the disadvantages of their particular size while maintaining its advantages. Some large schools have divided themselves into smaller subunits, sometimes creating schools-within-schools, in which a subset of students and teachers interact primarily with those in their unit. Such an arrangement may promote the more sustained and personal relationships between students and teachers and among teachers that are characteristic of a small school, while providing the better facilities and specialized services of a larger school.[26]

Some of the disadvantages of large schools also may be counteracted by smaller size classes. Research in the Tennessee schools indicates that the generally negative effects of large schools on student achievement are reduced when classes within each school are relatively small. (See section "Class Size" in this chapter.) However, even when classes are small, large schools appear to have a negative effect on student achievement.[27]

Just as a large school can try to gain the advantages of small size by subdividing, so small schools may gain some of the advantages of larger size by combining some resources with one or more other small schools—for example, offering joint courses in specialized or advanced subjects, or sharing a media specialist. Small schools also can try to supplement their own limited resources by making use of the resources of other institutions, such as libraries, museums, and colleges in their communities.[28]

CLASS SIZE

An aspect of schools that has received great attention in recent years is the size of classes. The belief that creating smaller classes will lead to better learning for students has become widespread and has gained strong political support. Many states have taken steps to reduce the size of classes in their schools. At the federal level, Congress has appropriated substantial money to help school districts to hire new teachers in order to reduce the size of primary-grade classes, especially in poor districts. In light of the attention and money being devoted to such efforts, it is especially important to review the evidence concerning the effects of class size on student achievement and on other outcomes.

NATURALLY OCCURRING DIFFERENCES

One type of study on this subject examines how the size of naturally occurring classes is related to changes in students' levels of achievement, controlling for the effects of other factors (such as students' ethnic membership and family socioeconomic status) that may be related to achievement. Eric Hanushek has summarized estimates of the effects of class size (over a range of 15 to 40 students per class) based on about 60 separate studies.[29] His tabulation of results shows little consistent effect of class size on student achievement. Only 12 percent of the estimates indicated that smaller class size had a statistically significant positive effect on achievement. About an equal proportion of results showed smaller class size related to *lower* student achievement. Hanushek concludes that "the econometric evidence as a whole gives little support to the idea that smaller classes will lead to general improvements in performance."[30]

Two other scholars, Alan Krueger and Diane Whitmore, have reviewed essentially the same set of studies of class size examined by Hanushek and reached a somewhat different conclusion.[31] They weighed the results of each study equally, rather than including multiple estimates of class size effects from some studies (as Hanushek did). When this method is used, the proportion of results showing that smaller class size had a significant positive effect on achievement rises to about 25 percent, while the proportion of results showing a negative effect drops slightly to about 10 percent. About two-thirds of the retabulated studies found that class size had no significant impact on student achievement.

Thus, both the Hanushek and the Krueger-Whitmore reviews find that most of the evidence they examined shows class size to have no significant effect on student achievement. But the latter review finds positive results considerably more often than negative results, and its authors believe that there is a clear tendency for smaller class size to raise student achievement.

EXPERIMENTAL STUDIES

The studies to which I just referred looked at naturally occurring classes of various sizes. Although these studies attempt to control for the effect of other factors that may affect achievement, it is possible that there were unmeasured initial differences between classes of different size that affected achievement. Thus, the best evidence concerning the effects of class size comes from experiments that compare classes of various sizes in which students do not differ initially.

In a paper published in 1989, Robert Slavin found eight studies in which the students in elementary school classes of different sizes were initially equivalent.[32] In one of these studies, students were randomly assigned to classes of different size. In the other seven studies, students assigned to classes of different sizes were matched with respect to prior achievement and background characteristics. In all of these studies, the smaller classes were at least 30 percent smaller than the larger classes and had no more than 20 students; class size was reduced from an average of 27 to about 16 (a 40% reduction). Most of these studies were conducted in schools attended by students from poor families.

Overall, these eight experimental studies found that substantial reductions in class size generally did have a positive effect on achievement, but that these effects were quite small. In several studies, positive effects of small class size in the first year faded out in later years. Slavin concludes: "The evidence . . . suggests that using Chapter 1 funds [federal funds to help disadvantaged students] to reduce class size will not in itself make a substantial difference in student achievement."[33]

The STAR Study

Since Slavin's review, results have been reported on experiments in several American states concerning the effects of smaller classes. The largest and most carefully done of these studies is Tennessee's Project STAR (Student/Teacher Achievement Ratio Study).[34] The STAR study randomly assigned teachers and students in each participating school to one of three types of classes: small (usually 13 to 17 students); regular (typically 22 to 25 students); and regular with a full-time teaching aide. The study began in 1985 in 79 schools within 42 school districts across the state. Students were followed from kindergarten through third grade, although different students participated for varying numbers of years. In all, 11,600 students took part in Project STAR, of whom 1,842 remained in the same size class for all four years.

Students in classes of different size were compared with respect to their achievement in reading and in math during their first four years of school. Researchers found that students in smaller classes in early grades had significantly higher achievement than those in both regular-sized classes and those in regular-sized classes with a teacher's aide. The overall advantage of students in smaller classes was moderate in each grade (about 0.20 of a standard deviation in scores.) The benefit of smaller classes for student achievement in the early grades was especially large in schools with a high proportion of African-American students. Promotion rates from each grade to the next also were somewhat higher in small classes than in regular-sized classes.

In a second phase of the Tennessee study, the academic progress of students who had been in different size classes in early grades were compared in later (fourth through eighth) grades when they were all in regular-sized classes. Students who had earlier been in smaller classes continued to achieve at a higher level than those in the same grade who had begun in larger classes, but their advantage was reduced to about half of what it had been earlier. By the tenth grade, students who had been in small classes in their early school years did not perform significantly better than other students on the Tennessee Competency Test. Nor did such students do better than others on college entrance tests, although they were more likely to take such tests.[35] Those who had earlier been in small classes were less likely to drop out of high school.

Encouraged by the achievement gains made in early school years by students in smaller classes, Tennessee also initiated a nonexperimental third phase of the STAR study in which class sizes in early grades were reduced for all students in the state's 17 lowest-income school districts. The average rank of these districts in both mathematics and reading scores for students in early grades rose steadily and substantially in the three years following the reduction in class sizes.

Other State Studies

Programs to reduce class size in the early years of school also have been studied in other states.[36] In 1984, Indiana provided state funds to pay for additional teachers and teacher aides in order to reduce average first grade class size to 18 (24 if a teacher's aide was present). Still in operation many years later, this program has subsidized staff salaries to try to reach an average class size of 18 in grades K–1 and 20 in grades 2 to 3. Studies of the effects of this program to reduce class size on student achievement have shown mixed results. While some positive effects have been reported, a review of four studies of the Indiana class size reduction program concluded that it had not improved student achievement.[37]

Nevada reduced class sizes in early grades during the 1990s. The effects of this class reduction appear to have been inconsistent, varying with students' ethnicity, socioeconomic status, and geographic area.[38] In the late 1990s, Wisconsin introduced a program that reduced the student–teacher ratio to 15:1 in kindergarten through third grade in some schools.[39] Early results from this program have shown some benefits in achievement for students in small classes compared to those in larger classes. However, the schools with smaller classes also have introduced other changes (including a more rigorous academic curriculum) that make comparisons based on class size problematic.

Two small studies of reductions in class size were conducted in two counties of North Carolina during the 1990s. In both localities, class sizes were reduced to 15 students in some classes. Achievement of students in the smaller classes in both studies was substantially better than that of students in matched comparison groups.[40]

In summary, the substantial amount of research on class size (most of it focused on early grades) indicates that smaller classes sometimes improve student achievement (as well as other outcomes) but that these positive outcomes generally are modest in size and are not found consistently. We need to focus our attention, then, on the circumstances under which smaller classes have positive effects and why such effects may or may not occur.

WHEN CLASS SIZE MAY MATTER

When do smaller classes lead to higher student achievement? The answer to this question relates largely to the way in which class size may affect the behavior of teachers and the interaction between teachers and students. A number of studies have found that, in general, teachers in smaller classes spend less time on discipline and on managing classroom activities; they spend more time on instruction than do teachers in larger classes. Teachers in smaller classes also tend to provide more individual instruction and more small-group instruction. They generally have more interaction with individual students and get to know each student—her strengths and weaknesses—better than in larger classes. Students tend to spend more time on task and appear more engaged in their work.[41]

However, while teachers' behavior tends to change as class size changes, often the behavior of teachers in small classes does not vary much from that of teachers in larger classes.[42] Slavin states: ". . . teachers do change their behavior in small classes, but the changes are relatively subtle and unlikely to make important differences in student achievement."[43] In discussing the modest changes that they found teachers making in smaller classes, Julian Betts and Jamie Shkolnik comment: "Overall, this set of findings raises the possibility that CSR [class size reduction] might become more effective if teachers adjusted their teaching styles more radically so as to take advantage of smaller classes."[44]

The effects of class size also depend on the characteristics and particular needs of students. A review of studies on the effects of class size by G. E. Robinson concluded that "the research rather consistently finds that students who are economically disadvantaged or from some ethnic minorities perform better in smaller classes."[45] Results from the experiments in Tennessee and Wisconsin also indicate that poor and minority students benefit most from small classes.[46] Students from poor and minority backgrounds generally have more difficulty adjusting to school and doing their schoolwork successfully. It appears that they benefit most from the more well-ordered environment and individualized attention that is possible in smaller classes.

The review by Robinson also suggests that small classes are most beneficial in reading and mathematics in the early grades. However, other research indicates that class size does matter in later grades as well as in earlier grades.[47]

Results from the Tennessee STAR experiment show also that smaller class size had a positive effect on student achievement both in larger and in smaller schools. Smaller classes counteracted the negative effects of large schools on achievement to a considerable extent.[48]

In sum, smaller class size tends to benefit student learning in a variety of school settings; it appears to benefit learning most for students from minority and poor backgrounds and when teachers take advantage of the smaller class size to interact more with students.

HOW SMALL IS SMALL ENOUGH?

In one major review of research on class size effects, G. V. Glass and M. L. Smith concluded that the major benefits from reduced class size occur when the number of students is reduced to below 20.[49] Examining a smaller number of studies done with the best methodology, Robert Slavin concluded that even cutting class size in half, from an average of 31 to an average of 16, resulted in trivial gains in achievement.[50] However, results from the Tennessee STAR experiment, as well as some other results (e.g., the North Carolina studies) indicate that class sizes of about 15 may raise achievement levels fairly substantially above that in classes of 25 or more.

Other studies of variations in class size in math and science classes of middle schools and high schools indicate that reductions in class size have a substantial effect on teachers' instructional practices (time working with small groups, use of innovative practices) only when the number of students goes below 20.[51] Overall, while there has been little research that systematically relates achievement to variations in class size, it appears that reducing classes to below 20 (perhaps to about 15) is necessary to get a clear boost in achievement.

Class Size Effects in Context

While smaller classes—especially those with fewer than 20 students—may raise achievement, there is considerable evidence that smaller class size sometimes may be less important than other school factors. The very mixed evidence from systematic studies of class size effects has already been described. Even in Project STAR in Tennessee, the experiment that has provided the most support for class size reduction, smaller classes did not improve achievement in all schools. For example, students in small kindergarten classes had higher reading scores than those in larger classes in only about half of the schools (40 of 79 schools). As Eric Hanushek notes, such variations in results across schools "demonstrates that other things are very important in determining achievement."[52] Other research finds that, even when reducing class size has some positive effects on student achievement, these effects are completely overshadowed by variations in teacher quality.[53]

Further indication that class size sometimes is not crucial in determining achievement levels comes from two other kinds of data. First are the trends in class size and student achievement over time. Between 1950 and 1997, average pupil-teacher ratios in the United States fell from about 27:1 to about 16:1.[54] However, student scores on achievement tests in various subjects showed little change during this period. These results do not necessarily show that class size has no effect on student achievement. Pupil–teacher ratios are not the same as class sizes (although they tend to be correlated). And factors other than class size (other changes in schools, family, and society) may have interfered with any impact of smaller class sizes. However, these data do suggest that smaller class size cannot be expected, in itself, to produce better student achievement.

A second kind of evidence suggesting that any effects of class size may be outweighed by other factors comes from international comparisons. For the 17 nations that report consistent data on pupil–teacher ratios and on test scores, test scores tend to rise as the ratio of pupils to teachers *increases*. For example, class sizes in Japan are much larger than in the United States but student performance is, on average, much better.[55] The greater individual attention that is possible in small classes may be less important in some countries, such as Japan, because students in that cultural setting have greater help, encouragement, and pressure from their parents than is generally true of American students.[56]

COSTS AND PROBLEMS OF SMALLER CLASSES

Reducing class size is expensive. Costs include paying for new teachers, additional support staff, and new buildings. Exact costs vary with such factors as the number of students in each class and the comprehensiveness of the program. In 1997–1998, the state of California spent $1.5 billion dollars on its program to reduce class sizes to 20, and this amount was supplemented by local district funds. Reducing class size to 18 in grades 1 to 3 throughout the country, as President Clinton proposed, would require hiring about 100,000 teachers at a cost of $5 to $6 billion dollars each year. Reducing class size to 15 would cost much more.[57]

Aside from its monetary cost, programs to reduce class size have presented other problems. In California, the greatly increased demand for teachers that its program created led to sharp declines in the average educational level, experience, and credentials of teachers. This decline in teacher qualifications was greatest in schools serving low-income and minority students. In addition, the demands for extra classroom space created by the program led to reductions in space for special education, child care, music and art programs, libraries, and computer labs.

Reviewing the effects of the California class size reduction (CSR) program, Brian Stecher and his colleagues assert: "CSR's negative effects are more dramatic than its modest gains."[58] A broader analysis of CSR programs concludes that the potential achievement gains stemming from reduced class size may be threatened by physically inferior classrooms and especially by less qualified teachers—problems that tend to be exacerbated by these same programs.[59]

Because of the high costs and difficulties associated with large-scale programs to reduce class size, some observers have suggested that class size reduction should be focused on students who are most academically at-risk, such as low-income and minority students. These students are most likely to benefit from the individual attention and orderly atmosphere that often occurs in smaller classes.

STUDENT BODY CHARACTERISTICS

Outcomes for students in a school may depend not only on the individual student's own background (particularly his family's socioeconomic status and his ethnicity) but also on the background characteristics of the student body as a whole. Whether the student body generally is composed of the children of affluent, well-educated parents or of low-income, poorly educated parents may affect the academic achievement and school career of individual students. Similarly, the racial and ethnic composition of the student body—whether it is predominantly white, or African-American, or Hispanic—may affect outcomes for individual students. The socioeconomic and ethnic characteristics of the overall student body may have such effects on individual students in a variety of ways—for example, by affecting the school's curriculum, order and discipline, teaching methods, and types of influence from peers.

In this section, I examine first the effects of the socioeconomic status of the student body, and then the effects of its ethnic composition. In doing so, I consider why these student body characteristics may be important.

SOCIOECONOMIC STATUS

In 1965, the United States government sponsored a massive study of elementary and high schools in the United States, primarily to find the reasons for disparity in school achievement between white students and black students. Data were gathered from more than 645,000 pupils in 4,000 public schools. The report of that study's findings, entitled *Equality of Educational Oportunity*,[60] indicated that most of the variation in achievement among students was related to differences among students *within* schools (especially to the family background of individual students), rather than to differences between schools. However, a fairly substantial proportion of variation in individual student achievement (e.g., about 22 percent for 9th-grade students) was accounted for by differences in the schools they attended. And what mattered most about the particular school that students attended were the characteristics of the student body. For example, when a student attended a school with peers who, on average, came from families that owned an encyclopedia and who themselves planned to go to college, that student did better academically, even controlling for his own family background and other personal characteristics. The characteristics of their fellow students had greater effects on the learning of those groups that generally performed most poorly—blacks, Mexican-Americans, Puerto Ricans, and Native Americans—than they did on the achievement of non-Hispanic white students or Asian students.

Later research has continued to show that the socioeconomic status of the student body of a school has an impact on the achievement of individual students. One large-scale study done in the 1980s used information from students and staff in about 500 high schools throughout the United States.[61] The researchers obtained data on the gains in achievement that students made from their sophomore to senior years in several English language skills, in math, and in science; they combined these data into an index of gain in achievement. They then related each individual student's gain in achievement to the average socioeconomic status of the student body at her school, based on average parental income, education, occupation, and home learning tools (e.g., encyclopedias and books). Holding constant the individual student's own family's socioeconomic status (as well as many other correlates of student achievement), the higher the average socioeconomic status of the student body at a school, the higher the achievement gains of the individual students. This "school peer effect" was statistically significant and its magnitude, although modest, was not trivial.

Additional later research also has found that, independent of their own family background, students tend to achieve better in schools whose student body is drawn mostly from affluent, better-educated families and achieve less well in schools whose students come from lower-status backgrounds.[62] Research has been consistent in finding that the social class of the student body of a school has a greater impact on the achievement of students from lower-achieving minority groups than it does on that of non-Hispanic white students.[63]

Why should the social class background of a student's schoolmates affect his academic achievement? First, the social class of a student body may affect what is taught and how it is taught in classes. When most students come from poor, low-education families, difficulties in learning are more common. Therefore, teachers tend to cover material at a slower pace and cover less material.[64] Also, high schools whose students mostly come from poor families generally offer fewer advanced courses than schools whose students come from a more affluent background.

The ways in which teachers conduct classes, and the orderliness of classes, also tend to vary in schools with students from different social class backgrounds. One study by Morton Deutsch and his colleagues[65] found that in schools whose students came from poor backgrounds, teachers spent only about half as much time actually teaching as did teachers in middle-class schools. Also, while dividing classes into ability groups appears generally to benefit student learning (see Chapter 3), this common practice does not appear to work well when classes have a high proportion of low achievers.[66] In such situations, the teacher is not able to give much individual attention to each low-achieving student.

In addition to differences in what is taught and how it is taught, higher-status schools and lower-status schools are apt to differ in the kinds of influences that students exert on each other. The higher the average socioeconomic status of the student body, the higher are the educational aspirations of the average student.[67] Thus, students in more affluent schools are apt to have more contacts with friends who are planning to go to college.[68] The result is that attending a school where the students generally come from a high socioeconomic status raises the educational aspirations of individual students, independent of their own family background.[69]

The influences of a student's peers go beyond their effect on her educational aspirations. Peers also exert pressures on students to conform to a variety of norms, including those concerning effort and success in school. In her review of research on peer cultures in schools, Barbara Bank notes that a large literature contrasts the positive educational orientation of middle-class groups with the negative orientation of those who come from working-class homes.[70] For example, working-class youths, especially boys, have been found to be more resentful of and rebellious against, school authority; middle-class youths are more likely to accept the educational system and to become involved in a competition for academic achievement. Such class-related differences in attitudes toward school tend to result either in pro-school norms (work hard, get good grades) or in anti-school norms (do as little as possible to get by). Each student's friends often exert pressure on him to conform to its norms in order to win acceptance by his peers.[71]

In sum, the social class of the student body appears to affect both the educational program of the school and peer influences on individual students. These effects, in combination, appear to explain the fact that the social class of the student body affects the achievement of individual students, apart from their own family background.

RACIAL AND ETHNIC COMPOSITION

Following the landmark decision by the U.S. Supreme Court in 1954 that racial segregation of schools by law is unconstitutional, much public attention has focused on how the racial composition of schools affects the academic achievement of black students and other racial and ethnic minorities. Efforts to increase racial mixing in the schools, which has often included busing of students, led to heated—sometimes violent—controversies. The subject of the racial and ethnic composition of the schools, especially the question of whether it is desirable to mandate the mixing of students of different races and ethnicities, continues to be debated. What is the relevant evidence?

The large-scale national study in the 1960s on "Equality of Educational Opportunity" (the EEO study)[72] found that achievement scores of black students generally rose as the proportion of whites in their classes increased. Those black students who entered desegregated schools in early grades had slightly higher average grades than those who entered desegregated schools in later grades. However, the racial composition of classes explained little (less than 2%) of the variations in test performance among black students.

To provide more evidence about the impact of racial mixing on student achievement and on other outcomes, dozens of additional studies have been carried out. Many of these studies were experiments, comparing those in desegregated settings to similar students in racially segregated settings.

This body of evidence indicates first that desegregation tended to have negative effects on the self-esteem of minority students. After reviewing a large number of studies, Nancy St. John concluded that "the effect of school desegregation on the general or academic self-concept of minority group members tends to be negative or mixed more often than positive."[73] W. G. Stephan also concluded that blacks in desegregated schools have lower self-esteem than those in segregated schools.[74] (Other reviewers find evidence on this matter inconsistent.[75]) The tendency of black self-esteem to become lower in predominantly white settings probably is due, at least in part, to the fact that their grades tend to be lower than those of white schoolmates.

With respect to the effects of desegregation on achievement, some reviewers see more consistent benefits than do others. All agree that the impact of desegregation varies; sometimes attending racially mixed classes is associated with higher achievement for minority students and sometimes it is not.[76] However, desegregation appears to have positive effects on achievement more often than not.

Richard Crain and Rita Mahard reviewed the relationship between deseg-regation and achievement test scores in 323 samples of students from 93 studies in 67 cities.[77] They found that gains for black students on standard-ized tests or equivalent measures outnumbered losses 173 to 98. Moreover, positive gains in achievement were more common and were larger in stud-ies that had the most rigorous research designs.[78] Attending racially-mixed classes appears generally to have the most positive effects when it occurs in early grades and in settings with a high proportion of whites.[79]

P. M. Wortman and F. B. Bryant reviewed the best (most methodological-ly sound) studies of desegregation and found that, on average, black stu-dents in desegregated settings appeared to be about two months ahead in achievement, compared to those in segregated settings.[80] However, this esti-mated achievement gain from desegregation still left black students, on average, considerably behind whites. Also, the gain from desegregated class-es appears to be small compared to other educational interventions, such as improved teaching methods.

There has been relatively little research on the effects of desegregation on Hispanic students. The information that is available shows a pattern sim-ilar to that for black students. The national EEO study found that Hispanics had higher achievement scores in schools with more white students.[81] A later national study of high school students found that attending mostly white schools was correlated with higher achievement for students of Mexican, Puerto Rican, or Cuban background.[82]

More rigorous studies of the effects of desegregation in specific areas have shown more mixed results. A study in Riverside, California, found that attending school with "Anglos" (non-Hispanic whites) did not improve the achievement of Hispanic children in grade school.[83] Another study of Hispanic children who were desegregated in the third grade found that they initially had lower test scores than Hispanics in segregated schools; however, by the eighth grade they were about one year ahead of the segregated group.[84] The school situation for Hispanic children is complicated by the fact that many of them do not speak fluent English. (Bilingual education is discussed in Chapter 4.)

Why does attending school with white classmates sometimes appear to have a positive effect, even if a modest one, on the achievement of minority students? Part of the answer appears to stem from the fact that white schoolmates generally come from higher social class backgrounds than do black schoolmates. As we have seen, students tend to achieve at a higher level when most of their schoolmates come from middle-class families. The national EEO study found that, when the average family educational background and aspirations of the student body were held constant, the apparent effect of school racial composition on student achievement largely disappeared.[85]

Some scholars have emphasized the positive influences that white schoolmates may exert on their black peers. They suggest that middle-class white students generally have positive attitudes toward learning and good study habits and that they can influence black classmates in these directions. Such helpful influences from white peers might be expected to occur especially when minority students are socially accepted by the whites.

However, some research has failed to find evidence that improved school performance by minority students is due to the influence of white schoolmates. For example, a study in Indianapolis found that the achievement of black high school students was *not* related to the characteristics of white peers (the education of the whites' parents or white peers' own academic values), to friendship with white peers, or to the combination of these factors. The effort and grades of black students were related more strongly to the academic values of their *black* peers than to those of their white peers.[86]

While the presence of many middle-class white schoolmates may not directly affect blacks, their presence may affect the types of demands that administrators and teachers make of students. As the proportion of whites in Indianapolis high school classes rose, the strictness of discipline increased. Also, as the proportion of whites in classes rose, the amount of work (especially homework) done by both black and white students generally rose. These results suggest that teacher expectations and academic standards tend to be higher in mostly white than in mostly black classes. Thus, black (and other minority) students may benefit somewhat from being in mostly white classes not so much because of contact with middle-class peers but, rather, because of the more rigorous education provided in such classes.

Whatever its possible advantages, greater racial mixing in the schools has been and continues to be hard to arrange. In fact, despite efforts of the courts, governments, and school boards, segregation of blacks in schools has not decreased since the 1970s and segregation of Hispanics has increased since that time.[87] However, even where changing the racial or ethnic composition of schools is not possible, improving the achievement of minority students still may be accomplished. The quality of the school program (especially the curriculum) and the standards and expectations of administrators and teachers appear to have a greater impact on achievement than does the racial or ethnic composition of the school. There are many examples of predominantly minority schools in which a high level of learning takes place.[88] (The general gap in achievement between white students and minority students is discussed further in Chapter 9.)

SCHOOL SPENDING

Poor academic performance by students often is attributed to lack of money and resulting scanty resources in the schools they attend. Poor facilities, crowded buildings and classes, low-paid teachers, and other deficits related to limited budgets, have been seen as leading to inadequate learning. But skeptics have questioned whether increased spending really produces better schools. What is the evidence concerning the impact of school spending on student achievement?

Several summary analyses of the relevant research present somewhat different overall results, depending on the criteria that different researchers use for including studies and on other differences in the reviewers' methodologies.[89] However, the reviewers are consistent in finding that: (1) higher spending on schools tends to be associated with higher student achievement, even after taking into account students' backgrounds; (2) only a minority of studies—although a substantial minority—have found a marked, statistically significant positive relationship between school spending and measures of student achievement.

A review by Rob Greenwald, Larry Hedges, and Richard Laine is especially rigorous in selecting high-quality studies concerning this relationship.[90] They included only studies that controlled for students' socioeconomic characteristics, had data at several points in time, and aggregated data at the level of school districts or smaller units. Of 34 studies included in their review, 73 percent found a positive relationship and 27 percent found a negative relationship between per-pupil expenditures and student achievement. A significant positive association between expenditures and achievement was found in 44 percent of the studies, while a significant negative association was found in only 3 percent of the studies. Greenwald and his associates estimate that the median effect of increasing per-pupil expenditures by $500 is an increase in achievement measures of one-sixth of a standard deviation—a modest but not insignificant improvement.

They conclude: "The general conclusion of the meta-analysis presented in this article is that student resources are systematically related to student achievement and that these relationships are large enough to be educationally important."[91] Another reviewer of relevant research, Eric Hanushek, believes that the work of Greenwald and his colleagues has exaggerated the association between school expenditures and student achievement.[92] However, he agrees that there does tend to be a positive relationship.

Findings regarding the association between spending and student performance vary widely when different levels of school organization are studied. Studies that examine variations in spending by individual schools or districts *within* individual states do not find consistent evidence that higher spending results in higher student achievement. But studies that include variations in spending *across* states generally do find that more school spending is associated with better student performance.[93]

The reasons for the different pattern of results in within-state studies versus across-state studies is not clear. The difference in results may be due to the fact that spending varies more across state lines than within states. It may be also that other differences across states that are associated with spending differences—for example, in curriculum and in ethnic composition—are responsible for some of the between-state differences in achievement.

Another perspective on the relationship between school spending and student achievement is obtained by examining changes in school spending over time. Public school spending, per pupil, in the United States has risen dramatically in recent times.[94] A graph of this spending (in constant dollars) shows per-pupil expenditures of $1,388 in 1951–1952, rising sharply and steadily to $6,584 in 1999–2000, an overall increase of 474 percent (see Figure 6-2).

These data overstate the increases in money actually available for providing education for most students. First, while comparisons of spending are adjusted for the overall level of inflation, it is likely that educational costs, including teachers' salaries, have risen faster than the general price level. Second, much of the increase in educational spending in recent decades has been targeted for special student groups, such as those in special education and bilingual education programs, and for supplementary services (food services, transportation, etc.). Still, even after adjustments have been made for increases in special and noninstructional purposes, increases in spending for the instruction of mainstream students have been substantial.[95]

While school spending has steadily increased over recent decades, the scores of American students on tests of their learning have shown little change. About every two years The National Assessment of Educational Progress tests representative national samples of students aged 9, 13, and 17 in a number of subjects, including mathematics, science, reading, and writing. Results of these national tests have shown little overall change over

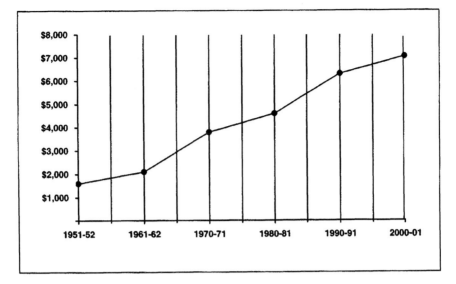

Figure 6-2 Expenditure per pupil in public elementary and secondary schools in the United States, in constant 2000–2001 dollars. *Source:* National Center for Education Statistics.

time. For example, after reviewing results from the previous 20 years, the Educational Testing Service concluded in 1990: "There have been various declines and improvements from assessment to assessment, but over the long term, achievement levels are quite stable." More recent results from these national tests continue to show little, if any, overall improvement.[96]

Of course, there are many factors, in addition to spending, that may affect student learning. But it seems evident that even substantial increases in national spending on schools do not necessarily lead to higher student achievement.

TYPES OF SPENDING

The effect of money spent on the schools depends on the uses to which the money is spent. Among the ways in which schools may spend money are: hiring more teachers; paying teachers higher salaries; getting (and developing) more highly qualified teachers; building better facilities; and upgrading instructional materials.

Hiring More Teachers

Much of new school spending in recent decades has been targeted at hiring more teachers in order to reduce class size. Between 1969 and 1997, the average pupil–teacher ratio in all American schools declined from almost

23:1 to less than 17:1, or 26 percent.[97] We have seen that smaller classes sometimes improve student learning but that positive effects of small classes are inconsistent and, when they occur, are generally modest. Small classes appear to be most helpful for raising the achievement of poor and minority students. (See the section "Class Size" earlier in this chapter.)

Paying Teachers More

Teachers' salaries usually are the biggest category of school expenditures and schools that spend more money overall generally pay their teachers more than other schools do.[98] Does such spending result in better outcomes for students?

Several reviews of studies on this subject find that higher teacher salaries sometimes are associated with higher achievement for students. But a significant relationship is not found in most studies.[99] For example, one reviewer considered 119 studies in which the relationship between teacher salary and student performance is reported. Only 20 percent of the studies found that higher teacher salaries predicted significantly higher student performance. In 7 percent of these studies, higher teacher salaries were associated with significantly *lower* student performance.[100] A recent detailed study of school spending and achievement in over 2,800 elementary schools in Texas found that, with other determinants of achievement controlled, spending on teacher salaries did not have a significant effect on student achievement in either reading or math.[101] Thus, while higher teacher salaries may be desirable for other reasons (such as raising teacher morale and reducing teacher turnover), they do not appear to have much direct effect on student learning.

Teacher Qualifications

Support for raising teachers' salaries often is based on the belief that higher salaries will attract better qualified teachers—teachers who are better educated, are more able, and have more experience. Do such teacher characteristics result in more student learning?

Teachers' Education

The amount of education that teachers have—for example, whether they have a master's degree—does not generally seem to affect students' achievement.[102] One reviewer examined 40 studies that related teachers' characteristics to improvements in students' academic performance from a previous time (thus controlling for family background and students' abilities). None of these 40 studies reported a significant relationship between the amount of teacher education and student achievement.[103] However, there is some evidence from other studies that when teachers of math and of science are better educated in their subjects, their students achieve at a higher level.[104] Extensive knowledge of their subject matter may be more important for teachers in technical or highly specialized subjects, such as math and science, than in other subjects, especially at the high school level.

Teachers' Abilities

The general knowledge and ability of teachers, as shown in tests taken by teachers, often show a positive association with student achievement. For example, one large study of Texas schools found that the strongest determinant of student test scores was their teachers' performance on a statewide recertification exam.[105] While not all studies show such a relationship,[106] one review of research found teacher ability to "have the strongest relation with student achievement of any of the [school] resource variables. . . ."[107] Teachers' verbal abilities are prominent among the abilities that relate to student achievement.

Teacher Experience

Having more experienced teachers also often contributes to student learning. Of 61 studies examined in one review of relevant research, 22 studies (36%) found that more teacher experience was related to significantly higher student performance; only one study found a significant relation in the opposite direction.[108] Other reviewers concur that students often learn more when their teachers are more experienced.[109]

Teacher Qualifications and Salaries

The evidence just outlined indicates that highly qualified teachers, especially those who have high general ability and are experienced, often contribute to greater learning for students. It is generally believed that, in order to attract and keep highly qualified teachers, it is necessary to pay good salaries. However, as we have seen, there is little evidence that higher teacher salaries generally lead to increased student achievement. How can we explain these seemingly inconsistent sets of results?

Paying higher salaries to teachers may not necessarily lead to having more able, more experienced teachers. Salary increases may be based in part on how many years of education (or how many degrees) teachers have, which, as we have seen, is generally not related much to student achievement. Increases may go equally to teachers who have the most knowledge and ability and those who have the least. More years of experience may bring only modest increases in salary. Moreover, features of their jobs other than salary—student engagement, student discipline, teachers' roles in decision making, faculty collegiality, and so on—may be equally important or more important than salary in attracting and keeping highly qualified teachers.

Salary cannot be ignored as an important factor in attracting and keeping good teachers. But salary incentives have to be used most effectively— for example, to attract teachers with high ability (not necessarily those with the most education) and to keep the most able and experienced teachers. Salary also has to be seen as only one type of incentive for getting and retaining the best teachers.

School Facilities

The national EEO study in the 1960s found that school facilities, such as laboratories and libraries, generally had little effect on students' achievement scores.[110] Similarly, a much more recent national study found that capital spending per pupil by school districts (that is, spending on buildings and other facilities) had no significant relation to academic achievement.[111] Apparently, good education does not depend on the amount of bricks and mortar that a school has.

Instructional Materials and Equipment

More spending for instructional materials, books, and equipment does generally contribute to higher student achievement. One review found that, in 12 of 18 studies examined, higher spending by schools on instructional materials and supplies and the library was significantly related to higher student achievement.[112] A national study found that, after controlling for other factors affecting science achievement, the achievement of high school students in science rose as more science equipment in good condition was available in classes.[113]

Other Types of Spending

Evidence concerning the effects of other types of school spending comes from the Texas study of elementary schools in that state.[114] The researchers found that, while higher teacher salaries did not generally improve student achievement, spending more on career ladder supplements for teachers did raise achievement. More spending on salaries for substitute teachers and for support personnel, such as teachers' aides, was associated with lower student achievement, especially in high-poverty schools. Apparently targeting spending to promote highly skilled teaching contributes to higher student achievement, while targeting spending on less skilled personnel lowers achievement.

The study of Texas elementary schools also found that, with other determinants of achievement controlled, more spending on the upkeep of the school raised student achievement, both in low-poverty and high-poverty schools. Why better-maintained schools should raise student achievement is an interesting question. Good upkeep may reflect a general school atmosphere of high standards and high concern for students.

Reallocating Spending

Some schools have changed the ways in which they spend available funds. A recent study looked at spending changes in three elementary schools and two high schools in low-income urban districts across the country.[115] These schools reallocated their spending in a variety of ways, including increasing the number of regular classroom teachers, reducing the number of "specialist" teachers and administrative positions, varying class sizes for different subjects, and increasing professional development for teachers. After the changes in spending patterns and other school changes, these schools had improved attendance and graduation rates and higher student achievement. Other schools also have modified usual patterns of school spending and reported improved student performance.[116]

Overall, the evidence reviewed in this section indicates that spending priorities should focus on improving the quality of classroom instruction, especially on recruiting and keeping able, experienced teachers (which may require more than monetary incentives); providing effective professional development programs; and providing teachers and students with ample instructional material and equipment.

OVERVIEW OF EFFECTS OF SCHOOL CHARACTERISTICS

Figure 6-3 provides a graphic overview of this chapter's discussion of how school characteristics affect teachers and students. The figure shows, first, that certain basic school characteristics affect the organization of the school. For example, schools that are smaller are apt to have more shared decision making and more collegiality among their staff; higher school spending may be used to provide career ladders and mentoring programs for faculty.

School characteristics also affect interactions among faculty and students. For example, more contacts and closer bonds tend to occur among faculty and between faculty and students as schools and as classes become smaller; more spending may be used to provide extra time for teachers to attend planning meetings with other teachers.

Figure 6-3 also shows that school characteristics may have direct effects on the academic program of the school and on the motivation, norms, and skills of both teachers and students. For example, the academic program of

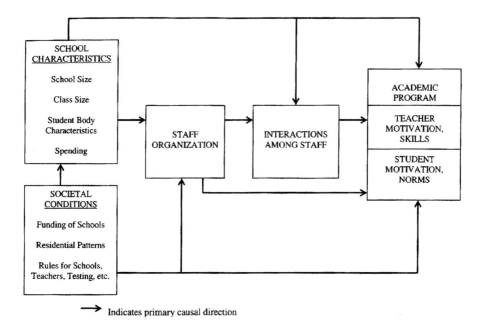

Figure 6-3 Some effects of, and influences on, school characteristics.

the school is likely to include a limited number of courses in small schools and to include more advanced placement courses in schools that serve students from high-income families; teacher norms of responsibility for student learning tend to be stronger in small schools, and their teaching skills are likely to be stronger when schools spend more on mentoring programs; students' academic motivation tends to be higher in small schools and in schools whose student bodies come from middle-class backgrounds.

Figure 6-3 shows that school characteristics also affect a school's programs and its teachers and students in indirect ways, through its effects on school organization and on staff and student interactions. The ways in which school organization, teacher interactions, and student interactions affect school outcomes are discussed in previous chapters.

Finally, Figure 6-3 shows that various conditions and regulations of the larger society affect schools in a number of ways. First, societal circumstances have direct impacts on schools' academic programs and on their teachers and students. For example, state regulations may require that high schools include a certain number of years of mathematics in their academic programs; rules for teacher certification may help determine the level and types of teacher skills; and a state mandate that students pass a competency exam in order to graduate from high school may affect students' motivation to learn certain material.

In addition, aspects of the larger society affect the characteristics of schools. Thus, for example, the overall level of school funding determines the spending of each school, residential patterns affect the composition of each individual school's student body, and government rules affect student body composition and class size. Variations in state and district laws concerning creation of charter schools and use of public vouchers for private schools affect a number of school characteristics, including the size of schools and the composition of their student bodies. These public policies and others that give parents a choice among schools are discussed in Chapter 8.

SUMMARY AND CONCLUSIONS

In this chapter, we have looked at some of the basic conditions under which a school operates—its overall size, the size of its classes, the social background of its student body, and its spending—as these conditions may be related to outcomes (especially academic achievement) for its students.

Large schools have a greater variety of courses and activities, have more specialized curricula, and offer more specialized services than do small schools. However, as schools become bigger, the relationships between administrators and teachers, among teachers, and between students and teachers, tend to become more formal and more impersonal; also, teachers participate less in school decision making and take less collective responsibility for students at the school. Students in large schools generally participate less in school activities and have less engagement in their schoolwork than do those in smaller schools.

The relationship between the size of high schools and student achievement is curvilinear (holding constant other factors related to achievement). Students in large high schools, and especially those in the largest schools, make much smaller gains in reading and math than those in medium-sized schools. Students in small high schools, especially the smallest schools, also score considerably below those in medium-sized schools. The advantage of attending medium-sized high schools appears to be greatest in schools with student bodies drawn primarily from low socioeconomic backgrounds.

The relation of school size to student learning in elementary schools—at least as shown in one large study—appears to be somewhat different than is true at the high school level. Elementary students in the smallest schools score considerably higher in math achievement than students attending either medium-sized or relatively large schools.

Overall, the evidence suggests that schools promote student learning best when they are neither very large nor very small. They should be large enough to provide sufficient facilities, courses, and services to their students but small enough to involve both faculty and students actively in the life of the school. The optimal size for elementary schools appears to be smaller than for high schools, probably because fewer specialized courses and activities are needed in elementary schools. Large schools can promote more intimate relationships and more active participation among faculty and students by dividing into subunits, such as semi-autonomous "schools within schools."

The size of *classes*, more than the size of schools, has received great attention in recent years and there have been widespread efforts to reduce class size. Although smaller classes are widely assumed to result in more student learning, the overall evidence in support of this expectation is weak. Smaller classes sometimes are associated with higher student achievement, but the connections are inconsistent and, when positive effects of small class size are found, these effects generally are modest.

As classes become smaller, teachers do tend to spend more time on instruction and less time on class management and discipline. However, teachers often do not adapt their teaching methods (e.g., time spent lecturing) appreciably to take full advantage of reduced class size.

Students from disadvantaged backgrounds and minority students seem to gain most from being in small classes. Students from these backgrounds may be especially likely to benefit from the greater proportion of time given to instruction and from the more individual attention that is possible in these settings.

Benefits of smaller classes are most likely to occur when there are fewer than 20 students—perhaps about 15—in a class. Both small schools and small classes may benefit student achievement, independently of each other.

Reducing the size of classes is costly, because it requires hiring more teachers and providing more classrooms. Programs to reduce class size may lead to a reduction in the quality of teachers (their preparation and experience) and to the crowding out of other useful school facilities (music rooms, libraries, labs, etc.).

Given the generally small and inconsistent impact of reduced class size on student achievement and the high costs of programs to reduce class size, it seems wise to be cautious in pushing sweeping programs of this type. Since smaller classes seem to benefit poor and minority students most, efforts to reduce class size might best be focused on these groups of students.

Another salient characteristic of a school is the composition of its student body, especially in terms of its social class and ethnic composition. Going to school with peers who come from families of relatively high social class (in terms of education, occupation, and income) raises the academic achievement of individual students, independent of their own family status. This positive effect is especially marked for minority students.

Having schoolmates from middle-class (or above) families appears to promote students' achievement in several ways. Schools with a predominantly middle-class student body tend to have a richer curriculum, and teachers in such settings spend more time on instruction and less on maintaining order. In addition, in a mostly middle-class school, students are more likely to have friends who plan to go to college (raising their own aspirations) and peers are more likely to encourage them to do well in school.

A racially mixed student body tends to raise the achievement of minority students. But this positive effect of racial diversity is inconsistent and, when it occurs, generally is quite small. The main reason why black students sometimes benefit from attending school together with whites does not appear to be that they are influenced in positive ways by their white peers. Rather, when classes are mostly white (and thus mainly middle class as well), discipline and standards imposed by teachers appear to be higher than when classes are mostly black (particularly when students are mostly black and also lower class).

Overall, evidence regarding the effects of student body characteristics on student learning suggests that, where possible, school systems should avoid concentrating low-SES students or minority students (especially when minority students are from poor backgrounds) in the same schools. However, given the concentration of socioeconomic and racial and ethnic groups in certain areas, it often is very difficult, if not impossible, to create schools that are ethnically mixed and/or have mostly middle-class students. But it is possible to maintain a good curriculum, effective discipline, and high standards in every school. Without a doubt, it is more difficult to do this in a school that has a high proportion of students from disadvantaged backgrounds. But there are many examples of such schools that, despite this handicap, have maintained high expectations and high standards for their students and have succeeded in having their students achieve well.

Differences in the amount of money spent on different schools have often been said to explain differences in student performance. Higher spending does tend to be associated with higher student achievement but the relationship is inconsistent—that is, higher spending often is associated with greater student learning but often it is not.

When the various *types* of school expenditures are related to student performance, we see that spending on physical facilities and on teacher salaries has little relation to student achievement. Having more teachers to create smaller classes tends to increase student achievement but this effect generally is small and inconsistent. Having teachers with high general ability, who have extensive knowledge when teaching technical subjects and who are experienced, appears to contribute most to student learning.

Overall, the evidence suggests that most schools should focus their spending priorities on improving the quality of classroom instruction, especially on recruiting and keeping able, experienced teachers (for which purpose salary incentives play some, but not the only, role); providing effective professional development; and giving teachers and students the instructional materials and equipment they need. Spending to reduce class size seems most useful where a high proportion of the students are from disadvantaged and minority families.

An overview of the school characteristics discussed in this chapter (size of the school and classes; student body composition, and spending) shows that they affect teachers and students directly and also indirectly through their impact on the organization of the school and on interactions of the people in it.

NOTES

1. National Association of Secondary School Principals, *Breaking Ranks: Changing an American Institution*. Reston, VA: Author, 1996.
2. V. Lee, School Size and the Organization of Secondary Schools. In M. Hallinan, *Handbook of the Sociology of Education*. New York: Kluwer, 2000, pp. 327–344.
3. J. Buzacott, *Scale in Production Systems*. New York: Pergamon, 1982.
4. W. Fox, Reviewing Economics of Size in Education. *Journal of Education Finance, 6,* 1981, 273–296.
5. D. Monk and E. Haller, Predictors of High School Academic Course Offerings: The Role of School Size. *American Educational Research Journal, 30,* 1993, 3–21.
6. V. Lee and A. Bryk, A Multilevel Model of the Social Distribution of High School Achievement. *Sociology of Education, 62,* 1989, 172–192.
7. V. Lee and A. Bryk, Curriculum Tracking as Mediating the Social Distribution of High School Achievement. *Sociology of Education, 61,* 1988, 78–94.
8. Lee, School Size and the Organization of Secondary Schools, p. 338.
9. See, for example, C. Anderson, The Search for School Climate: A Review of the Research. *Review of Educational Research, 52,* 1982, 368–420; W. Fowler and H. Walberg, School Size, Characteristics and Outcomes. *Educational Evaluation and Policy Analysis, 13,* 1991, 189–202.
10. D. Meier, *The Power of Their Ideas: Lessons for America from a Small School in Harlem*. Boston: Beacon Press, 1995, p. 108.
11. Meier, Ibid, p. 109.
12. V. Lee and S. Loeb, School Size in Chicago Elementary Schools: Effects on Teachers' Attitudes and Students' Achievement. *American Educational Research Journal, 37,* 2000, 3–31.
13. V. Lee and J. Smith, Collective Responsibility for Learning and Its Effects on Gains in Achievement for Early Secondary School Students. *American Journal of Education, 104,* 1996, 103–147.
14. V. Lee, B. Smerdon, C. Alfeld-Liro, and S. Brown, Inside Large and Small High Schools: Curriculum and Social Relations. Paper presented at Annual Meeting of American Sociological Association, New York, NY, August 1996.
15. Meier, *Power of Their Ideas*, p. 113.
16. J. Griffith, An Empirical Examination of a Model of Social Climate in Elementary Schools. *Basic and Applied Social Psychology, 17,* 1995, 97–117.
17. See, for example, R. Barker and R. Gump, *Big School, Small School: High School Size and Student Behavior*. Stanford, CA: Stanford University Press, 1964.
18. V. Lee and J. Smith, The Effects of High School Restructuring and Size on Gains in Achievement and Engagement for Early Secondary School Students. *Sociology of Education, 68,* 1995, 271–290.

19. V. Lee and J. Smith, High School Size: Which Works Best and for Whom? *Educational Evaluation and Policy Analysis, 19,* 1997, 205–227.

20. V. Lee, Using Hierarchical Linear Modeling to Study Social Contexts: The Case of School Effects. *Educational Psychologist, 35,* 2000, 125–141.

21. Lee and Loeb, School Size in Chicago Elementary Schools; V. Lee, Using Hierarchical Linear Modeling to Study Social Contexts.

22. Lee, et al., Inside Large and Small High Schools.

23. See, for example, Meier, *The Power of Their Ideas,* Chapter 6; C. Glickman, *Revolutionizing America's Schools.* San Francisco: Jossey-Bass, 1998, pp. 40–43.

24. Meier, *The Power of Their Ideas,* Chapter 6.

25. L. Schorr, *Common Purpose.* New York: Doubleday, 1997, Chapter 8.

26. D. Muncie and P. McQuillan, School-Within-a-School Restructuring and Faculty Divisiveness. Report Number 6, School Ethnography Project. Providence, RI: Annenberg Institute for School Reform, Brown University, 1991.

27. K. Nye, The Effect of School Size and the Interaction of School Size and Class Type on Selected Student Achievement Measures in Tennessee Elementary Schools. Ph.D. Dissertation, University of Tennessee, Knoxville, 1995.

28. Lee, School Size and the Organization of Secondary Schools.

29. E. Hanushek, Some Findings from an Independent Investigation of the Tennessee STAR Experiment and from Other Investigations of Class Size Effects. *Educational Evaluation and Policy Analysis, 21,* 1999, 143–163.

30. Hanushek, Ibid, p. 148

31. A. Krueger and D. Whitmore, Would Smaller Classes Help Close the Black-White Achievement Gap? Princeton, NJ: Industrial Relations Section, Princeton University, March 2001.

32. R. Slavin, Class Size and Student Achievement: Small Effects of Small Classes. *Educational Psychologist, 24,* 1989, 99–110.

33. Slavin, Ibid., p. 107.

34. J. Finn and C. Achilles, Tennessee's Class Size Study: Findings, Implications, Misconceptions. *Educational Evaluation and Policy Analysis, 21,* 1999, 97–109.

35. Krueger and Whitmore, in Would Smaller Classes Help . . .?, state that when the college entrance test scores of students who had earlier been in small classes are adjusted for the greater proportion of such students who take these tests, their average score is above that of other students.

36. A. Molnar, *Vouchers, Class Size Reduction, and Student Achievement.* Bloomington, IN: Phi Delta Kappa Educational Foundation, 2000; J. Finn, *Class Size and Students at Risk: What Is Known?* Office of Educational Research and Improvement, U.S. Department of Education, 1998; D. Grissmer, Class Size Effects: Assessing the Evidence, Its Policy Implications, and Future Research Agenda. *Educational Evaluation and Policy Analysis, 21,* 1999, 231–248.

37. D. Gilman and C. Tillitski, The Longitudinal Effects of Smaller Classes: Four Studies. ERIC Document Reproduction Service No. ED 326313, 1990.

38. Molnar, *Vouchers, Class Size Reduction, and Student Achievement,* p. 40.

39. A. Molnar, et al., Evaluating the SAGE Program: A Pilot Program in Targeted Pupil-Teacher Reduction in Wisconsin. *Educational Evaluation and Policy Analysis, 21,* 1999, 165–177.

40. Finn, *Class Size and Students at Risk,* p. 12.

41. Finn, Ibid.; Grissmer, Class Size Effects; Molnar, *Vouchers, Class Size Reduction, and Student Achievement*; J. Betts and J. Shkolnik, The Behavioral Effects of Variations in Class Size: The Case of Math Teachers. *Educational Evaluation and Policy Analysis, 21*, 1999, 193–213; J. Rice, The Impact of Class Size on Instructional Strategies and the Use of Time in High School Mathematics and Science Courses. *Educational Evaluation and Policy Analysis, 21*, 1999, 215–229.

42. Betts and Shkolnik, Behavioral Effects of Variations in Class Size.

43. Slavin, Class Size and Student Achievement, p. 106.

44. Betts and Shkolnik, Behavioral Effects of Variations in Class Size, p. 209.

45. G. Robinson, Synthesis of Research on Effects of Class Size. *Educational Leadership, 47*, 1990, 80–90, p. 85.

46. Grissmer, Class Size Effects.

47. Finn, *Class Size and Students at Risk*, p. 15.

48. K. Nye, The Effect of School Size and the Interaction of School Size and Class Type.

49. G. Glass and M. Smith, Meta-Analysis of Research on Class Size and Achievement. *Educational Evaluation and Policy Analysis, 1*, 1979, 2–16.

50. Slavin, Class Size and Student Achievement.

51. Rice, Impact of Class Size; Betts and Shkolnik, Behavioral Effects of Variations in Class Size.

52. Hanushek, Some Findings from an Independent Investigation, p. 157.

53. S. Rivkin, G. Hanushek, and J. Kain, Teachers, Schools, and Academic Achievement (Working paper 6691). Cambridge, MA: National Bureau of Economic Research, 1998.

54. U.S. Department of Education, National Center for Education Statistics, *Digest of Education Statistics*, 2000. Washington, DC: 2001.

55. Hanushek, Some Findings from an Independent Investigation.

56. See H. Stevenson and J. Stigler, *The Learning Gap*. New York: Summit Books, 1992.

57. See Grissmer, Class Size Effects; B. Stecher, G. Bohrnstedt, M. Kirst, J. McRobbie, and T. Williams, Class Size Reduction in California. *Kappan, 82*, 2001, 670–674.

58. Stecher, et al., p. 673.

59. D. Brewer, C. Krop, B. Gill, and R. Reichardt, Estimating the Cost of National Class Size Reductions Under Different Policy Alternatives. *Educational Evaluation and Policy Analysis, 21*, 1999, 179–192.

60. J. Coleman, E. Campbell, C. Hobson, J. McPartland, A. Mood, F. Weinfeld, and R. York, *Equality of Educational Opportunity*. Washington, DC: U.S. Government Printing Office, 1966.

61. J. Chubb and T. Moe, *Politics, Markets, and America's Schools*. Washington, DC: Brookings Institution Press, 1990.

62. L. Mussoline and R. Shouse, School Restructuring as a Policy Agenda. *Sociology of Education, 74*, 2001, 44–58; M. Kennedy, R. Jung, and M. Orland, *Poverty, Achievement, and the Distribution of Compensatory Education Services*. Washington, DC: U.S. Department of Education, 1986.

63. E. Campbell and C. Alexander, Structural Effects and Interpersonal Relationships. *American Journal of Sociology, 71*, 1965, 284–289.

64. M. Adams, *Beginning to Read: Thinking and Learning About Print*. Urbana: Center for the Study of Reading, University of Illinois, 1990.

65. M. Deutsch, *Communication of Information in the Elementary Classroom.* New York: Institute for Developmental Studies, 1964.

66. R. Dreeben and R. Barr, Classroom Composition and the Design of Instruction. *Sociology of Education, 61,* 1988, 129–142.

67. Coleman, et al., *Equality of Educational Opportunity.*

68. D. Alwin and L. Otto, High School Context Effects on Aspirations. *Sociology of Education, 50,* 1977, 259–273; V. Lee and A. Bryk, A Multilevel Model of the Social Distribution of High School Achievement.

69. R. Boyle, The Effects of the High School on Students' Aspirations. *American Journal of Sociology, 71,* 1966, 628–639.

70. B. Bank, Peer Cultures and Their Challenge for Teaching. In B. Biddle, et al., (eds.), *International Handbook of Teachers and Teaching.* Boston: Kluwer, 1997, pp. 879–937, p. 890.

71. Bank, Ibid.; J. Coleman, *The Adolescent Society.* Glencoe, IL: Free Press, 1961.

72. Coleman, et al., *Equality of Educational Opportunity.*

73. N. St. John, *School Desegregation: Outcomes for Children.* New York: Wiley, 1975, p. 54.

74. W. Stephan, School Desegregation: An Evaluation of Predictions Made in Brown vs. Board of Education. *Psychological Bulletin, 85,* 1978, 217–238.

75. P. Zirkel, Self-Concept and the Disadvantage of Ethnic Group Membership and Mixture. *Review of Educational Research, 41,* 1971, 211–225; M. Weinberg, *Minority Students: A Research Appraisal.* Washington, DC: National Institute of Education, 1977.

76. St. John, School Desegregation; Weinberg, *Minority Students;* L. Bradley and G. Bradley, The Academic Achievement of Blacks in Desegregated Schools. *Review of Educational Research, 47,* 1977, 399–499.

77. R. Crain and R. Mahard, The Effect of Research Methodology on Desegregation-Achievement Studies: A Meta-Analysis. *American Journal of Sociology, 88,* 1983, 839–854.

78. Crain and Mahard, Ibid.; Coleman, et al., *Equality of Educational Opportunity.*

79. P. Wortman and F. Bryant, School Desegregation and Black Achievement: An Integrative Review. *Sociological Methods and Research, 13,* 1985, 298–324.

80. Wortman and Bryant, Ibid.

81. Coleman, et al., *Equality of Educational Opportunity.*

82. R. Mahard and R. Crain, The Influence of High School Racial Composition on the Academic Achievement and College Attendance of Hispanics. Paper presented at annual meeting of the American Sociological Association, New York, 1980.

83. H. Gerard and N. Miller, *School Desegregation: A Long-Range Study.* New York: Plenum, 1975.

84. G. Morrison, Jr., An Analysis of Academic Achievement Trends for Anglo-American, Mexican-American and Negro-American Students in a Desegregated School Environment. Ph.D. Dissertation, University of Houston, 1972.

85. Coleman, et al., *Equality of Educational Opportunity,* p. 307.

86. M. Patchen, *Black-White Contact in Schools: Its Social and Academic Effects.* West Lafayette, IN: Purdue University Press, 1982.

87. J. Farley, *Majority-Minority Relations,* 4th edition. Upper Saddle River, NJ: Prentice Hall, 2000, Chapter 12.

88. See, for example, U.S. Department of Education, *Hope for Urban Education.* Washington, DC, 1999.

89. See D. Verstegen and R. King, The Relationship Between School Spending and Student Achievement. *Journal of Education Finance, 24,* 1998, 243–262.

90. R. Greenwald, L. Hedges, and R. Laine, The Effect of School Resources on School Achievement. *Review of Educational Research, 66,* 1996, 361–396.

91. Greenwald, et al., Ibid., p. 384.

92. E. Hanushek, A More Complete Picture of School Resource Policies. *Review of Educational Research, 66,* 1996, 397–409.

93. E. Hanushek, Assessing the Effects of School Resources on Student Performance: An Update. *Educational Evaluation and Policy Analysis, 19,* 1997, 141–164.

94. U.S. Department of Education, National Center for Education Statistics. *Digest of Education Statistics,* 2000, Table 170.

95. R. Rothstein, Why Spending Doesn't Improve Test Scores. *Principal, 81,* 2001, 62–63; S. Ceci, P. Papierno, and K. Mueller-Johnson, The Twisted Relationship Between School Spending and Academic Outputs. *Journal of School Psychology, 40,* 2002, 477–484.

96. R. Ehrenberg, D. Brewer, A. Gamoran, and J. Willms, Class Size and Student Achievement. *Psychological Science in the Public Interest, 2,* 2001, 1–30.

97. Ehrenberg, et al., Ibid.

98. Verstegen and King, The Relationship Between School Spending and Student Achievement; M. Elliott, School Finance and Opportunities to Learn. *Sociology of Education, 71,* 1998, 223–245.

99. Verstegen and King, Ibid.

100. Hanushek, Assessing the Effects of School Resources.

101. Elliott, School Finance and Opportunities to Learn.

102. Verstegen and King, The Relationship Between School Spending and Student Achievement.

103. Hanushek, Assessing the Effects of School Resources.

104. D. Monk, Subject Area Preparation of Secondary Mathematics and Science Teachers and Student Achievement. *Economics of Education Review, 13,* 1994, 125–145; A. Wayne and P. Youngs, Teacher Characteristics and Student Achievement Gains. *Review of Educational Research, 73,* 2003, 89–122; Elliott, School Finance and Opportunities to Learn.

105. R. Ferguson, Paying for Public Education: New Evidence on How and Why Money Matters. *Harvard Journal on Legislation,* 28, 1991, 465–498.

106. Hanushek, Assessing the Effects of School Resources.

107. R. Laine, R. Greenwald, and L. Hedges, The Use of Global Education Indicators. Paper presented at Annual Meeting of American Educational Research Association, New Orleans, April 1994; See also Wayne and Youngs, Teacher Characteristics.

108. Hanushek, Assessing the Effects of School Resources.

109. Verstegen and King, The Relationship Between School Spending and Student Achievement.

110. D. Coleman, et al., Equality of Economic Opportunity.

111. H. Wenglinsky, *When Money Matters: How Educational Expenditures Improve Student Performance and How They Don't.* Princeton, NJ: Educational Testing Service, 1997.

112. B. McPhail-Wilcox and R. King, Production Functions Revisited in the Context of Educational Reform. *Journal of Education Finance, 12,* 1986, 191–222.
113. Elliott, School Finance and Opportunities to Learn.
114. E. Harter, How Educational Expenditures Relate to Student Achievement. *Journal of Education Finance, 24,* 1999, 281–302.
115. A. Odden and C. Busch, *Financing Schools for High Performance.* San Francisco: Jossey-Bass, 1998.
116. Odden and Busch, Ibid.

Chapter 7

STANDARDS AND TESTING: ASSESSING STUDENTS AND SCHOOLS

The biggest and most controversial development in American education in recent years has been the successful drive—led by business and political leaders—to establish specific standards for learning and to assess students and schools in terms of those standards. Those who advocate standards and testing argue that schools are no exception to the general organizational principle that people work more effectively when there are good measures of their success.[1]

The traditional standard for judging students' learning progress has been whether they have passed a set of required courses. But some observers of the schools, such as Albert Shanker, past president of the American Federation of Teachers, have noted that many students can graduate from high school after four years of simply showing up and doing the minimal amount of work needed to pass.

Schools were judged and accredited in the past primarily by so-called "input" factors, including their facilities, staff, and curriculum. Many of those dissatisfied with the "product" of schools—the education of their graduates—have argued successfully that schools, instead, should be assessed primarily by the outcomes they have achieved for their students. This type of assessment, they say, creates pressures on underperforming schools to improve. Public knowledge about each school's degree of success leads to widespread demands that subpar schools be upgraded. Other pressures come from tangible rewards and penalties to schools that may result from success or failure. Thus, advocates say, standards-based assessment of schools gives school personnel greater incentives to provide better and more equal education to their students.[2]

By 2001. most states had voluntarily created standards for education in some basic subjects, such as reading and mathematics, and mandated that schools test students' achievement in these subjects. Many states also require high school students to pass a test of minimal competency in order to receive a regular high school diploma. In 2001, creating standards and testing for their achievement became national policy with passage of the federal No Child Left Behind Act. This law requires that, in order to receive federal funds for education, states must develop content standards in reading and mathematics (and later in science) and develop tests linked to those standards for grades 3 through 8. Testing students against state standards, publicly assessing the performance of individual schools, and giving rewards or penalties for students and schools according to test results, have become prominent features of life in American schools.

The recent wave of additional testing in American schools has led to dismay, anger, and even resistance among many parents and educators. Critics charge that increased testing has weakened curricula and teaching by focusing teachers' and students' attention on low-level rote learning of facts. They say that students are spending more time on test preparation and on taking tests and less time on learning. They question the validity of some standardized tests as good measures of learning. They charge that high-stakes testing is hurting poor and minority children by causing more of them to drop out of school or not to get a regular high school diploma.[3]

In an article discussing problems with high-stakes testing, John Merrow says: "Unchecked, they will choke the life out of many excellent schools and drive gifted teachers out of classrooms. Furthermore, they will lead to debased and unnecessarily low standards, undermining the very cause for which they were instituted in the first place."[4]

Given the major impact of new standards and additional testing in American schools and the intense controversies about these developments, it is important to examine as objectively as possible what is being done and what the effects on students and schools have been.

This chapter discusses various kinds of standards and measures that are being used to assess the performance of individual students and of schools. It considers the effects of testing programs on students and on schools, including their effects on curriculum, instruction, student motivation, and students staying in school. Ways in which programs of standards and assessments can be tailored to contribute to students' learning, rather than to detract from genuine learning, are discussed. The chapter begins with a brief consideration of standards for what young people should learn in school.

CURRICULUM STANDARDS

What do we want our children to learn in school? School has always been seen as a place where young people should learn the information, skills, attitudes, and habits that will prepare them for successful lives as adults. Not all of such learning involves knowledge of academic subjects. For example, skills in driving a car and in woodworking and responsible attitudes toward drugs are useful for leading successful lives. However, because academic knowledge and credentials are seen by most people as especially important for individuals' occupational success and also for the economic health of the nation, students' academic learning (in reading and writing skills, mathematics, science, history, etc.) has been the focus of attention for educators and the public alike.

Because of its decentralized system of education, the United States, unlike many other countries, has no national standards for curriculum content. Nonofficial curriculum standards have been developed by national groups representing professional disciplines, such as mathematics, science, history, and social studies. The standards developed for different subject disciplines differ in the extent to which they: (1) emphasize concepts and generalizations, as opposed to sets of facts; (2) identify the sequence of topics that should be taught in successive grades; (3) clearly link the content to the important concepts and principles of the discipline; and (4) identify clearly the key skills to be taught.[5]

The curriculum content standards developed by subject disciplines may influence, but have not necessarily been adopted by, the agencies that set curricula standards in the various states. The content standards used by states differ in specificity and rigor. Robert Linn and his associates note that "content standards and associated tests are much more ambitious in some states than others."[6] They also point out that the "cut scores" used to define proficient performance also vary widely from one state to another. For example, in 2001 the percentage of students who scored as proficient on their states' grade 8 mathematics test was 7 percent in Louisiana and 39 percent in Mississippi, while in Texas 92 percent of students passed the state math test for that same grade. Linn and his colleagues comment: "Clearly proficient or passing have quite different meaning in these three states."[7]

The No Child Left Behind Act of 2001 requires all states to develop content standards in reading and math and to give tests linked to those standards for grades 3 through 8 by 2005. Science content standards and tests are to follow by 2007. However, the specific standards set by various states may continue to differ.

STANDARDS FOR STANDARDS

What types of standards for curriculum content are desirable?

Studies of human cognition show that people are more likely to learn and to remember information when they are given a conceptual framework within which specific facts and ideas are interrelated.[8] Thus, many educators have called for curricula that emphasize key concepts and principles.

A number of studies of students' learning, especially in math classes, support the importance of conceptual understanding. Curricula that emphasize conceptual thinking have been found consistently to lead to higher student achievement than curricula that emphasize computation.[9]

Commenting on results of these studies, James Hiebert and his colleagues say: "Understanding is crucial because things learned with understanding can be used flexibly, adapted to new situations, and used to learn new things."[10]

Educators generally agree on several additional criteria for desirable curriculum standards.[11] First, since conceptual frameworks and principles have been developed most clearly in core academic disciplines (such as math, science, and history), content standards should focus on these disciplines, rather than on interdisciplinary topics (such as the environment).

Second, rather than trying to include all topics, content standards should focus on the essentials. Donald Gratz comments: "A laundry list that satisfies everyone will leave teachers right where they are now—facing the impossible task of trying to rush through overstuffed textbooks and ridiculously long lists of curriculum objectives."[12] Limiting the material covered permits students to cover important topics in depth, rather than study a larger number of topics superficially.

Third, there is wide agreement among educators that standards should not prescribe teaching methods or substitute for teachers' lesson plans. While standards can be useful to teachers, by providing them with clear expectations of what students should know, teachers should have the flexibility to meet curriculum goals in ways that are best for their particular students.

Curriculum standards used by different states and for different subjects differ widely in the extent to which they meet these criteria.

ASSESSING STUDENTS' LEARNING

After standards of what students should know are defined, some assessment of what they do know needs to be made. Students' learning may be assessed in a number of ways, including objective tests, performance tests, and grades. Students also may be assessed to see if they have met some minimum level of proficiency required for promotion or graduation. I next discuss these measures of student performance in terms of their advantages, problems, and effects on students. (The effects of assessment methods on schools, especially on curriculum and teaching, are discussed later in this chapter.)

OBJECTIVE TESTS

Traditionally most tests given to students have been so-called "objective" tests, asking the student to choose the correct answer from among several possible alternatives (multiple choice), to say whether a statement is true or false, or to fill in a correct word, number, or other short answer. Such tests have the advantage of reliability. An answer is (usually) either correct or incorrect. The first president of the U.S. was George Washington, not Abraham Lincoln. Brazil is in South America, not Africa. Ten minus seven is three, not four. Also, objective tests—especially multiple-choice tests, which can be machine-scored—are easy and cheap to mark.

Scores on many objective tests are reported with reference to how they compare to the average for some designated large group, for example, all fifth graders in the American public schools in the year 2004. The ease of administering and scoring multiple-choice tests make possible such comparisons to a large base group. (These are known as "norm-referenced" tests).

An alternative way to report results of tests is to compare the scores to some criterion of performance ("criterion-referenced" tests). If the criterion of adequate knowledge of arithmetic is being able to answer correctly 7 out of 10 questions, and the criterion of excellent arithmetic knowledge is giving 9 correct answers out of 10, then students will be judged by these criteria, regardless of how other students perform. Tests of minimum competency are of this type. So too are the National Assessment of Educational Progress tests that judge students' performance as basic, proficient, or advanced. Criterion-referenced tests have the advantage of giving some indication of the adequacy of a student's knowledge, although not of how he compared to some larger group.[13]

Criticisms of Objective Tests

Objective tests have been criticized on a number of grounds. One important charge is that tests of cognitive abilities are biased against students from minority subcultures, such as African-Americans and Hispanic-Americans.

Some culturally biased items have been found on some cognitive tests (e.g., asking about golf rather than basketball). However, such items, which increasingly are screened out, do not appear to account for much of the racial differences found on such tests.[14]

In addition, large racial differences are found on tests, such as math and science tests, where cultural differences are not likely to be important, as well as on language tests.[15] Moreover, average differences between races remain large even when scores are adjusted for the social class of students. Thus, while it is always necessary to guard against cultural biases in tests, such biases do not appear to have major effects on test results. (For a discussion of reasons for racial and ethnic differences in school achievement, see Chapter 9.)

A more compelling criticism of objective tests concerns the level of learning they measure. Many educators and other critics complain that most objective tests seek to assess narrow and disconnected facts, learned by rote, that do not reflect real understanding. Kenneth Wilson and Bennett Davis say: "Ironically, as standardized tests have become more pervasive, they've also become less meaningful . . . the most widely used conventional standardized tests continue to measure fact retention and the isolated performance of rote skills. Most have not yet acknowledged the need to measure students' growth in the creative application of knowledge."[16] A Boston College study asserts: "The tests most commonly taken by students—both standardized tests and textbook tests—emphasize and mutually reinforce low-level thinking and knowledge."[17]

The validity of standardized objective tests as a measure of student learning also may be weakened by lack of effort on tests by some students. Peter Behuniak has pointed out that long and boring preparation for taking standardized tests can lead students to feel resentment toward the testing. He says: "These attitudes can have a powerful depressive effect on student performance on the tests. . . ."[18] Such a depressive effect on scores is most likely when standardized test scores have no consequences for individual students, as is often the case.

Effects on Motivation and Learning

Taking the primarily objective tests given by states does not appear to motivate most students to learn. A recent national survey of more than 4,000 teachers asked the teachers whether they agreed that "the state-mandated test motivates previously unmotivated students to learn." Only 6 percent of elementary school teachers, 9 percent of middle school teachers, and 10 percent of high school teachers said they thought this was true.[19]

Standardized tests that are "norm-referenced," as well as classroom tests that are marked "on a curve," may have undesirable effects on overall student motivation. Because the tests are scored in ways that will "spread" the scores, many students will score poorly regardless of how much knowledge they may have. Grant Wiggins comments: "This has implications for incentives and for future performance: curved scoring ensures that, by design, at least half of the student population is made to feel inept and discouraged about their work, while the upper-half often has an illusory feeling of achievement."[20]

Such an illusory feeling of achievement appears to be reflected in the fact that African-American and Hispanic-American students judge their own ability in math more highly than do white students, while white students judge themselves more able in math than do Asian-American students.[21] In actual fact, Asian-Americans perform best in math and whites perform next best, while African-Americans and Hispanic-Americans do less well.[22] This discrepancy between actual and perceived achievement may seem strange until we reflect that most grades on tests and in courses reflect achievement relative to classmates and not amount of knowledge *per se*. The unfortunate result is that many students whose actual achievement is low do not realize the need for them to do better.

PERFORMANCE ASSESSMENT

Many educators, business leaders, and other citizens have urged that education, and assessment of student achievement, should go beyond rote learning of facts and focus on students' ability to think. A U.S. Department of Education study found that employers wanted workers with thinking skills, including problem solving, creativity, decision making, and learning how to learn, as well as interpersonal and teaming skills.[23] Educator Grant Wiggins writes: "In the assessment of intellectual outcomes, substantial attention should be devoted to more sophisticated skills, such as understanding principles, applying skill and knowledge to new tasks, and investigating, analyzing, and discussing complex issues and problems.[24]

It is possible for objective tests to assess such higher-level thinking to some extent. As Myron Dembo notes, multiple-choice, matching, or short-answer questions can be designed to "tap high levels of reasoning such as required in inference, organization of ideas, comparison and contrast."[25] For example, the item "Harriet Beecher Stowe was to freedom for slaves as Susan B. Anthony was to _____" (Answer: the right to vote for women) requires a comparison of historical figures and events and some use of abstract concepts (e.g., advocating rights for a group).

However, a substantial assessment of students' abilities to analyze, reason, and apply information in new situations usually requires a less restrictive, more individualized assessment of performance than is possible with objective tests. Many different types of performances may be assessed. Students may be asked to write an essay on the causes of the American Revolution, conduct a science experiment to show how chemicals combine, explain the methods they used to answer a math problem, show a biological process (such as evolution) by a graphic display, apply the principles of electricity to the design of a system to light a backyard, and so on.

The activities assigned are designed to stimulate a student to seek understanding, to be creative, to solve problems, and to apply general ideas to current and real-life situations. For example, high schools in Littleton, Colorado, created performance-based systems that included requirements that students write effectively, conduct experiments and apply mathematical principles and operations to solve a wide range of problems.[26]

To document student performance over time (e.g., a semester), some schools have instituted the use of portfolios. A portfolio is a collection of student's work in one or more subject areas. For example, a given portfolio might include essays, reports on research projects, and description of an experiment conducted by the student. In Vermont, fourth graders and eighth graders have been required to compile portfolios of classroom work in writing and mathematics. The writing portfolios must include a poem, story, play, or narrative; a personal response to a cultural event, current issue, math problem, or scientific phenomenon; writing from subject areas other than English; a "best piece" chosen by the student; and a letter that explains the best piece and why it was chosen. In math, students choose five to seven pieces of their classroom work for their portfolios. The portfolios should include math applications to problems and investigations (usually involving data analysis or research) that result in conclusions.[27] In some schools, assessment of students by final exams has been replaced with "exhibitions" or "mastery demonstrations" by graduating seniors.

Many states have used assessment of student writing samples or other types of performance-based assessments as part of their overall programs to assess student achievement. As of the year 2000, over 40 states had adopted some form of performance assessment.[28]

Criticisms, Problems of Performance Assessment

Performance assessment has not escaped criticism and attack. Efforts to develop innovative standards and assessments for students have disturbed those who emphasize basic skill and knowledge in education. These critics see such new approaches as weakening learning. They call for a return to "traditional education." In Littleton, Colorado, for example, opponents of performance-based education succeeded in gaining control of the local school board in order to reverse the changes that had been made.[29]

Conservative critics of performance-based education also have contended that required performances, such as essays based on students' own experiences and ideas, assess attitudes and beliefs, rather than knowledge, and intrude on the privacy of the family. In California, challenges to the state learning assessment tests led to court decisions allowing students and local districts to withdraw from the test.[30]

In addition to dealing with objections from conservative critics to their basic approach, advocates of performance testing also must address major problems with scoring the assessments. First, scoring performances, such as essays, is costly in time and money. For example, when performance-based assessment was begun in California, about 2,500 teachers met during the summer of 1993 at 37 sites around the state for four days of training in scoring student papers.[31] The state aimed to train a cadre of teachers who would return to their own schools to train other teachers.

Schools must pay the teachers involved for their additional time spent in training or else pay for substitute teachers during regular class times. Costs should decrease after a new assessment program is well established, since less training will have to be done. However, it will almost always take more teacher time to assess various student performances—essays, experiments, graphic displays, research projects, and so on—than to score multiple-choice tests. (On the other hand, multiple-choice and other objective tests may take more time to prepare.)

A very central issue with performance tests is the reliability of the scoring. It will help assessment little if performance tests are more valid than objective tests (i.e., are better at measuring what is important) but are largely subjective, dependent on the scorer's personal judgment and biases. Qualitative judgments need to be converted into quantitative scores and those scores must be pretty much the same, regardless of who the particular scorer is. The task, as Wilson and Davis note, is to devise "the fairest and most accurate ways to quantify and systematize . . . subjective judgments of quality."[32]

States and localities that have adopted some form of performance testing have also developed systems to score the students' work. For example, in Vermont, the pieces of each student's portfolio in math have been scored on a 4-point scale according to seven criteria, including mathematical language, how the student solved the problem, and the extent to which the student explained her reasoning.

An initial study of Vermont's portfolio assessment program by an outside research group found serious problems of inadequate reliability (i.e., lack of sufficient agreement) in ratings of both writing and math portfolios. The researchers pointed to three possible reasons for low agreement among raters: (1) a rather complex system—for example, math raters had to score papers on each of seven different criteria and there was a lack of clarity about what raters should look for; (2) inadequate training of teachers who did the ratings; and (3) since portfolios included a variety of materials prepared in response to varied classroom assignments, scorers had no uniform "anchor" to which to refer their scoring.

In response to these findings, Vermont school officials made changes in their assessment procedures, including adding a standard item to serve as an anchor for judgment and using more highly trained raters. Following these changes, agreement among raters improved, especially in math.[33] More generally, raters of students' work usually have been found to have high levels of agreement in their judgments when the tasks are the same for all students and when scoring procedures are well defined.[34]

Efforts to create reliable and valid performance tests continue. The work of the New Standards Project and of the College Board to develop national tests of performance have been part of the effort. Other efforts to develop good measures of student performance are part of curriculum projects being conducted around the United States. In addition, commercial test publishers—which have in the past developed only objective tests—have begun to bring their technical expertise to the development of reliable tests of performance.[35]

Effects on Motivation and Learning

The process of performance assessment often involves students in activities that are motivating and that contribute to their learning. For example, students in an elementary school in Littleton, Colorado, chose a topic to research, on which they then gave an oral presentation that was judged by the teacher. Describing these activities, Robert Rothman observes: "'Taking' the assessment becomes doing interesting and instructive classroom work; preparing students for the assessment becomes good teaching."[36]

As the preceding quotation suggests, the process of engaging students to participate actively in learning, often in specific projects of their own choice, may increase their interest and motivation in their schoolwork. The beneficial effect of performance evaluation should also be increased if teachers follow their assessment of each student's performance with feedback on the strengths and weaknesses of her performance and if the student is encouraged to revise and improve her work. Grant Wiggins has emphasized this aspect of assessment, saying: ". . . assessment should be designed to *improve* performance, not just monitor it."[37] He adds, "Successful learning depends on adjustment in response to feedback; no task worth mastering can be done right on the first try."[38] (It may be noted that some objective tests—so called "diagnostic tests"—also may be used to give certain types of feedback to students on their strengths and weaknesses.)

Consistent with an emphasis on feedback, students' work on performance tests tends to be judged in terms of progress, rather than (or in addition to) an absolute standard of excellence. This type of emphasis is part of a national assessment system recently adopted by Great Britain. A report of the task force that made recommendations for the new system said, "Formative assessment must be in terms to which students can respond and which clearly indicate what has been and what remains to be achieved. . . . Many pupils seem to need short-term objectives which are clear and which they perceive to be attainable. The possibility of achieving these builds enthusiasm for progress in learning. . . ."[39]

There is only limited direct evidence that this type of assessment—which elicits active student involvement and then gives students feedback on their progress toward clear standards—will increase student motivation and achievement. Research in schools that are members of the Coalition of Essential Schools indicates that, under a program that assesses students through their exhibitions, students become "more invested in their studies. . . ."[40] Most of the additional supporting evidence is indirect, coming from research on achievement motivation in a variety of situations, including schools and work. This substantial body of work shows that motivation, effort, and performance are raised by a combination of clear standards of excellence, medium difficulty (a task that is challenging but possible to succeed in), control by the person over methods of doing the task, and full feedback to the person on his performance and progress toward success.[41]

COMBINING DIFFERENT TYPES OF ASSESSMENT

Although there often has been argument about whether performance tests or traditional objective tests are better, it is not necessary to use one type of test to the exclusion of the other. Objective tests are good at assessing students' mastery of facts and basic skills. Performance tests are especially useful for assessing higher-level thinking. These types of achievement are complementary. A student must have essential information and basic skills before he can analyze, organize, and solve problems.

Many states and districts that have used tests of performance have continued to use objective tests as well. For example, in California, a history/social science assessment included multiple-choice questions; questions that ask students to select an answer and then justify it with historical evidence; short-answer questions; and essay questions. In Maine, all students are given a standard state test but students have been evaluated primarily by locally developed assessments. These may include performances, portfolios, demonstrations, standardized tests and other indicators of achievement.[42] An advisory group to the Maine Department of Education has recommended that assessment systems in that state should use multiple ways to assess learning, including "selected-response formats," such as, multiple-choice or true-false questions; "constructed-responses," such as short answers or essays; and other performance measures, such as projects or demonstrations.[43]

On a national level, the National Assessment of Educational Progress has combined the use of multiple-choice questions (on which it relied at first) with open-ended questions and essays.[44] The use of a number of different types of tests may provide a better overall picture of students' knowledge and skills than the use of only one method of assessment.

TESTING FOR PROMOTION AND GRADUATION

Many advocates of standards and testing assert that tests should have important consequences for students, especially in determining whether they should be promoted to a higher grade or receive a high school diploma. Such consequences, they believe, will motivate students to take their studies seriously and to learn what they should learn. Requiring students to show competency on tests in order to advance through school would, they say, end the phenomenon of poorly educated and even semi-illiterate students graduating from high school without the knowledge and skills they need to lead successful lives.

By the end of the 2000–2001 school year, 18 states and the District of Columbia had tied student promotion to performance on state exams.[45] At least 28 states now have a test that students must pass in order to get a high school diploma or plan to have such a test.[46]

Critics of such high-stakes tests have protested that these tests are having devastating consequences for students, especially many from minority groups, who are being denied promotion or high school diplomas. Civil rights groups and groups of parents (e.g., in Florida and Michigan) have mounted legal challenges and have lobbied state legislatures to stop the administration of tests of minimum competency or to make then easier to pass.

What are the effects of high stakes tests on students? Since such tests may lead to students being denied promotion, research on the effects of retention in grades is relevant. This body of research is not entirely consistent with regard to how retention affects achievement. One careful study of Baltimore elementary school children found that repeating a grade helped retainees to do better in their repeated year and for some years later.[47] However, most studies have found that, even with student background and prior test scores controlled, children who are required to repeat a grade do more poorly in their studies than similar students who are promoted with their age cohort.[48] The Baltimore study suggests that retention in grade may have positive effects on achievement when students are held back only once and after the first grade.

While the evidence concerning the effects of retention in grade on student learning is not entirely consistent, it is clear that retaining students in grade results in many students leaving school earlier than they otherwise would. Studies in Chicago and two national studies have found that, even after controlling for students' backgrounds and earlier academic achievement, students who were retained in their grade were far more likely than others to drop out of high school. One national study found that students who were held back before the eighth grade were more than four times as likely as students who were not held back to leave high school or else to receive a less prestigious General Education Development (GED) diploma.[49] Another study found that students who were required to take exams for promotion in the 8th grade were more likely than others to drop out of school by the 10th grade.[50]

With regard to exams required to graduate from high school, there is little systematic evidence concerning their impact on student achievement. One study based on national data found that, in high schools with minimum competency requirements for graduation, students took more courses (although often very basic courses) in math, science, vocational education, and computer science.[51]

While having to demonstrate minimum competence on tests may lead students to take more courses in core academic subjects, and may increase motivation and learning for some students, high-stakes tests lead many students to leave school or to fail to get a standard high school diploma. In Boston, for example, where students must pass a state achievement test in order to graduate from high school, nearly one-third of the high school class of 2003 dropped out before their senior year. Of those remaining, a large number had not passed the required state exam by their senior year, and it was estimated that only about one-third of those who began high school would receive their diplomas at the end of four years.[52]

After high-stakes testing was begun in New York State, the number of students receiving "special education" diplomas (rather than regular high school diplomas) increased about 22 percent.[53] Similar increases in the number of students dropping out of high school completely, or receiving lower-level diplomas, have occurred around the United States, especially among poor and minority students. Writing about the high-stakes testing program in Massachusetts, Linda Nathan comments: "High stakes environments push drop-out rates up, particularly for the most vulnerable students. The state's current policy will hurt most grievously the very students who are supposed to benefit most from it."[54]

Some of the controversy about minimum competency tests seems to assume that we must choose between turning out large numbers of poorly educated high school graduates or withholding high school diplomas from a substantial proportion of potential graduates. An alternative perspective, such as that proposed by the National Commission on Educational Excellence, emphasizes educating all (or almost all) students up to an adequate level of knowledge and skills. Such an approach would emphasize efforts to avoid school failure from the earliest grades, frequent assessment throughout the school years, and remediation for those students who are falling behind in their studies.

Of course, by the time a student is in the 10th grade or higher (when tests for graduation are taken), it may be difficult to remedy academic deficiencies. Assessment, diagnosis, feedback, and remediation needs to start much earlier in the student's school career.[55]

Retention in grade or denial of a high school diploma may be necessary and appropriate for a few students. But many educators have pointed out that an educational system that emphasizes the sorting of winners and losers, especially at the end of their school careers, would not serve either its students or the public well.

COURSE GRADES

In addition to taking tests, students are, of course, assessed for their work over a period of time by course grades.

The use of grades is almost universal in American schools. Despite attack from critics who believe that grades often reduce motivation and learning, the practice of grading has continued and, where occasionally suspended, usually has been reinstated.[56] What are the uses and advantages of assigning grades? What problems may grading bring?

A student's grades are, of course, intended to assess his overall learning. Grades may be used by teachers and school administrators to make necessary decisions—about honors for particular students, about promotion, about placement in ability groups or academic tracks, about graduation, about admission to colleges. While past grades are far from a perfect predictor of future success in school (or in jobs), students with higher grades at one school level do tend also to get better grades at higher levels. For example, high school grades are the best single predictor of college grades.[57]

Most parents want the schools to assign grades to students so that they can judge how well their children are doing. Many students as well want to get grades to know how they are doing. Also, some employers find grades useful, if only as an indication of prospective employees' habits of applying themselves to tasks.[58]

But how well do grades really indicate the extent of students' learning? And what impact do grades have on students' motivation, effort, and further learning?

In general, teachers are able to make fairly valid judgments of their students' level of achievement. A review of research on this subject shows that teachers' judgments correlate fairly highly (median correlation was .65) with objective measures of student performance.[59] However, as we have already noted, the meaning of a grade depends in part on how it is based—especially on whether it shows the extent to which a student has mastered a given body of knowledge or whether it shows how he compares to some set of other students (regardless of how much he knows). In addition, when assigning a grade, teachers may consider a variety of factors other than the student's knowledge. These include the student's effort, her cooperation, her attentiveness, her past grades, her (presumed) ability, the neatness of her work, her attendance, and so on.[60]

Girls tend to be given higher grades than boys, even when their achievement levels are the same. This result probably is due to the fact that girls tend to conform more to teachers' expectations about "good conduct." A related finding is that students who are most liked by their teachers tend to get better grades. Other studies in colleges show that when a number of instructors teach the same course to similar students, the grading distributions for students vary greatly, depending on their particular instructor.[61]

Grades and Motivation

Many teachers see grades as necessary to motivate students to try hard and to reward them for their efforts. A teacher interviewed in one study commented: "Kids choose not to bother to learn, study, or even consider stuff that is not being graded."[62] Parents also often use grades as a motivator—rewarding good grades with praise, money, presents, and privileges and/or penalizing poor grades with disapproval, loss of privileges, even physical punishment. And many students describe themselves being motivated by grades. For example, a student quoted by one researcher said: "They make you work hard to prove you're smart."[63]

In addition to being (or bringing) rewards and/or penalties, grades may increase students' motivation by helping them to judge their progress toward academic goals (such as a high grade point average). Such positive effects of grades on motivation are most likely to occur among students who are doing well in school—that is, students who generally are getting good grades.[64]

While grades may help to motivate some students, there are ways in which grades may reduce motivation, especially for students who get low grades. First, there is evidence that extrinsic motivators, such as grades, may reduce the motivation to do a task for its intrinsic enjoyment. For example, rewarding students for reading may reduce their interest in reading once the external rewards end.[65]

More important, the goal of better grades usually does not seem to motivate those students who get poor grades.[66] Students who receive poor grades tend to get discouraged, may stop trying, and may try to build their self-esteem by disruptive activities. Writing about students who do not receive good grades, or other rewards, John Bonstingle says: "Those who do not receive such rewards most often become discouraged about their abilities. Rather than working harder to achieve the "A," they gradually drop out, first psychologically, and later physically.[67] Discussions in focus groups with older students and high school dropouts led one researcher to these conclusions: "Students who receive good grades tend to think grades are important. Those who receive poor marks become discouraged about learning. Poor grades are a major reason why students drop out."[68]

Rather than viewing grades as always good or always bad for motivation, it is important to specify the *conditions* under which grades, and other evaluations (such as comments from teachers) are most likely to raise (or lower) students' motivation and effort. General research on achievement motivation, and research on the motivation and effort of students specifically,[69] suggest that the following conditions increase motivation:

1. Grades are important to students; they are seen as helping them to reach important personal goals—getting into college or getting a good job, getting parental and/or peer approval, etc.
2. Students see their behavior as affecting their grades.
3. Students believe that there is a substantial chance (but not a certainty) that trying hard will result in good grades.

In other words, grades are likely to motivate students to try hard if grades matter to them, if they see a connection between their effort and grades, and if they think that they have a good chance to get good grades if they try hard.

In order for grades to be a motivator, students who try harder and achieve more should get higher grades. But this is not necessarily true. Research in schools indicates that grades tend to be highest in those classrooms where student effort is lowest.[70] This phenomenon appears to result from the fact that grades generally are given on the basis of a student's performance relative to his classmates. Classes in which students are from poor, perhaps minority, backgrounds often are not challenged greatly by teachers and are given relatively good grades for little effort. Both students and their parents may be unaware of their low level of achievement.

Summarizing results from their studies, Natriello and Dornbusch state: ". . . the teachers appear to employ a strategy of evaluation designed to motivate effort among lower-achieving students by distributing more praise. . . . At the same time they appear to shy away from making real demands on these students. Praise and warmth in the absence of challenging standards inflate student assessments of their effort, without really fostering effort-engagement behavior."[71] These authors also found that black and Spanish-surname students assessed their own efforts as higher, but scored lower on actual behaviors indicating effort, than did white and Asian-origin students. They conclude that teachers' evaluations, although perhaps well-meaning, distort students assessments of their own effort and permit them to be satisfied with low levels of effort.

In their discussion of conditions for effective systems of education, Natriello and Dornbusch mention several circumstances under which evaluations of students will raise their motivation. One is that "students must receive evaluations that are sufficiently frequent and challenging to direct their efforts on school tasks." To direct their efforts, the evaluations need to indicate to the student the ways in which she can improve her performance. Natriello and Dornbusch add: "The difficult tasks faced by teachers include demanding a level of performance by each student that is within that student's capacity and yet requires additional effort if the student is to reach that standard."[72]

Grades that are given only after a student has completed his work represent what Carol Sager calls "grades as inspection."[73] Much like inspection in factories, grades often have been used to judge the final product and see how many are defective. But business firms increasingly have learned that it is less costly and more effective to try to build quality into their products by checking and, if necessary, improving them, throughout the production process.

Similarly, grades can help to improve the "production"—that is, learning—process in schools if they are part of a process that gives students frequent feedback on what they are doing right, what they are doing wrong, and what they need to do in order to improve their performance. In other words, to have the most positive effect on students' motivation and effort, grades must be part of a broader learning process.

Different Methods of Grading

Letter grades—usually a 5-point scale of A, B, C, D, and F—are the most commonly used system of grading in American schools.[74] While some schools have used other ways of assessing students, the letter grade system has persisted in the great majority of schools. Carol Sager, a critic of letter grades, comments: "Even in systems where letter grades have been successfully eliminated in elementary schools, they are almost always reinstated by the middle grades. For the purposes of this study, it was almost impossible to find a high school that had eliminated grades or attempted to eliminate grades in school."[75] Grades appear to persist because they are less time-consuming than alternatives, because parents typically protest an absence of grades (many parents believe that grades give them important information about how their children are doing in school), and because some alternatives to grades (e.g., portfolio assessment, or mastery learning) require other substantial changes in the school.

A number of alternatives to using traditional letter grades have been proposed. These include a pass-fail (or credit–non-credit) system; written evaluations of each students' work; the contract system; and the mastery approach. Each of these grading systems has advantages and disadvantages.[76] However, there appears to be little hard evidence about the effects that pass-fail grades, written evaluations, and self-evaluations have on students' motivation and learning.

There is some evidence about the effect of mastery learning systems. Since the contract system and the mastery learning system have some important similarities, we may consider them together. The contract system and the mastery approach both link student grades directly to specific learning goals. Under the contract system, if the student does a certain type, quantity, and ideally quality, of work, she will automatically receive a certain grade. The same contract may apply to the whole class or may vary for different students, depending on what they wish to do and perhaps on their interests and abilities. The terms of the contract may be stated by the teacher alone, may be reached for the whole class by a group decision, or may be designed by each student, with the teacher's agreement.

The mastery approach uses a different method of grading as part of a broadly different approach to teaching and learning. At the beginning of the course, the teacher tells the students what they are expected to learn (in a series of subject units), how their learning will be tested, and what the criteria are for different levels of proficiency (C, B, A, etc.). Each student may learn in his own way and at his own pace and be examined when he thinks he is ready. A student who wants to earn a B or an A grade will continue to study a unit until he has reached his desired level of proficiency. He may take retake exams (in a different form each time) until he is satisfied with his grade.

A number of types of mastery learning programs have been used in many school districts around the United States. Two separate reviews of research on the effectiveness of mastery learning programs have found that students in such programs show larger achievement gains than students in non-mastery programs, although there are wide differences in gains from study to study. One review of group-based mastery learning found that long-term experiments lasting one or more months were less effective than programs of four weeks or less. Other research and reviews on mastery learning programs have suggested that slower-learning students may be helped at the expense of faster-learning students and that achievement gains may decline over time.[77]

One form of mastery learning is called the Personalized System of Instruction (PSI). A comparison of 75 courses taught both conventionally and by PSI found that PSI produced higher achievement, less variation in achievement, and higher student ratings of courses. PSI did not affect frequency of withdrawal from courses or amount of study time. Most students in PSI courses liked the self-pacing, the ability to earn a high grade if specific requirements are met, and the availability of personal tutoring (a feature of PSI). The program seems to work best for students with enough self-discipline and motivation to work independently.[78]

EVALUATING SCHOOLS

The strategy of establishing standards for learning and measuring achievement emphasizes holding schools accountable for the performance of their students.

For several decades, most states have been publicly reporting information about educational outcomes on a school level. Many have attached rewards, such as monetary rewards to teachers and/or schools, and penalties, such as limiting the autonomy of school administrators, to varying levels of school performance. New national legislation requires public disclosure of information about every school's performance and attaches sanctions to poor performance.

MEASURES OF SCHOOL PERFORMANCE

How do we assess how good a job a given school is doing? Such intangible outcomes as producing graduates who have good character and are good citizens often are cited, but schools are rarely evaluated on these criteria. A school also may be assessed by its success in getting its students to attend and to complete their education, as indicated by attendance rates and dropout rates. Another possible indicator of a school's success (especially for high schools) is the proportion of its students who go on to higher education. The outcome that now is receiving most attention, by the public and by legislation, is the academic achievement of the school's students.

In trying to judge schools by the academic performance of their students, a number of problems arise.

What Is Measured

First, the meaning of any assessment depends on what is being measured. Standardized objective tests, such as those using many multiple-choice items, are often used. But performance tests also have been used—for example, in Vermont and Maine and in the early stages of Kentucky's school assessment program. Some states have assessed test performance against fixed criteria of proficiency, while other states have used a "norm-referenced" system, which judges the performance of each group of students against the performance of other students.

Use of different types of tests and different criteria for judging students' performance raises questions about just what a constitutes good academic performance by a school's students. Do we judge academic achievement by recall of facts or by understanding of general principles? By whether a group of students generally is proficient in a subject or by how they compare to other groups of students?

Adjusting for Students' Backgrounds

A school's showing on a measure of school performance may not take into account the characteristics of its student body. For example, Mississippi awarded each school district one of five accreditation levels based on the absolute performance of that district's students on a standardized achievement test. The ratings earned by districts matched closely the proportion of poor students (those eligible for free lunch) in each district.[79] Clearly, student achievement is affected not only by what happens in school but also by the student's background and home situation, especially the income and education of his family and his ethnicity. Therefore, most school recognition and reward programs measure the performance of a school's student body in a way that adjusts for the students' backgrounds.

One approach is to focus on the amount of improvement in each school—how much change occurs over time in student outcomes, such as achievement scores, attendance rates, and graduation rates. For example, in South Carolina, a test score has been predicted for each student based on her test scores in the previous year. The median of the gains of all students in a school has been used as a "school gain index."[80]

A limitation of this approach is that a school that begins at a low level of student outcomes, and stays the same, will rate as highly as a school having a similar student body that begins with excellent student outcomes and maintains this high level. In addition, schools serving students of low socioeconomic status (SES) may be unable to make gains equal to those of schools with more affluent students. In South Carolina, for example, schools serving students of low SES showed smaller gains than other schools and could seldom qualify for awards. Apparently, gains were more difficult to attain in schools that started out at a low level. As a result, South Carolina adjusted its school assessment system by classifying schools into groups based on their students' SES and also by adjusting a school's actual gains by the absolute level of prior scores at the school.[81]

An alternative approach to making fair comparisons among schools is to adjust measures of performance by the social and economic characteristics of their students. For example, the city of Dallas adjusted each student's scores on standardized achievement tests by whether the student was black, Hispanic, limited English-proficient, male, and approved for free or reduced-price lunch. Also, school scores were adjusted for the mobility rate among its students (the rate of students entering or leaving) and the degree of overcrowding. A later stage of the Dallas assessment calculated the gains in achievement for each school's student body compared to a predicted value, based on a complex formula.[82]

While adjustment of school performance measures by the background of its student body has been advocated as fair, some observers have questioned the wisdom of this procedure. In Mississippi, for example, some state officials opposed introducing adjustments for socioeconomic status on the grounds that such action would create a double standard. Critics of adjustments for student background say that these procedures legitimize low expectations for poor and minority students. They argue that it is important to identify clearly the schools in which students (whatever their backgrounds) are not learning enough, so that pressures to help and to improve such schools may be increased.

Elmore, Abelmann, and Fuhrman comment: "If performance accountability systems are seen as ways of rewarding and penalizing schools for what they are able to do, then it is fair to control for student background and prior achievement. On the other hand, if the systems are supposed to be useful in driving resources toward schools that have the largest gap between performance standards and actual performance, then controlling for student background or prior performance is counterproductive, because it allows schools and school systems to, in effect, conceal the pockets of greatest need by adjusting standards."[83]

To try to resolve this dilemma, it seems desirable to give attention to a number of measures that show: (1) the absolute level of student performance, (2) student performance in relation to their backgrounds, and(3) improvements over time. Such information will become more readily available under the federal No Child Left Behind Act of 2001. States now must develop objectives for improved achievement, and measure yearly progress, for specific groups, including those who are economically disadvantaged, those from major racial and ethnic groups, and those with limited English proficiency. Progress for these groups, as well as for all students, will be assessed for each school.

Fluctuations in School Results

Under the No Child Left Behind (NCLB) Act, all students must be at the proficient level in reading and math by the end of the 2013–2014 school year. To meet this goal, schools must improve their performance every year and schools that do not meet their objective for two consecutive years will be identified for improvement.

It is important to recognize, however, that school-level measures of student achievement fluctuate from year to year for a number of reasons unrelated to a school's program or the efforts of its staff. In many areas, a large proportion of a school's students are different from year to year because their families move from one place to another. Also, cohorts of students change each year, as last year's eighth graders become this year's high school freshmen, and so on. Moreover, school scores for each year are subject to errors of measurement.

Results from the Student Assessment Program in Colorado in the three school years from 1997 to 2000 illustrate the instability of school-level results.[84] Data from about 750 schools were tabulated according to the number of years (zero, one, two, or three) in which they met their targeted increase in students scoring at the proficient level. While about 43 percent of the schools met their improvement target in one year, and another 49 percent met it for two years, less than 5 percent of the schools consistently showed improvement in all three years. These data indicate that year-to-year fluctuations in school-level test results do not necessarily show real change in school quality, and that schools cannot show consistent improvements in test results. The NCLB Act permits states to aggregate several years of data in assessing school improvement, but considerable volatility in test results remains. To be most meaningful, change must be assessed on a long-term basis.

Comparability of Results Across States

As noted earlier, content standards, tests, and standards that define proficient performance vary widely across states. The result is that the percentage of students in each state who score at the proficient level also varies greatly.

The extent to which schools can show "adequate yearly progress" on tests of student proficiency depends on the stringency of the standards and of the accompanying tests in their state. Schools in states with rigorous standards and tests will have more difficulty demonstrating progress than schools in states that have lower content standards and easier tests. Thus, Linn and his colleagues assert that the federal law may be "providing states with incentives to adopt less challenging content standards, to develop tests aimed more at minimums than at higher-level understanding, and to set cut scores at levels familiar in the era of minimum competency testing."[85] Linn and his colleagues argue there is a need to create common benchmarks against which the achievement of students in different states can be compared.

EFFECTS OF TESTING PROGRAMS ON SCHOOLS

What effects have programs of standards and testing had on schools—on school curriculum, on instructional methods, on teachers, and on students?

Incentives to Raise Test Scores

The dissemination of data concerning the performance of students in each school on tests of academic achievement creates pressures on administrators and teachers to have their students do well on the tests. School staff members are judged by the public and by their superiors on the basis of these results. Test results usually attract wide interest and scrutiny by the press and the public. When the first results came out in Mississippi, a journalist there said: "I mean nobody could keep them. It was probably the most read thing in the state."[86]

Having one's school publicly identified as outstanding may cause administrators and teachers to feel proud, while a low rating is likely to make them feel embarrassed. More tangible rewards and/or penalties also may be consequences of school test performance. Some states have awarded flags or plaques to high-performing schools. Some have given extra money to the school or to administrators or teachers when student test scores are high. For example, in California, Kentucky, Texas, and other parts of the country, principals and superintendents often have been paid a bonus if their students scored well on standardized tests.

In some states, poor test performance by a school's students may lead to a reduction in the school's autonomy, restriction of athletic participation by its students, or permission to its students to transfer to another school. Moreover, school superintendents, principals, and teachers may have to forgo salary increases or even face loss of their jobs if their students do not test well.

Incentives for school staff to raise test scores have varied among states, districts, and particular schools. Schools in the middle range of student performance, with little chance to gain attention as either outstanding or deficient, have had less incentive to try to improve scores than either the best schools or those with the most problems.[87] Also, political pressures have led some states, such as Kentucky and Mississippi, to postpone or soften penalties against poorly performing schools, while retaining rewards for high performance.

Passage of the federal NCLB Act in 2001 has created additional and more widespread incentives for school staff to try to attain high student scores on state tests. Schools that fail to meet state objectives for yearly improvements in test scores will suffer penalties that may include school restructuring and facilitating students' transfer to other schools.

The pressures that school accountability programs put on school staff lead them to try to raise the test scores of their students. Among the actions they may take are the following: (1) change the curriculum, (2) change teaching methods, and (3) manipulate the test scores.

Effects on Curriculum

Those who have worked to establish clearer curricula standards often have wanted such standards to be rigorous and to provide students an understanding of concepts and principles. However, what is actually taught to students in classrooms has been shaped less by formal curriculum objectives than by the kinds of tests that are used to measure student achievement. As a report by the Southern Regional Education Board notes: "What gets measured gets taught."[88]

Some state tests, or portions of them, do measure the kinds of skills and knowledge that students need to be successful in life and push school curricula in these directions.[89] For example, where states require students to demonstrate writing skills as part of their assessment, schools generally include more writing in their curricula. However, the major portions of many state tests measure primarily the acquisition of isolated facts and simple skills. Such tests tend to shape curricula and teaching methods that emphasize rote learning of facts at the expense of higher-level understanding and developing skills of analysis and problem solving.

A recent national survey of over 4,000 teachers found that state testing programs have resulted in a "narrowing of the curriculum," especially in the 19 states where the stakes of tests are high for teachers and students. Overall, 79 percent of elementary school teachers, 77 percent of middle school teachers, and 61 percent of high school teachers agreed with the statement "There is so much pressure for high scores on the state-mandated test that teachers have little time to teach anything not on the test."[90] An earlier national survey of math and science teachers found similar results. One fifth grade teacher interviewed in the earlier study said that "eighty to ninety percent of class time in math is based on preparation for proficiency tests. Testing restricts my teaching to a narrow range of objectives. The exercises are dull and unimaginative and do not encourage thinking or doing."[91]

The amount of time in schools devoted to subjects other than those emphasized by state tests often is reduced. Although state curriculum standards commonly cover many subjects, mandated tests usually focus on

English language skills, especially reading, and math. Time devoted to other subjects, such as social studies, foreign languages, music, and even science, often is reduced.[92] For example, a study in Houston, Texas, found that teachers in history, art, and science were told that they had to spend a sizable part of their class time drilling students to prepare for the state math test.[93]

In addition to spending more time on those subjects and topics covered by state tests, many schools also are devoting considerable time to teaching students skills of test-taking. For example, after Massachusetts required that students pass a state exam in order to graduate from high school, students in a Boston high school had to take test-prep classes and forgo foreign language or science or theatre.[94] A study of schools in Houston, Texas, found that students were spending much of the school day studying not subject content but, rather, how to take tests. The author of that study asserts that ". . . TASS (Texas Assessment of Academic Skills)-prep is replacing the curriculum"[95] in many schools. A national study in 1992, when mandatory testing was less widespread than it is today, found that about half of teachers surveyed said they took time away from regular course work to teach test-taking skills.[96]

When the time that students spend in test preparation is added to the time they spend taking tests, the total represents a substantial part of their total time in school. In some Arizona districts, for example, about 20 percent of a student's total time in class is devoted to testing.[97]

The focus on standardized tests is strongest in schools with high proportions of minority students. Teachers in such schools are far more likely to "teach to the test" and to drill students in test-taking than are teachers in schools with primarily white students.[98] Some educators believe that the focus on tests is especially detrimental to the education of poor and minority students. Writing about the effects of testing in the Houston schools, Linda McNeil says that the testing program "creates a new form of discrimination as teaching to the fragmented and narrow information on the test comes to substitute for a substantive curriculum in the schools of poor and minority youth."[99]

Effects on Teaching

Related to their effects on curricula, testing programs also affect teaching practices and teacher morale.

Sometimes teachers are motivated to work toward reaching their school's achievement goals for students. A study of 20 schools in Kentucky and the Charlotte–Mecklenberg area of North Carolina found that new accountability systems provided many teachers with a focus for their work and increased the energy they devoted to instruction. Teachers valued professional recognition and "thank yous" for doing a good job and getting salary bonuses.

However, this study also found some negative effects of the accountability programs that tended to reduce teachers' motivation and effectiveness. Negative effects included higher pressure and stress on teachers and loss of freedom through state-directed assistance or "takeovers" of their schools.[100]

Other research has found that many teachers have been forced to downgrade or abandon what they believe are the most effective teaching methods in order to focus on raising students' scores on state tests. The recent national study of teachers asked teachers whether they agreed with this statement: "The state-mandated testing program leads some teachers in my school to teach in ways that contradict their own ideas of good educational practice." Eighty-two percent of elementary school teachers, 77 percent of middle school teachers and 69 percent of high school teachers agreed.[101]

An Arizona educator has described how the "fixation" on preparing students for basic skills tests in that state and elsewhere threatens the continued use of inquiry-based methods of teaching science. Inquiry methods engage students actively and collaboratively in scientific work and promote critical thinking and problem solving. However, schools are now reluctant to devote resources to such learning, which does not contribute to their test scores in reading and math.[102]

Another educator describes how the drive to improve test scores has led many schools and districts—for example, the Chicago public schools—to try to "teacher-proof" instructional programs. Describing such programs, Beverly Falk says that they "place teachers in the role of compliant technicians who must follow the rules to produce better results. Some educators have even abandoned teaching practices that have been nationally recognized and recommended."[103]

The pressures on teachers to improve test scores and restrictions put on their freedom to use methods they think contribute most to genuine learning have undermined some teachers' morale. Writing about the Kentucky testing programs, Betty Lou Whitford and Ken Jones state that the morale of Kentucky educators has declined. They say:

> Attention is on what the state demands more than on what the student needs. More and more teachers talk about the enormous pressure they are living with. They look and act tired. The sense of efficacy is on the wane as teachers struggle with the insecurity of not knowing how to keep getting higher and higher test scores, especially as their students come to them with increasing social and personal problems.[104]

The effect of school accountability systems on teacher morale may also be affected by the clarity and perceived fairness of the system. If a school's scores are computed in a way that teachers understand, and if teachers can see a clear connection between their efforts and the school's scores, their motivation and effort are likely to rise. However, school scores sometimes are computed in complex ways that make it hard for teachers to understand what the scores mean and how these scores relate to their own work.

Moreover, teachers sometimes are frustrated when, by working hard, they succeed in raising student performance, only to get no recognition because other schools have improved more.[105] In Dallas, dissatisfaction among teachers whose schools repeatedly failed to win competitive awards led the school system to increase the proportion of schools winning each year, from 20 percent to about 50 percent (based on gains in student performance).

Performance Testing

Just as objective state tests have major effects on schooling, assessments that require students to demonstrate knowledge and skills by performance tend to affect curricula and how teachers teach. A study by the RAND Corporation, done for the National Center for Research on Evaluation, Standards, and Student Testing, indicates that the type of portfolio assessment adopted in Vermont leads to changes in teaching.[106] Math teachers surveyed and principals interviewed agreed that the program took considerable teacher time to implement. However, they also generally agreed that the program had changed instruction for the better. Principals mentioned increased emphasis on problem solving, less emphasis on the textbook and on drill and practice, and more attention to communication in math. Teachers said they were giving more emphasis to problem-solving and communication skills, often including written reports on math-related projects.

A survey in California found that most teachers said they assigned more writing tasks than they had previously after a writing assessment was introduced.[107] In a San Diego middle school, where portfolios of performances have been an important part of student assessment, teachers could no longer simply assign chapters in textbooks; they also assigned tasks (research projects, etc.) that gave students a chance to show and apply their understanding. In addition, the assessment system led teachers at this school to work together on specific themes. For example, if the overall theme was the study of different cultures, the students might read and analyze literature from different cultures; in social studies they might investigate the history of several cultures; and in science they might research how physical traits pass from generation to generation within a culture.

Effects on Student Achievement

When schools give standard achievement tests regularly, and when the results have consequences for students and/or schools, students' scores on the tests tend to rise over time. For example, in Kentucky and Texas, average test scores on tests of reading and math rose in many districts after mandatory state tests were introduced.[108] In Kentucky, there also is evidence that, as a result of the inclusion of writing in the assessment program, the quality of students' writing improved.[109]

Testing programs that are accompanied by incentives for school personnel seem especially likely to raise scores. In Dallas, Texas, cash bonuses have
been provided to the entire staff of schools whose students performed well
on state and other achievement tests. Researchers examining effects of the
Dallas school assessment and incentive program compared the pass rates of
Dallas students on various state tests, including reading and math, with the
pass rates of students in five other large Texas cities. Student performance
in each school was controlled by the race and ethnicity of students, the percentage who are economically disadvantaged, and the mobility rate of students. Pass rates in Dallas schools increased by about 11 percent more than
they did in the other five cities. Consistently higher gains in achievement
were apparent among both white students and Hispanic students, although
not among black students in Dallas.[110]

Some researchers have suggested that gains in test scores may be due to
students getting better at taking state tests rather than to greater knowledge.
Other critics of school accountability and testing systems point to areas and
subgroups in which achievement scores have remained low. While such
qualifications are valid, it seems clear that long and repeated study of certain information and basic skills can raise students' competency in subjects
such as reading and simple math. Such an outcome is important for many
young people, including those from poor or minority families who might
not otherwise develop such basic knowledge and skills.

But while testing programs may encourage schools to teach their students
certain information and basic skills, they may leave students with, and even
encourage, a very superficial level of learning. Writing about schools in
Houston, Linda McNeil says:

> . . . teachers report that even though many more students are passing TAAS
> reading, few of their students are actually readers. Few of them can use read-
> ing for assignments in literature, science, or history classes; few of them
> choose to read; few of them can make meaning of literature or connect writ-
> ing and discussing to reading. In schools where TAAS reading scores are
> going up, there is little or no will to address this gap.[111]

Other writers and researchers also have observed that while standardized
testing may improve some basic knowledge and skills, it usually contributes
little to developing real understanding. This conclusion is bolstered by the
results of a recent national study that compared the achievement of students in those states that now require exams with high stakes (for students
and/or schools) with the achievement of students in other states. Students
in states with high-stakes exams consistently improved on the state exams
but generally did less well on other independent measures of academic
achievement, such as the SAT exams and the National Assessment of
Educational Progress (NAEP). The study's lead author is quoted as commenting: "In theory, high-stakes tests should work, because they advance the
notions of high standards and accountability. But students are being trained

so narrowly because of it, they are having a hard time branching out and understanding general problem-solving."[112]

Efforts to Manipulate Test Scores

Testing programs that evaluate and sanction schools on the basis of their students' test scores create pressures on administrators and teachers that sometimes lead them to manipulate these scores.

Actual tampering with test results has been reported in a number of schools around the United States. For example, the Dallas school district found that, in at least two situations, school personnel had altered test papers in order to raise the achievement scores of their school's students. In some districts elsewhere, school officials have been under criminal investigation for tampering with the scores they reported on state tests.[113]

Schools also may try to enroll or to keep only students who they believe are likely to do well on tests.[114] Schools in Houston, for example, have been reported to advise low-performing students to leave after the ninth grade or not to discourage those who may wish to leave. Linda McNeil notes: "The school's scores will be higher if these students exit before taking the tenth grade TAAS."[115]

Another strategy that has been used by schools in several states is to classify students in ways that improve the school's showing. Some schools have classified a large number of students as retarded or "special education" and thus not included in computing the regular school score.[116] Also, schools may artificially raise the proportion of their students who are classified as poor and who, therefore, may be judged by a lower standard. For example, in South Carolina, which has given awards to schools based on the family income of their students, principals may enroll as many students as possible in the free and reduced-price lunch program.[117]

IMPROVING LOW-RATING SCHOOLS

Schools whose students score low on state tests may not be able to improve on their own. Studies of school accountability systems by a group of Harvard researchers has found that low-performing schools often do not respond to the resulting consequences by improving their organization or instructional program. "Instead, they often respond by doing the same things they were doing, only doing them harder," the researchers say.[118]

For a school assessment system to have a positive impact on education, it is important that effective procedures be in place for helping the poorest-performing schools to improve. Commenting on rewards for good performance, David Cohen says "The success of such schemes depends heavily on whether state or local school systems could enhance the capacity of the worst schools to respond constructively to more powerful incentives, for those would be the schools least likely to be able to respond well on their own."[119]

Sometimes the help provided to low-performing schools by districts or states is inadequate. In Mississippi, districts that scored on the lowest level of performance had to develop an improvement plan. The state was able to provide some assistance to low-performing schools by providing consultants, making field visits, setting up training programs, and in other ways. But such help usually did not last long. A state official said: "With limited resources, both human resources and financial resources . . . our inability to stay with those districts is a weakness of the system."[120]

Where states have the authority to take over the running of poorly performing schools, state agencies may lack the technical and/or administrative expertise to run schools effectively. A state official in Mississippi remarked that ". . . before you take over a district, you better be real sure that you can do a better job running it than the people who are there."[121]

There are some good examples of what states can do to help low-performing schools to improve. For example, Maryland has regional centers for staff development, and school districts in other states have provided support for teacher learning and professional development. Some districts have provided curriculum guidance and materials to schools.[122] In Kentucky, the State Department of Education has selected and further trained distinguished educators to advise personnel in "declining" schools on matters such as curriculum, student assessment, personnel evaluation, and school budget and finance.

There is a danger, however, that the changes and "improvements" introduced to raise test scores will narrow the curriculum and emphasize rote learning. For example, researchers examining the Kentucky system of school accountability express doubt about whether the changes introduced into low-performing schools there are necessarily desirable ones. They quote the principal of a school that had been put under the control of a Distinguished Educator (DE) as saying about teachers in his school:

> Because the system is all about improving test scores, they stopped doing things for kids that they wanted to do. We lost a lot of great integrated curriculum stuff that was really turning kids on when the DEs took over, because that was all seen as not necessary. The DEs told us not to do that stuff, to concentrate instead on the content areas for the assessment.[123]

Whether a system of accountability for schools will improve schools depends on the nature of that system—the types of standards, tests, and incentives—as well as on efforts to help those schools that score poorly. In the final "Summary and Conclusions" section of this chapter, I discuss ways in which school assessment and accountability systems can be made most effective.

SUMMARY AND CONCLUSIONS

Creating standards for learning, testing students' knowledge, and holding schools accountable for their students' performance have become the cornerstones of recent government efforts to improve American schools.

Standards for curriculum content and for student performance on tests differ widely among states. Curriculum standards that emphasize conceptual understanding lead to higher levels of student achievement.

Objective tests, such as those with multiple-choice items, are relatively inexpensive and easy to administer and scoring of answers is reliable. However, they generally measure fairly low-level learning, such as recall of facts. Performance tests, such as essays and reports, are better suited than objective tests to assess students' abilities to solve problems and to apply concepts and principles to specific situations. The kinds of learning assessed by objective tests and by performance tests —information and basic skills by the former, analysis and problem solving by the latter—are complementary. A combination of the two types of tests usually is most useful for assessing overall learning.

"High-stakes" testing, which requires students to pass a test in order to be promoted to a higher grade or to graduate from high school, may lead some students to attend more to their studies or to take additional course work. However, research evidence generally does not find that retention in grade leads to greater student learning. High-stakes testing does lead to more students dropping out of school.

Schools do not have to choose between graduating students who lack minimum learning proficiency versus having a large number of students drop out of high school or fail to graduate. An alternative strategy is to try to make all students proficient in learning by early and continued assessment, and remediation where necessary, throughout their school careers.

Being assessed in another way, by course grades, raises the motivation of some students, especially those who are able to do well in their studies. But for students who generally do not do well in school, grades tend to discourage effort. A different type of problem occurs when teachers of low-performing classes give high grades that do not reflect actual student achievement, thus not challenging their students to do better. A grading system, such as mastery learning, that permits students to earn a high grade by reaching set goals, working at their own pace until completion, usually has been found to lead to larger achievement gains than occur otherwise.

In general, assessments of student learning, including both tests and grades, may be seen not just as a way of checking on what each student knows, but as an important part of the learning process. Assessments contribute most to learning when students have a clear idea of what they will be assessed on and why; they are encouraged to set meaningful learning goals for themselves; results of assessments are used to diagnose each student's strengths and weaknesses; students are given feedback on their perform-ance and counseled on how to improve; and each student sees that he has a good chance to do well if he tries hard. In short, to be most useful for stu-dent learning, assessment should fit into the process of effective teaching, as discussed in Chapter 3.

In addition to linking each student's progress through school to meas-ures of her learning, the movement to develop standards and testing aims to make schools more accountable for their students' learning.

When a school is judged and its personnel are rewarded or penalized on the basis of its test scores, the school is likely to change its educational pro-gram in order to raise its scores. Schools that are being judged primarily by objective tests of achievement, as is usually the case, generally have modified their curricula to emphasize the isolated facts and simple skills that such tests usually measure. They reduce time devoted to subjects and topics not tested and devote considerable time to drilling students on the likely con-tent of the tests and preparing them in skills of test-taking. In some cases, the tests essentially become the curriculum.

Teachers are sometimes energized by the goals their school's staff may set to improve the school's test scores. But a focus on raising students' scores on mandatory state tests has forced many teachers to abandon the teaching methods that they have found to be most effective and lowered their morale. There is some evidence that when school accountability programs are introduced, student scores on state tests that assess basic information and skills tend to increase. While such gains may be important for low-achieving groups, these students may be gaining only low-level knowledge and skills and not deep understanding of subjects or higher skills, such as analysis and problem solving.

Overall, evidence concerning the effects of programs to make schools accountable for their students' learning indicates that such programs pose the following dilemma for educators, parents, and the public: How can we hold school principals and teachers responsible for their students' scores on tests without causing them to focus their curriculum and teaching on these tests in ways that degrade, rather than upgrade, the quality of education?

While answers to this question are not easy, a review of the evidence sug-gests that the following guidelines can contribute to a good system of school accountability:

1. Tests are tied to curriculum content standards that place specific facts in the context of central concepts and general principles.
2. Both objective tests that assess primarily knowledge of specific facts and basic skills, and performance tests that are better able to assess thinking skills (analysis, problem solving, applications of principles, etc.), are used. Using several kinds of tests not only gives a better pic-ture of student learning but also keeps the school program from becoming too narrow.

3. Schools make public, and are evaluated in part on, the number of their students who drop out or leave the school for other reasons. Otherwise, high test scores may be bought at the price of losing, or forcing out, many students.

4. The methods of evaluating school performance are clearly understandable to, and seen as fair by, school staff and the public. Otherwise, they will not give their full support to the program.

5. School staff are given incentives, such as getting more resources for the school, monetary bonuses, and public recognition, to work for good performance by their school.

6. Test results are used to improve the school's educational program. Specific areas in which the knowledge or skills of students generally are weak are identified and needed improvements in curriculum and instruction are made accordingly.

7. Low-performing schools are given the resources and expertise they need to improve. Changes in such schools are aimed not only at improving scores on standardized tests but also at giving students the broad understanding and problem-solving skills that they need to have.

These specific guidelines may be modified or improved. The goal would remain to get a good assessment of more than just superficial student learning and to use this information to improve the school's capacities to produce genuine learning for all students.

NOTES

1. J. Coleman, et al., *Redesigning American Education.* Boulder, CO: Westview Press, 1997.

2. For a discussion of the pros and cons on this issue, see B. Falk, Standards-Based Reforms: Problems and Possibilities. *Phi Delta Kappan, 83,* 2002, 612–620.

3. For one critique, see A. Kohn, *The Case Against Standardized Testing.* Portsmouth, NH: Heinemann, 2000.

4. J. Merrow, Undermining Standards. *Phi Delta Kappan, 82,* 2001, 653–659.

5. See H. Erickson, *Concept-Based Curriculum and Instruction.* Thousand Oaks, CA: Corwin Press, 1998.

6. R. Linn, E. Baker and D. Betebenner, Accountability Systems: Implications of Requirements of the No Child Left Behind Act of 2001. *Educational Researcher, 31,* 2002, 3–16, p. 4.

7. Linn and others, op cit., p. 4.

8. See C. Bereiter and M. Scardemalia, Cognition and Curriculum. In P. Jackson, ed., *Handbook of Research on Curriculum.* New York: Macmillan, 1992, pp. 486–516.

9. J. Hiebert and Others, *Making Sense: Teaching and Learning Mathematics with Understanding.* Portsmouth, NH: Heineman, 1997; K. Fuson, W. Carroll, and J.

Drueck, Achievement Results for Second and Third Graders Using the Standards-Based Curriculum, *Everyday Mathematics. Journal for Research in Mathematics Education, 11*, 2000, 277–295.

10. Hiebert, et al., Ibid., p. 1.
11. D. Gratz, High Standards for Whom? *Phi Delta Kappan, 81*, 2000, 681–687.
12. Gratz, Ibid., p. 682.
13. See M. Dembo, *Applying Educational Psychology.* New York: Longman, 1994, Chapter 12.
14. See Dembo, Ibid.; J. Travers, S. Elliott, and T. Kratochwill, *Educational Psychology.* Madison, WI: Brown and Benchmark, 1993.
15. See, for example, M. Patchen, *Black-White Contact in School: Its Social and Academic Effects.* W. Lafayette, IN: Purdue University Press, 1982.
16. K. Wilson and B. Daviss, *Redesigning Education.* New York: Henry Holt, 1994, p. 140.
17. G. Madaus et al., *The Influence of Testing on Teaching Math and Science in Grades 4–12.* Boston: Center for the Study of Testing, Evaluation and Educational Policy, Boston College, 1992.
18. P. Behuniak, Consumer-Referenced Testing. *Phi Delta Kappan, 84*, 2002, 204.
19. J. Pedulla et al., *Perceived Effects of State-Mandated Testing Programs on Teaching and Learning.* Chestnut Hill, MA: National Board on Educational Testing and Public Policy, School of Education, Boston College, 2003.
20. G. Wiggins, *Assessing Student Performance.* San Francisco: Jossey-Bass, 1993, p. 154.
21. Wiggins, Ibid., p. 153.
22. M. Patchen, *Diversity and Unity: Relations Between Racial and Ethnic Groups.* Thousand Oaks, CA: Wadsworth, 1999.
23. National Center for Research on Evaluations, Standards, and Student Testing, *Measurement of Workforce Readiness Competencies.* Washington, DC: U.S. Department of Education, 1992.
24. Wiggins, *Assessing Student Performance*, p. 77.
25. Dembo, *Applying Educational Psychology*, p. 574.
26. See R. Rothman, *Measuring Up: Standards, Assessment, and School Reform.* San Francisco, Jossey-Bass, 1995.
27. Rothman, Ibid., Chapter 3.
28. R. Hambleton et al., Setting Performance Standards on Complex Educational Assessments. *Applied Psychological Measurement, 24*, 2000, 355–366.
29. Rothman, *Measuring Up*, Chapter 1.
30. Rothman, *Measuring Up*, Chapter 4.
31. Rothman, *Measuring Up*, p. 100.
32. Wilson and Daviss, *Redesigning Education*, p. 147.
33. Rothman, *Measuring Up*, pp. 158–160.
34. R. Brennan, Performance Assessments from the Perspective of Generalizability Theory. *Applied Psychological Measurement, 24*, 2000, 339–353.
35. See Dembo, *Applying Educational Psychology*, p. 585; Rothman, Measuring Up, Chapter 4; B. Whitford and K. Jones, *Accountability, Assessment, and Teacher Commitment.* Albany: State University of New York Press, 2000, Chapter 15.
36. Rothman, *Measuring Up*, p. 12.
37. Wiggins, *Assessing Student Performance*, p. 6; italics in original.

38. Wiggins, Ibid., p. 12.

39. Department of Education and Science, *Task Group on Assessment and Testing Report.* London: Her Majesty's Stationery Office, 1988; pars. 37, 14.

40. J. Podl, et al., *The Process of Planning Backwards: Stories from Three Schools.* Providence, RI: Coalition of Essential Schools, Brown University, p. 12.

41. See M. Alderman, *Motivation for Achievement: Possibilities for Teaching and Learning.* Mahwah, NJ: Lawrence Erlbaum, 1999.

42. D. Ruff, D. Smith, and L. Miller, The View from Maine: Developing Learner-Centered Accountability in a Local Control State. In B. Whitford and K. Jones, eds., *Accountability, Assessment, and Teacher Commitment.* Albany: State University of New York Press, 2000, pp. 163–178.

43. T. Coladarci, Is It a House or a Pile of Bricks: Important Features of a Local Assessment System. *Phi Delta Kappan, 83,* 2002, 772–774.

44. Rothman, *Measuring Up,* pp. 97–98, 114.

45. B. Falk, Standards-Based Reforms: Problems and Possibilities. *Phi Delta Kappan, 83,* 2002, 612–620.

46. J. Merrow, Undermining Standards. *Phi Delta Kappan, 82,* 2001, 652–659.

47. G. Natriello and S. Dornbusch, *Teacher Evaluative Standards and Student Effort.* New York: Longman, 1984.

48. Natriello and Dornbusch, Ibid.; R. Hauser, What If We Ended Social Promotion? *Education Week,* April 7, 1999, pp. 64, 37.

49. Hauser, Ibid.

50. W. Mathis, No Child Left Behind: Costs and Benefits. *Phi Delta Kappan, 84,* 2003, 679–686.

51. B. Wilson and G. Rossman, *Mandating Academic Excellence: High School Responses to State Curriculum Reform.* New York: Teachers College Press, 1993, Chapter 2.

52. T. Wagner, Reinventing America's Schools. *Phi Delta Kappan, 84,* 2003, 665–668.

53. W. Cala, An Allegory on Educational Testing, *Phi Delta Kappan, 84,* 2003, 514–516.

54. L. Nathan, The Human Face of the High-Stakes Testing Story. *Phi Delta Kappan, 83,* 2002, 595–600.

55. See Merrow, Understanding Standards, regarding frequent absence of links between testing and remediation.

56. C. Sager, *Eliminating Grades in Schools.* Milwaukee, WI: ASQC Quality Press, 1995, Section 1.

57. Sager, Ibid.; H. Kirschenbaum, R. Napier, and S. Simon. *Wad-ja-get: The Grading Game in American Education.* New York: Hart Publishing, 1971, Chapter 12.

58. Sager, *Eliminating Grades,* Section 2.

59. R.D. Hoge and T. Coladarci, Teacher-Based Judgment of Academic Achievement: A Review of the Literature. *Review of Educational Research,* 1989, 297–313.

60. G. Robinson and J. Craver, *Assessing and Grading Student Achievement.* Arlington, VA: Educational Research Service, 1989.

61. Kirschenbaum, et al., *Wad-ja-get,* Chapter 12.

62. Sager, *Eliminating Grades,* p. 10.

63. Sager, *Eliminating Grades,* p. 7.

64. Kirschenbaum, et al., *Wad-ja-get*, Chapter 12.
65. Sager, *Eliminating Grades*, p. 23.
66. Kirschenbaum, et al., *Wad-ja-get*, p. 181.
67. Sager, *Eliminating Grades*, p. 22.
68. Sager, *Eliminating Grades*, p. 9.
69. Natriello and Dornbusch, *Teacher Evaluative Standards*.
70. Natriello and Dornbusch, *Teacher Evaluative Standards*, pp. 105–106.
71. Natriello and Dornbusch, *Teacher Evaluative Standards*, p. 141.
72. Natriello and Dornbusch, *Teacher Evaluative Standards*, p. 11.
73. Sager, *Eliminating Grades*.
74. Robinson and Craver, *Assessing and Grading*.
75. Sager, *Eliminating Grades*, p. 35.
76. See Kirschenbaum, et al., *Wad-ja-get*; Dembo, *Applying Educational Psychology*.
77. For a brief review of this research, see Dembo, *Applying Educational Psychology*, pp. 79–80.
78. Dembo, Ibid., pp. 80–81; this study focused on college courses.
79. R. Elmore, C. Abelmann, and S. Fuhrman. The New Accountability in State Education Reform. In H. Ladd, ed., *Holding Schools Accountable*. Washington, DC: Brookings Institution Press, 1996, p. 82.
80. See C. Clotfelter and H. Ladd. Recognizing and Rewarding Success in Public Schools. In Ladd, *Holding Schools Accountable*, pp. 30–31.
81. Clotfelter and Ladd, Ibid., pp. 31–32.
82. Clotfelter and Ladd, Recognizing and Rewarding Success.
83. Elmore, et al., The New Accountability, p. 94.
84. Linn, et al., Accountability Systems.
85. Linn, et al., Accountability Systems, p. 13.
86. Elmore, et al., The New Accountability, p. 79.
87. Elmore, et al., The New Accountability.
88. Quoted by Rothman, *Measuring Up*, p. 46.
89. See K. Marshall, A Principal Looks Back: Standards Matter. *Phi Delta Kappan, 85,* 2003, 104–113; R. Elmore and S. Fuhrman, Holding Schools Accountable: Is It Working? *Phi Delta Kappan, 83,* 2001, 67–72.
90. Pedulla, et al., Perceived Effects of State Mandated Testing Programs.
91. G. Madaus, et al., *The Influence of Testing on Teaching Math and Science in Grades 4–12.* Boston: Center for Study of Testing, Evaluation and Educational Policy, Boston College, 1992.
92. Mathis, No Child Left Behind: Costs and Benefits.
93. L. McNeil, *Contradictions of School Reform.* New York: Routledge, 2000.
94. Nathan, The Human Face of the High-Stakes Testing Story.
95. McNeil, *Contradictions of School Reform*.
96. Madaus, et al., *The Influence of Testing*.
97. O. Jorgenson and R. Vanosdall, The Death of Science? What We Risk in Our Rush to Standardized Testing and the Three R's. *Phi Delta Kappan, 83,* 2002, 601–605.
98. McNeil, *Contradictions of School Reform*.
99. McNeil, *Contradictions of School Reform*, XXVI
100. Elmore, Holding Schools Accountable.
101. Pedulla, et al., Perceived Effects of State-Mandated Testing Programs.

102. Jorgenson and Vanosdall, The Death of Science?

103. Falk, Standards-Based Reforms.

104. Whitford and Jones, *Accountability, Assessment, and Teacher Commitment*, p. 60.

105. Clotfelter and Ladd, Recognizing and Rewarding Success.

106. Rothman, *Measuring Up*, pp. 87–88.

107. R. Anderson, *California: The State of Assessment.* Sacramento, CA: California Department of Education, 1990.

108. J. Scheurich and L. Skrla, Continuing the Conversation on Equity and Accountability. *Phi Delta Kappan, 83*, 322–326; Whitford and Jones, Accountability, Assessment, and Teacher Commitment.

109. Elmore, et al., The New Accountability, p. 78.

110. Clotfelter and Ladd, Recognizing and Rewarding Success.

111. McNeil, *Contradictions of School Reform*, p. 237.

112. G. Winter, More Schools Rely on Tests, But Big Study Raises Doubts. *New York Times*, December 28, 2002; A1; quote A13.

113. D. Hoff, Standards at Crossroads After Decade. *Education Week*, September 22, 1999.

114. R. Meyer, Comments on Chapters Two, Three, and Four. In Ladd, *Holding Schools Accountable*; T. Lewin and J. Medina, To Cut Failure Rate, Schools Shed Students. *New York Times*, July 31, 2003, A1; McNeil, *Contradictions of School Reform*, p. 25.

115. McNeil, *Contradictions of School Reform*, p. 25.

116. R. Meyer, Comments.

117. Clotfelter and Ladd, Recognizing and Rewarding Success.

118. Elmore, *Holding Schools Accountable.*

119. D. Cohen, Standards-Based School Reform: Policy, Practice, and Performance. In Ladd, *Holding Schools Accountable*, p. 124.

120. Elmore, et al., The New Accountability, p. 83.

121. Elmore, et al., Ibid., p. 83.

122. Elmore, *Holding Schools Accountable.*

123. Whitford and Jones, *Accountability, Assessment, and Teacher Commitment*, p. 21.

Chapter 8

FAMILY CHOICE AMONG SCHOOLS: THE CONTROVERSY ABOUT CHOICE

Some people who are dissatisfied with the current performance of most American schools believe that efforts by public schools to reform themselves, or by state legislatures to mandate change, have very limited prospects of success. They argue that the fundamental condition that blocks effective school improvements is that public schools have a monopoly on free education and that most parents and students have no choice about the school that students will attend. Therefore, they contend, there is not sufficient pressure on school administrators and teachers to improve their schools. Parents—especially those of modest means—are "stuck" with the school to which their children have been assigned.

The remedy, say these critics of traditional public school systems, is to give each family a choice among a number of schools. Such choice, they say, would permit parents (and older students as well) to choose the school that best matches their own values, interests, and aspirations, and which they judge provides the best education available. Such a choice, proponents say, would be especially helpful to poor families (disproportionately minorities) who are not financially able to make the choices that affluent families now have available.

Giving families a choice among schools is seen by proponents of this idea as the best way to hold schools accountable and to force them to improve. If, in "voting with their feet," many families leave or do not enroll in a particular school, it will be forced to change in ways that meet the needs and wishes of its clientele (especially if funding is tied to enrollment).

Many advocates of school choice believe that the same mechanisms that work in markets—decentralization, competition, and consumer sovereignty—will work in schooling as well. In such an environment, schools would be autonomous and free to develop their own educational strategy and mission. In such schools, where educators, parents, and students share values and goals, a strong sense of community will develop. Students will be more highly motivated and they and their parents will be more satisfied than those in traditional schools.[1]

The high hopes pinned on the idea of school choice are shown in the following statement by two of its advocates, John Chubb and Terry Moe: "Choice . . . has the capacity *all by itself* to bring about the kind of transformation that, for years, reformers have been seeking to engineer in myriad other ways."[2]

Giving families choice among schools has been advocated especially by two groups. The first (and earlier) set of supporters are conservatives who generally see free-market solutions as superior to these devised by government. The second (and more recent) group of supporters are some advocates for low-income minority groups who see parental choice as a way of improving subpar inner-city schools.

In response to those who promote family choice among schools, advocates of the traditional common school make several major arguments. First, they maintain that, by providing a common education to children of all social classes and ethnic backgrounds, the public schools lay the groundwork for a unified and democratic society. Defenders of the common public school see school choice programs as leading to a segmenting of American youth—and ultimately adult society—into a variety of separate groups on the basis of talent, interests, economic status, gender, religion, and other social characteristics. Such a social division may occur not only because of different preferences and different resources among families, but also as a result of selection by "schools of choice" of those students (and families) whom they are willing to admit. Among other social divisions that school choice will foster, critics of such programs contend, is greater segregation of students by social class and by race and ethnicity.

Defenders of the common public school also see school choice programs as weakening the regular public school system. They point to the fact that money that might otherwise be used to maintain and improve the common public schools may be used for alternative schools instead. They argue also that alternative schools may remove from the common schools the more able and more motivated students and the most active and engaged parents. Thus, the common public schools may be weakened and have greater difficulty providing a quality education to the large number of students for whom they will retain responsibility.[3]

Some of the opposition to parental choice programs has come from many of those on the liberal side of the political spectrum, including some representatives of minority groups. These liberals see such programs as being intended primarily to benefit the affluent, as leading to greater stratification and segregation, and as undermining the public schools.

Opposition to school choice programs also has come from many educators, including administrators and teachers unions. Educators have been especially concerned about the effects of choice programs on the public schools, including possible effects on their own professional positions.

While debates about general principles of school choice may be useful, it is important to distinguish among various school choice programs. Such programs differ with respect to the number of options available to families; information about schools provided to families; public versus private control of schools; public accountability of schools; rules for selection of students by schools; and socioeconomic and other barriers to choice among schools by families. The major types of choice programs include intra-district choice plans, alternative and magnet schools, charter schools, and voucher plans. I next examine each of these types of programs, looking at their characteristics and at evidence of their effectiveness in improving education.

CHOICE WITHIN PUBLIC SCHOOL DISTRICTS

While assignment of children to their neighborhood public school is still common in American communities, some parents and students have been offered choices within the public school system. I consider first choices of schools—alternative schools, magnet schools, and other non-neighborhood schools—that are administered by the regular administration of a school district. (Charter schools, which are publicly supported schools that are more independent of the regular school administration, are considered in the next section).

ALTERNATIVE SCHOOLS

A few public schools offering specialized or nontraditional education operated early in the twentieth century. In the 1960s, when a general anti-establishment mood was widespread in the United States, parents who were dissatisfied with the constraints of traditional classrooms and wanted to give their children more freedom to develop their talents, succeeded in persuading many school systems to create some "alternative schools." Since that time, the number of alternative schools has expanded greatly. In addition to schools having a "progressive" style in curricula and pedagogy, alternative schools of other curricula types, designed to serve students with disciplinary problems; gifted students; students of a particular ethnicity; boys; girls; and other particular groups, have multiplied. Estimates of the number of alternative schools in the 1990s ranged from 2,000 to 6,000 and the numbers of such schools, especially those for "at-risk" students, has grown since then.[4]

MAGNET SCHOOLS

Starting in the 1970s, "magnet" schools that provided a specialized type of curriculum or emphasized a particular pedagogical approach were created. Their main purpose originally was to increase racial mixing in the public schools by drawing together families and students with similar interests but diverse ethnicity from all parts of each school district. At the elementary and middle school levels, magnet schools may focus, for example, on basic skills; on foreign languages; on visual performance and creative arts; on science, math, and computers; or on gifted and talented students. At the high school level, magnet schools are more likely to be oriented toward careers; they include, for example, schools giving special emphasis to science, engineering, aviation, business and marketing, creative and performing arts, medical careers, and college preparation.

By 1991, there were 2,433 magnet schools in 230 school districts serving 1.2 million students. Magnet schools are more likely to be found in central cities than elsewhere.[5]

Many magnet schools are selective in admitting students. A national study in 1994 found that about a quarter of magnet elementary schools and over half of magnet high schools had an admission test.[6]

OPEN ENROLLMENT AND CONTROLLED CHOICE

Alternative schools and magnet schools may provide at most a few alternatives to neighborhood schools which children may attend (if admitted). Open enrollment plans make choice among all the schools in a district—regular neighborhood schools as well as any alternative or magnet schools—available to all families. Students are assigned first to neighborhood schools, after which they may be enrolled in any other district school, so long as space is available.

Another way of permitting families to choose among schools is that of "controlled choice." Under this type of plan, there are no neighborhood schools. Most schools are alternative or magnet schools instead. Families rank-order their preferences among schools in their district. The district office or individual schools then assign students to schools, taking into account factors such as available space and the racial and ethnic composition of each school. Usually, most families get their first choice and about 90 percent get their first or second choice under this type of plan.[7]

A recent review of school choice developments estimated that there are about 1,200 school districts serving about 8 million students that operate under some type of open enrollment.[8]

OUTCOMES OF CHOICE AMONG DISTRICT PUBLIC SCHOOLS

What happens when families are able to choose among schools in their district rather than being assigned to a neighborhood school? We consider next the outcomes for parents, for students, and for the school system.

Exercise of Choice

When parents are able to choose among district schools, on what basis do they choose? Several studies find that most parents choose schools for their children mainly on academic criteria, such as high standards, teacher quality, and high student performance.[9] However, there are some differences in the choices of parents of different backgrounds.

First, where parents have the option of accepting a neighborhood school assignment or making a choice among schools, those of higher education and income are more likely to exercise their option to choose.[10] In addition, socioeconomic status and ethnicity may affect the type of school that parents prefer. A study of family choice of schools in two New York and New Jersey districts found that minority (mostly black and Hispanic) parents, and parents who have graduated from high school but not from college, are more likely than other parents to value discipline, safety, and high test scores. Whites and college graduates placed higher value than other parents on teacher quality, teaching of values, and diversity in the school.[11]

Commenting on the greater concern about strong academic performance shown by minorities and non-college graduates, Mark Schneider and his colleagues say: ". . . test scores act as gatekeepers to success in higher education and the labor market. While higher-status parents know this, their children have more options and alternatives when considering the future. . . . Because these parents can take the academic performance of their schools as a relative 'given,' they can ask their schools to emphasize other aspects of education—for example, humanistic approaches to learning."[12]

To make informed choices, families need information about various schools that their children may attend. But often parents do not have much accurate information about such matters as test scores and class sizes in the various schools that their children may attend. Lower-income and minority parents especially tend to know relatively little about non-neighborhood schools.[13] Commenting on parents' limited information about school choice options, Mark Schneider and his colleagues suggest that school planners "need to begin to think more carefully and creatively about outreach and information dissemination activities."[14]

Parental Involvement and Satisfaction

Several studies have found that parents of students in magnet schools and parents in intra-district choice programs are generally more involved in their children's schools than are parents of children in neighborhood schools.[15] For example, parents of public school students attending schools of choice in several New York and New Jersey districts were more likely than parents of students in neighborhood schools to be PTA members, to volunteer in school activities, to trust teachers, and to talk to other parents.[16]

Parents who choose a school are more likely than other parents to be involved even when their demographic characteristics (education, race, etc.) are held constant.[17]

The "choosers" may tend to have different personal characteristics (such as being more active) than others. In addition, public schools of choice may generally provide more inviting milieus for parent involvement. There is evidence, for example, that magnet school parents are more likely than other parents to see a supportive, caring climate that welcomes their involvement in the school.[18]

Parental involvement in public schools of choice also may reflect their positive attitudes toward their children's schools. Parents who choose a public school are more likely to be satisfied with their children's school than are the parents of children in neighborhood schools.[19] This higher satisfaction may stem from the fact that the schools these parents have chosen match their preferences better than do their neighborhood schools. Greater satisfaction among public school "choosers" also may stem from people's tendency to justify their choices (in order to reduce "dissonance" between the fact of their choice and the outcome of their choice).

One study, using a national sample of public high schools, found that parents generally were more satisfied with schools that have selective admissions procedures, even though those schools did not differ from matched schools in curricula, teaching methods, student achievement, and extracurricular activities.[20] In discussing the results of this study, Mary Driscoll suggests that—whatever the reasons for the greater satisfaction among parents—such parental satisfaction may contribute to a stronger school community.

Students' Attitudes and Behavior

A great deal of evidence shows consistently that students who attend alternative schools or magnet schools exhibit more positive attitudes and behavior in school than do their peers in neighborhood schools. Research on alternative schools has focused mainly on schools attended by at-risk students. One study found that 60 at-risk students in three alternative high schools were less disruptive and more positive about school than a matched group of students from regular high schools in the same districts.[21] Several studies have found that students in alternative high schools are absent less often than those in conventional schools. One researcher surveyed 1,200 alternative secondary schools and programs. Eighty-one percent of these schools reported that students' attendance had improved compared to their attendance in their previous schools.[22] Other studies have found that students in alternative schools are more satisfied with school than are those in conventional schools.[23]

Results from studies of magnet schools in New York State, Maryland, Los Angeles, and elsewhere are consistent with the results from the studies of alternative schools. They find magnet schools generally to have positive effects on student attitudes and behavior. These positive outcomes include more positive attitudes about teachers and school, fewer behavior problems, more on-task behavior, and better attendance compared to students in regular schools. In addition, several studies indicate that students in magnet schools generally have higher educational aspirations and are less likely to drop out of school than are students of similar backgrounds in regular schools.[24] For example, a New York State study of 41 magnet schools in eight school districts found that three-fourths of the magnet schools had lower dropout rates than their district averages.[25]

Student Achievement

Evidence concerning the academic achievement of students in public schools of choice also is almost uniformly positive. Most of the relevant evidence comes from studies that compare the scores on achievement tests of students in magnet schools and in regular public schools. Many of these studies have found the average scores of students in magnet schools on standardized tests of reading and mathematics to be above the average scores of schools in their district. Several of these studies, including studies in Montclair, New Jersey, and in Prince George County, Maryland, found that when magnet programs were instituted in a school district, test scores rose for both white students and black students. Moreover, in magnet elementary schools in Prince George County, the gap in scores between black students and white students narrowed in magnet schools.[26]

It should be noted that the higher achievement of students in magnet schools may sometimes be affected by differences in their family backgrounds or by students' own characteristics, such as previous achievement levels. However, several studies have held constant other factors that may affect achievement and still found that students in magnet schools achieved better than students in regular schools. One study compared the growth in achievement during high school of New York City students who won lotteries to attend magnet schools with similar students who were unsuccessful in these lotteries.[27] Since the winners and losers were chosen by chance, selection effects were absent and there was no reason to suspect these two groups differed in any way. Lottery winners who attended magnet schools improved their reading scores more, earned more course credits, and were less likely to drop out of school than those who lost in the lottery and attended regular public high schools.

A national survey compared the achievement of students in magnet high schools and in comprehensive high schools (all in central cities) on tests of mathematics, science, reading, and social studies.[28] Achievement scores of students in the two types of schools were adjusted, in turn, for differences in student characteristics (e.g., earlier achievement, race, and socioeconomic status) and for differences in school context (e.g., percentage

African-American, percentage receiving free lunch). Even with the effects of student characteristics and of school context held constant, students in magnet high schools had significantly higher scores on tests in science, reading, and social studies.

Why do students who attend magnet schools and other public schools of choice tend to do better in their studies than similar students in neighborhood schools? Differences in courses taken do not explain the magnet school advantage. Data from the national survey of high school students show that, compared to students in public comprehensive schools, students in public magnet schools took only slightly more math and science courses, the same number of English courses, and somewhat fewer social studies courses. Moreover, when student achievement scores were controlled for any differences in number of academic courses taken, magnet school students still scored significantly higher than those in regular high schools.

Results from the same national study also showed that the higher achievement of magnet high school students, compared to those in regular high schools, could not be explained by differences in the composition of schools' student bodies (e.g., percentage African-American, percentage Latino, percentage in single-parent families, and percentage receiving free or reduced-price lunches).

Another possible explanation for the higher achievement of students in public schools of choice—especially of those in magnet schools—is that staff and students in these schools have a sense of shared interests and purpose that bonds them together. One study of programs for at-risk students and magnet programs found that effective programs provided students a sense of membership in the school community.[29] Adam Gamoran states: "A sense of membership, reflecting the trust, norms, and obligations that constitute social capital, increases students' commitment to and engagement with school work, and is thus likely to promote achievement."[30] However, Gamoran's analysis of data from the national survey of high school students (referred to previously) did not find evidence to support the idea that greater student attachment to their schools is a cause of the higher achievement of magnet school students.

Still another possible explanation for the relatively high academic achievement of magnet school students is that the faculty of schools with a special curriculum or pedagogical focus may be more highly motivated and may have higher expectations for students than do teachers in regular schools. In a report on their study of career magnet high schools in New York City, Crain, Hebner and Si say: "the school's 'theme' . . . creates an identity for the school which gives faculty a meaningful purpose in education, motivates them to hold students to higher standards, and helps the school develop an integrated and coherent educational philosophy."[31]

A large-scale U.S. Department of Education study of more than 1,000 magnet schools found that, in general, teachers in magnet schools were more committed than were their peers in conventional public schools.[32] A smaller study that compared teacher attitudes in seven alternative schools and six conventional schools found that teachers in the alternative schools were generally more satisfied.[33] Thus, there is some evidence (although it is very limited) indicating that teachers in schools with a special educational focus generally may be more enthusiastic about their work and may have higher expectations for their students, as compared to teachers in regular schools.

Variations in Outcomes

The evidence reviewed in this section indicates that giving families choice among public schools has generally led to some positive outcomes. Parents who have chosen their children's school are more involved in and more satisfied with the school than are parents whose children are assigned to neighborhood schools. Students in public schools of choice generally have more positive attitudes toward school, appear more engaged in their schoolwork and, most significant, have higher achievement in academic subjects.

After reviewing the evidence from their study of intra-district choice in New York City and New Jersey, Mark Schneider and his colleagues suggest that choice among public schools can provide a stimulus to improved public education similar to that sometimes provided by private schools. They say;

> . . . by providing venues in which parents can signal greater interest and involvement in quality education and where parents with shared values can congregate, alternative public schools, like sectarian schools, provide the milieu in which functional communities can grow and where learning can increase. But unlike the separation between public schools and private schools, the fact that these alternative schools are *public* schools creates more competitive pressure on other public schools than private schools ever would.[34]

It is important to recognize, however, that giving families choice among public schools is not a "magic bullet" that will automatically produce improved or excellent schools. There is great variation among alternative schools, among magnet schools, and among schools in districts that have choice plans. For example, Mary Metz intensively studied three magnet middle schools in a midwestern city.[35] She found that these magnet schools differed widely in a number of important ways, including the kinds of activities in classrooms (e.g., whether lectures by teachers or cooperative student projects were emphasized); in the friendliness of relations between teachers and students and among students; in faculty culture (e.g., whether teachers generally had a sense of efficacy); and in the relations between teachers and the principal (e.g., whether they worked together to define the school's mission). These kinds of variations among magnet schools made a difference for their educational effectiveness. The operation and effectiveness of these schools also was affected by a variety of outside constraints, including school district rules and teacher union pressures.

Providing families with choice among public schools usually will increase the probability that parents, staff, and students will share common goals. But to reach these goals, school administrators and teachers must still fashion an effective school organization, good curriculum, and effective classroom methods.

Economic and Ethnic Divisions

When public school systems permit families to choose among schools, what effect does this system have on the grouping of students by social class and ethnicity? First, one may note that children from African-American and Hispanic families and from families with relatively low education and income are more likely than others to be in magnet schools and other public schools of choice. Data from the National Longitudinal Survey of 1988, for example, showed that 11.5 percent of African-American students and 11.3 percent of Hispanic students attended a magnet high school; among white students, only 2.9 percent attended a magnet school. Among students whose parents' income was under $25,000, 7.4 percent attended a magnet high school, but only 3.8 percent of students from families who earned over $50,000 were in magnet high schools. Similarly, African-American students, Hispanic students, and students from families with less education and lower incomes were more likely than whites and students from higher-status families to attend vocational or technical high schools. The greater likelihood that students from minority ethnic groups and those from lower socioeconomic backgrounds will attend magnet or vocational-technical schools seems mainly a result of the fact that most specialized schools of these types are located in central cities whose populations are heavily non-white and relatively low in education and income.[36]

Do schools of choice in a given school district "skim off" the better students and those students whose parents are better educated? There is some evidence that this is the case. A study in Cincinnati found that parents of students in magnet schools had higher socioeconomic status than parents of students in non-magnet schools. Several studies of intra-district choice programs in San Antonio and New York City found that parents of children in choice schools were better educated than those parents whose children stayed in their neighborhood schools. An analysis of an inter-district public school choice program in Massachusetts found that students who moved from one district to another had higher test scores and came from families of higher socioeconomic status than students who stayed in their district.[37]

Another study of magnet schools in school districts in Boston, Chicago, New York City, and Philadelphia found that these schools gave preference to students with good records of academic attainment, attendance, and behavior and tended to reject those with learning problems.[38] These schools often had complex application procedures that discouraged less sophisticated and motivated parents from signing up their children. They often sent undesirable students back to their neighborhood schools. Researchers Donald Moore and Suzanne Davenport comment: "A system that is supposed to provide students with choices has, too frequently, left the typical entering high school student in our big cities, and especially students at risk, out in the cold."[39] Other researchers have found that alternative schools for at-risk students have sometimes been used primarily to remove and isolate such students from mainstream schools and programs.[40]

A major purpose behind the establishment of magnet schools in the 1970s was to encourage racial integration in schools, primarily by keeping white families and students in central city school districts. In some areas, students choosing magnet schools or other specialized public schools over neighborhood schools have been disproportionately white. However, results from a national study indicate that both African-American students and Hispanic students who attended a public high school of choice (magnet, vocational-technical, or other) tended to have fewer white classmates than did minority students who attended a neighborhood school.[41] Commenting on these results, Stephen Plank and his colleagues say: ". . . a finding that . . . the various types of schools of choice may be more segregated than assigned schools or indistinguishable from assigned schools in their student composition indicates a failure of these schools of choice to achieve one of their stated purposes."[42]

To counter the tendency for school choice to lead to separation among social groups, many school districts have tried to "balance" enrollments, especially in terms of race and ethnicity. Districts sometimes have used a "controlled choice" plan, in which administrators override the first school choices of some families in order to get a desired racial and ethnic student composition. Administrators also may reduce or eliminate admission requirements for specialized schools.

Some writers on public schools of choice assert that every school should be "balanced" in terms of its student composition. For example, Timothy Young and Evans Clinchy state: "Every school should have a student population that is a cross section or microcosm of a district's total school population, including poor, minority, at-risk, and handicapped students."[43] Other writers point out that there are costs to such a policy—a limitation of family choice and much greater difficulty in creating schools that are distinctive in their goals and methods of education.[44] Thus, communities and schools are faced with a problem of trying to balance several social goods— family choice, distinctive school programs, and racial and class diversity— that are not fully compatible.

CHARTER SCHOOLS

THE CHARTER CONCEPT

A relatively new type of organization created to give families alternatives among public schools is the charter school.[45] A charter school is a public school that operates autonomously from the district school administration. Although supported by public funds, it has substantial control over its own budget, curriculum, instruction, hiring of staff, schedule, and other matters. It is open to all students who wish to attend (subject to space limitation).

A charter school may be operated by a number of different types of groups, such as a group of parents, a team of teachers, a community organization, a university, or (in some states) a private profit-making firm. It may be a new school or an existing school (either previously private or previously part of the public school system).

The school is given a charter for a specified period of time (typically five years) to educate children according to its own philosophy and design. It is supposed to be held accountable to the terms of its charter, which can be terminated if the school does not fulfill its terms.

The charter school concept has been appealing to a broad range of groups in American society. By providing families with more choice and promising more competition among schools, it appeals to social conservatives. By keeping schools of choice within the public school system, it is acceptable to liberals and to teacher unions that are dedicated to preserving public schools.

The first charter school law in the Unites States was passed by Minnesota in 1991. Most states (38 states by 1999) followed quickly with their own charter school laws. By September 1999, there were about 1,700 charter schools operating[46] and the number has been steadily rising since then.

The laws governing charter schools vary among states. Rules vary concerning the difficulty of opening a charter school, what kind of charter schools may earn a profit, whether a for-profit organization can run a charter school under contract with the founder, the level of public funding, the length of time for which charters are granted, and other matters.[47]

WHAT CHARTER SCHOOLS ARE LIKE

What are charter schools like? In what ways are they different from regular public schools?

Most charter schools are small. The median enrollment in 1996–1997 was 150 students, compared to 500 students in other public schools in states with charter schools. More than 60 percent of charter schools had fewer than 200 students; only 16 percent of regular public schools had fewer than 200 students.[48]

There is more variability among charter schools than among regular public schools in their curriculum emphasis and in the student populations they serve. For example, in Arizona, some charter schools are designed to serve at-risk adolescents, some are designed for college-bound high school students, and some have a special focus on a particular pedagogical approach (such as Montessori schools and other schools emphasizing active or cooperative learning). There also are content-centered elementary schools (such as those emphasizing high academic standards and mandatory homework); other elementary schools with diverse emphases, such as on bilingualism or on packaged computer courses; and junior and senior high schools that include schools focusing on native American language and culture and on performing arts.[49]

Innovation

A major rationale for creating charter schools is that such schools will be free to break out of traditional molds, to be innovative, and to provide new and better models of educational practice. Has this happened?

There are instances in which a charter school has used its autonomy to devise an innovative, effective program. One such positive example is a Minnesota charter school in which "students work through a competency-based curriculum, using a curricula guide and completing projects in nine curricula areas. Teachers serve as facilitators, advise groups of students on projects, consult with parents, and assess progress."[50] The regular school board in this district has been so impressed with the successful innovations at this charter school that it has introduced some of its program in the traditional public schools.

However, such exemplary schools appear to represent a minority of charter schools. Most research does not find much evidence that charter schools have been especially innovative in their curricula or instructional methods.[51] A study in Michigan found that little curriculum innovation occurred in charter schools, in part because teachers were excluded from making curriculum decisions. A study of 75 charter schools in Arizona found that none of their curricula was pathbreaking, although the curricula of charter schools did have a clearer focus and greater variation than those of other district schools. Many charter high schools in Arizona are managed by "chains" that used standardized curriculum and instructional methods.

In a report on the first few years of charter schools in New Mexico, Jean Casey and her associates said:

> For the most part, the curricula are traditional, and teachers employ rather
> standard methodologies. In some cases, commercially produced curriculum

programs have been substituted for original designs. The only true and successful innovations at this time seem to be service learning/community-based projects and mentoring programs, which are found in about half of the currently operating charter schools.[52]

Reports on California charter schools have presented somewhat differing pictures of their innovativeness. One study found that charter schools in that state were much more likely than comparison public schools to experiment with new instructional practices and to adopt new practices aimed at increasing parent participation.[53] However, another study found that 87 percent of charter schools in California reported using traditional classroom-based approaches to instruction. Also, an intensive study of two California charter schools, based on observations and interviews, found that teachers did not teach any differently then they did previously in non-charter schools.[54]

After reviewing many studies around the United States, Thomas Good and Jennifer Braden concluded: "Overall, innovation in curriculum and classroom instructional strategies was virtually non-existent in charter schools."[55] Advocates of charter schools dispute this assessment.[56] But at most there is only very limited evidence to date that charter schools have been innovative with respect to curriculum and instruction.

Teachers' Roles

Advocates of charter schools have argued that creating such schools will free teachers from restrictive rules and, by giving teachers more autonomy, empower them to function as full and more effective professionals. A number of studies have examined the perceptions of teachers in charter schools about the conditions of their work, often comparing their assessments to those of teachers in regular public schools.

The findings of these studies have been inconsistent. A Hudson Institute study found that, in charter schools across 10 states, a large majority of teachers were satisfied with most aspects of their schools, including teacher decision making.[57] Among Arizona elementary school teachers, a much larger percentage of teachers in charter schools, compared to those in regular district schools, reported having great influence on establishing curricula, selecting instructional materials, and determining class schedules.[58] Survey data and interviews with charter school teachers in Ohio and New Mexico also indicate that most of these teachers see themselves as enjoying a considerable amount of autonomy with respect to topics taught in class and instructional methods.[59]

Contrary to these results, studies in other states have found that teachers in charter schools experienced no more empowerment, or less empowerment, than teachers in regular public schools. One study surveyed teachers in 20 charter elementary schools and in 17 nearby traditional elementary schools in Colorado and Michigan. In Colorado, teachers in traditional schools reported significantly more autonomy over their work (e.g., scheduling, curriculum, textbooks) and greater participation in school decisions that directly affect their work than did charter school teachers. In Michigan there were no significant differences between charter school teachers and traditional school teachers with respect to either autonomy or participation in decision making.[60] A study of two charter schools in California found that, when comparing their present charter schools with regular schools in which they had previously taught, most teachers saw little difference in their degree of autonomy in the classroom. (Charter school teachers in this California study did think they presently had more influence on some school-level decisions.)[61]

While evidence is inconsistent concerning whether charter school teachers enjoy greater autonomy, there is more consistency in evidence indicating that they have high work loads and high levels of stress. For example, a study of charter schools in California found that, in addition to their regular teaching duties, teachers had to perform many tasks—security, cleanup, clerical work, and library tasks—that usually are done by others in traditional (and usually larger) schools.[62] Such problems are especially prominent in the first year or two of a charter school's life, but may persist in later years if support staff in the school is inadequate.

EFFECTIVENESS OF CHARTER SCHOOLS

How successful have charter schools been? Since this type of school is relatively new, evidence on its outcomes—for parents, students, and the schools—is somewhat limited. But some interesting results are available.

Outcomes for Parents

The Charter Schools in Action Project, sponsored by the Hudson Institute, obtained data from about 50 charter schools enrolling about 16,000 students in 10 states. The most common reasons parents gave for choosing charter schools were: small school size; higher standards; a program closer to their educational philosophies; greater opportunity for parent involvement; and better teachers. Asked about their satisfaction with various aspects of their charter schools, large majorities of parents said they were at least "somewhat satisfied" in every way and over 70 percent were "very satisfied" with opportunities for parent participation, class size, curriculum, school size, and individual attention by teachers. Also, a majority of parents rated their charter schools as better than the school their child would otherwise attend in almost every way mentioned.[63]

A study of charter schools in Arizona also found parents to be favorable about the charter schools their children were attending. Large majorities of parents thought that, compared to their child's experiences in his or her previous school, the child was doing either a lot better or a little better in several ways: academically; in attitude toward school learning; in feelings about his or her teachers; and in liking for classmates. Some parents of students in the Arizona charter schools did have concerns about such matters as improvement of the school building and grounds; lack of sports or extracurricular programs; and transportation.[64]

In addition to their generally high satisfaction, parents of students in charter schools have a high level of participation in their children's schools. Studies in California, Michigan, and Arizona have found that parents of charter school students took a more active part in their school's activities, had more communication with the school, and reported more opportunities to be involved than they had in their child's previous school. Parents in charter schools were involved in such activities as volunteering in classrooms, participating in parent training programs, assisting with fund-raising, and serving on governing boards.[65]

The high involvement of charter school parents is not always voluntary. Many charter schools require certain types of participation by parents (e.g., attending parent meetings) and/or require that parents volunteer for a minimum number of hours. Some charter schools have denied admission to, or dismissed, students whose parents were not willing to meet the schools' requirements.[66]

Student Attitudes

Like their parents, most students who have been studied compare their experiences at charter schools favorably with those at other schools. In the Arizona study, large majorities of students in charter schools said they felt better than they had in their previous school concerning how they are doing in their classes; how they feel about going to school; how they like their teachers; and how they like the other students. A study in Michigan found that 64 percent of students attending charter schools said they were learning more than they had at their previous school. The Hudson Institute's survey of students from 39 charter schools in 10 states found that 61 percent said that teachers in their present charter school were better than teachers in their previous school; only 5 percent thought their present teachers were worse. With respect to their interest in schoolwork, 50 percent of charter school students said their present interest was higher, while only 8 percent said their interest had been higher in their previous school. However, a substantial number of charter school students surveyed in several studies expressed dissatisfaction with a perceived lack of enough sports and other extracurricular activities.[67]

Student Achievement

Do charter schools improve students' academic achievement? The limited amount of evidence bearing on this question is mixed.

The Hudson Institute study of students from 39 charter schools in 10 states indicates that students themselves think that they are doing better work in their current charter schools than they did in their previous schools. While about 43 percent of the charter students thought that they had done "excellent" or "good" work in their previous school, 62 percent said they were doing good or excellent work in their current charter school. And while almost 24 percent of the students said they had done "poor" or failing work at their previous school, only 8 percent gave a similar negative view of their work in their present charter school. A more positive judgment about their work at their present school was found among students of all racial and ethnic groups (whites, African-Americans, Hispanics, Asians, and Native Americans). Parents of children in charter schools (including students with learning problems, gifted students, and students with limited English proficiency) also rated their children's performance in their current charter school as better than that in their previous school.[68]

However, evidence from student scores on tests of achievement is mixed. On the positive side, a Colorado study of 32 charter schools that had been operating for at least two years found the average achievement of students in those schools to be higher than that of students at other schools in their districts that serve a similar population of students. In Massachusetts, the academic performance of students attending each of 21 charter schools was compared to the performance of other students in their districts. Students in most charter schools scored as well or better than other students in English and in science in both the fourth and eighth grades. (Comparisons between charter school students and other students in math did not differ consistently.[69])

Less positive results come from studies of charter schools in other states. Several studies of student achievement in Arizona show little difference between scores of students in charter schools and those in regular public schools. In one of these studies, students in 14 charter high schools for at-risk students, 20 special-focus elementary schools (including content-centered schools), and three special-focus high schools all had scores on a state achievement test that were similar to the scores of comparable students in regular district schools.[70]

Several studies in Michigan found that students in charter schools performed either no better or more poorly than students in neighborhood traditional schools. One of these studies found that, based on the percentage of students who achieved satisfactory achievement scores, only 4 percent of charter schools placed in the top quartile (25%) of all schools in their district, 14 percent were in the second quartile, 27 percent in the third, and 43 percent in the fourth, or lowest, quartile.

Overall, the evidence indicates wide variations in the kind of impact that charter schools have on student learning. Chester Finn and his colleagues note some examples of charter schools that appear to have produced dramatic gains in reading and math, while also noting that low student scores at other charter schools have dismayed both parents and school administrators.[71]

Effects on Social Integration

Do charter schools, as some charge, generally serve the most advantaged segments of the school population—whites, the middle-class, and those without special problems—while leaving behind the children of minorities and the poor and those who have disabilities?

On a national level, charter schools enroll minority, poor, disabled, and at-risk students in proportions roughly equal to the proportions of these groups in all schools. National studies that compared the student population in charter schools to that of all public school students found an equal or slightly higher proportion of charter students who were eligible for the federal lunch program, were minorities, had limited English proficiency, and were special education students.[72]

However, if one examines the student composition of schools at a more local level—comparing charter schools to other schools in their own districts—some differences emerge. In Michigan, some charter schools were found to have no or very few students with special education needs while other charter schools had more special education students than other district schools. In Arizona, of all the funds that charter schools spent on special education, almost half was spent by one school. Similarly, charter school students who are academically at-risk are mostly concentrated in schools that cater to such students.[73]

On a local level, there also is some clustering of charter school students by ethnicity and social class. A study in Arizona matched 55 urban charter schools and 57 rural charter schools with nearby schools in their districts.[74] Some findings: 46 percent of the charter schools had substantial ethnic segregation; for example, Hispanic students were greatly underrepresented in charter schools as compared to traditional public schools. The proportion of white students in charter schools was typically 20 percentage points higher than in public schools. The charter schools that were disproportionately white usually emphasized college-preparatory programs while charters with a large proportion of minority students tended to offer vocational education or special programs for students who had been expelled from a public school.

A study in California found that in about 40 percent of charter schools, students were more likely to be white than at other schools in the same district. The same California study found that in about 60 percent of charter schools, students were less likely to come from low-income families than were students at other district schools.[75] A national study found that, while most charter schools were not "racially distinct" from their surrounding school district, 28 percent of the charter schools were disproportionately either white or non-white.

Overall, the evidence indicates that there tends to be some clustering of students in charter schools by ethnicity and social class. Some advocates for charter schools have suggested that it may be acceptable, and even desirable, for charter schools to serve particular types of students. They argue, for example, that at-risk students often benefit from programs devised specifically for them. They say that some charter schools serve well particular kinds of disabled students (e.g., a charter school for the deaf in Minnesota) but that most charter schools cannot offer the best specialized help needed by many disabled students. They also point out that a basic rationale for charter schools is to provide distinctive educational programs, often for a distinctive clientele—such as families that want a more "child-centered" education, an education focused more on "the basics," a vocationally oriented education, an academically accelerated program, or an Afrocentric emphasis. Chester Finn and his colleagues note that "some 26 percent of U.S. charters report that serving a special population was one of the primary reasons for founding a charter school, with one-fifth of these schools saying that was their most important motivation."[76]

Some states have charter laws that attempt to enforce "acceptable" ethnic distributions in schools. Such legal provisions restrict the extent to which charter schools are able to shape their educational programs. Lawmakers, educators, and other citizens must decide on the relative value they wish to give to having schools that are socially diverse versus having schools with distinctive educational programs.

Impact on Regular Public Schools

One of the rationales for establishing charter schools is that these schools can serve as laboratories that will try out new ideas and methods, which may then be adopted by a much larger number of public schools.

There is some anecdotal evidence from school districts in a number of states (including Massachusetts, Michigan, and Arizona) that the opening of new charter schools has stimulated the public school system to begin new educational programs of their own, such as a full-day kindergarten and magnet schools.[77] In Arizona, researchers asked 30 educators and policymakers how district schools had reacted to competition from charters.[78] Many districts, especially those that had overflow enrollments, did nothing. However, officials in other districts reacted in one or more of the following ways: (1) by trying to improve their "customer relations" (e.g., by soliciting more input from parents); (2) by advertising their strengths (such as high test scores and low costs) in newspapers and other outlets; (3) by trying to undermine charter schools in their district (e.g., by pressuring a zoning board to deny use of a building to a charter school); and (4) by making changes in their educational programs, such as opening magnet schools or modifying their curricula (e.g., increasing the use of phonics in reading instruction).

Researchers also assessed the impact of charter school competition in Arizona by comparing changes in 45 public schools in Nevada (which had no charter school competition) with changes in traditional public schools in Arizona, 21 of which had little or no competition from charter schools and 24 of which had substantial competition from charter schools in their districts. The greater the competition from charter schools, the more teachers reported that their school principal showed a growing propensity to encourage teacher experimentation, consult with teachers, follow up on new policies, help teachers to upgrade the curriculum, inform parents of school programs, and promote in-service training. Summarizing these findings, Robert Maranto and his colleagues say: "Arizona schools facing potential competition experienced greater change than Nevada schools lacking competitive concerns, and Arizona schools that faced higher levels of actual competition were the most likely to have changed in significant ways."[79]

Another study, sponsored by the U.S. Department of Education, investigated the impact of charter schools on 49 school districts in five states (Arizona, California, Colorado, Massachusetts, and Michigan).[80] Nearly half of the district leaders said that charter schools had negatively affected their funding; the transfer of students from regular district schools to charter schools meant reduced revenues for the district. In reaction to the appearance of charter schools, nearly half of the district leaders said that their schools had given more attention to their relationships with parents and others in the community—for example, having more frequent communication with parents and increasing their public relations efforts. In addition, in response to competition from charter schools, most districts (61%) tried to improve their educational programs—for example, by introducing extended-day kindergarten, new music and art classes, programs for gifted students, or programs for at-risk youth. One in five districts in the study responded to charter schools by starting new specialty schools, such as a "back to basics" school or a school for academically advanced students.

The impact of charter schools on a school district was affected by trends in student enrollment in that district. In districts where enrollment was declining, charter schools had a more negative effect on district budgets. In these situations, charters were seen as a threat and districts responded competitively, including putting new emphasis on customer service and adding new educational programs. Districts that had increasing student enrollments usually did not see charter schools as a competitive threat. These districts generally made few changes in their operations, and a few saw charter schools as providing a tool to promote educational improvements in their district.

In order for regular public schools to get maximum benefit from any innovative or different programs used in charter schools (and vice versa), there must be effective communication between charter and non-charter schools and a willingness by those in each type of school to learn from the other. However, such communication often does not occur or is not valued. In one study, 40 public school superintendents were asked their views about how charter schools might inform public education.[81] A majority of the superintendents said that charter schools cannot inform public education, while only one-fourth thought that charters could serve this function. Superintendents who said charter schools had little to offer saw differences in the circumstances of charter schools and regular schools, thought that charter schools were not really very different or innovative, or thought that charter school practices were not desirable.

A study of 10 California school districts found little sharing of ideas between charter and non-charter schools. Amy Wells explains:

> One reason for this lack of sharing was a general lack of communication across the schools, especially in situations where the charter schools were more independent from the districts and where the charters were established to be in direct competition with the public schools . . . we found little evidence that educators in public schools are learning about new innovative ideas from charter school educators.[82]

Overall, the evidence indicates that the presence of charter schools often does cause public school districts to try to compete harder for students and that sometimes they do this by trying to expand their program offerings. The influence of charters does *not* seem to result often from direct communication, consultation, and sharing of ideas between charters and other district schools.

VARIABILITY AMONG CHARTER SCHOOLS

Our review of the literature on charter schools makes it clear that there are great differences among these schools, not only in their programs, but also in their effectiveness.

Thomas Toch, who has studied charter schools in Arizona and Michigan, has written that "the best charter schools pursue innovation and educational excellence with an enthusiasm sorely lacking in many traditional schools."[83] However, Toch also notes that in many charter schools there are problems that are rarely found in regular public schools. He states that ". . . in scores of charters in Arizona and Michigan, curricula and teaching are weak, buildings are substandard, and financial abuses are surprisingly prevalent."[84]

Other researchers also have noted wide variations in the quality of charter schools. Robert Maranto and his colleagues state: "Arizona's charter school law has allowed 272 flowers (and weeds) to bloom . . . the very freedom that has allowed capable operators to open their schools has also allowed an unknown number of corrupt or incompetent operators."[85] Echoing this theme of variability, a book chapter about charter schools nationally by Thomas Good and Jennifer Braden is titled "Charter Schools: Some of the Best and Worst in American Education."[86]

There are, as we have seen, some ways in which charter schools tend to be similar to each other and different from most public schools—for example, being smaller in size and having greater parental involvement. But the fact that a school is a charter school tells one very little, if anything, about how effective an educational program that school has. Moreover, because the programs of charter schools vary so widely, and because they have more autonomy than regular public schools in carrying out their programs, differences in educational outcomes (achievement, dropouts, etc.) are likely to vary more among charter schools than among schools in the regular public school system.

PROBLEMS OF CHARTER SCHOOLS

Charter schools generally have encountered some special problems and challenges. Of particular importance are problems of finances, management, and accountability.[87]

Finances

A number of major studies have found that charter schools often lack adequate funding. Funding formulas vary among states. In most states, the funding formula is designed to provide a charter school with the average per-pupil cost of the school district in which its students live. However, even where this is true, charter schools often face several special financial problems. Although they receive money for operating expenses, they may not receive capital funds or have bonding authority to help pay the costs of buildings and other facilities. They may not receive as much money from non-state sources (such as local property taxes) as regular public schools. In addition, individual (and typically quite small) charter schools usually have to pay out of their own budgets the costs of administrative and support services that are provided to regular public schools by a central office.

To cope with their financial problems, charter schools have employed a number of strategies, including obtaining federal grants, contracting with public school districts for some services, and—most significantly—privatizing their public schools to some extent. Amy Wells and Janelle Scott have described a number of privatization strategies that charter schools in California and elsewhere have used.[88] These include private fund-raising, contracting with private firms (including curriculum specialists), and partnerships with major corporations. In addition, many charter schools are run by private firms such as Edison Schools and Advantage Schools. Thus, while charter schools are almost always public schools (in the sense that they are publicly funded and free), the line between the public and the private spheres has become blurred in many of these schools.

Management

Operators and administrators of charter schools often lack sufficient training or experience to deal with a host of managerial tasks: financial planning, accounting and reporting systems (some mandated by state law), purchasing, providing transportation, maintenance and renovation of facilities, providing custodial services, food preparation, and many other tasks. In his study of charter schools in four states (Colorado, Georgia, Massachusetts, and Michigan), Bryan Hassel says:

> Charter school leaders interviewed for this study recalled being shocked by the administrative burdens of starting and operating an autonomous public school. Many charter school founders entered the charter arena because they wanted to put some kind of educational philosophy into action, but they quickly found their time consumed not by curriculum and instructional practice but by the renovation of facilities, the contracting out of numerous services, the management of their states' complicated accounting and reporting systems, the intricacies of providing transportation to far-flung students, and the like.[89]

A consultant to some Connecticut charter schools has asserted that many of the people who began charter schools in that state had neither the experience nor the skills to administer these schools. These operators have been overwhelmed by having to handle varied administrative responsibilities, at the same time that they try to develop curricula and deal with educational issues.[90]

At least some charter schools also spend a larger proportion of their budgets for administration than do regular public schools. A study of expenditures of charter schools and of regular public schools in Michigan (in a year when revenues of the two types of schools were about equal) found that charter schools spent 30 percent of their operating expenditures for business and administration as compared to 12 percent for non-charter public schools. Charter schools spent a smaller proportion of their operating expenditures on instruction (54%) than did other public schools (63%).[91]

Hassel has suggested that charter schools need to develop an "infrastructure" to support their educational programs. Such an infrastructure might include such entities as charter school resource centers (to provide train-ing, consultation, and other services), charter school associations (to help members with such activities as joint purchasing of services for the school), and use of government programs for technical assistance.[92]

Accountability

The charters granted to charter schools are based in part on a bargain between the school and public authorities: in exchange for being given sub-stantial autonomy, the school will be accountable for good financial man-agement and good educational results. Charters are granted to schools for a specified number of years (in most states, three to five years) and when it is time for renewal of a school's charter, the charter-granting agency is sup-posed to evaluate the school's performance against the goals stated in its charter.

In some locations, such as Chicago and the District of Columbia, charter-granting agencies have developed detailed policies for evaluating the per-formance of charter schools. For example, a policy adopted in Chicago in 1998 provided for the annual evaluation of charter schools based on test scores, attendance, financial stability, and compliance with applicable laws.[93] However, most states and localities have not established clear or effective systems for assessing the performance of charter schools. For example, in Arizona, the Department of Education was unable to check reports from charter schools for accuracy and thus "unable to hold charters accountable."[94] The national study of charter schools by the Hudson Institute concluded that "today's charter school accountability systems remain underdeveloped, often clumsy and ill-fitting, and are themselves beset by dilemmas."[95]

Of all charter schools that opened since 1992, 3 percent (32 schools) had closed by the beginning of the 1998–1999 school year.[96] Most were closed because of organizational problems or financial mismanagement (or fraud). It has been very rare for a charter school to be closed because of educational deficiencies. A number of researchers have observed that fail-ing charter schools often are allowed to continue to operate, sometimes because of political pressures.

It should be noted that poorly performing schools in the regular public system also are often allowed to continue without much change. However, the fact that charter schools are granted a degree of freedom from many of the rules and regulations that apply to most public schools makes the prob-lem of accountability especially acute for them. As Bryan Hassel points out, in the absence of clear procedures for judging the performance of charter schools, taxpayers cannot feel confident that these schools are using public money effectively, and the charter schools themselves may be uncertain about how to develop their programs.[97]

VOUCHERS TO ATTEND PRIVATE SCHOOLS

Vouchers are grants of money that are given to parents that they can apply toward the cost of tuition at private schools.

About a quarter of all elementary and secondary schools in the United States are private schools. About one in eight American students is educated in a private school. Most private schools are religious schools. Compared to public schools, private schools more often draw their students from relatively high socioeconomic backgrounds and less often enroll minorities.[98]

Supporters of voucher programs maintain that all students—especially those who are getting an inadequate education in inferior schools—should be given the opportunity to attend private schools of their choice. Voucher advocates believe that such programs will lead to higher achievement for students who are able to attend private schools. Moreover, they argue, public schools will be forced to improve because of the need to compete for students with private schools. The voucher movement has brought together conservative advocates of free-market principles and some advocates for the poor and minorities who see private school vouchers as the best way to improve education for inner-city youth.

Voucher proposals have aroused strong opposition from defenders of the tradition and values of the public school system. Opponents believe that voucher programs would seriously damage the public schools, by taking away many of their children (including the most able and motivated students) and by siphoning off badly needed money.[99]

EMERGENCE OF VOUCHER PROGRAMS

Aside from a rare example in a small California community in the 1960s, voucher plans actually began to be introduced in some American communities in the 1990s. Public funds were used in Milwaukee and Cleveland to give vouchers to a limited number of families to help them pay the costs of private schools. A larger number of voucher programs have been funded by private sources, such as wealthy individuals or foundations. About 80 private voucher programs, serving more than 60,000 children, have been established around the United States, by a recent estimate.[100] Typically, these programs are targeted at low-income, often minority, children in inner cities. Since the number of available vouchers almost always is fewer than the number of applicants, winners usually are selected by lottery. Vouchers usually can be used at either a religious or nonreligious private school. The dollar amount of a voucher varies among programs; it typically is not enough to cover the entire cost of tuition.

The number of publicly funded voucher programs has been very small for two main reasons. One reason is the strength of organized opposition to the idea of using public money to pay for private, especially religious, schools. Because of this opposition, ballot initiatives to provide vouchers or tuition tax credits for private school education have been defeated in a number of states, including California, Oregon, Colorado, Washington, and Michigan. The second reason is that the legality of providing money that goes to religious schools (which educate most private school students) has been in serious question. The legal status of vouchers, at least on a federal level, was clarified in 2002 when the U.S. Supreme Court ruled that it is constitutional to give public money to parents for payment of tuition to any private school, including religious schools. The legal battle on this issue continues in some states regarding whether the state constitutions permit public funds to be given to religious schools. However, the U.S. Supreme Court decision means that the question of vouchers becomes one of "Is this a good idea?" rather than "Is it legal?" in much of the United States.

PUBLIC OPINION ABOUT VOUCHERS

Most Americans have had positive views about private schools and about giving students vouchers to attend private schools. One national survey explored peoples' attitudes on this subject in great detail.[101] It found that, while most parents of public school students were fairly satisfied with their local schools, about half of all public school parents thought that private schools and parochial schools usually were better than public schools with respect to academic quality, safety, discipline, teaching moral values, and providing individual attention to students. Only about 4 percent thought private schools were worse in each of these ways. A majority both of parents of schoolchildren and of non-parents supported the idea of vouchers to be used for private schools.

While no demographic group is greatly dissatisfied with their public schools, dissatisfaction is highest among low-income people, African-Americans, and those in districts with low-performing schools. Support for vouchers also is strongest among these disadvantaged groups. People in these social groups tend to see vouchers in terms of the issue of equity—whether their children have the chance to get as good an education as the children of more affluent people. Summarizing some of these survey responses, Terry Moe says ". . . these results reinforce the connection between vouchers and the socially disadvantaged, which is at the heart of the modern movement."[102] One should add that the voucher movement also is backed by free-market conservatives; by those already in private schools who would like some of their tuition costs defrayed; and by some affluent whites who want more choice of schools for additional reasons, including some who wish to avoid schools with a large number of minority students.

EFFECTIVENESS OF PRIVATE SCHOOLS

Are private schools really better than public schools? Let us first consider the evidence for Catholic schools and then that for nonreligious private schools.

Catholic Schools

A number of studies have compared students in schools run by the Catholic Church to students in the public schools. These studies generally have found that Catholic school students score higher than public school students on standardized tests in math, reading, and other subjects. The advantage of Catholic school students is reduced (and sometimes is not evident) when effective controls for students' prior achievement and socioeconomic status are introduced. However, even with such controls for students' backgrounds (including race), Catholic school students still tend to achieve at a significantly higher level than their public school peers.[103]

The generally higher achievement of Catholic school students appears to result from some distinctive features of these schools. Discipline in Catholic schools is stricter than that in public schools and students are given more homework. Yet students tend to be more engaged in their schoolwork and feel more bonds to their schools. Catholic schools create a strong academic atmosphere that emphasizes learning and achievement. Consistent with this emphasis, Catholic school students are more likely to be enrolled in an academic program and take more academic courses than their public school peers.[104]

Analysis of data from a national study of high school students found that the higher achievement scores of Catholic school students (compared to students in public schools) could be explained by some of these differences. Specifically, the stronger academic climate, the stronger feelings of bonding that students had with their schools, and the greater number of academic courses taken accounted for the higher achievement displayed by Catholic school students.[105]

In addition to their generally high academic performance, students attending Catholic schools are more likely than similar public school students to complete high school. They also are more likely to attend college, especially selective private colleges. These effects of Catholic schools on student attainment are particularly marked for students who are from urban areas and who are from racial minorities.[106]

Nonreligious Schools

Most of the evidence on the academic effects of private schools comes from religious (mostly Catholic) schools. However, data from a national study of schools permitted a comparison of students in 39 nonreligious private high schools with those from students in 213 comprehensive public high schools.[107] Those in the private schools had significantly higher scores on tests of achievement in math, science, reading, and social studies. (Students from these non-religious private schools also scored higher than students in Catholic schools and in public magnet schools.)

Why did students in nonreligious private schools achieve at a higher level than those in public schools? Private schools differ from public schools in a number of ways. Students in private schools were less likely to be African-American or Latino and generally were higher in socioeconomic status. Private school students took more academic courses, especially in math and science and also in English and social studies, than those in public schools. The academic climate of the private schools, as described by school principals—including emphasis on learning and achievement—was higher than in public schools. In addition, students' responses indicated that students felt a stronger bonding to private schools than to public schools.

When the differences in achievement between nonreligious private schools and public schools were controlled by the characteristics of their student bodies (e.g., the proportions that are African-American, Latino, and low-income), the gap in achievement between the private and public schools disappeared. In addition, when the private-public school differences in student achievement were controlled (in turn) for differences in school academic climate and for differences in student bonding and in course-taking, the advantage of private schools over public schools also disappeared, and was even reversed in some instances. These findings indicate that the achievement advantage of nonreligious private schools may be explained both by the background advantages of their students and by these special features of the private schools.

EFFECTS OF VOUCHERS ON ACHIEVEMENT

Voucher programs that give public money to some students to attend private schools have been studied in only a few locations. In the early 1990s, a small initial voucher program in Milwaukee permitted some students to attend nonreligious private schools. A number of separate analyses of achievement gains made by these students, compared to a control group of non-voucher students in the public schools, were performed. Results of these analyses varied but, according to one reviewer, "the preponderance of evidence from evaluations of the Milwaukee plan produced small annual gains in mathematics scores among a group of low-income children in the elementary or middle school grades. However, it did not improve reading scores."[108] The results of these studies are of limited generality, since most of the voucher students attended one of only three private nonreligious schools.

An evaluation of the voucher program in Cleveland found that public school students started first grade with test scores in language and math that were below those of voucher students. However, by the end of third grade, the overall gap in test scores had been reduced by almost 80 percent; that is, the public school students largely caught up to the voucher students. The evaluators say: "The most recent results do not reveal any significant impacts of participation in the voucher program on student achievement."[109]

More extensive information has come from a recent study of similar voucher programs in New York City, Dayton, Ohio, and Washington, D.C. In each of these cities, private organizations provided scholarships for some public school students to attend a private school of their (family's) choice. Most of these were religious schools. Eligible grades varied by city (grades 1–4 in New York, K–12 in Dayton, and K–8 in Washington). In each of these cities, students from low-income families were eligible for the program.

Since the number of applications was greater than the number of scholarships available in each city (about 2,000 in New York, about 800 in Dayton, and about 1,600 in Washington), awards were made by lottery. This system made it possible to compare the achievement of those students who won scholarships and attended private schools with similar students who also applied for the awards but did not win in the random lottery drawing and therefore remained in public schools. In all three cities, students were tested in math and reading prior to the lottery and then again one year later and two years later.

Separate analyses of data from this study have led to somewhat different conclusions. The researchers who conducted the study reported that, in all three cities, African-American students who used vouchers to attend private schools scored higher in math and/or reading (usually both) than similar African-American students in the control groups in the public schools. However, white students and Hispanic students who attended private schools did not achieve any better than their control groups in public schools in any of these cities.[110]

Two other researchers did a reanalysis of the data for New York, the city that the original report showed to have the most notable overall gains for voucher recipients. When they included a larger sample of students in their analysis, they found that achievement differences between African-American voucher students in private schools and comparable students in public schools were smaller than those originally reported and statistically nonsignificant.[111]

Overall, the three-city study indicates that African-American students may have benefited somewhat from attending private schools through voucher programs (although it is not clear how much) but that students from other ethnic groups did not. The reasons why only African-American students may have benefited from attending private schools are not clear. The result does not appear to be due to any special deficiencies of their neighborhood schools, since in New York non-black students from the same neighborhoods did not benefit from attending private schools.[112] It may be that, for other reasons, African-American children were more in need of the special features that private schools often provided—such as small school size, perhaps smaller class size (shown in other research to benefit African-American students most), strict discipline, and academic emphasis. (See Chapter 9 for a discussion of the academic achievement of black students.)

Some evidence on the effects of voucher programs also is available from countries other than the United States.[113] As in the United States, such programs have been targeted mainly at low-income students. In Chile, students who used vouchers to attend Catholic schools had slightly higher achievement scores than those in public schools (after scores were controlled for students' socioeconomic status and other background factors). However, students who attended *nonreligious* private schools under the voucher programs had *lower* achievement scores than comparable students in public schools.

Under the voucher plan in Colombia, the academic performance of students in private schools did not differ much from that of students in public schools. Studies of for-profit schools that were created in Colombia, with voucher students as their main clientele, found some of them to have serious difficulties.

The studies of voucher programs in Chile and in Colombia both indicate that the effects of attending private schools is likely to vary across different types of schools. Martin Carnoy and Patrick McEwan suggest that these results have important implications for U.S. policymakers. They comment: "It is misleading to predict the impact of large-scale voucher plans [in the U.S.] by relying on current comparisons of public and Catholic schools. Vouchers will probably lead to the creation of many new private schools. . . . The objectives, resources, constraints, and outcomes of new private schools (especially nonreligious and for-profit schools) may bear only a passing resemblance to those of existing Catholic schools."[114]

EFFECTS OF VOUCHERS ON PUBLIC SCHOOLS

What effects do private schools, and voucher programs specifically, have on the public schools? There is evidence that the presence of many other schools exerts competitive pressures on public schools to be more effective. One study found that when public school systems are near a large number of private schools (or close to many other public school systems), the test scores of their students rise and their per-pupil costs decrease. Another study compared the achievement test scores of students in public schools in Milwaukee, where these schools had competition from voucher schools and charter schools, with student test scores in similar schools elsewhere in Wisconsin that did not face such competition. Test scores of students in the public schools subject to competition rose more rapidly than the test scores of students in the other Wisconsin schools.[115]

Clive Belfield and Henry Levin recently reviewed 25 separate studies in the United States that looked at the effects of competition (either from private schools or from other public schools) on students' academic achievement.[116] These studies included 206 estimates of relationships between specific measures of competition and specific measures of student achievement. About one-third of these estimates indicated that increased competition among schools was significantly correlated with higher student achievement. Greater competition among schools was only rarely associated with lower student achievement. The reviewers conclude that greater competition among schools tends to make schools more effective, although they note that such gains generally are modest.

Research in Chile shows that the impact of voucher plans on the public schools may vary for schools that serve students of different social backgrounds.[117] Increased enrollment in private schools was associated with an increase in the achievement of students who attended public schools that served middle-class students. However, in public schools whose students were from lower socioeconomic levels, increased competition from private schools appeared to reduce achievement scores. Apparently, the middle-class public schools had the capacity to respond effectively to a competitive challenge from private schools, while those with low-SES student bodies did not.

The response of public schools in three cities (Milwaukee, Cleveland, and Englewood, Texas) where voucher programs were begun has been studied by Frederick Hess.[118] One response of public school systems in these cities was to launch outreach public relations or advertising campaigns. For example: flyers or radio spots were used to advertise the schools' services or performance, their high standards, and the choices available within the pubic school system; some attempts were made to make it easier for parents to communicate with the school; and simplified forms and registration were provided. There also was some effort by public schools in these cities—especially in Milwaukee, where voucher competition was strongest—to begin some new programs or new themed schools.

However, Hess concludes that, while some new programs were added to these public school systems, standard practices in most of each city's schools and classrooms were not changed. He states: "There was no evidence that competition bulldozed away inefficiencies or forced systemic efforts to reform policy or improve practice, as officials had neither the incentive nor the ability to mount aggressive assaults on organizational culture or procedure."[119]

Hess argues that the limited response to voucher programs in the public school systems he studied was due in part to a very limited threat perceived by administrators and teachers. The voucher programs were limited to relatively small numbers of students. Teacher shortages meant there was little danger that reduced enrollments would cause teachers to lose their jobs. In

Wisconsin, the state funding formulas provided little penalty for reduced enrollments to the public schools. In addition, Hess points out several other reasons that the public schools did not make substantial changes in the organization and procedures of most of their schools. These reasons include a lack of clear evidence that voucher schools outperformed public schools in these cities and resistance to changes by teacher unions.

Regarding the effects of competition, Hess says: "Markets are not magic—they drive change only when producers have the motive and the means to change."[120] Competition from voucher programs, he argues, will lead to substantial change in public schools only when it constitutes a serious threat to funds and jobs and when public school administrators have the power and means to effect change.

EFFECTS OF VOUCHERS ON SOCIAL INTEGRATION

As with other school choice programs, voucher programs that help students to attend private schools may affect the social class composition of schools. Voucher programs to date have targeted their assistance to low-income families, but—within these low-income groups—parents with relatively high education have been more apt than others to participate.[121] Thus, these voucher programs probably tend to draw off the most able and most motivated students from the public schools.

If voucher programs were made available to all parents—as most supporters of such programs advocate—much larger "sorting" effects, by the social class of students, would be likely to occur. Vouchers usually provide only a portion of the money necessary to attend a chosen private school. Moreover, even if a voucher provided enough money to attend private school A, it would not cover all expenses at a more expensive private school B. Therefore, the students in various private schools would tend to cluster by their families' wealth.

SUMMARY AND CONCLUSIONS

A broad movement for school choice has developed in the United States and in some other countries. This movement is based on the proposition that giving families a choice among schools will introduce competitive pressures that will force schools to improve dramatically.

Several types of school choice programs have been introduced in some school districts. These include: (1) programs that permit families to choose non-neighborhood schools (alternative schools, magnet schools, or other) within the regular school system; (2) creation of charter schools, which—although publicly funded—are relatively independent of the regular school system; and (3) providing vouchers that help families send their children to private schools.

There is enormous variation across these "schools of choice." They differ widely in the types of students they attract, their curricula, the teaching methods they use, and many other ways. Not surprisingly, outcomes for students also vary. Nevertheless, there are some general findings that emerge from relevant research.

Overall, the evidence to date provides some basis for optimism about the effects of allowing families greater choice of schools. First, evidence from parents taking part in intra-district choice programs, from those whose children attended magnet schools, and from those whose children attended charter schools all show that parents were more satisfied with "schools of choice" than with traditional neighborhood schools. Parents who had chosen a school also were more highly involved with their children's school, such as by volunteering to help with school activities.

Like their parents, students attending schools of choice (alternative schools, magnet schools, or charter schools) generally are more satisfied with their teachers and with their school than are their counterparts in regular public schools. Also, students in alternative schools or magnet schools and students in Catholic schools are more engaged in their schoolwork and better behaved than students in regular public schools.

Outcomes on measures of academic achievement vary for different types of schools of choice. Compared to students in regular public schools, those in magnet schools and in private schools (both religious and nonreligious) tend to score higher on tests of academic achievement. Also, both white students and black students tend to have higher achievement in magnet schools and in Catholic schools, compared to their peers in regular public schools. Students in these types of schools of choice—especially those in magnet schools and Catholic schools—tend to achieve better even when the effect of students' background is controlled.

The boost in academic achievement given by some schools of choice (both public and private) seems to result from several common features of schools. These schools generally have a strong "academic climate"—that is, their staff gives great emphasis to high academic achievement and conveys high expectations to the students. Related to this strong academic emphasis, these schools (especially both religious and secular private schools) require their students to take more academic courses than are required in most public schools. In addition, all of these types of schools appear to have a strong sense of community—among staff, parents, and students—and students tend to feel more strongly bonded to their schools than do students in most regular public schools.

While student achievement generally is higher in several types of schools of choice (public magnets, private religious, and private secular) than in traditional public schools, this advantage has not been found consistently for charter schools. The inconsistent impacts of charter schools on student achievement appear to result from wide differences in the quality of their instructional programs and from problems that many charter schools have had with financing, management, and support systems.

Evidence about the impact of voucher programs is very limited. Studies in Milwaukee and Cleveland have found vouchers to have small or no effects on student achievement. The most extensive evidence on American schools comes from programs in three cities that used lotteries to award scholarships to some low-income students to attend private schools of their families' choice. Compared to similar students in public schools, achievement scores for voucher winners in private schools tended to be higher for African-American students but not for Hispanics or for non-Hispanic white students. It may be that African-American students benefited most from the more orderly atmosphere, higher standards, and more personal attention often found in private schools.

In Chile and Colombia, low-income students who used vouchers to attend Catholic schools had somewhat higher academic achievement than those in public schools. However, voucher students attending nonreligious schools—including for-profit schools created to serve the new voucher clientele—had *lower* achievement than those in the public schools. These different effects of vouchers on student achievement appear to reflect variations in the quality of private schools in these countries.

While giving families greater choice among schools generally increases the satisfaction of both parents and students, and sometimes raises student achievement as well, such programs have some limitations and present some problems. First, it is clear that the education provided by some schools of choice—especially some charter schools and some private schools—is no better and sometimes worse than that of the regular public schools. There is no magic in being a private school, a charter school, a magnet school, or an alternative school. Like regular public schools, they can be successful only with effective school organization, curricula, instructional methods, assessment methods, and other components of a good school.

The variations in the effectiveness of schools of choice, and some evidence that new, quickly organized schools often are substandard schools, suggest that there are risks in trying to quickly create a large number of alternative schools. Nontraditional schools funded by public money—such as charter schools—need to have well-developed instructional plans, management plans, and sufficient resources (financial, human, and technical) to do their jobs well. Both nontraditional, publicly funded schools and private schools in which public funds are used for tuition, need to be fully accountable, providing information to the public about their educational programs and about educational outcomes for their students.

Another problem is that giving families choice among schools tends to segment students by ability, race, social class, religion, and other characteristics. Better-educated parents, even within low-income groups, are more likely than other parents to participate in choice programs. Many magnet schools select only better students for admission, and some alternative schools isolate at-risk students from others. Charter schools, at the local level, tend to cluster students by race and social class, and special education students tend to be grouped together in a very small number of charter schools.

The sorting effects of voucher programs are less clear at present. Existing voucher programs help some low-income students attend private schools, thus increasing economic diversity. However, since vouchers do not cover all tuition costs, they may tend to leave the poorest students in the public schools. If vouchers are expanded to cover families within a wider income range, the relatively affluent will be more able than poorer families to make up the tuition difference necessary to attend private schools.

Voucher programs also will tend to segment students by religion. In some countries, such as the Netherlands, most students attend schools operated by the religious groups with which their families are affiliated. While extreme segmentation by religious affiliation is less likely in the United States, support for voucher plans is stronger among Catholics and "born-again" Christians than among "mainline" Protestants.[122] Probably Catholics and more fundamentalist Protestants would be more likely than others to participate in voucher programs and to choose private schools sponsored by their own religions.

Thus, there is a trade-off between giving families maximum choice among schools and maintaining schools that are diverse by social class, religion, race, and other social characteristics. Citizens of each state and local community need to decide what balance they wish to strike between these two goals.

Another important question is how programs that give families a choice among schools affect the operation and effectiveness of traditional public schools. There is some evidence that, where effective competition exists, the achievement of students in the regular public schools may improve. But whether the appearance of schools and programs that give families choice among schools leads to much change in regular public schools depends on how serious the competitive threat is. Charter schools have provoked the greatest changes in regular public school districts when total enrollment in districts has declined and schools are concerned about keeping up enrollments.

However, competition from other schools sometimes leads to *poorer* performance by schools in the regular public school system. If larger-scale voucher programs and more charter schools draw off the best students and the best-educated, most active parents from the regular public schools, those schools may find it very difficult to improve themselves sufficiently to meet the competitive challenges. To meet such challenges, regular public schools need to be given the resources—facilities, operating funds, skilled staff members, technical assistance, and so on—to enable them to make improvements and compete effectively.

NOTES

1. For a summary of arguments in support of school choice, see, T. Young and E. Clinchy, *Choice in Public Education.* New York: Teachers College Press, 1992; and M. Schneider, P. Teske, and M. Marschall, *Choosing Schools: Consumer Choice and the Quality of American Schools.* Princeton, NJ: Princeton University Press, 2000.

2. J. Chubb and T. Moe, *Politics, Markets, and America's Schools.* Washington, DC: Brookings Institution Press, 1990, p. 217; emphasis in original.

3. See Young and Clinchy, *Choice in Public Education.*

4. For descriptive information on alternative schools, see Young and Clinchy, *Choice in Public Education*; Schneider, et al., *Choosing Schools.*

5. For descriptive information on magnet schools, see R. Blank, R. Levine, and L. Steel, After Fifteen Years, Magnet Schools in Urban Education. In B. Fuller and R. Elmore, eds., *Who Chooses? Who Loses? Culture, Institutions and the Unequal Effects of School Choice.* New York: Teachers College Press, 1996; Young and Clinchy, *Choice in Public Education*; Schneider, et al., *Choosing Schools.*

6. J. Nathan, *Charter Schools.* San Francisco: Jossey-Bass, 1996, p. 7.

7. Young and Clinchy, *Choice in Public Education.*

8. Schneider, et al., *Choosing Schools*, p. 23.

9. P. Teske and M. Schneider, What Research Can Tell Policymakers About School Choice. *Journal of Policy Analysis and Management*, 20, 2001, 609–631.

10. Teske and Schneider, Ibid.

11. Schneider, et al., *Choosing Schools*, Chapter 4.

12. Schneider, et al., Ibid., p. 264.

13. Teske and Schneider, What Researchers Can Tell Policymakers About School Choice.

14. Schneider, et al., *Choosing Schools*, p. 265.

15. Teske and Schneider, What Researchers Can Tell Policymakers About School Choice.

16. Schneider, et al., *Choosing Schools*, Chapter 12.

17. Schneider, et al., Ibid.

18. C. Smrekar and E. Goldring, *School Choice in Urban America: Magnet Schools and the Pursuit of Equity.* New York: Teachers College Press, 1999.

19. Teske and Schneider, What Research Can Tell Policymakers About School Choice.

20. M. Driscoll, Change, Achievement, and School Community. In E. Rasell and R. Rothstein, eds., *School Choice: Examining the Evidence.* Washington, DC: Economic Policy Institute, 1993, pp. 147–169.

21. M. Gold and D. Mann, *Expelled to a Friendlier Place: A Study of Effective Alternative Schools.* Ann Arbor: University of Michigan Press, 1984.

22. M. Raywid, *The Current Status of Schools of Choice.* Hempstead, NY: Project on Alternatives in Education, 1982.

23. Young and Clinchy, *Choice in Public Education.*
24. Young and Clinchy, Ibid.
25. New York State Education Department, *New York State Magnet School Research Study.* Albany: MAGI Educational Services, 1985.
26. Young and Clinchy, *Choice in Public Education.*
27. R. Crain, A. Heebner, and Y. Si, *The Effectiveness of New York City's Career Magnet Schools.* Berkeley, CA: National Center for Research in Vocational Education, 1992.
28. A. Gamoran, Student Achievement in Public Magnet, Public Comprehensive, and Private City High Schools. *Educational Evaluation and Policy Analysis, 18,* 1996, 1–18.
29. G. Wehlage and G. Smith. Building New Programs for Students at Risk. In F. Newmann, ed., *Student Engagement and Achievement in American Secondary Schools.* New York: Teachers College Press, 1992, pp. 92–118.
30. Gamoran, Student Achievement, p. 3.
31. Crain, et al., *Effectiveness of New York City's Career Magnet Schools,* p. 3.
32. P. Fleming, R. Blank, R. Dentler, and D. Baltzell, *Survey of Magnet Schools.* Washington, DC: James Lowry and Associates, 1982.
33. G. Smith, T. Gregory, and R. Pugh, Meeting Student Needs: Evidence for the Superiority of Alternative Schools. *Phi Delta Kappan, 62,* 1981, 561–564.
34. Schneider, et al., *Choosing Schools,* p. 272.
35. M. Metz, *Different by Design: The Context and Character of Three Magnet Schools.* New York: Routledge and Kegan Paul, 1986.
36. S. Plank, K. Schiller, B. Schneider, and J. Coleman, Effects of Choice in Education. In Rasell and Rothstein, *School Choice,* pp. 111–134.
37. Teske and Schneider, What Research Can Tell Policymakers About School Choice.
38. D. Moore and S. Davenport, High School Choice and Students at Risk. *Equity and Choice, 5,* 1989, 5–10.
39. Moore and Davenport, Ibid., p. 7.
40. Young and Clinchy, *Choice in Public Education.*
41. Plank, et al., Effects of Choice in Education.
42. Plank, et al., Ibid., p. 130.
43. Young and Clinchy, *Choice in Public Education,* p. 38.
44. Schneider, et al., *Choosing Schools.*
45. See T. Good and J. Braden, *The Great School Debate: Choice, Vouchers, and Charters.* Mahwah, NJ: Lawrence Erlbaum, 2000; C. Finn, Jr., B. Manno, and G. Vanourek, *Charter Schools in Action.* Princeton, NJ: Princeton University Press, 2000.
46. Finn, Jr., et al., Ibid., p. 23.
47. Good and Braden, *The Great School Debate;* B. Hassel, *The Charter School Challenge.* Washington, DC: Brookings Institution Press, 1999.
48. D. Weil, *Charter Schools: A Reference Handbook.* Santa Barbara, CA: ABC-CLIO, 2000, Chapter 1.
49. R. Stout and G. Garn, Nothing New: Curricula in Arizona. In R. Maranto, S. Milliman, F. Hess, and A. Gresham, eds., *School Choice in the Real World: Lessons from Arizona Charter Schools.* Boulder, CO: Westview, 2001, pp. 159–172.
50. Good and Braden, *The Great School Debate,* p. 193.
51. Good and Braden, Ibid.

52. J. Casey, K. Andreson, B. Yelverton, and L. Wedeen. A Status Report on Charter Schools in New Mexico. *Phi Delta Kappan, 83,* 2002, p. 520.

53. R. Corwin and J. Flaherty, *Freedom and Innovation in California's Charter Schools.* Los Alamitos, CA: SWRL, 1995.

54. Good and Braden, *The Great School Debate,* pp. 143, 147.

55. Good and Braden, Ibid., p. 148.

56. See Finn, Jr., et al., *Charter Schools in Action.*

57. Finn, Jr., et al., Ibid., p. 277.

58. R. Maranto and A. Gresham, The Wild West of Education Reform: Arizona Charter Schools. In Maranto, et al., eds., *School Choice in the Real World,* pp. 99–114.

59. J. Fox, Organizational Structures and Perceived Cultures of Community— Charter Schools in Ohio. *Phi Delta Kappan, 83,* 2002, 525–531; Casey, et al., A Status Report on Charter Schools in New Mexico.

60. J. Crawford, Teacher Autonomy and Accountability in Charter Schools. *Education and Urban Society, 33,* 2001, 186–200.

61. R. Pack, Charter Schools: Innovation, Autonomy, and Decision-Making. Unpublished Ph.D. Dissertation, University of Arizona, 1999.

62. Pack, Ibid.; see also Finn, Jr., et al., *Charter Schools in Action,* p. 115.

63. G. Vanourek, B. Manno, C. Finn, and L. Bierlein, Charter Schools as Seen by Students, Teachers, and Parents. In P. Peterson and B. Hassel, eds., *Learning from School Choice.* Washington, DC: Brookings Institution Press, 1998, pp. 187–211; Finn, Jr., et al., *Charter Schools in Action,* p. 271.

64. L. Mulholland, *Arizona Charter School Progress Education.* Phoenix: Morrison Institute for Public Policy, 1999.

65. Good and Braden, *The Great School Debate,* Chapter 6.

66. Good and Braden, Ibid.

67. Good and Braden, Ibid.; Finn, Jr., et al., *Charter Schools in Action,* pp. 84–85.

68. Finn, Jr., et al., Ibid., Appendix.

69. Finn, Jr., et al., Ibid, Chapter 4.

70. Stout and Garn, Nothing New: Curricula in Arizona Charter Schools; Finn, Jr., *Charter Schools in Action,* p. 76; Good and Braden, *The Great School Debate,* Chapter 6.

71. Finn, Jr., et al., *Charter Schools in Action,* Chapter 4.

72. Finn, Jr., et al., Ibid.

73. Good and Braden, *The Great School Debate,* Chapter 6; Finn, Jr., et al., Ibid.

74. C. Cobb and C. Glass, Ethnic Segregation in Arizona Charter Schools. *Education Policy Analysis Archives, 7,* 1999, 8.

75. SRI International, *Evaluation of Charter School Effectiveness: Part 1.* Online: http://www.lao.ca.gov/sri_charter_schools_1297-part1.html.

76. Finn, Jr., et al., *Charter Schools in Action,* p. 162.

77. Finn, Jr., et al., Ibid., Chapter 9.

78. R. Maranto, S. Milliman, F. Hess, and A. Gresham, Do Charter Schools Improve District Schools? In Maranto, et al., *School Choice in the Real World,* pp. 129–141.

79. Maranto, et al., Ibid., p. 139.

80. J. Ericson, D. Silverman, P. Berman, B. Nelson, and D. Solomon, *Challenge and Opportunity: The Impact of Charter Schools on School Districts.* Jessup, MD: U.S. Department of Education, 2001.

81. Good and Braden, *Charter Schools in Action*, p. 163.
82. A. Wells, UCLA Charter School Study. Los Angeles: Author, 1998, p. 62.
83. T. Toch, The New Education Bazaar. *U.S. News and World Report*, April 27, 1998, p. 36.
84. Toch, Ibid., p. 37.
85. R. Maranto, S. Milliman, F. Hess, and A. Gresham, In Lieu of Conclusions: Tentative Lessons from a Contested Frontier. In Maranto, et al., *School Choice in the Real World*, pp. 237–247; p. 239.
86. Good and Braden, *The Great School Debate*, Chapter 7.
87. B. Hassel, *The Charter School Challenge: Avoiding the Pitfalls, Fulfilling the Promise.* Washington, DC: Brookings Institution Press, 1999; A. Wells and J. Scott, Privatization and Charter School Reform. In H. Levin, ed., *Privatizing Education.* Boulder, CO: Westview, 2001, pp. 234–262.
88. Wells and Scott, Ibid.
89. Hassel, *The Charter School Challenge*, p. 156.
90. S. Sarason, *Charter Schools: Another Flawed Educational Reform?* New York: Teachers College Press, 1998, p. 106.
91. Good and Braden, *The Great School Debate*, p. 169.
92. Hassel, *The Charter School Challenge*, Chapter 7.
93. Finn, Jr., et al., *Charter Schools in Action*, p. 132.
94. Maranto, et al., Tentative Lessons, p. 241.
95. B. Manno and Others. Charter School Accountability; Part IV of C. Finn, Jr. and Others, *Charter Schools in Action: A Final Report.* Washington, DC: Hudson Institute, 1997, p. 1.
96. Finn, Jr., et al., *Charter Schools, in Action*, p. 135.
97. Hassel, *The Charter School Challenge*, Chapter 7.
98. P. Cookson, Jr., Assessing Private School Effects. In Rasell and Rothstein, *School Choice*, pp. 173–184; By the Numbers. *Lafayette Journal-Courier*, August 18, 2002, A12.
99. J. Hanus and P. Cookson, Jr. *Choosing Schools: Vouchers and American Education.* Washington, DC: American University Press, 1996.
100. T. Moe, *Schools, Vouchers, and the American Public.* Washington, DC: Brookings Institution Press, 2001, p. 3.
101. Moe, Ibid.
102. Moe, Ibid., p. 351.
103. P. McEwan, The Potential Impact of Large-Scale Voucher Programs. *Review of Educational Research, 70,* 2000, 103–149; A. Gamoran, Student Achievement in Public Magnet, Public Comprehensive, and Private City High Schools.
104. J. Coleman, T. Hoffer and S. Kilgore, *High School Achievement: Public, Catholic, and Private Schools Compared.* New York: Basic Books, 1982; A. Bryk, V. Lee, and P. Holland, *Catholic Schools and the Common Good.* Cambridge, MA: Harvard University Press, 1993; Gamoran, Student Achievement.
105. Gamoran, Student Achievement.
106. McEwan, The Potential Impact of Large-Scale Voucher Programs; Cookson, Jr., *School Choice.*
107. Gamoran, Student Achievement.
108. McEwan, The Potential Impact of Large-Scale Voucher Programs.

109. K. Metcalf, et al., Evaluation of the Cleveland Scholarship and Tutoring Program, Summary Report 1998–2001. Bloomington, IN: Indiana Center for Education, Indiana University, March 2003; quote from p. 7.

110. W. Howell, P. Wolf, P. Peterson, and D. Campbell, Effects of School Vouchers on Student Test Scores. In P. Peterson and D. Campbell, editors, *Charters, Vouchers, and Public Education*, pp. 136–159. Washington, DC: Brookings Institution Press, 2001.

111. A. Krueger and P. Zhu, *Another Look at the New York City School Voucher Experiment.* Princeton, NJ: Education Research Center, Princeton University, January 2003. See also K. Zernike, New Doubt Is Cast on Study That Backs Voucher Efforts. *New York Times*, November 15, 2000, A21.

112. Krueger and Zhu, Ibid.

113. M. Carnoy and P. McEwan, Privatization Through Vouchers in Developing Countries: The Cases of Chile and Colombia. In H. Levin, ed., *Privatizing Education.* Boulder, CO: Westview, 2001, pp. 151–177.

114. Carnoy and McEwan, Ibid., p. 172.

115. F. Hess, *Revolution at the Margins: The Impact of Competition on Urban School Systems.* Washington, DC: Brookings Institution Press, 2002, Chapter 1.

116. C. Belfield and H. Levin, The Effects of Competition Between Schools on Educational Outcomes. *Review of Educational Research, 72*, 2002, 279–341.

117. Carnoy and McEwan, Privatization Through Vouchers in Developing Countries.

118. F. Hess, *Revolution at the Margins.*

119. Hess, Ibid., p. 197.

120. Hess, Ibid., p. 70.

121. McEwan, The Potential Impact of Large-Scale Voucher Programs.

122. Moe, *Schools, Vouchers, and the American Public.*

Chapter 9

THE EDUCATION GAP BETWEEN MINORITY STUDENTS AND WHITE STUDENTS

Students of different races and ethnic groups differ, on average, both in the years of education they complete and in their proficiency in academic subjects as indicated by their scores on achievement tests. These differences among groups—African-Americans, those of Hispanic heritage, those of Asian background, non-Hispanic whites, and others—are important for the students themselves and for society as a whole.

The more schooling students complete, the more able they are to enter skilled occupations and the higher their incomes are likely to be.[1] Apart from the amount of schooling completed, higher cognitive proficiency—in verbal, math, and other skills—also contributes to higher earnings for individuals.[2] On a societal level, large gaps in education among racial and ethnic groups perpetuate group differences in social class, which, in turn, contribute to negative stereotypes, to separation of groups, and to conflicts among these groups.[3]

This chapter begins by examining the educational differences that exist among racial and ethnic groups in the United States. Next I consider possible reasons why such gaps in attainment and achievement occur, including students' home backgrounds, various aspects of schools, and the attitudes and behaviors of students themselves. Since most relevant research has dealt with differences between African-American students and white students, my own focus also is on the "black-white gap." However, some attention also is given to research on Hispanic-American students and those from other minorities. The final section of the chapter summarizes relevant research findings and suggests ways to reduce educational gaps among racial and ethnic groups.

YEARS OF SCHOOLING

The amount of education that Americans receive increased dramatically during the twentieth century, especially after World War II. The rise has been marked for people of all races, but especially for minorities. In 1940,

266

among all young adults (those from 25 to 29 years old), 22 percent had completed high school and 4.5 percent had completed four or more years of college. Among young black adults, only 7.7 percent had completed high school and only 1.3 percent had four or more years of college. (Persons of Hispanic origin were not counted separately until about 1980.)

The proportion of all youth who completed high school rose steadily over time and the racial gap in high school completion steadily shrank. By 2001, 93.3 percent of young white non-Hispanic adults and 87 percent of black non-Hispanic adults were high school graduates. However, young adults of Hispanic origin were less likely than others to have finished high school; 63.2 percent were high school graduates.

With respect to completion of college, racial and ethnic differences remain large. Among young adults who were 25 to 29 years old in 2001, 33 percent of non-Hispanic whites, 17.9 percent of non-Hispanic blacks, and only 11.1 percent of Hispanics had a bachelor's degree or higher.[4]

The U.S. government reports from which these data are taken do not show school completion percentages separately for people of Asian background. However, other data indicate that Asian-Americans complete more years of education than any other group. A U.S. Census Bureau report in 1998 showed that slightly more young Asian adults than young whites had graduated from high school. Over half of young Asians (51%), as compared to 28 percent of young whites, had obtained at least a bachelors degree.[5]

Overall, then, while Americans of all racial and ethnic groups are completing more schooling than in the past, blacks still lag somewhat behind whites in high school completion and are only about half as likely to complete college. Hispanics are far behind non-Hispanics—both white and black—in both high school and college completion. Students of Asian background complete the most years of education.

PROFICIENCY IN SCHOOL SUBJECTS

Racial and ethnic groups differ not only in the years of education they complete but also in the proficiency that students achieve in subjects they study at any given grade level. The National Assessment of Educational Progress (NAEP) measures the proficiency of American children and youth in reading, mathematics, and other subjects. Non-Hispanic white students and Asian students consistently have scored considerably higher on these tests (as well as on other tests) than non-Hispanic black students, Hispanic students, and Native American students.

The achievement gap between whites and blacks, and between whites and Hispanics, generally shrank somewhat during the 1980s. From 1990 to 2003 the achievement scores of all three of these groups rose slightly. However, the racial and ethnic gaps in achievement did not decline in this most recent period.[6]

To get a better sense of the magnitude of the differences in achievement scores among racial and ethnic groups, we look next at some recent NAEP results on tests of reading and mathematics.[7]

Achievement levels in each subject are defined as follows:

"Basic: This level denotes partial mastery of prerequisite knowledge and skills that are fundamental for proficient work at each grade.

Proficient: This level represents solid academic performance for each grade assessed. Students reaching this level have demonstrated competency over challenging subject matter, including subject-matter knowledge, application of such knowledge to real-world situations, and analytical skills appropriate to the subject matter.

Advanced: This level signifies superior performance."[8]

READING PROFICIENCY

The nationally given NAEP reading test assesses students' understanding of reading materials from typical sources available to students (such as children's magazines and informational books). Students read these materials and then answer comprehension questions (some multiple-choice and some requiring written answers) about them.

The tests assess students' skills in tasks that range (as grade-appropriate) from the more simple, such as following brief written directions and being able to understand short uncomplicated passages, to the more difficult, such as interrelating ideas and being able to explain relatively complicated informational material.

Table 9-1 shows the percentage of students who scored at different levels of reading achievement in 2003 (for fourth and eighth graders) and in 2002 (for twelfth graders).[9] Results are shown separately for non-Hispanic whites, non-Hispanic blacks, Hispanics, Asians, and (for fourth and eighth grades) American Indians.

At each grade level, a much smaller percentage of white students and of Asian students than of students in the other three groups scored below the Basic level of proficiency in reading for their grade. Much larger proportions of white and of Asian students were at the Proficient and the Advanced reading levels. In general, black students did slightly more poorly than either Hispanic students or American Indian students.

MATH PROFICIENCY

The nationally given NAEP test in mathematics assesses students' proficiency in five content areas: (1) number sense, properties, and operations;

Table 9-1 Percentage of Students At or Above Different Reading Achievement Levels, for Students of Different Race and Ethnicity[a]

Fourth Graders, 2003

	Below Basic	Basic	Proficient	Advanced
White	25	34	30	11
Black	60	27	11	2
Hispanic	56	29	13	2
Asian	30	32	26	12
American Indian	53	31	14	2

Eighth Graders, 2003

	Below Basic	Basic	Proficient	Advanced
White	17	42	37	4
Black	46	41	12	1
Hispanic	44	41	14	1
Asian	21	39	35	5
American Indian	43	40	16	1

Twelfth Graders, 2002[b]

	Below Basic	Basic	Proficient	Advanced
White	21	37	36	6
Black	46	38	15	1
Hispanic	39	39	21	1
Asian	27	39	30	4

[a]Students with disabilities or limited proficiency in English were permitted to use certain accommodations (such as extended time or small-group testing).
[b]Data for American Indians were not available for twelfth graders in 2002.
Source: National Center for Education Statistics.

(2) measurement; (3) geometry and spatial sense; (4) data analysis, statistics, and probability; and (5) algebra and functions. Each question is intended to measure one of three mathematical abilities: conceptual understanding, procedural knowledge, or problem solving. Some questions are multiple-choice while others require written answers.

Table 9-2 shows the percentage of students who scored at different levels of math achievement for their grade, in 2003 for fourth and eighth graders and in 2000 for twelfth graders.[10]

As was true for reading achievement, white students and Asian students generally scored higher in math than did blacks, Hispanics, and American Indians. Much larger percentages of the latter groups were at a Below Basic level and much smaller proportions scored at the Proficient or Advanced

Table 9-2 Percentage of Students At or Above Different Mathematics Achievement Levels, for Students of Different Race and Ethnicity[a]

Fourth Graders, 2003

	Below Basic	Basic	Proficient	Advanced
White	13	44	38	5
Black	46	44	10	0
Hispanic	38	46	15	1
Asian	13	39	38	10
American Indian	36	47	16	1

Eighth Graders, 2003

	Below Basic	Basic	Proficient	Advanced
White	20	43	30	7
Black	61	32	6	1
Hispanic	52	36	11	1
Asian	22	35	30	13
American Indian	48	37	13	2

Twelfth Graders, 2000

	Below Basic	Basic	Proficient	Advanced
White	28	52	17	3
Black	69	28	3	0
Hispanic	57	39	4	0
Asian	25	43	25	7
American Indian	45	47	8	0

[a]Students with disabilities or limited proficiency in English were permitted to use certain accommodations (such as extended time or small-group testing).
Source: National Center for Education Statistics.

levels, compared to whites and Asians. (Asian students outpaced white students somewhat.)

Among the three lower-achieving groups, American Indians did somewhat better in math than either Hispanics or blacks. Hispanic students scored somewhat higher than black students.

To summarize the results that compare the academic proficiencies of students from different racial and ethnic groups, whites and Asians consistently have scored considerably higher than blacks, Hispanics, or American Indians on tests of reading, mathematics, and other subjects. Of the three lower-performing groups, blacks recently score somewhat below Hispanics and American Indians. While the proportion of students who fall into categories such as Basic and Proficient will vary with different tests, the high proportion of students (especially among some ethnic groups) who score as Below Basic on the NAEP tests, as well as the large differences in achievement across groups, indicate that serious educational problems exist.

EXPLANATIONS OF RACIAL/ETHNIC DIFFERENCES IN ACHIEVEMENT SCORES

A variety of possible explanations have been advanced for the observed differences in test scores among students of different racial and ethnic groups. These include: (1) test bias; (2) hereditary differences in ability; (3) differences in home background; (4) differences in the kinds of schools attended; and (5) differences in students: their aspirations, expectations of success, and motivation.

TEST BIAS

The question of possible bias in tests has been studied, especially with regard to the test scores of black students and white students.[11] The type of possible bias that has received the most attention is content bias. Content bias may be present when a test contains questions that favor one group over another. This could occur if the questions concerned topics that were more within the life experiences or culture of one group than another or that used language that was distinctive to one group.

While content bias may affect the performance of some students, it does not appear to explain very much of the gap in test performance between whites and blacks. Test-makers recently have been concerned about the possibility of content bias and have combed their tests to eliminate items where such bias might be present. Black children and slightly younger white children find the same words easy or difficult. Moreover, the black-white gap in test scores on tests that are relatively nonverbal and culture-free, such as those in mathematics and science, are about as large as the gaps on tests, such as reading comprehension, that rely more on language.

With respect to differences between Hispanic students and non-Hispanic white students, there is insufficient evidence regarding the possible effect of test bias. Although English is the first language of most Hispanic students, those whose families have come to the United States recently may not know the English language well. For students who are not adequately proficient in English, standardized tests—especially those measuring English verbal skills—may underestimate what the students know.[12] The extent to which such language problems bias the overall results for Hispanic students is unclear. Any such biases should be less serious for tests on subjects, such as mathematics, that do not require fluent knowledge of English.

Overall, while test bias sometimes may be a problem, substantial differences in achievement scores between racial and ethnic groups appear to be real.

HEREDITY

Some writers have asserted that the gap in achievement scores between blacks and whites (and between other ethnic groups) reflects genetic differences in intelligence.[13] Most social and behavioral scientists reject this explanation, pointing to contrary evidence. For example, two studies compared the IQ scores of mixed-race children (one white parent, one black parent) who were living with a white mother with the scores of mixed-race children living with a black mother. The IQ scores of the children living with a white mother were considerably higher and similar to the scores of white children. Since the genetic makeup of the two groups of mixed-race children was similar, these results suggest that differences in the parenting practices of white mothers and black mothers, not genetic differences, were the main influence on their children's scores. Two other studies used blood markers to estimate the percentage of Europeans in the ancestry of mixed-race (black and white) children. Neither study found an association between the extent of European ancestry and childrens' IQ.[14]

There is a substantial literature concerning the relationship, if any, between race and intelligence.[15] I do not attempt to summarize this literature. Rather, I only note the general consensus among scholars that there is not convincing evidence of hereditary differences in intelligence across racial and ethnic groups. Thus, we need to look to environmental causes to explain the differences in school achievement that we observe.

HOME BACKGROUND

The home background of minority students, including the social class and the composition of their families, tends to differ from that of white students.

Social Class

How well students do in school is related to the education and income of their families. Students whose achievement in school is low are more likely to come from low-income families and to have parents with relatively little education.[16] An analysis of the achievement gap between black students and white students found that the gap typically is reduced by about one-third when students' social class is controlled. The relative improvement in blacks' social class position in recent decades was found to be responsible for some overall reduction of the test score gap during the same period.[17]

Children who grow up in a family at the lower end of the socioeconomic ladder are more apt than higher-SES children to suffer a number of practical disadvantages that may affect their schooling.[18] They are more likely than children from families of higher social class to have been victims of preventable health conditions that may affect their school performance, including prenatal exposure to alcohol or drugs, low birth weight, lead poisoning, and child abuse and neglect. Their families are more likely than other families to move often, thus disrupting the continuity of their education. Even if they do well in school, a lack of money may make going to college more difficult and dropping out of school to take a job more attractive.

Parenting Practices

The educational disadvantages of minority children begin even before they start school. The National Longitudinal Survey of Youth assessed the vocabulary scores of three- and four-year-olds from 1986 to 1994. The median vocabulary scores of the black children was found to be far below the median scores of white children.[19]

The vocabulary scores of young children are influenced by their parents' practices in interacting with their children. A child's vocabulary tends to be richer when her parents reads to her, provide cognitively stimulating activities (such as recognition of letters and numbers) in the home, praise the child's accomplishments, and provide a stimulating learning environment in other ways. Such a stimulating learning environment is more likely to be provided by middle-class parents. The fact that blacks are less likely than whites to be middle-class explains part of the difference in vocabulary in parenting practices between the races.

However, even when parents' social class (and some other parent characteristics) are controlled, there remain some black-white differences in parenting practices that explain an additional portion of the racial gap in vocabulary among young children. With other variables, including social class, controlled, racial differences in parenting practices account for 20 to 25 percent of the racial gap in vocabulary scores between black and white five- and six-year-olds.[20]

Discussing these findings, Christoper Jencks and Meredith Phillips comment: "This suggests that changes in parenting practices might do more to reduce the black-white test score gap than changes in parents' educational attainment or income."[21] Since social class, as well as race, affects parenting practices, social class will continue to play at least an indirect role.

Educational Resources

The social class and the race of students' families may also affect the educational resources—such as books, newspapers, magazines, encyclopedias, and computers—that are available to children in their homes. Drawing on data from a national study of middle school students, Vincent Rosigno and James Ainsworth-Darnell obtained information about the educational resources in each student's home and about students' participation in trips to museums and in cultural classes (in art, music, or dance) outside of school.[22] Black students were found to have, on average, significantly fewer educational resources in their homes and to be less likely to visit museums or to attend outside-school cultural classes than their white counterparts. Most of these racial differences were explained by social class differences but, even with social class controlled, black students had fewer educational resources and less exposure to outside educational experiences than did whites.

For students of all races combined, having more educational resources in the home, making more trips to museums, and attending more cultural classes outside school all were associated with higher grade-point averages and higher scores on achievement tests. Such home-linked educational experiences had positive effects on student performance even when the effect of family socioeconomic status was held constant. However, the researchers note that family educational resources and experiences "only moderately explain racial and social-class gaps in performance."[23]

Parents' Aspirations

The expectations that parents have concerning how far their children will go in school have some influence on students' attachment to and engagement in school.[24] However, compared to parents of white students, parents of students from minority groups do *not* appear to have much different aspirations or expectations about their children's educational attainment.

In a national study, 10th-grade students were asked, "How far in school do you think your father and your mother want you to go?" Each student answered the question separately for each parent. Slightly smaller percentages of black students and of Hispanic students than of non-Hispanic white students said that each of their parents wants them to get a four-year college degree or more. But, compared to white students, more minority students— especially African-Americans—said that their parents wanted them to do at least some graduate studies. (Asian-American students reported the highest educational aspirations by parents.)

For students of all racial and ethnic groups, students' perceptions of their parents' aspirations appeared to affect their own educational expectations. The more education parents wanted for them, the more education students expected to complete, even after controlling for students' socioeconomic status and their school performance.[25]

In addition to having high educational aspirations for their children, parents from all racial and ethnic groups report talking regularly with their children about their school experiences and encouraging their children to do well in school.[26] However, despite their positive attitudes toward education, many low-income minority parents are not able to provide the same level of help or educational resources that middle-class white parents can give.

Middle-Class Minority Students

Low educational achievement, in comparison to whites (and also to Asians) is not a problem only for minority students from poor or low-education families. The lower academic achievement of most minority students, in comparison to non-Hispanic white peers, is found at each level of parents' social class.

National samples of student achievement scores show that differences between whites and blacks and Hispanics still remained among students from these groups whose parents had similar education. For example, the average reading and math scores of white students whose parents had graduated from high school were higher than those of black and Hispanic students whose parents had the same amount of education.

The difference among students from different ethnic groups but similar social class background was most noticeable in the SAT scores of the high school students applying to college. At both extremes of parental education (either the parents have no high school degree or at least one parent has a graduate degree), there were sizable ethnic group differences in both reading and math scores. At either extreme of parental education, white and Asian-American students scored much higher than black and Puerto Rican students and considerably above Mexican-American and Native American students.

The same pattern was also found when SAT scores of students from different ethnic groups at each extreme of income were compared. Both among students whose parents were the poorest and among those whose parents were the richest, similar differences in achievement among ethnic groups were found.[27]

Why do achievement scores of students in some ethnic groups tend to be low even though they come from middle-class families? While the answer to this question is not completely clear, some clues come from research that shows that, among all ethnic groups, students perform best when their academic achievement is encouraged by both their parents and their friends. This research also shows that white and Asian-American students are more likely than African-American and Hispanic-American students to have the combined support of both parents and peers for high achievement in school.[28]

PEER NORMS

The peer groups of black students and of some other racial minorities sometimes give little encouragement to, or even oppose, high achievement in school. Some studies have found that the peers of African-American students rejected behavior that was seen as "acting white." Behaviors defined as "white" included speaking standard English, studying hard, and getting good grades. Black students who worked hard in school sometimes were harassed by their peers.[29] Such anti-achievement attitudes have been described as part of a broader "opposition orientation" to a white-dominated society. While this oppositional orientation is strongest among the most disadvantaged blacks, it also appears to affect middle-class black children who sometimes are under peer pressure not to "act white" accademically.[30]

Similar norms of opposition to school authorities and to academic achievement have been found to be fairly widespread among Mexican-American youth.[31] Peer pressure against school achievement also has been described among Native Americans. Academically oriented Navaho and Ute students were discouraged by both school peers and adults from doing well in school; high achievement was considered a "white" attribute. Native American students who aspired to attend college also were seen by some as "acting white." Those who went away to college tended to feel they were rejecting their cultural identity.[32]

To what extent peer norms that oppose high academic achievement are widespread among minority students is not clear. A national survey asked 10th-graders: "Among the friends you hang out with, how important is it to study, get good grades, finish high school, and continue their education beyond high school?" African-American students reported more pro-school values among their peers than did white students. Moreover, African-American students reported being especially popular when they also are seen as very good students. These results, say researchers James Ainsworth-Darnell and Douglas Downey, "contradict the oppositional culture model."[33]

However, using the same data set as Ainsworth-Darnell, another group of researchers found that in schools with a high percentage of minorities (less than 25% white students), black students who were very good students had a heightened chance of being "put down by other students."[34] Another national study asked 4th-graders whether "my friends make fun of people who try to do well." Blacks and Hispanics experienced significantly more peer ridicule for school effort than did whites; Native Americans also reported more peer opposition than did whites, while Asians did not differ from whites in this respect. Students from families with relatively little education, boys, and those attending schools in high-poverty and urban areas also were more likely than others to experience peer ridicule for trying hard in school.[35]

Reporting these results, George Farkas and his colleagues say:

> These additive effects cumulate quite powerfully for any student possessing multiple risk factors. For example, an African American or a Hispanic male student who comes from a poor family, has a parent who dropped out of high school, and who attends a low-income, central-city public school would have a very high risk of finding himself within a peer group that negatively sanctions school effort.[36]

The question of how widespread an oppositional peer culture is among black students and other minority students continues to be debated.[37] It seems safe to conclude that opposition by peers to trying hard and to being a good student is a factor in pushing down the achievement of at least some minority students, including some of those from middle-class families.

PARENTAL SUPPORT

The degree of support for academic achievement from the parents of minority students also may impact the students. There is evidence that black male students whose parents push them to do well in school, while also giving help and support, are high-achievers in school.[38] However, at least some middle-class black parents appear to be somewhat nonchalant about their children's school performance. In a recent study of black students from middle-class families attending school in an affluent suburb (Shaker Heights, Ohio), John Ogbu found that affluent black parents spent no more time on homework or on keeping track of their children's schooling than did poor white parents.[39] Ogbu says, "The parents work two jobs, three jobs, to give their children everything, but they are not guiding their children."[40] Whether the parents studied by Ogbu are representative of most middle-class African-American parents is not known.

Some researchers also have pointed out that middle-class minority parents are likely to have reached middle-class status more recently than middle-class white parents. The more recent arrivals into the middle class may carry over some of the parenting practices of their relatively low-education families. There is evidence that racial differences in parenting practices are partly due to the fact that even when black and white parents have the same test scores, education attainment, and income, black parents are likely to have grown up in less advantaged households.

In addition, those minority parents who have achieved middle-class status in terms of education, occupation, and income, generally have accumulated much less family wealth than have middle-class white parents. There is evidence that, even with the usual measures of social class held constant, the net worth of parents (particularly their income-producing assets) affects the cultural opportunities they provide their children (such as special lessons or activities) and contributes to the children's academic achievement.[41]

In addition to the effect of parents' characteristics on their children's achievement, there appears to be an additional "grandparent effect." For children whose grandparents had similar characteristics (such as education and occupation), the gap in vocabulary between young black children and young white children shrinks by about 25 percent. Meredith Phillips and her colleagues comment: "This suggests that changes in families' class position take more than one generation to alter parenting practices. It could therefore take several generations for educational or economic changes to exert their full effect on the black-white test score gap."[42]

THE ROLE OF TEACHERS

Is the achievement gap between whites and minorities affected by the types of teachers the students have? And what about the kinds of relationships that students have with teachers—do teacher–student relationships have an impact on racial and ethnic differences in achievement?

Teacher Qualifications

The qualifications of teachers—especially their amount of experience in teaching—often have an effect on student achievement.[43] Are those who teach in predominantly minority schools less qualified than teachers in mostly white schools? The evidence on this question is somewhat mixed.

One report found that new teachers hired without meeting certification standards are usually assigned to low-income and high-minority schools. A study of 900 Texas school districts found that differences in achievement between black students and white students were strongly affected by differences in the qualifications of their teachers (as measured by scores on a licensing exam, master's degrees, and experience).[44]

Somewhat inconsistent evidence comes from national data on secondary schools. These data show that mostly black and mostly white schools have the same average number of teachers per pupil, the same pay scales, and teachers with almost the same amount of formal education and teaching experience.[45] Thus, it appears that differences in teacher qualifications sometimes contribute to racial and ethnic achievement differences but that major differences in teacher qualifications are not always found. (See Chapter 6 for a discussion of the relationship between teacher characteristics and student achievement.)

Race of Teachers

Do minority students do better in school when their teachers are of the same race or ethnicity? Some authors, writing about Hispanic as well as black students, have emphasized the importance of teachers sharing a racial or cultural identity with their students.[46] However, there is only weak and inconsistent evidence that minority children learn more from minority teachers than non-Hispanic white teachers.

Moreover, while matching teachers and students with respect to race or culture may have some advantages, such a policy may have the unwanted effect of lowering teacher competency. Minority individuals, on average, score lower than non-Hispanic whites on teacher competency exams.[47] Thus, at present there appears to be a trade-off between matching teachers with student ethnicity and having the most competent teachers.

Teacher Expectations

Teachers generally perceive some students as having more academic ability and as likely to perform better than others. In forming their expectations, teachers tend to rely on students' records (test scores and grades), on the reports of other teachers, and on their own classroom experiences with students. However, teacher expectations are sometimes influenced by the students' social class and race; they may have higher expectations of middle- or upper-class students than of lower-class students and higher expectations of non-Hispanic whites than of blacks or Hispanics.[48]

The expectations that teachers have for students' academic performance affect their behavior toward their students. When they have low expectations of students, they tend, for example, to call on them less often to answer questions; give them the answers to questions more often, rather than helping them to find the right answers themselves; criticize them more often when they fail at a task; praise them less often when they succeed; place fewer academic demands on them; and pay less overall attention to them. Some studies have found that teachers give black students less positive feedback and more negative feedback than white students, although this has not always been found to be true.[49]

The expectations that teachers have of their students do appear to affect the students' academic performance. Low teacher expectations tend to lower students' performance, while high expectations tend to raise performance. These effects undoubtedly occur in part because of the links between teacher expectations and teacher behavior. Teacher expectations may also have an impact on students' performance because they affect students' own expectations. Students become aware of their teachers' expectations for them and they tend to have expectations for themselves that are similar to those of their teachers.[50]

While teacher expectations appear to have some effect on students' performance in school, generally this effect is not large for individual students. Brophy concludes from his own research, and from that of others, that a typical student's academic performance is lowered or raised 5 to 10 percent as a result of teacher expectations.[51]

However, teacher expectations, and those of school administrators as well, do not affect only individual students. They also may affect the programs and the atmosphere of the entire school. Especially in schools that enroll mostly low-income minority students, the teaching staff and administrators may have basically given up on providing a good education. Their low expectations are reflected in the few demands placed on their students.[52]

Kati Haycock and her colleagues observed class activities in high-poverty, high-minority classrooms and compared these activities to those in other classrooms. She says:

> We have come away stunned. Stunned, first, by how little is expected in high-poverty schools—how few assignments they get in a given school week or month. Stunned, second, by the low level of the few assignments they do get. In high-poverty urban middle schools, for example, we see a lot of coloring assignments, rather than writing or mathematics assignments.[53]

Poor minority students often are given relatively good grades for minimal levels of effort and performance. Summarizing results from their own studies, Gary Natriello and Sanford Dornbusch state "The teachers . . . shy away from making real demands on these students. Praise and warmth in the absence of challenging standards inflate student assessments of their effort, without really fostering effort-engagement behavior."[54] Students may not realize that they are doing little and learning little.

A review of teaching practices used with African-American males finds that a combination of high standards, high expectations, and supportiveness is most effective. Michele Foster and Trypheni Peele conclude: "In their dealings with [African-American] students, expert teachers express concern and have respect for their pupils, command respect in return, and expect their students to meet high behavioral and academic standards."[55]

Studies of the reactions of African-American males to their teachers indicate that these students prefer teachers who are both strict and caring—personally supportive but insistent that their students perform well academically. Foster and Peele quote one student as saying: "I don't really feel the teachers were pushing and encouraging us to succeed. . . . Mrs. Jackson . . . was great and Mr. Rubinstein was good too. He challenged us in a way. . . . [Mrs. Jackson] pushed me to do better. The majority of the other teachers did next to nothing."[56]

SCHOOL CHARACTERISTICS

While individual teachers affect students' performance in school, so also do the characteristics of the schools they attend. We next consider a number of school characteristics that have been investigated as possibly affecting the achievement gap between non-Hispanic whites and minorities.

Resources

In general, the racial gap in school achievement cannot be explained by differences in school spending. While there are examples of glaring inequality of spending and resources between rich suburbs and nearby poor central cities, the average white child and the average black child live in school districts that spend almost exactly the same amount of money for each student. Also, there is, in general, little difference between predominantly white schools and predominantly black schools with respect to the average number of teachers per pupil and teacher pay scales.[57]

Composition of the Student Body

Research evidence (summarized in Chapter 6) shows that both the ethnic composition and the social class composition of the student body have some effects on the achievement of minority students. In general, the academic achievement of black and Hispanic students tends to rise when they attend schools whose students are mostly non-Hispanic whites. However, these positive effects are not found consistently and are quite modest in magnitude. The tendency for minority students to do better when in mostly white classes appears to be due mostly to higher standards and higher teacher expectations in such settings.

The social class makeup of the student body has a clear impact on student achievement. The higher the socioeconomic status of a student's schoolmates, the higher his achievement tends to be—independent of the student's own social class background. We have noted in (in Chapter 6) a number of ways in which the social class of a student body may affect a school's operation—including the curriculum offered, the pace of learning, the orderliness of classes, and the norms of students regarding learning.

Minority students are more likely to attend schools with classmates from lower-class backgrounds. Moreover, minority students—blacks, Hispanics, and Native Americans—are affected more than non-Hispanic white students by the average social class of their schoolmates. It may be that because minority students tend to have less preparation, fewer educational resources, and less support outside of school, they are more vulnerable to the deficiencies of schools with large concentrations of poor students.

In sum, one reason why minority students generally perform less well than white students is that they are more likely to attend schools with high proportions of poor minority students. Academic standards and expectations in such schools tend to be lower than in schools with mostly white and affluent student bodies.

Ability Grouping and Tracking

The academic achievement of minority students also is affected by the widespread school practices of ability grouping and tracking. (See Chapter 2 for a general review of evidence on this subject.)

Because minority children begin school with poorer skills, especially in English language, they are more likely than non-Hispanic white students to be put in low-ability classes or low-ability groups within classes. Careful experimental studies have found that, in elementary schools, ability grouping raises the achievement level of students at all ability levels. At the same time, the gap in achievement between pupils in the low- and the high- ability groups widens. In other words, elementary students at all ability levels do better in ability groups than in heterogeneous classes, but those in the high-ability group progress at a faster rate.

At the secondary school level, African-American and Hispanic students are more likely than non-Hispanic whites (and Asians) to be in non-college preparatory tracks—that is, in low-ability classes and in more basic and less advanced courses. Their placement in (or choice of) such programs appears to be based primarily on their prior records of achievement (grades, test scores, etc.).

Thus, students in different high school tracks begin at different levels of academic achievement. However, in addition to starting out at a higher achievement level, those in a college-preparatory program *gain* more in achievement during high school than do those who follow other programs. Thus, the gap between the low-track and high-track students widens between their sophomore and senior years. Those in the college-preparatory program may gain more partly because they take more courses or more advanced courses. In addition, there are other differences between tracks— such as in teaching methods or disciplinary problems—that may lead to greater gains for students in the higher track.

In sum, the presence of many minority students in low-ability and low-track classes and programs appears to widen the achievement gap between those students and students in "higher level" classes and programs.

Other Characteristics of Schools

In earlier chapters (see especially Chapters 6 and 8), I have noted a number of school situations in which the gap in achievement between white students and minority students has been found to narrow.

1. Racial differences in achievement are less in Catholic schools than in public schools.
2. Racial differences in achievement are less in magnet schools than in other schools.
3. Vouchers to attend private schools tend to lead to higher achievement for black students but not for white (or Hispanic) students.
4. The average socioeconomic status of the student body affects the achievement of minorities more than it does that of white students.
5. Reducing the size of classes benefits the achievement of black students more than that of white students.

These favorable conditions for minority achievement appear to have some common elements. Catholic schools, magnet schools, and private schools all are relatively small and tend to create bonds of support and trust between students and school staff. Likewise, small classes facilitate more staff–student interaction and more support and help from teachers. These more intimate, more communal type of school settings also reduce problems of maintaining good order and discipline that are sometimes detrimental to minority student achievement. A primarily middle-class student body also may help to maintain good order, as well as provide peer support for learning.

In each of the ways listed, minority students, especially black students, appear to be more affected by the school context than are whites. It may be that, because they are more likely to have had academic difficulties and may have less help and support from family, minority students react more strongly to variations in the school situation. In the favorable settings noted, the racial achievement gap declines.

STUDENT EFFORT AND STUDENT ATTITUDES

Do black and Hispanic students try less hard than non-Hispanic white students? Do they have lower aspirations and expectations regarding their future educational and occupational attainments?

Effort

Although research findings vary, they tend to show that minority students put forth somewhat less effort than white students. A study of Indianapolis high schools found that black students were much more likely than white students to say that they often were late to class and also were more likely to miss a class without permission.[58] African-American and Hispanic students in California and in Wisconsin also reported spending less time on homework than their non-Hispanic white schoolmates.[59]

One study obtained data relevant to student effort from a national sample of high school sophomores and from their teachers. Each student was asked several questions concerning whether he had gotten into any trouble during the first half of the school year (e.g., for not following school rules) and about the number of hours he spent on homework per week. Two teachers assessed each student's classroom effort and whether the student was disruptive in the classroom. Compared to white students, African-American students were significantly more likely to report having been in trouble in school and reported spending fewer hours on homework. Teachers judged African-American students as putting forth less effort and also as being more disruptive than the white students.[60]

While African-American students tended to devote less actual effort to their school work, they saw themselves as trying hard in their classes. They were, in fact, significantly more likely than white students to say that they try hard in class. Black students also were more likely to say they "think that other students see you as a good student."[61] These results may indicate that the standards by which black students judge their own effort and success as students are different from those of whites.

Attitudes Toward School

Some scholars have depicted minority students as often rejecting the schools as agents of an oppressive society.[62] Such strongly negative attitudes toward their schools do not appear to be typical of most minority students. A national study of high school sophomores asked students about their treatment by teachers, their attitudes toward teachers, the fairness of discipline, and whether they thought it was okay to break certain school rules. Compared to white students, African-American students perceived themselves as being treated well by teachers, had somewhat more positive attitudes toward their teachers, and were less likely to think it was okay to break school rules. However, African-American students were less likely than white students to think that school discipline was fair.[63]

A national study of American students in grades 7 to 12 included a measure of students' attachment to school. This measure was based on the extent to which students agreed that, in the past school year, they felt close to people at their schools, felt a part of their schools, and were happy to be at their schools.

Among students in middle schools, neither African-Americans nor Hispanic-Americans had significantly less (or more) attachment to their schools than did white students. Among those in high schools, Hispanic-American students again did not differ significantly from non-Hispanic whites in school attachment. African-American high school students were slightly lower in school attachment than white students; this racial difference, although reaching statistical significance, was small.[64]

Overall, these results do not suggest major differences in the attitudes toward school of minority students versus those of non-Hispanic white students.

Aspirations and Expectancies

There is evidence from a number of studies that the educational and occupational aspirations of black students generally have been as high as those of white students.[65] For example, in the 1970s, Indianapolis high school students were asked "How far would you *like* to go in school? The answers of black students and of white students were similar, with blacks wanting slightly more schooling beyond high school than whites did.

Students also were asked about the kind of work they would "*really like* to do in your later life." Black students were only slightly less likely than white students to choose an occupation of the highest prestige (such as professional).[66]

Of course, a student's expectancies about her future education or occupation may be different from her aspirations. Do students from different racial and ethnic groups have similar expectations about being able to fulfill their aspirations?

In 1990, high school sophomores taking part in the National Education Longitudinal Study were asked: "As things stand now, how far in school do you think you will get?" Results have been reported separately for whites, African-Americans, Hispanic-Americans, and Asian-Americans.[67]

Asian-American students expected to complete the most education. Differences between whites and African-Americans were quite small. Fewer than one in eight whites and fewer than one in six blacks expected to get only a high school diploma or less. Most whites (59%) and most blacks (55%) expected to obtain a four-year college degree or more; slightly more blacks than whites said they expected to get a Ph.D. degree.

Among Hispanic-American students, educational expectations were somewhat lower than those of whites and blacks. The great majority of Hispanics (81%, compared to 88% of whites and 84%of blacks) said they expected to get some education beyond high school. Almost half of Hispanics (45%) compared to 59 percent of whites and 55 percent of blacks, expected to get a college degree or more.

In another study, a national sample of seniors was asked in 1992 about their plans after high school. The proportion of blacks and of non-Hispanic whites who said they planned to attend college right after high school was almost identical (about three quarters in each group). The proportion of Asians with such plans was a little higher (83%) and that of Hispanics a little lower (66%).

Asked about the occupations they expected to be in at the age of 30, a slightly higher proportion of blacks than whites said they expected to have a professional, business, or managerial position (55% to 50%); Asian-Americans were slightly more likely (61%) and Hispanics and Native Americans slightly less likely (47 and 43%, respectively) than other groups to expect to attain one of these relatively high-level occupations. Other differences in occupational expectations among the ethnic groups were small.[68]

Aspirations and Behaviors

The evidence reviewed in this section indicates that the aspirations and expectations of minority students, especially African-Americans, do not differ greatly from those of non-Hispanic whites. However, the aspirations of minority students often are not related closely to their position and performance in school.

Among black students in the Indianapolis schools, expectations about getting the kind of jobs they wanted was less strongly related to school performance than was the case for whites.[69] Moreover, black and Hispanic students are more likely than white and Asian-American students to be optimistic about getting the kind of jobs they want even if they are doing poorly in school.[70] Apparently, black and Hispanic students often are not well informed about what needs to be done in order to attain the occupational positions to which they aspire. L. Scott Miller comments: "Black students may also be unable to assess the level of academic performance it takes to prepare for good jobs or to avoid bad jobs, possibly in part because the students know few adults who have excellent education and the associated desirable jobs."[71]

The apparent lack of realistic understanding by many minority students about what they would need to do to reach their aspirations may help to explain the relatively low level of effort described earlier. An additional explanation is suggested by James Ainsworth-Darnell and Douglas Downey who suggest that the neighborhoods in which many poor African-American students live (e.g., those with high rates of unemployment and nontraditional family structures) "are less likely to foster the kinds of skills, habits, and styles that lead to school success."[72]

MINORITY SCHOOLS WITH HIGH ACHIEVEMENT

There are some schools with mostly-minority student bodies in which students "beat the odds" and have high levels of academic achievement. For example, a study by the U.S. Department of Education identified nine urban public elementary schools serving mostly poor students of color in which student achievement scores in math and reading were higher than the average of all schools in their state (or above the 50th percentile on a nationally normed test).[73] Another study looked at 21 schools, at varying grade levels, in which most students were poor and (usually) minority, and which had median test scores above the 65th percentile on national achievement tests; most of these high-achieving schools were public schools.[74] A third study examined eight Texas public schools at different levels (three elementary schools, three middle schools, and three high schools) in which two-thirds or more of the students were Mexican-American (many having limited backgrounds in English), most students were poor, but average test scores on the state Assessment of Academic Skills were well above average for all state schools.[75]

These studies and others, including earlier research on effective schools in poor minority areas,[76] have shown that schools that are effective in teaching poor minority children tend to have some common characteristics:

1. The staff of the school shares measurable goals that reflect a vision of success.
2. There is a high level of interaction, collaboration, and joint planning by the faculty.
3. Standards for student learning are high, as shown, for example, in course requirements, in time devoted to learning tasks, and in effort required of students.
4. Great emphasis is placed on effective instruction. Specific practices used include (among others): using a culturally responsive pedagogy that relates to student interests and experience; cooperative learning; peer tutoring; and giving teachers constructive feedback on their classroom performance.
5. There is continual development of teacher skills. Interaction among teachers on instructional issues (such as discussion, critiquing each other, and mentoring by master teachers) has been one effective approach.
6. The school environment is disciplined and orderly. The effectiveness of discipline is enhanced by the fact that most students think that they are learning successfully.
7. Parents are involved, as partners with the school, in students' learning activities.
8. There is regular assessment of student learning. While objective tests often are used, assessments of student performance on more complex tasks also are used in some effective schools. Results of tests are used diagnostically to promote improvement by students and by teachers.

These characteristics of effective schools are not unique to schools that serve mostly poor and minority students. They are prominent among the features of all effective schools.

The specific ways in which general guidelines for good education are applied to schools with poor and minority students will sometimes need to be different from the way that they are applied to schools with mostly middle-class white students. For example, teachers of minority students may need to tailor their instructional methods to fit the cultural background and learning styles of these students.

Moreover, there may be more difficulty in putting some of these ideas into effect in schools with poor and minority students. For example, school administrators and teachers may find it harder to communicate and collaborate with parents who are poorly educated and/or speak poor English than they do with middle-class white parents.

But while it may be more difficult to shape schools in ways that provide a good education for poor and minority students, the examples provided by the schools discussed earlier in this section show that it can be done. The "achievement gap" can be closed.

SUMMARY AND CONCLUSIONS

African-American and Hispanic students complete fewer years of education than non-Hispanic white students and, among students at the same educational level, do less well on tests of academic achievement. Racial and ethnic differences in achievement are due in part to average differences in social class between these groups. Children who grow up in poor families, with parents who have relatively little education, suffer a number of disadvantages that make them less well prepared for learning than middle-class children when they enter school.

Low school achievement by minority students is not limited to students who come from poor families with little education. Middle-class black and Hispanic students score considerably lower than non-Hispanic white students whose parents have similar income and education. The relatively low academic achievement of middle-class minority students appears to be influenced sometimes by the antiacademic norms of their minority peers, who ridicule high effort and high achievement. Also, some middle-class minority parents do not give enough guidance to their children's schoolwork.

In school, the learning progress of minority students is affected, and often limited, by the attitudes and actions of their teachers. Teachers often have low expectations of minority students, assign them little and simple work, and may give students good grades for work of a low level. Teachers who are most effective in promoting high achievement by minority students combine high standards—insisting that their students do well academically—with caring and supportiveness for students' efforts.

Characteristics of the schools they attend also affect the achievement of minority students. Regardless of their own social class background, students, especially minority students, do better academically as the socioeconomic level of the school's student body rises. Minority students also tend to have slightly higher achievement when they attend schools and classes with mostly white schoolmates. Schools with relatively affluent and mostly white students are more likely than schools with high concentrations of poor and minority students to have high standards, to be orderly, and to have students who give support to their peers for high achievement.

School programs that create separate ability-level classes and separate curriculum tracks generally result in large proportions of minority students in low-ability classes and noncollege curriculum tracks. Differences in the quality of education provided to these students, compared to those in "higher" classes and tracks, widen the initial achievement gap between minority students and non-Hispanic white students.

The aspirations and expectations of minority students for higher education and for careers are similar to those of non-Hispanic white students. Moreover, minority students' attitudes toward school are, in general, equally positive to those of other students. However, the school grades and the program of courses taken by minority students often are inconsistent with their high aspirations. Also, the amount of effort by minority students, such as time spent on homework, tends to be lower than the effort of non-Hispanic white students. Minority students often seem to be unaware of the kind of school record necessary for higher education and better careers and also are not aware that their effort is relatively low.

Low academic achievement by minority students is not found everywhere. In some schools in which most students are poor and minority, average achievement scores are above those for the general student population in their state or nationally. These high-achieving minority schools generally share some common characteristics, including high standards, effective instructional practices, an orderly environment, parent involvement, and using assessments of student learning to improve student and teacher performance.

The evidence that indicates some of the reasons for the gap in achievement between minority students and other students suggests some approaches that should help to reduce, and eventually close, this gap. First, more must be done to help develop the cognitive abilities of preschool minority children, such as their vocabulary, so that they are as ready to learn as other children when they begin school. More information and counseling about cognitive development could be given to the parents of young children. Programs for preschool children, such as Head Start, could be expanded to cover more poor and minority children and to focus more on developing children's cognitive abilities than they usually have done.

Within the regular school, principals and teachers must have high standards and high expectations about the behavior and performance of minority students. Teachers need to combine insistence on high achievement with being supportive, being caring, and helping students to be successful in their schoolwork.

The quality of education provided to students in lower-skill classes and non-college tracks needs to be greatly improved. While the specific material covered and the pace of coverage may appropriately differ somewhat in different classes, students in lower-skill classes and lower tracks should be held to high standards of performance. Those who do not want to go to college can be offered career-preparation programs that include core academic subjects and that, by linking their studies to desirable careers, can motivate students to achieve at a high level.

School personnel and others must give minority students more information about the kinds of courses they need to take and the level of effort and grades they need to attain in order, realistically, to fulfill their career aspirations. Schools and those outside the schools also need to do more to encourage minority students to support each other in their school efforts, rather than to ridicule those who try hard and do well. Cooperative learning activities, in which students work together on a group task, and in which they may compete with other groups, is one usually effective way of getting students to help and encourage each other to do well in their schoolwork.

Finally, schools can do a number of other things to improve the achievement of minority students. These include setting specific goals for student achievement, having programs to continually develop teacher skills, having good discipline and order, and using regular assessment of student learning to improve teacher methods and student learning. These and other characteristics of all effective schools are sometimes harder to put in place in high-poverty and minority schools. But, as the example of some schools shows, these things can be done and the racial and ethnic achievement gap can be closed.

NOTES

1. J. Ballantine, *The Sociology of Education*, 5th edition. Upper Saddle River, NJ: Prentice-Hall, 2001, pp. 213–214.
2. A. Cancio, T. Evans, and D. Maume, Jr. Reconsidering the Declining Significance of Race: Racial Differences in Early Career Wages. *American Sociological Review, 61*, 1996, 541–556.
3. M. Patchen, *Diversity and Unity: Relations Between Racial and Ethnic Groups.* Belmont, CA: Wadsworth, 1999.
4. U.S. Office of Education, *Digest of Education Statistics 2001.* Washington, DC, 2002, Table 8; U.S. Bureau of the Census, *March Current Population Surveys, 1971–2001.* Washington, DC: 2002, Tables 25-1 and 25-3.
5. K. Haycock. Closing the Achievement Gap. *Educational Leadership, 58,* 2001, 6–11.
6. U.S. Office of Education, *Digest of Education Statistics 2001.* Washington, DC, 2002; National Assessment of Educational Progress, *The Nation's Report Card.* Jessup, MD, 2003.
7. For evidence concerning how blacks and whites differ on additional measures of achievement, see L. Hedges and A. Nowell, Changes in the Black-White Gap in Achievement Test Scores. *Sociology of Education, 72,* 1999, 111–135.
8. National Assessment of Educational Progress, *The Nation's Report Card; Ibid,* Reading Highlights, 2003; Mathematic Highlights, 2003.
9. Data for this table were provided to the author by the National Center for Education Statistics.
10. Data for this table were provided to the author by the National Center for Education Statistics.
11. See C. Jencks and M. Phillips, eds., *The Black-White Test Score Gap.* Washington, DC: Brookings Institution Press, 1998, Chapter 2.
12. A. Scribner, Using Student Advocacy Assessment Practices. In P. Reyes, J. Scribner, and A. Scribner, eds., *Lessons from High-Performing Hispanic Schools.* New York: Teachers College Press, 1999. Chapter 7.
13. See, for example, R. Herrnstein and C. Murray, *The Bell Curve: Intelligence and Class Structure in American Life.* New York: Free Press, 1994.
14. C. Jencks, Racial Bias in Testing. In C. Jencks and M. Phillips, *The Black-White Test Score Gap,* pp. 55–85.

15. See, for example, J. Loehlin, G. Lindzey, and J. Spuhler, *Race Differences in Intelligence*. San Francisco: W. H. Freeman, 1975.

16. L. Miller, *An American Imperative: Accelerating Minority Educational Advancement*. New Haven, CT: Yale University Press, 1995.

17. Hedges and Nowell, *Changes in the Black-White Gap in Achievement*.

18. Miller, *An American Imperative*.

19. C. Jencks and M. Phillips, Introduction. In C. Jencks and M. Phillips, *The Black-White Test Score Gap*, p. 2.

20. M. Phillips, et al., Family Background, Parenting Practices, and the Black-White Test Score Gap. In C. Jencks and M. Phillips, eds., *The Black-White Test Score Gap*, pp. 103–148; see also A. Lareau, Invisible Inequality: Social Class and Childrearing in Black Families and White Families. *American Sociological Review, 67*, 2002, 747–776.

21. Jencks and Phillips, Ibid., p. 24.

22. V. Roscigno and J. Ainsworth-Darnell, Race, Cultural Capital, and Educational Resources: Persistent Inequalities and Achievement Returns. *Sociology of Education, 72*, 1999, 158–178.

23. Roscigno and Ainsworth-Darnell, Ibid., p. 171.

24. M. Johnson, R. Crosnoe, and G. Elder, Jr., Students' Attachment and Academic Engagement: The Role of Race and Ethnicity. *Sociology of Education, 74*, 2001, 318–340.

25. S. Cheng and B. Starks, Racial Differences in the Effects of Significant Others on Students' Educational Expectations. *Sociology of Education, 75*, 2002, 306–327.

26. U.S. Department of Education, *Digest of Education Statistics*. Washington, DC: Government Printing Office, 1994.

27. Miller, *An American Imperative*.

28. L. Steinberg, S. Dornbusch, and B. Brown, Ethnic Differences in Adolescent Achievement: An Ecological Perspective. *American Psychologist, 47*, 1992, 728.

29. S. Fordham and J. Ogbu, Black Students' School Success: Coping with the Burden of "Acting White". *Urban Review, 18*, 1986, 10–11, 13–23.

30. C. Steele, Race and the Schooling of Black Americans. *Atlantic Monthly*, April 1992, 68–78.

31. M. Gibson and J. Ogbu, *Minority Students and Schooling*. New York: Garland Press, 1991.

32. D. Deyhle, Constructing Failure and Maintaining Cultural Identity: Navajo and Ute School Leavers. *Journal of American Indian Education, 31*, 1992, 24–27, 45.

33. J. Ainsworth-Darnell and D. Downey, Assessing the Oppositional Culture Explanation for Racial/Ethnic Differences in School Performance. *American Sociological Review, 63*, 1998, 536–553.

34. G. Farkas, C. Lleras, and S. Maczuga, Does Oppositional Culture Exist in Minority and Poverty Peer Groups? *American Sociological Review, 67*, 2002, 148–155.

35. Farkas, et al., Ibid.

36. Farkas, et al., Ibid., p. 152.

37. See D. Downey and J. Ainsworth-Darnell, Reply to Farkas, Lleras, and Maczuga. *American Sociological Review, 67*, 2002, 156–164.

38. F. Hrabowski III, K. Maton, G. Greif, *Beating the Odds: Raising Academically Successful African-American Males*. New York: Oxford University Press, 1998.

39. J. Ogbu, *Black American Students in an Affluent Suburb: A Study of Disengagement*. Mahwah, NJ: Lawrence Erlbaum, 2003.

40. F. Lee, Why Are Black Students Lagging? *New York Times*, November 30, 2002, A17.

41. M. Phillips, et al., Family Background, Parenting Practices, and the Black-White Test Score Gap; A. Orr, Black-White Differences in Achievement: The Importance of Wealth. *Sociology of Education, 76*, 2003, 281–304.

42. Phillips, et al., Ibid., p. 126.

43. E. Hanushek, Assessing the Effects of School Resources on Student Performance: An Update. *Educational Evaluation and Policy Analysis, 19*, 1997, 141–164.

44. L. Darling-Hammond, Race, Education, and Equal Opportunity. In C. Foreman, Jr., ed., *The African-American Predicament*. Washington, DC: Brookings Institution Press, 1999, pp. 71–81.

45. C. Jencks and L. Phillips, Introduction, *The Black-White Test Score Gap*, p. 10.

46. P. Reyes, et al., *Lessons from High-Performing Hispanic Schools*. New York: Teachers College Press, 1999.

47. R. Ferguson, Can Schools Narrow the Black-White Test Score Gap. In Jencks and Phillips, *The Black-White Test Score Gap*, pp. 318–374.

48. J. Dusek and G. Joseph, The Bases of Teacher Expectancies: A Meta-Analysis. *Journal of Educational Psychology, 75*, 1983, 327–346.

49. See, for example, B. Means and M. Knapp, Cognitive Approaches to Teaching Advanced Skills to Educationally Disadvantaged Students. *Phi Delta Kappan*, December, 1991, 282–289; J. Irvine, *Black Students and School Failure*. Westport, CT: Greenwood, 1990.

50. Miller, *An American Imperative*.

51. J. Brophy, Research on the Self-Fulfilling Prophecy and Teacher Expectations. *Journal of Educational Psychology, 75*, 1983, 327–346.

52. See, for example, J. Kozol, *Savage Inequalities: Children in America's Schools*. New York: Crown, 1991.

53. Haycock, Closing the Achievement Gap, p. 8.

54. G. Natriello and S. Dornbusch, *Teacher Evaluative Standards and Student Effort*. New York: Longman, 1984, p. 11.

55. M. Foster and T. Peele, Teaching Black Males: Lessons from the Experts. In V. Polite and J. Davis, eds., *African-American Males in School and Society*. New York: Teachers College Press, pp. 8–19; quote from p. 13.

56. Foster and Peele, Ibid., p. 16.

57. Jencks and Phillips, *The Black-White Test Score Gap*, pp. 8–9.

58. M. Patchen, *Black-White Contact in Schools: Its Social and Academic Effects*. W. Lafayette, IN, Purdue University Press, 1982, Chapter 10.

59. L. Steinberg, B. Brown and S. Dornbusch, *Beyond the Classroom*. New York: Simon & Schuster, 1996.

60. Ainsworth-Darnell and Downey, Assessing the Oppositional Culture Explanation. See also R. Solomon *Black Resistance in High School*. Albany: State University of New York Press, 1992; for a somewhat different view, see M. Johnson, R. Crosnoe, and G. Elder, Jr. Students' Attachment and Academic Engagement, *Sociology of Education, 74*, 2001, 318–340.

61. Ainsworth-Darnell and Downey, Assessing the Oppositional Culture Explanation.

62. M. Hallinan, Sociological Perspectives on Black-White Inequalities in American Schooling. *Sociology of Education*, Extra Issue 2001, 50–70.

63. Ainsworth-Darnell and Downey, Assessing the Oppositional Culture Explanation.

64. M. Johnson, et al., Students' Attachment and Academic Engagement.

65. See, for example, W. Boykin, Academic Performance of Afro-American Children. In J. Spence, ed., *Achievement and Achievement Motives*. San Francisco: W. H. Freeman, 1983.

66. Patchen, *Black-White Contact in Schools*, Chapter 10.

67. Cheng and Starks, Racial Differences in the Effects of Significant Others.

68. National Center for Education Statistics, *Digest of Educational Statistics*, Washington, DC: U.S. Government Printing Office, 1994.

69. Patchen, *Black White Contact in Schools*, Chapter 10; see also D. Mark, Discrepancies Between Aspirations and Preparation of Low SES Students. In S. Gregory, ed., *The Academic Achievement of Minority Students*. Lanham, MD: University Press of America, 2000.

70. Steinberg, et al., Ethnic Differences in Adolescent Achievement.

71. Miller, *An American Imperative*, p. 210.

72. Ainsworth-Darnell and Downey, Assessing the Oppositional Culture Explanation, p. 551.

73. U.S. Department of Education, *Hope for Education: A Study of Nine High-Performing, High-Poverty, Urban Elementary Schools*. Washington, DC, 1999.

74. S. Carter, *No Excuses: Lessons from 21 High-Performing, High-Poverty Schools*. Washington, DC: The Heritage Foundation, 2001.

75. Reyes and Others, *Lessons from High-Performing Hispanic Schools*.

76. S. Rosenholtz, Effective Schools: Interpreting the Evidence. *American Journal of Education, 93*, 1985, 352–388.

Chapter 10

OVERVIEW: MAKING OUR
SCHOOLS MORE EFFECTIVE

Outcomes for students, including how much schooling they complete and how much they learn in school, depends on what happens in a number of settings: students' home situations, the classroom, the school as a whole, and the wider society. To improve educational outcomes, we need to pay attention to what happens in each of these settings and to how those events are related.

The previous chapters have reviewed research that has examined the practices that appear to work best in the classroom, in the school, and in the broader society. In summarizing the research results and my conclusions based on these results, I will organize the discussion around the questions raised in Chapter 1, as follows:

1. What should students be taught? And should the curriculum be the same for all students?
2. How should classrooms be run? For example, what kinds of activities, instructional methods, and grouping of students are most effective?
3. How do various characteristics of schools—such as school size, the composition (economic and ethnic) of the student body, and the amount and patterns of spending—affect student outcomes?
4. What kinds of school organization and programs—such as staff participation in decision making, collaborative activities among teachers, and programs to involve parents in their children's education—make schools more effective?
5. How should students and schools be assessed? And how is such assessment related to student motivation and to curriculum and teaching?
6. What effect have programs that give parents and students more choice among schools (such as those for charter schools and for vouchers) had on schools and on students?
7. How can the gap in achievement between minority students and non-Hispanic white students be explained and reduced?

In the next sections, I discuss each of the issues listed as questions above. In doing so, I consider the policies and practices that contribute to good outcomes for students; the processes through which these results occur; and some of the ways in which the various aspects of schooling (at the classroom, school, and societal levels) are interrelated.

THE CURRICULUM: WHAT SHOULD STUDENTS BE TAUGHT?

It is not surprising, but nevertheless important, that the more time students spend studying a particular subject and the more extensive the coverage, the greater their knowledge in that subject area. When students take more courses in core academic subjects (such as math and science), are exposed to more extensive coverage of topics in that subject and to a high level of content (e.g., geometry rather than simple arithmetic), and spend more homework time on that subject, their level of achievement rises.

To counter a decline in enrollments in academic courses, many states have increased their requirements for graduation from high school, adding courses in core academic subjects, especially math and science. However, the additional courses that students take often are basic or remedial courses. Raising students' level of learning in a given subject requires not only their taking more credit hours but also covering content that is sufficiently extensive and at a high enough level of understanding.

There has been a continuing debate between those who advocate teaching "the basics" in each subject (e.g., the rules of spelling and grammar in English, the important dates and events of American history) and those who emphasize teaching students "thinking skills," such as forming generalizations and hypotheses, solving problems, and applying principles to new settings. Studies of cognition show that people quickly forget isolated and disconnected facts. For specific information to be meaningful, it must fit into organizing frameworks of concepts and relationships. Thus, a curriculum that focuses on the memorization of discrete facts and disconnected skills is likely to produce only a low level of learning.

On the other hand, schools cannot promote effective analytical thinking and problem solving among their students without building the base of information and basic skills that is necessary for such high-level thinking. Students need to learn both essential information and skills and the conceptual understandings and thinking skills that permit them to use these "basics" most effectively.

A central issue of curriculum design, especially at the high school level, is whether all young people should learn the same things or whether schools should offer varied programs of study. Most teachers prefer grouping students by skill level, believing that it makes it easier for them to plan and teach a curriculum. Moreover, providing a number of programs or "tracks" sometimes helps schools to better serve students with different interests, abilities, and aspirations.

However, the practice of tracking often has some negative effects on the quality of education experienced by students in "lower" non-college tracks. Students in non-college tracks have smaller gains in achievement during high school than students in college tracks. This smaller gain appears to be due, at least in part, to their taking fewer advanced academic courses and receiving less effective instruction. The use of vocational and other non-college tracks also has not usually had its intended results of keeping students in high school until graduation or enhancing their career success.

The effects of separate curriculum programs on student achievement vary depending on differences in teaching practices, the kind and content of courses taught, the ease of transferring across tracks, and many other aspects of a tracking system. Moreover, there are some separate curricula programs, such as those in magnet schools and some vocational programs, that have been successful in raising student motivation and achievement.

Thus, there is no uniform answer to the often-debated question of whether tracking harms or benefits students, particularly those in non-college programs. If separate curriculum programs result in courses of inadequate content, poor instruction, low expectations, and stigmatization of students in "lower" tracks, they will reduce the motivation and achievement of these students. However, if students are offered programs of study that they perceive as opportunities for fulfilling their aspirations for meaningful careers, and such programs provide courses of solid content, effective instruction, and recognition of student achievement, their motivation and achievement may be enhanced.

WHAT MAKES FOR EFFECTIVE CLASSROOMS?

The focal point for education is the classroom. Learning in the classroom is shaped primarily by the kinds of learning activities that take place and by the kinds of interactions that occur between students and teachers and among students.

Traditionally, classroom activities center around the teacher, who lectures and leads students in "recitations." Such direct instruction by teachers often promotes student achievement, especially in the early grades, for students with low skills, and when teaching a well-structured body of knowledge. However, students often are more attentive and learn better when they are actively engaged in schoolwork, rather than passively listening to the teacher.

Teachers do not have to choose between using only direct instruction and using only methods that emphasize independent activity by students. They often can get the advantages of both methods by combining lecture with related student activities (such as students applying ideas from the lecture to a particular problem).

A class activity is most conducive to high student motivation and to learning when it has the following characteristics: (1) It not only imparts information and basic skills but also promotes skills of analysis and problem solving; (2) The activity interests the student or is seen as useful in her own life; (3) The task is of moderate difficulty—hard enough to be challenging but not so hard as to discourage effort or prevent success. (Students from poverty backgrounds and low-achieving students usually require smaller steps in the task and a higher ratio of success in their work than do other students.); (4) While it is best for teachers to maintain general control over the activity, students should have some autonomy or participation in decisions about how to do a task.

As students engage in learning activities, their interaction with the teacher is important in maintaining their motivation and in promoting success experiences for them. Teachers need first to monitor the progress of their students, especially when students have been low achievers and when students are engaged in challenging tasks and/or working independently. As the teacher monitors students' work, he needs to give them feedback on how they are doing and help as needed. Corrective feedback from teachers to students about their performance, including homework, is one of the strongest contributors to high student achievement.

High expectations by the teacher about students' performance; clear standards for evaluating students' work that emphasize each student's own mastery of certain goals, rather than his performance relative to others; and teacher praise for good work, all can help to provide students with experiences of success in their schoolwork. Such success experiences are especially important for students of low socioeconomic background and for others whose prior academic difficulties have caused them to lose confidence in their own abilities and to become frustrated with the learning process.

Teachers sometimes have to punish students who break rules or engage in other undesirable behavior. Punishment is most likely to be effective when it is consistent, is seen by students as legitimate, and is combined with rewards for positive behavior. However, order in the classroom derives primarily not from punishments but from engaging students' interest in learning activities.

To match teaching methods to different levels of student skill, students often are grouped in, or within, classes according to their skill level. Students in elementary school who are assigned to homogeneous ability groups—both those in low-skill groups and those in high-skill groups—have been found consistently to achieve better than comparable students in mixed-ability groups. However, the initial gap in achievement between the higher-skill and the lower-skill groups tends to increase when students are taught in homogeneous groups. Ability grouping appears to be most useful under particular conditions, including flexibility in the grouping plan so that students can be readily moved to a different group as their performance changes.

Another basis for dividing students into subgroups within a class is the creation of groups of students who cooperate in their learning, earning rewards for the group as well as for each individual. Cooperative learning generally has been found to be effective in promoting learning for many different types of students and at many different grade levels. Students participating in cooperative groups usually are friendly to others in their group (even across racial lines) and encourage each other to do their best work. To make cooperative groups effective in promoting learning, it is helpful to arrange tasks that require unique contributions from each member; to make outcomes (such as grades) for each student depend on her own work, as well as that of the group; and to teach students the skills necessary for them to work together effectively.

Computers can contribute to student learning in many ways. However, the benefits that many have expected from the use of computers in schools have been largely unrealized to date. Studies that have compared the learning of students using various computer technologies with those used in traditional classrooms generally have not found differences in student achievement. Computer applications need to be improved, guided by an understanding of learning and of higher-order thinking and how they are developed. When computers are used in classes, the teacher is less the primary provider of knowledge than she is in traditional classes; however, her role as a guide and coach in obtaining knowledge, as well as in other ways, remains important.

In sum, teachers in effective classrooms: (1) get students involved in challenging activities that develop both basic information and skills and skills of analysis and problem solving; (2) create conditions that lead to success (and expectancy of future success) for students, including high but reachable standards, feedback on progress, help, and reward for good work; (3) involve students in cooperative interactions with each other, so that the power of peer group norms operates in support of learning goals.

The research on teaching and classroom life provides only some general guidelines concerning effective practice. Teaching must be tailored to the varying and changing requirements of specific groups of students in specific circumstances. Thus, providing a high level of learning in classrooms requires ongoing discussion, planning, and innovation among the faculty of each school.

HOW SHOULD A SCHOOL BE ORGANIZED TO MAKE IT MOST EFFECTIVE?

What happens in each classroom is influenced by the academic program of the school. The school's academic program is shaped, at least in part, by the way in which its staff members make decisions and relate to each other. Both the academic program and staff relationships are, in turn, affected by other basic characteristics of the school, such as its size and the composition of its student body.

THE ACADEMIC PROGRAM

Schools produce good outcomes for students when they complement a good curriculum with plans and procedures for learning that energize teachers, facilitate effective classroom instruction, and engage students in their studies.

School effectiveness is enhanced when the staff agrees on clear and specific goals for their students' learning. Having shared goals—for example, all their first-grade students knowing how to read or 90 percent of their students completing high school—helps to focus and motivate teachers' efforts and leads to better student outcomes.

The effectiveness of learning in a school also is affected by the way in which it organizes available time. Block schedules have fewer but longer class periods than traditional school schedules. They are intended to permit both students and teachers to focus their attention and effort on a small number of classes (often three) each day. Block schedules generally are liked more than traditional schedules by both students and teachers; they make it easier for teachers to manage class activities; and they reduce the number of negative behaviors, such as disciplinary infractions and absences, by students. (There also is some evidence of higher achievement for students following block schedules, although the evidence on this point is not consistent.) For block scheduling to be most effective, teachers need to take full advantage of longer class periods by using more varied and interactive methods of instruction than may be possible in shorter classes.

For students whose home language is not English, bilingual education at the beginning of their schooling has a positive effect on learning. However, to help students learn English well and to learn other academic subjects, long-term bilingual programs that last most of the elementary school years do not appear to be effective. Rather, programs that provide students with some home-language help at the start of school, but move them fairly quickly to all-English instruction, appear to be superior.

A school also can enhance student learning by making parents partners in their children's learning. Programs that have increased parental involvement—by establishing more personal contacts, providing opportunities for parents to participate in school activities, and in other ways—have had positive effects on students' achievement.

Engaging Students

In order for the academic program of a school to be effective, students must be engaged in, rather than indifferent to, or even resistant to, their studies. As a first step, schools must restrain off-task or disruptive behavior. Students learn more in schools that are orderly. Rules should be clear, consistent, and effectively enforced, but not overly restrictive, and need to be seen as fair by students. In addition to helping to keep students "on task," the presence of effective discipline in a school leads teachers to feel a greater sense of effectiveness and to have more enthusiasm and commitment to their work.

Motivating students' effort in their schoolwork, of course, requires more than disciplinary procedures to control inappropriate behavior. It especially requires that students see learning and doing well in school as bringing important rewards to them. Schools can provide information and counseling that shows students more clearly how doing well in school can help them to fulfill their educational and occupational aspirations. They can give public recognition to students who are academically successful; such recognition helps promote a high level of achievement in a school. Perhaps most important, schools can enlist the power of peer norms in support of academic success. Greatest approval and respect from students' peers usually have gone to those who excel in nonacademic activities, such as sports. By structuring group activities and competitions around academic goals (such as science competitions or management games), schools can increase the peer approval and esteem that go to those who excel in learning.

DECISION MAKING IN SCHOOLS

The academic program of the school and the morale and instructional methods of teachers are shaped to a considerable extent by the ways in which school staff—the principal, teachers, and others—work together. How decisions in the school are made, the way in which teachers are evaluated and rewarded, and the extent to which staff members work collaboratively together, help determine whether the school is a place where effective teaching and learning occur.

To try to overcome the problems of centralized and often rigid decision-making procedures, some school systems have adopted "site-based management" (SBM), in which most decisions (about staffing, budget, curriculum, professional development, etc.) are made by those directly involved in each school or their representatives (usually including teachers, administrators, and parents and/or community members). Teachers in schools with SBM, especially those who participate actively in school decision making, establish more collegial relationships with other teachers and have a stronger belief that they can promote positive change in their school than is generally found among teachers in non-SBM schools.

However, SBM often has not improved student learning. This frequent lack of impact on learning appears to be due to a frequent failure of decentralized decision making to improve classroom practice in significant ways. However, in some schools, SBM has led to substantial changes in curriculum and instructional methods intended to improve learning in the classroom. Those schools with SBM programs that have succeeded in changing classroom practices have drawn on the energies and ideas of a wide range of people (rather than having only limited participation). The SBM programs in these schools also have focused major attention on improvements in classroom practice and on the professional development of teachers, rather than on more peripheral matters.

Problems of bureaucracy led some big city school systems to move decision-making authority to a more local community level. However, there is little evidence that community control of schools generally has improved student learning. Nor has recentralization of authority in many school systems consistently improved classroom practice and student learning. Both centralization and decentralization have advantages and disadvantages. By combining local control of schools with an oversight body that monitors and assists local schools, school systems may be able to gain some of the advantages and minimize the disadvantages of each decision-making approach.

The way a school is organized often is also influenced by a teacher union. Unions sometimes have had a negative impact on school effectiveness. But in other cases, unions have collaborated with administrators to improve schools' instructional programs. For such collaboration to occur, unions must be willing to broaden their traditional concerns (with pay and teacher protections) and administrators must be willing to share power with teachers.

INCENTIVES FOR TEACHERS

Participation in school decision making may help induce teachers to contribute greater effort toward school success. There are, in addition, many other reasons—including pride in their craft and the desire to help students—that may lead teachers to improve their skills, to work hard, and to remain in their profession. Some schools also have tried to use financial and career incentives—including "merit pay," linking pay to teacher certification, and providing career ladders—in order to motivate teachers.

Evidence on teacher incentive programs is limited but generally finds them to have very little effect on teacher motivation and performance or on student learning. Teachers often have reacted negatively to incentive programs, seeing the evaluations of their work as unreliable or unfair and as promoting competition and division with the school faculty.

Teachers are more likely to accept a system for evaluating them if they have a role in developing the system and if they are judged, at least in part, by their peers. Incentive systems can avoid fostering destructive competition by making rewards potentially available to all teachers who meet some criterion of excellence (rather than to only a few) and/or by giving rewards to all teachers if the school as a whole meets some goal. To be most effective, incentive programs for teachers should be part of a broader plan to provide professional growth for teachers—through mentoring programs, workshops, faculty discussions, and other means.

RELATIONSHIPS AMONG TEACHERS

The amount and types of interaction that take place among school staff members—such as participation in decision-making groups to plan aspects of the school program, meetings to discuss particular students whom teachers share, mentoring of newer teachers by more experienced colleagues, visits by peers to each others classes, and team teaching—shape the kind of relationships that teachers and other staff members have with their colleagues. In schools that provide little opportunity for faculty members to interact about professional matters, teachers tend to feel isolated and alienated from their colleagues.

In schools that give rewards to teachers and/or to departments on a competitive basis, there may be some suspicion and rancor among faculty members. But where teachers are brought together often in cooperative activities, working toward common goals, they develop a strong sense of community with other faculty members. Where such a sense of community exists, teachers are more satisfied with their jobs, are more enthusiastic and more committed to their work and to school goals, and put forth greater effort than teachers who have less collegial relationships. Where a strong professional community exists in a school, teachers also are likely to use information and ideas from their colleagues to improve their teaching methods.

The evidence that stronger bonds of collegiality among teachers leads to higher teacher motivation and to improvements in their teaching methods suggests that the end result of a stronger teacher community should be better outcomes for students. This indeed is the case; where bonds of collegiality among teachers are stronger, student test scores have been found to be higher and dropout rates among students lower. Creating opportunities for faculty members to work together cooperatively and build strong collegial relationships is one of the most important ways in which schools can improve their effectiveness.

OTHER SCHOOL CHARACTERISTICS

The organization of a school—including its academic program, decision-making procedures, and staff relationships—as well as other aspects of school life that affect both staff and students, are influenced by some of the basic characteristics of the school. The size of the school (and its classes), the composition of the student body (especially with respect to social class and ethnicity), and the amount and types of school spending are among the most important of such basic school characteristics.

School Size

The size of a school affects both teachers and students, as well as their relationships. As schools get bigger, the relationships between administrators and teachers, and among teachers, tend to become more formal and more impersonal; also, teachers participate less in school decision making and take less collective responsibility for students at the school.

Personal relationships between teachers and students are more common in small schools than in larger high schools. Such close contacts between students and teachers make it more likely that students will share the norms and "academic culture" of the school's faculty, rather than being immersed solely in a peer culture that may not support learning. Students in small schools also tend to be more engaged in their schoolwork and to participate more in school activities than those in larger schools.

Among high school students, achievement appears to be highest in high schools of medium size (between 600 and 900 students). It may be that medium-sized high schools enjoy some advantages of larger size (such as wider curriculum offerings and more specialized services) while still retaining much personalized interaction among faculty and students that is characteristic of smaller schools. More limited evidence at the elementary school level indicates that achievement gains are greatest in the smallest elementary schools. The possible advantages of larger size (such as wider course offerings) probably are less relevant in elementary schools than in high schools.

In general, schools need to balance the advantages of bigness and smallness. They should be big enough to provide good facilities and enough courses and services to students. They should be small enough to encourage participation by faculty and by students, as well as close personal relationships among teachers and between teachers and students. Large schools may be able to overcome some of their disadvantages by subdividing into smaller units. Small schools may gain some of the advantages of larger size by sharing some of their resources.

Class Size

The size of classes has received much recent attention, and many efforts are being made to reduce class size. The best evidence on the effects of class size on student achievement comes from experimental studies that compare equivalent groups of elementary school students who have attended classes of different size. Most of these experimental studies have found smaller class size (usually fewer than 20 students) to have positive but small effects on student achievement. The benefits of attending small classes have been greatest for minority students.

The positive, if modest, effect that smaller class size often has on student achievement appears to be the result of the ways in which class size may affect teacher behavior and the interaction between teachers and students. In general, teachers in smaller classes spend less time on discipline and on managing classroom activities and more time on instruction than do teachers in larger classes; they also tend to provide more individual and small group instruction and to have more interaction with individual students. However, the behavior of many teachers in small classes does not differ much from those of teachers in larger classes. Reducing class size may have greater effects if teachers change their teaching styles more to take greater advantage of smaller class size.

While reducing class size often has some benefits, it also has costs— high financial costs, sometimes hiring less qualified teachers in order to staff more classrooms, and sometimes reducing the space allotted to other school programs in order to provide space for more classes. One possible solution to this dilemma is to focus efforts to reduce class size primarily on students who are most academically at risk, such as low-income and minority students. These students are likely to benefit most from the individual attention and orderly atmosphere that often occurs in smaller classes.

Student Body Backgrounds

What happens in a school—what is taught, the interaction between teachers and students, and the relationships among students—also is affected by the typical backgrounds of students in that school.

Going to school with peers who generally come from affluent, well-educated families raises the academic achievement of individual students, independent of their own families' status. This positive effect is especially marked for minority students.

Schools in which most students come from lower-class families differ from those whose students come from more advantaged backgrounds in a number of ways. Teachers cover subjects at a slower pace and cover less material; fewer advanced courses are offered at the high school level; teachers spend less time on instruction and more time on maintaining order; and students' friends are less likely to encourage them to do well in school. In combination, these factors create a less positive environment for learning in schools with students from a predominantly lower-class background than is found in schools serving higher-status students.

The racial and ethnic composition of schools has received great attention, and debates continue about policies that require school districts to maintain specified percentages of black students and white students. Minority students who attend racially mixed schools tend to have higher achievement than those who attend primarily segregated schools. However, the positive effect of racial diversity on achievement is inconsistent and, when it occurs, usually is quite small. Attending racially mixed classes generally helps minority students' achievement most when it occurs in early grades and in schools with a high proportion of whites. Blacks and other minority students may benefit somewhat from being in mostly white classes because teachers tend to have higher expectations and set higher standards for students in such settings than they do in mostly minority classes.

Evidence about the effects of student body characteristics on learning suggests that school systems should try to avoid concentrating low-SES or minority students (especially those from poor families) in the same schools. However, residential patterns and other constraints often make it difficult for school systems to avoid such social class and ethnic groupings. In such circumstances, high-quality education can be maintained by trying to duplicate the key conditions for learning commonly found in middle-class white schools—especially a strong curriculum, orderly classrooms, and high standards for student performance.

Spending

Poor academic performance by students often is attributed to schools not having an adequate level of funding. Research on this subject shows that higher spending tends to be associated with higher student achievement but that this relationship usually is weak. Spending on physical facilities or on raising teacher salaries has little effect on student achievement (although it may have other benefits, such as helping to retain teachers). Higher spending to reduce class size, to hire more able and more experienced teachers, and to increase mentoring of teachers, are likely to have somewhat greater impacts on student learning. However, while more money for schools—effectively targeted—undoubtedly can be beneficial, the evidence indicates that more spending is not necessarily the key to providing students a good education. Other aspects of schools—such as curriculum, instructional methods, and faculty collaboration—have greater impact. Such aspects of schools can be affected by spending levels but depend on many other factors as well.

HOW SHOULD STUDENTS AND SCHOOLS BE ASSESSED?

The effectiveness of education, for individual students and for schools as a whole, cannot be judged without some measures of outcomes for students, especially of their learning. Nor are strong pressures for any needed improvement of schools likely to be generated in the absence of some measures of educational outcomes. However, the recent emphasis on testing of students in American schools has provoked strong controversy about its possible benefits and its possible negative effects.

TYPES OF TESTS

As some educators have noted, "What is measured gets taught." Some tests measure primarily whether the student remembers the answers to questions about somewhat disconnected facts or can perform certain basic skills (such as dividing one number by another or spelling particular words). Where testing emphasizes memorization of facts and performance of routine skills, school administrators and teachers (who themselves may be judged by student performance on the tests) often adapt their curriculum and the instruction to this type of low-level content.

Another type of measure of student learning is performance assessment. Performances such as writing an essay, conducting a science experiment, or applying mathematical principles to solve problems, are more likely than most objective tests to assess students' capacities to understand and organize information and ideas, to reason, and to apply information in new situations.

Assessing student learning through performances generally is more time-consuming and more costly than using objective tests. It also requires developing well-defined scoring procedures in order to make judgments of performance reliable. However, when performance assessment has been used, curriculum and teaching change to reflect the emphasis on student understanding and thinking; for example, principals and teachers have reported less emphasis on drill, more emphasis on writing and oral communication skills, and more assignment of tasks (such as research projects) that give students a chance to develop and show understanding of the topic.

The use of objective tests and of performance tests are not mutually exclusive. Using several different types of tests can provide a better overall picture of students' knowledge and understanding than the use of only one method of assessment.

When states require that high school students pass a minimum competency test in order to graduate, schools often increase the number of courses they require in basic academic subjects such as math and science. However, in schools with minimum competency requirements, a large proportion of students may take basic or remedial courses in required subjects and teachers may devote great attention to routine drill on subjects that will be tested. One educational commission concluded that the minimum tends to become the maximum, lowering education standards for all students. Thus, when schools test for a minimum level of knowledge and skills, they need also to maintain standards for higher levels of attainment, and to measure such higher attainments, as well.

Another problem with "high stakes" testing is that it results in many students dropping out of school. The number of dropouts can be reduced if crucial assessments are not delayed until the end of schooling—as may occur when competency exams are given midway through high school or later. A continuing process throughout the school years, in which testing is used to diagnose students' strengths and weaknesses, and to provide guidance for improvement, should help to reduce the number of students who fail tests of competency in high school.

ASSESSMENT AND STUDENT MOTIVATION

Assessment of student's work—by test scores and by grades, as well as in more informal evaluations by teachers—often affects students' motivation. When doing well in school is important to students and when they believe that high effort is likely to lead to good marks, students are likely to try hard in their schoolwork. When they are evaluated on the basis of performances (such as doing experiments and research projects) that get them actively involved in their work, students are further motivated to do well.

Under some conditions, however, assessments of student learning reduce students' motivation. Students who consistently receive poor marks on tests and low grades in their courses tend to become discouraged and stop trying; these students often "drop out," first psychologically and then physically. The problem is made more serious by the use of assessment methods that grade each student according to how his performance compares to that of others, rather than according to how much he has learned.

Use of "norm-referenced" tests and assigning grades "on a curve" are prime examples of assessment methods that judge students comparatively. Such methods guarantee that some students will receive low evaluations of their work—regardless of how much they have tried or how much they have learned. Use of methods that assess how well each student has mastered a given body of material is much more likely to lead to high student motivation.

Assessment should not be viewed as "inspection" that follows learning, but rather as part of the learning process. Test results and evaluations of student performance can be used to provide students with important feedback on their strengths and weaknesses in understanding a subject. Such feedback is most likely to foster further learning if it is combined with suggestions to, and work with, the student to improve her performance. The feedback is most likely to foster further learning when it takes place in the context of other conditions that promote motivation for achievement—clear standards of excellence, tasks that are challenging but doable, some control by the student over her methods of work, and the prospect that further effort will lead to greater success.

TESTING AND SCHOOL IMPROVEMENT

Those who advocate obtaining measures of school effectiveness maintain that such information will lead to improvement of subpar schools, through public pressures and through rewards and penalties that can be attached to evidence of school performance. Mandated testing in schools, with testing outcomes resulting in rewards or penalties, does create great pressures on school staff to do everything possible to raise test scores. However, the changes that schools have made in their curriculum and instruction as a result of testing programs often do not represent genuine improvements.

Schools that are being judged primarily by objective tests of achievement, as is usually the case, generally have modified their curricula to emphasize the isolated facts and simple skills that such tests usually measure. They reduce time devoted to subjects and topics not tested and devote considerable time to drilling students on the likely content of the tests and preparing them in skills of test-taking. In some cases, the tests essentially become the curriculum. In addition, some schools have tried to reclassify, reject, or force out low-performing students in order to raise their school test scores.

Teachers are sometimes energized by the goals their school's staff may set to improve the school's test scores. But a focus on raising students' scores on mandatory state tests has forced many teachers to abandon the teaching methods that they have found to be most effective and lowered their morale.

There is some evidence that when school accountability programs are introduced, student scores on state tests that assess basic information and skills do tend to increase. However, while such gains may be beneficial for low-achieving groups, these students may be gaining only low-level knowledge and skills and not a deep understanding of subjects or higher skills, such as analysis and problem solving, that they also are likely to need.

The challenge we face is how to assess students' learning without causing principals and teachers to focus their curricula and teaching on testing in ways that degrade, rather than improve, the quality of education. A key to resolving this dilemma appears to be the use of both objective tests and performance tests to assess not only knowledge of specific facts and basic skills but also thinking skills, such as analysis, application of principles, and problem solving. When schools are judged by such broad and well-rounded assessments of learning, they are under pressure to improve their programs in ways that produce genuine and not merely superficial learning. In addition, making the number of dropouts from school an important criterion of school performance can encourage school staff to try to improve learning outcomes for all their students.

SCHOOL CHOICE: HOW DOES IT AFFECT STUDENTS AND SCHOOLS?

The characteristics and organization of individual schools—their financing, their size, the composition of their student body, the way in which decisions are made, the academic program, and so on—are shaped by societal forces and arrangements beyond each individual school. These outside forces include pressures from influential groups (such as business and religious organizations), school financing systems, the organizational structure of the local school district, and rules and directives from legislatures, administrative agencies, and courts.

I have given some, but usually limited, attention to various outside-the-school forces throughout this book. Among outside influences, I have given greatest scrutiny to societal and school system arrangements that permit parents and students to choose a school, rather than to be assigned to one. "School choice" has become a rallying cry for many people who want to improve schools, but it has been seen by many others as a threat to the public school system.

Programs that permit people to choose schools include those that: (1) permit families to choose non-neighborhood schools (magnet schools, alternative schools, or other) within the regular public school system; (2) create charter schools, which, although publicly funded, are relatively independent of the public school system; or (3) provide vouchers that help families send their children to private schools. There is great variation both among and within each of these types of schools of choice. Nevertheless, relevant research finds some common outcomes, as well as some differences, resulting from different choice plans.

Parents taking part in a variety of school choice plans have been more satisfied with, and more highly involved with, their children's schools than they were with their neighborhood schools. Students attending schools of choice (both public and private) generally are more satisfied with their teachers and schools, more engaged in their schoolwork, and better behaved than students in regular public schools.

Compared to students in regular public schools, those in magnet schools and in private schools tend to score higher on tests of academic achievement—even when the effects of students' background are controlled. The higher academic achievement found in these schools of choice appears to result from several features that these schools share: a strong "academic climate" that emphasizes high standards and high expectations; more academic courses required; and a strong sense of community that leads students to feel strongly bonded to their schools.

While student achievement generally is higher in several types of schools of choice (public magnets, private religious, and private secular schools) than in traditional public schools, this advantage has *not* been found consistently for charter schools. Charter schools differ widely with respect to the quality of their instructional programs, and many charter schools have had serious problems with financing, management, and support systems.

The few studies so far about the effects of voucher programs in American cities have found only slight and mixed evidence that such programs raise student achievement. In Chile and Colombia, low-income students who used vouchers to attend Catholic schools had somewhat higher achievement than students in the public schools. But voucher students attending nonreligious schools—including for-profit schools created to serve the new voucher clientele—had lower achievement than those in the public schools. The effects of voucher programs on student achievement varies both with the needs of students who use them and with the quality of the private schools that they attend.

While giving families greater choice among schools generally increases the satisfaction and involvement of both parents and students, and sometimes raises student achievement, such programs have some limitations and present some problems. First, the fact that a school is different from a traditional public school—with the name of magnet school, alternative school, charter school, or private school—does not necessarily mean that it is a better school. The education provided by some schools of choice—especially some charter schools and some private schools—is no better and sometimes worse than that in regular public schools. For this reason, it is risky to try to create alternative schools quickly, especially in large numbers. Nontraditional schools need to have well-developed instructional plans, effective management plans, and sufficient resources in order to provide a good education to students. Also, publicly funded schools, such as charter schools, and private schools in which public funds are used, need to be fully accountable, providing information to the public about their educational programs and about outcomes for their students.

A problematic aspect of school choice programs is that they tend to segment students in a number of ways: by ability, race, social class, religion, and other characteristics. Thus, there is a trade-off between giving families maximum choice among schools and maintaining schools that are socially diverse, bringing together youth from many parts of the community. People in each state and community must decide what balance they wish to strike between these two goals.

Another important question is how programs that give families a choice among schools affect the traditional public schools. There is some evidence that, where alternative schools offer effective competition, the achievement of students in the regular public schools may improve. However, strong competitive pressures from other schools have sometimes led to poorer performance by students in regular public schools. If charter schools and/or large-scale voucher programs draw off money, the best students, and the best-educated, most active parents from the regular public schools, these schools may find it very difficult to improve themselves enough to meet the competitive challenges. While traditional public schools sometimes can benefit from competition, they need to be given the resources—financial, human, and technical—to enable them to make improvements and compete effectively.

THE ACHIEVEMENT GAP FOR MINORITIES: HOW CAN IT BE EXPLAINED AND REDUCED?

African-American students and Hispanic students do less well in their studies and complete less schooling than non-Hispanic white students or Asian students. Most notably, differences among these groups on tests of achievement in reading, mathematics, and other subjects have been large and persistent. Gaps in the amount and quality of education received by students from different racial and ethnic groups lead to differences in individuals' own life chances and contribute to cleavage and conflict between groups in society.

To try to understand existing differences in academic achievement among racial and ethnic groups, it is helpful to look at the same set of educational influences that we have discussed throughout this book—including students' home backgrounds, the interaction between students and teachers, the academic program of the school, and other characteristics of each school. These factors affect the educational experiences and success of all students, but may have varying impacts on students from different racial and ethnic groups.

Part of the group differences in school achievement is attributable to the fact that minority children are more likely to come from families of lower social class (i.e., families having low income and relatively little education). Children from lower social class families are more likely than others to suffer a number of practical disadvantages, including health problems and frequent changes of residence, that may interfere with schooling. In addition, lower-class parents are less likely than middle-class parents to provide a stimulating learning environment for their children. Among preschoolers, minority children generally have much poorer English vocabularies than non-Hispanic white children and also may know less other information (such as numbers and letters) than middle-class white children. Thus, minority children already tend to be behind other children when they enter school.

After children begin school, a number of processes tend to reinforce and widen the achievement gaps that are present initially. Teachers tend to have low expectations of poor and minority students. Teachers, therefore, often have low standards of performance for, and place relatively few demands on, these students. Teachers often give minority students good grades for low-level performance.

Because they often have early difficulty with their schoolwork, minority students are disproportionately placed in low-ability classes or groups and later follow "tracks" designed for students who will not go to college. While grouping by ability has some educational advantages, it increases the gap in achievement between students in the low-ability and those in the high-ability groups or tracks.

Minority students also are more likely than non-Hispanic white students to attend schools whose student bodies come from lower-class backgrounds and are predominantly minority. Such schools are likely to have less emphasis on academic excellence, more discipline problems, and less encouragement from peers to do well in school. These school characteristics tend to widen the achievement gap between minority students and non-Hispanic white students.

Differences in academic achievement between racial and ethnic groups are not entirely due to average differences in social class among these groups. African-American students and Hispanic students score considerably lower than non-Hispanic whites on tests of achievement even when their parents have comparable income and education. Minority students whose parents are solidly middle-class score quite a bit lower than non-Hispanic white students from similar families. The reasons why middle-class minority students lag behind other students in achievement are not completely clear. Minority parents who are middle-class themselves often were raised in lower-class families and may carry over the parenting practices common to this social stratum. Also, there is evidence that minority students, including those from middle-class families, are more likely to be ridiculed by their peers for trying hard and for doing well in school.

The lower academic achievement of minority students is not due to their having negative attitudes toward school or to having low aspirations. The educational and occupational aspirations of African-American students, and their expectations about fulfilling their aspirations, are about as high as those of white students; the aspirations and expectations of Hispanic students are almost as high.

However, high aspirations and expectations often are held by minority students who have low school grades and/or are following a program of courses that does not prepare them for college. Moreover, African-American students tend to put less effort into their schoolwork than white students do. Many minority students do not seem to have a clear understanding of what they need to do to fulfill their aspirations. Often, despite relatively low effort, they believe that they are trying hard, suggesting that they—and perhaps their teachers—have low standards for judging their effort. In addition, pressures from peers to not try hard in school may reduce minority students' effort despite the high aspirations they may have.

The evidence that indicates why minority students often lag behind other students in achievement suggests some directions for efforts to reduce this gap. First, it is important to help minority children of preschool age to develop their cognitive abilities—to learn many English words, to be able to do simple reasoning, to recognize letters and numbers, and so on—so that they begin school as ready to learn as other children. Programs that give information and counseling to parents about the importance of providing activities that are mentally stimulating to young children—reading, talking, doing puzzles, and so forth—will help some children. More general impact can come from preschool programs such as Head Start. These programs can be expanded to cover more poor and minority children and can focus more on developing children's cognitive abilities than they usually have done in the past.

Within the school, much can be done by teachers and administrators to raise the motivation and academic achievement of minority students. Teachers need to have high expectations and standards for students' behavior and performance but also to be supportive and caring. Teachers also need to create conditions—through appropriate activities, feedback, help, and methods of evaluation—that promote success, rather than the low evaluations or failure frequently experienced by minority students.

To promote high achievement by minority students, it is desirable for schools and classes to be relatively small. Such settings facilitate closer contacts between faculty and students and also help to reduce problems of maintaining order and discipline that are sometimes detrimental to the achievement of minority students.

Some changes in the courses and curricula of schools, especially high schools, seem desirable. Some differentiation of students into different courses and programs on the basis of their abilities, interests, and goals may often help in serving students' different needs. However, the caliber of education offered to students in lower-skill classes in non-college tracks often needs improvement. Courses for these students should cover as much material as possible at the highest level of understanding as possible. Rather than relying on drill and memorization, teachers should use instructional methods that challenge students' understanding. Students in lower-skill classes and "lower" tracks, no less than others, should be held to high standards of performance and be recognized and rewarded for academic success.

For those students who do not want to go to college, improved programs that link their education to a good career path can help to motivate students. In addition, schools should fully inform students about the possibility of switching to a college-preparatory track and facilitate such a move for those students who want to make it.

Finally, school personnel and others need to give minority students more information about the kinds of courses they need to take, the level of grades they need to attain, the level of effort they need to put forth, and the educational path they need to follow if they are, realistically, to be able to fulfill their career aspirations. In addition, schools and those outside the schools should try to reduce pressures that minority students often feel from their peers to not work hard in school. One way to do this is to involve students in group academic activities, including competitions, that provide rewards to group members for team success and which, as we have seen, lead group members to encourage each other's efforts.

Raising achievement levels of minority students is easier in schools that have a substantial proportion of middle-class white students, primarily because academic standards tend to be higher and order maintained better in such schools. Residential patterns and other constraints make it difficult to create schools with such student body composition. However, many predominantly minority schools have succeeded in turning out students who achieve well academically. Other mostly minority schools also can do so by creating similar conditions—including high academic standards, an orderly atmosphere, and support and help for students in being successful in school.

LINKS BETWEEN THE CLASSROOM, SCHOOL ORGANIZATION, AND SOCIETY

Concern about the public schools and discussion about how to improve schools has been ongoing for many years. Individuals and groups have advocated a variety of specific policies or programs as the keys to remedying our educational problems. Recently, prominent proposals have included comprehensive testing of students, greater choice of schools by parents (including charter schools and voucher programs), smaller classes, and more decentralized management of each school.

While such specific proposals often have merit, each is limited in its effects and unlikely to be fully successful unless coordinated with other important aspects of education. For example, frequent testing of students can improve education only if such testing is linked to an effective curriculum and effective instructional methods and if the test results lead to efforts to improve the performance of individual students and of the school. An effective program to improve many of our schools requires a comprehensive examination of what happens in the home, in the classroom, in each school, and in the total school system.

Students' learning in school is influenced first by their home environments and especially by the actions of their parents: stimulating their early vocabulary and other cognitive skills; providing learning resources, such as books and magazines in the home; encouraging and helping students to do homework, and so on. It is not easy for schools and the community to influence children's' home environment, and efforts to do so need to be made with respect for the autonomy of parents.

But there are things that can be done and that will be seen by most parents as helpful. Schools can work more closely with parents, especially those with young children, to inform them of what the teacher and school are trying to accomplish and to enlist their help. For example, parents can collaborate with teachers in helping children to reach specific learning goals, such as recognizing simple words. At a broader societal level, preschool education to give children basic skills—recognizing letters and numbers, for example—can be expanded. Since children spend many hours at home watching television, it also would be desirable to provide more educational programs for children of all ages. Teachers could link some school assignments to such television programs.

In the school itself, the center of the learning experience for most students is the classroom. This book has devoted considerable attention to the kinds of classrooms—the learning activities, instructional methods of teachers, types of interaction among students, and so on—that have been found generally to be most effective in raising students' engagement and their learning. What has been said here about the classroom are generalizations intended as broad guidelines. The specifics of what makes for effective learning in classrooms will differ in different situations, depending on such factors as the characteristics of students (their cultural background, their skill level, their interests, their initial commitment to learning, etc.); the grade level; the subject matter; and the teacher's goals. Teachers need to adapt general principles of good instruction to the specific and often changing circumstances of each school and each particular class.

We have seen that what happens in the classroom is influenced in many ways by the characteristics and organizational features of the school. The academic program, the participation of faculty in school decisions, the extent of collaboration among teachers, and other school characteristics have both direct and indirect effects on student motivation and learning. These school features affect the rewards students get for academic success, the costs to students of misbehavior or lack of effort, the motivation of teachers, and the instructional skills of teachers, among other results.

To create effective classroom environments, schools must be organized in ways that will motivate their faculty, continually improve the faculty's skills, lead the school staff to share common goals, and facilitate collaboration to reach those goals. Earlier chapters of this book have described in detail some of the features of schools that have been found to contribute to effective student learning.

However, simply instituting a particular type of organization or procedure in a school will not automatically bring desired benefits. For example, we have seen that instituting site-based management, block time schedules, or smaller classes in a school, does not necessarily lead to improved education. Changes in school organization improve student learning only when these organizational changes have positive impacts on classroom life—such as improved teacher skills, better instructional methods, or increased student motivation. Changes in school characteristics or organization need to be carefully designed and monitored to show clearly how they affect teachers and students.

Just as instituting particular kinds of school organization does not automatically bring desired results, the same is true of particular kinds of societal intervention in schools. We have seen, for example, that creating new charter schools leads to better student learning only when such schools have effective organization and instructional programs. Similarly, state mandates for more extensive testing of students lead to improved learning only if the tests are assessing meaningful knowledge and have the effect of strengthening, rather than diluting or "dumbing down," curriculum and instruction.

An overall strategy for improving our nation's schools is most likely to be effective if it: (1) keeps the ultimate focus of change efforts on what happens in the classroom, such as what content students are taught, what activities students engage in, and what instructional methods teachers use; (2) considers the ways in which the overall characteristics and operation of the school—the academic program, the ways in which decisions are made, the relationships among staff members, and so on—influence teachers and students in the classroom; and (3) assesses proposed educational programs of the broader society—such as spending programs, school choice plans, and testing programs—by carefully tracing their effects on the characteristics and organization of individual schools and ultimately on teachers and students in the classroom.

The task of improving our schools is not an easy one. There are no simple answers, no panaceas. Research of the kind summarized in this book tell us what generally is likely to work best in producing good educational outcomes. But this body of research and this book do not provide a "cookbook" whose recipes, if followed, will produce the desired results. To be effective, school structures or procedures that generally have positive results usually have to be tailored and adapted to the special circumstances of particular schools or particular classrooms. Moreover, particular types of procedures—by teachers, by schools, or by society—do not have desired effects automatically. Policies and procedures, even those with good research evidence supporting them, need to be carefully crafted and monitored in terms of their effects on teachers and classrooms, and ultimately on students, in a particular situation.

Giving careful attention to how educational practices work in particular situations does not mean that general findings and general principles should be ignored. The large body of research evidence and experience that is available can provide many useful ideas and guidelines for educators and others about what kinds of schools and classrooms are most likely to be effective. By summarizing the relevant evidence, this book is intended to help provide the reader with such useful ideas and guidelines for effective education.

INDEX

317